Historical Introduction

TO THE

ROMAN LAW

BY

FREDERICK PARKER WALTON

K.C. (Quebec), B.A. (Oxon.), LL.B. (Edin.), LL.D. (Aberdeen and McGill); Hon. Member American Bar Association; Director of the Sultanieh School of Law, Cairo Formerly Dean of the Law Faculty, McGill University, Montreal.

Author of "Handbook of Husband and Wife according to the Law of Scotland" "Scotch Marriages, Regular and Irregular"; "Scope and Interpretation of the Civil Code of Lower Canada"; "Workmen's Compensation Act, 1909, of the Province of Quebec, with a Commentary"; "Egyptian Law of Obligations," Etc.

FOURTH EDITION, REVISED

With a new introduction by
Michael H. Hoeflich
University of Kansas School of Law

THE LAWBOOK EXCHANGE, LTD.
Clark, New Jersey

ISBN 978-1-58477-966-7

Lawbook Exchange edition 2016

The quality of this reprint is equivalent to the quality of the original work.

The Lawbook Exchange, Ltd.
33 Terminal Avenue
Clark, New Jersey 07066-1321

Please see our website for a selection of our other publications and fine facsimile reprints of classic works of legal history:
www.lawbookexchange.com

Library of Congress Cataloging-in-Publication Data

Names: Walton, Frederick Parker, 1858-1948 author. | Hoeflich, Michael H., writer of introduction.
Title: Historical introduction to the Roman law / by Frederick Parker Walton ; with a new introduction by Michael H. Hoeflich, John H. & John M. Kane Professor of Law, University of Kansas, School of Law.
Description: Fourth edition. | Clark, NJ : Lawbook Exchange, Ltd., 2016. | Includes bibliographical references and index.
Identifiers: LCCN 2016034677| ISBN 9781584779667 (hardcover : alk. paper) ISBN 1584779667 (hardcover : alk. paper)
Subjects: LCSH: Roman law--History.
Classification: LCC KJA190 .W35 2016 | DDC 340.5/4--dc23
LC record available at https://lccn.loc.gov/2016034677

Printed in the United States of America on acid-free paper

INTRODUCTION

Michael H. Hoeflich*

Frederick Parker Walton's *Historical Introduction to Roman Law* is a magisterial work that was part of the movement for the revival of Roman law teaching in the Anglo-American world which took place during the latter years of the nineteenth and the early years of the twentieth century.[1] But unlike the works of his contemporary English Romanists like Bryce or Amos, Walton wrote his great work in Quebec, Canada, a mixed jurisdiction in which French law, and through it, Roman law, played a significant role in the contemporary legal system.[2] Walton makes clear his focus on Canadian readers in his introduction to the volume. He also makes it clear that he sees the importance of learning Roman law as going beyond simple domestic legal knowledge. For Walton, the study of Roman law also opened up the immense possibilities of comparative legal studies as well as the ability to understand—and, if desired, master—all national legal systems based upon Roman law.

---

* John H. & John M. Kane Professor of Law, University of Kansas School of Law, 2016.

[1] See, M.H. Hoeflich, *Roman and Civil Law and the Development of Anglo-American Jurisprudence in the Nineteenth Century* (Athens, Ga., 1988).

[2] On Bryce, see, H.A.L. Fisher, *James Bryce* (N.Y.: Macmillan,1927); on Amos, see, T. Legg, "Sheldon Amos," in Matthew & Harrison, edd., *Oxford Dictionary of National Biography*, v. 2, *s.v.* " Amos, Sir. M.M. Sheldon."

Walton was perfectly positioned for the task he set himself. He was born in Nottingham, England in 1858 and graduated from Lincoln College, Oxford in 1883 having studied the classical curriculum there. From Oxford he moved to Edinburgh to study law and received his LLB in 1886 and became an advocate that year. During the next few years Walton served as a lecturer in Roman law at the University of Glasgow. He was appointed to the deanship at McGill University in 1897 and moved to Canada in order to take up the post. He remained at McGill until 1915 when he moved to Cairo to lead the law school there. In 1923 he returned to England and Oxford where he spent the rest of his life. He died in 1948.[3]

It is hard to imagine someone better qualified to write a handbook on Roman law designed to train French Canadian law students than Walton. His training in classics at Oxford and his legal training at Edinburgh assured that he possessed all of the scholarly skills necessary to master the complexities of ancient law. His time spent in Scotland as an advocate and as a Roman Law teacher meant that he not only was qualified in Roman law but, as a Scottish advocate, he was also qualified in a mixed jurisdiction similar to what he would find in Quebec. The diversity of his training and legal experience made it possible for Walton to see the study of Roman law from a broad perspective, one that could significantly enrich Roman law scholarship and teaching as well as train students for practice in Quebec.

Indeed, very soon after Walton arrived at McGill he made this broad perspective clear to his faculty, his students, and the bar. In a lecture he delivered to the university he said:

---

[3] This account is based upon that given by H.B. Hanbury, in Matthew & Harrison, edd., *Oxford Dictionary of National Biography* (2004), v. 57, *s.v.* "Walton, Frederick Parker."

> What the law faculty could do...was to teach fundamental principles to accustom the student to reason upon the principles of things, and to enable him to refer isolated cases to general rules...as was natural the Dean made a strong plea for the thorough study of Roman law, and showed most clearly how useful and even how necessary was its study in the Province of Quebec.[4]

In the words of Vernon Palmer:

> Walton compared Quebec to Louisiana and concluded that these jurisdictions "occupy a position midway between the Common law and the Civil law." He estimated that Scotland could no longer be classified as a civil law country.... He pictured Quebec in much the same position as Scotland.[5]

The official *History of the Institute of Comparative Law* at McGill further emphasizes both Walton's superb understanding of the needs of lawyers and law students in mixed jurisdictions, but, also, the value of the study of Roman law both as a basis for the study of comparative law and as a practical necessity fro practice:

> At the turn of the nineteenth century, the comparativist focus of the faculty was further bolstered by the appointment of Frederick Parker Walton as dean (1897–1914). As a scholar of Roman law rather than as a practicing lawyer as all previous Deans had been, the

---

[4] "Dean Walton's Speech" [extracted for the *McGill Fortnightly Review*, January 20, 1898] reprinted in *The Social Contributions of McGill Law* (2010), http://iancpilarczyk.com/wp-content/uploads/2010/10/ChapterVII.pdf, p.152.

[5] See, Vernon V. Palmer, "Quebec and the Third Legal Family," *Revue de Droit de McGill/McGill Law Journal*, v. 54 (2009) pp. 323-351, at 326.

> Oxford-trained Walton emphasized the importance of legal history and the emerging field of comparative law—as tools in the formation of legal professionals...[6]

In a nutshell, Walton brought three strengths to his work: expertise in the history of Roman law and Roman legal thought, expertise in comparative law based on his mastery of Roman law and the civil law/common law hybrid systems of mixed jurisdictions, and a belief that a thorough knowledge of Roman law could provide a strong basis for the practice of law in mixed jurisdictions like Scotland, Louisiana, and Quebec.

Although Walton's *Historical Introduction* was written for his students in Quebec and those in other mixed jurisdictions, the book found wider fame precisely because it provided an expert history and analysis of Roman law suitable for English speakers at a time when legal scholars and law teachers in Common law jurisdictions had come to believe that a thorough grounding in Roman law would benefit Common law students and lawyers. Many scholars and jurists such as Bryce and Amos in England and Pound and Sherman in the United States believed that Roman law was a superior basis for Common law students understanding general jurisprudence.[7]

Walton's book was a great success as is evidenced both by the fact that it went through four editions and by contemporary reviews. The book was first published in 1903 by William Green & Sons and carries an Edinburgh imprint. In itself, it is quite interesting that the book was first published in Scotland rather than Canada and may reflect both Walton's continuing ties to Scotland and the publisher's belief that the book would be of equal interest to

---

[6] *History of the Institute of Comparative Law, www.mcgill.ca/Institute of Comparative Law.*

[7] See, M.H. Hoeflich, Op. Cit., n.1, above.

Scottish lawyers and law students as to Canadians. A revised second edition was published by Green in 1912 but this edition carries the imprint of both Edinburgh and London, as does the third edition published in 1916. The addition of London to the place of publication information may well indicate the increasing success of the book outside of the mixed jurisdictions. Finally, the fourth and final edition of the book was published in 1920, now, again carrying the Edinburgh place of publication. That the book would go through four editions in fewer than twenty years is a strong indicator of it market success.

In addition to the evidence of reprinting, the success of Walton's volume is made clear by the positive reviews it received. Most important of these must stand the review of the first edition published in the *Harvard Law Review* in 1904:

> ...as an introduction to the study in Montreal of the Roman law as it appears today in the law of the Province of Quebec, it is equally valuable for one who is to learn the modern Civil law and for one to whom Roman law is of interest only as a wonderful and effective example of the human intellect applied to the complex affairs of an imperial civilization. Dean Walton describes clearly and convincingly not only the history of important legal doctrines, but also the constitutional history of Rome...The author's learning is evident...his grasp of the subject is complete...In publishing in so handy a form just the facts about the history of Roman law that we most need to know, Dean Walton has deserved the thanks of the profession.[8]

The judgment of the reviewer in the *Harvard Law Review* in 1904 is as true today as it was more than a century ago.

---

[8] *Harvard Law Review*, vol. 17 (1904), p. 294.

Historical Introduction

TO THE

ROMAN LAW

BY

FREDERICK PARKER WALTON

K.C. (Quebec), B.A. (Oxon.), LL.B. (Edin.), LL.D. (Aberdeen and McGill); Hon. Member American Bar Association; Director of the Sultanieh School of Law, Cairo
Formerly Dean of the Law Faculty, McGill University, Montreal.

Author of "Handbook of Husband and Wife according to the Law of Scotland" "Scotch Marriages, Regular and Irregular"; "Scope and Interpretation of the Civil Code of Lower Canada"; "Workmen's Compensation Act, 1909, of the Province of Quebec, with a Commentary"; "Egyptian Law of Obligations," Etc.

FOURTH EDITION, REVISED

EDINBURGH
W. GREEN & SON, LIMITED
LAW PUBLISHERS
1920

PREFACE TO FOURTH EDITION

THE facts that another edition of this book has been called for, and that the second edition has been translated into Portuguese indicate that it makes an appeal to students who are attending lectures upon the *Institutes*. It does not pretend to be a systematic history of the Roman law, nor is it intended in any way to take the place of a commentary on the *Institutes* of Justinian. It is rather a series of chapters on problems, mainly historical, which confront the student who is beginning the Roman law. Its aim is to be complementary to a course of lectures, and to supply a historical background.

The historical notices contained in the *Institutes* of Justinian are so fragmentary that without more information the student does not see the law in its true perspective. He has to be reminded that the law of Justinian is the culmination of a long history, and that the Romans started with a little body of Aryan customs, out of which their extraordinary genius was able by slow degrees to shape a legal system of the greatest refinement.

Unfortunately the pressure of other subjects renders it impossible for most students to make a detailed study of the history of Roman law. If the "introduction" is not to encroach upon the time assigned to the practical law it must be kept within narrow limits. The difficulty is largely one of selection. One of the topics which cannot be neglected is clearly that of the sources of the law, in the sense of a description of the various ways in which, at one time or another, laws were made at Rome. As to the relative importance of other chapters in the history there is room for difference of opinion. I am inclined to think that the period of the Kings and the Early Republic, obscure as some of it is, offers most of interest and value. The intermediate stages between the early law and the law of Justinian are generally noticed in the *Institutes* themselves. It is for this reason that I have given a comparatively full account of the early law, and that I have ventured with some hesitation to devote a few pages to the ethnology of the Romans, to the archæological evidence which is being so rapidly accumulated, and to the Etruscan influence upon the early city. The origin of the Romans, the character of the civilisation which they brought with them, and the nature of the environment of the infant State, are subjects to which the student of the Roman law cannot be indifferent.

So far as space has permitted I have tried to compare the early Roman law with that of some of the other Aryan peoples. Brief and inadequate as such references must be in a work of this kind, they may, nevertheless, serve to arouse the interest of some students in the fascinating subject of comparative law, and to direct them to ampler sources of information.

I am indebted for several suggestions to my former colleague, Professor S. B. Slack, of M'Gill University.

I regret that Part III. of the work of the late Professor E. C. Clark, dealing with the Regal Period, has appeared too late for me to avail myself of it.

SULTANIEH SCHOOL OF LAW,
CAIRO, *September* 1920.

LIST OF WORKS MOST FREQUENTLY CITED OR CONSULTED

1. General Works of Reference

Zeitschrift der Savigny Stiftung für Rechtsgeschichte. (Romanistische Abtheilung.)

Nouvelle Revue Historique de Droit Français et Étranger.

Zeitschrift für vergleichende Rechtswissenschaft.

Pauly-Wissowa, *Realencyclopædie der classischen Alterthumswissenschaft.*

Daremberg et Saglio, *Dictionnaire d'Antiquités Grecques et Romaines.*

Bruns, *Fontes*, 6th edition, Freiburg, 1893.

Girard, *Textes de droit Romain*, 2nd edition, Paris, 1895.

Companion to Latin Studies, Cambridge, 1910.

2. Special Works

Appleton, C., *Le Testament Romain*, Paris, 1903.

Bernhöft, F., *Staat und Recht der Römischen Königszeit*, Stuttgart, 1882.

Binder, J., *Die Plebs*, Liepzig, 1909.

Botsford, G. W., *The Roman Assemblies*, New York, 1909.

Brunner, H., *Deutsche Rechtsgeschichte*, Leipzig, 1887.

Bruns, C. G., *Geschichte und Quellen des Römischen Rechts*; revised and brought down to date by Pernice in Holtzendorff, *Encyclopædie der Rechtswissenschaft*, 5th edition, Leipzig, 1889.

Calisse, Carlo, *Storia del Diritto Italiano*, Firenze, 1903.

Clark, E. C., *History of Roman Private Law*, Part I., "Sources," Cambridge, 1906.

Continental Legal History Series, Vol. I. (General Survey), Boston, 1912.

Costa, E., *Storia delle Fonti*, Torino, 1909.

Costa, E., *Storia del Diritto Romano Privato*, Torino, 1911.

Cuq, E., *Les Institutions Juridiques des Romains*, 2nd edition, Paris, 1904.

Cuq, E., *Manuel des Institutions Juridiques des Romains.*

Dareste, R., *Études d'Histoire du Droit*, Paris, 1889.

Dareste, R., *Nouvelles Études d'Histoire du Droit*, Paris, 1902.

Esmein, A., *Mélanges d'Histoire du Droit et de Critique*, Paris, 1886.

Gide, P., *Condition Privée de la Femme*, Paris, 1885.

Girard, P. F., *Manuel Elementaire de Droit Romain*, 5th edition, Paris, 1911.

Girard, P. F., *Organisation Judiciaire des Romains*, Paris, 1901.

Greenidge, A. H. J., *Legal Procedure of Cicero's Time*, Oxford, 1901.

Grimm, J., *Deutsche Rechtsalterthümer*, 4th edition, Leipzig, 1899.

Howard, G. E., *History of Matrimonial Institutions*, London, 1904.

Jhering, R. von, *L'Esprit du Droit Romain*, translated by Meulenaere, 2nd edition, Paris, 1880.

Jhering, R. von, *Vorgeschichte der Indoeuropäer*, Leipzig, 1894.

Jörs, P., *Römische Rechtswissenschaft zur Zeit der Republik*, unfinished, Berlin, 1888.

Karlowa, O., *Römische Rechtsgeschichte*, unfinished, Leipzig, 1901.

Kohler, J., *Shakespeare vor dem Forum der Jurisprudenz*, Wurzburg, 1883.

Kovalewsky, M., *Modern Customs and Ancient Laws of Russia*, London, 1891.

Kovalewsky, M., *Coutume Contemporaine et Loi Ancienne*, Paris, 1893.

Krüger, P., *Geschichte der Quellen des Römischen Rechts*, Leipzig, 1888.

Kuklenbeck, L., *Entwicklungsgeschichte des Römischen Rechts*, unfinished, Munich, 1910.

Lambert, E., *Études de Droit Commun Législatif, Fonction du Droit Civil Comparé*, Paris, 1903.

Launspach, C. W. L., *State and Family in Early Rome*, London, 1908.

Leist, B. W., *Alt-Arisches Jus Civile*, Jena, 1892.

Maine, Sir H. S., *Ancient Law*, edited by Pollock, London, 1907.

Maine, Sir H. S., *Village Communities*, London, 1871.

Maine, Sir H. S., *Early History of Institutions*, London, 1875.

Manu, Laws of, Edition Bühler, in Sacred Books of the East, Oxford, 1886.

Meyer, E., *Geschichte des Alterthums*, Stuttgart, 1893.

Mitteis, L., *Reichsrecht und Volksrecht, in den Östlichen Provinzen des Römischen Reiches*, Leipzig, 1891.

Modestov, B., *Introduction à l'Histoire Romaine*, French translation, Paris, 1907.

Mommsen, Th., *Römisches Strafrecht*, Leipzig, 1899.

Mommsen, Th., *Römisches Staatsrecht*, 3rd edition, Leipzig, 1887.

Mommsen, Th., *Römische Forschungen*, Berlin, 1864, 1879.

Mommsen, Th., *Abriss des Römischen Staatsrechts*, Leipzig, 1893.

Muirhead, J., *Roman Law*, edited by Goudy, London, 1899.

Pais, E., *Storia di Roma*, unfinished, Turin, 1898.

Peet, T. E., *Stone and Bronze Ages in Italy*, Oxford, 1909.

Rein, W., *Criminalrecht der Römer*, Leipzig, 1844.

Ridgeway, W., *Early Age of Greece*, Cambridge, 1901.

Ridgeway, W., *Who were the Romans?* London, 1907.

Ripley, W. Z., *Races of Europe*, New York, 1899.

Roby, H. J., *Introduction to the Digest*, Cambridge, 1884.

Roby, H. J., *Roman Private Law*, Cambridge, 1902.

Rossbach, A., *Untersuchungen über die Römische Ehe*, Stuttgart, 1853.

Schrader, O., *Sprachvergleichung und Urgeschichte*, 2nd edition, Jena, 1890.

Schulin, F., *Geschichte des Römischen Rechtes*, Stuttgart, 1889.

Soltau, W., *Römische Geschichtschreibung*, Leipzig, 1909.

Soltau, W., *Altrömische Volksversammlungen*, Berlin, 1880.

Soltau, W., *Die Gültigkeit der Plebiscite*, Berlin, 1884.

Strachan-Davidson, J. L., *Problems of the Roman Criminal Law*, Oxford, 1912.

Viollet, P., *Histoire du Droit Civil Français*, 2nd edition, Paris, 1893.

Voigt, M., *Die XII. Tafeln*, Leipzig, 1883.

Westermarck, E., *History of Human Marriage*, 2nd edition, London, 1894.

PERIODS IN THE HISTORY

THE history of the law stretches over thirteen hundred years—that is, from 753 B.C., the assumed date of the foundation of the city, to 565 A.D., the date of Justinian's death. It is convenient to break up the history into shorter periods, and the divisions usually adopted are those of the political history, that is to say :—

First Period—	
The Kings . .	753 B.C.–509 B.C.
Second Period—	
The Republic . .	509 B.C.–27 B.C.
Third Period—	
The Constitutional Monarchy or Principate . . .	27 B.C.–284 A.D.
Fourth Period—	
Absolute Monarchy .	284 A.D. – 565 A.D. — *i.e.*, from the commencement of the reign of Diocletian to the death of Justinian.

I have followed these in the headings of the chapters, but for the purpose of the law-student there is no advantage in dividing the period of the Kings, which is really in the main pre-historic, from that of the Republic.

The most natural divisions are :—

First Period—	
The Kings and the Early Republic, Period of the *Jus Civile* . . .	753 B.C.–242 B.C.

Second Period—	
The Later Republic, Period of the Rise of the *Jus Gentium* .	242 B.C.–27 B.C.
Third Period—	
The Principate, Period of the Classical Jurists . .	27 B.C.–284 A.D.
Fourth Period—	
Absolute Monarchy, Period of Imperial Legislation and Codification . .	284 A.D.–565 A.D.—*i.e.*, from the commencement of the reign of Diocletian to the death of Justinian.

The date 242 B.C., which I have taken as the break between the second and the third period, is the date generally assigned as that of the creation of the office of *praetor peregrinus*, after which the growth of the *jus gentium* became much more rapid.

TABLE OF CONTENTS

ROMAN LAW

CHAPTER I

The Value of the Roman Law and the Causes of its Success

With the exception of the Bible there is no book which has so profoundly affected western civilisation as the Corpus Juris. It has given to the modern law much of its substance, and a form, an arrangement and a method which will last as long as society itself. It has become, as Jhering says, an element of our civilisation.[1] The Roman law is the greatest single legacy which the ancient world has bequeathed to the modern. In Art, in Literature, in Philosophy, in Science, our debt to the ancient civilisation is incalculable. The intellectual ferment out of which progress is born, the restless striving after something better, which is the mark of the western world, was the gift of Greece. She is the spiritual mother of Europe, and through Europe of America. But for the brilliant genius of that extraordinary people it seems not impossible that Europe might have remained no less indissolubly bound by the chains of custom than Asia. But in Art, in Literature, in Philosophy, and most of all in the Physical Sciences, there is a great breach of continuity between the ancient and the modern world. It would not be correct to say that our Art, or our Philosophy, or our Science is ancient art, or ancient philosophy, or ancient science, modified and adapted to a new environment. But it is not incorrect to say that

[1] *Esprit du Droit Romain*, i. 14.

the modern civil law is the Roman law, so modified and adapted.

The history of the civil law might be compared with the course of a large river which after flowing for a long distance breaks up into several channels. Each of these new channels receives affluents great and small, and each of them becomes a river with a character of its own. But if we trace any one of them back, we ultimately come to the parent stream. So, if we trace back the French, or the German, or the Italian, or the Roman-Dutch law, we come to the old Roman law out of which they all flowed.

In the countries which derive their law from the Roman, innumerable changes have been made in detail. Some of these have been made openly by statute, others have been introduced stealthily by judges or commentators. Sometimes a whole stream of new law has flowed in—*e.g.* there was a time when the feudal system almost drowned the Roman law in some countries. But feudalism in its extreme form could not last. And the French law at the Revolution swept away many of the feudal rules—*e.g.* the rule that a son excludes daughters in succession to a fief, and that the eldest son excludes the younger.[1] In this, as in some other questions of great importance, the modern French law is nearer to the Roman than the old French law was. And, notwithstanding all the changes which have been made in one country and another, the essential unity of the civil law has not been lost. The differences are differences of detail; the principle, the methods, and the terminology are the same. A French lawyer who began to practise in Italy, or a Quebec lawyer who transferred himself to New Orleans, would have to learn something of the statute law of his new home, and to inquire the views of the Courts as to certain moot questions of the civil law which for centuries have agitated the breasts

[1] See, for distinctions, Glasson, *Histoire du Droit et des Institutions de la France*, 7, 430, 466.

of the commentators. But his main stock of legal knowledge would not need to be renewed, the technical phraseology would be the same, and the legal method which he had painfully learned would stand him in as good stead in his new country as in his old one.

In the Province of Quebec we may get a rough notion of the extent to which the Civil Code is based on the Roman law, by turning over an edition which gives the commissioners' references to authorities. If one looks at any Book of the Code, except Book IV. which deals with Commercial Law, one will find continual references to the Roman law. In some parts of Book I., which deals with persons, they are less frequent. One would hardly expect the formalities of marriage or the official rules as to acts of civil status to be those of the Roman Empire.

And the profound change in the character of our society since the sixth century has brought with it corresponding changes in the law of persons. The patriarchal household in which the *paterfamilias* rules as king and priest has long since passed away. The Roman law of persons has its centre in that singular and primitive institution, and its fall has made obsolete a great part of the old law. Again, the institution of slavery which affected most intimately every part of the social organism at Rome has, happily, disappeared. And, still again, the influence of the Church has altered profoundly the law of marriage and divorce. So that in the law of persons we shall not be surprised to find that a new order has taken the place of the old. Still, the new order has grown out of the old and is a development of it. The very word "person" in its legal sense is Roman, and we owe to the Roman law the discussions as to the requisites of personality, and the fruitful distinction between physical and jural persons. The law of Tutory is also mainly Roman. Our law of persons, like our law of obligations, is built upon the Roman, but as to persons the modifications have been much greater. But, frequent as are the references of the commissioners to the Roman law, these, notwithstanding, afford only a very rude test of the indebtedness of our code to the law of Rome. For the commissioners often content themselves with citing Domat, Ricard, Pothier, or other old French writers. If we turn to these we find that they support every argument by Roman authority. To a very considerable extent indeed, the Civil Code of Lower Canada simply reproduces in an abridged and abstract form the conclusions reached by the Roman lawyers fifteen or sixteen hundred years ago.

Sir Henry Maine says that the Code Napoléon "may be described without great inaccuracy as a compendium of the rules of Roman law then practised in France, cleared of all feudal admixture, such rules, however, being in all cases taken with the extensions given to them, and the interpretations put upon them by one or two eminent French jurists, and particularly by Pothier."[1] The description applies equally to the Civil Code of Lower Canada. It is very significant of the permanent value of the Roman law that two great codes, one drawn up at the beginning and one at the end of this century, should consist to so great an extent of Roman law. The new code for the German Empire, which came into effect on 1st January 1900, is full of Roman law. And if the whole code may be roughly called a compendium or abstract of the rules of Roman law, especially is this the case as to the parts of the code which deal with obligations and with some of the special contracts, such as sale, lease, mandate, and deposit. This is almost all pure Roman law. I do not mean that no changes have been made, but the changes are trifling when compared with the mass of rules which have remained unaltered. The *Coutume de Paris*, upon which the old civil law of Quebec is based, contains nothing about these subjects. That *coutume*, like the other *coutumes* of the *ancien régime* in France, had not any

[1] *Village Communities, etc.*, 357.

general theory of obligations, nor any special theory as to particular contracts. Some of them had a few peculiar rules as to the sale of certain kinds of property, or local customs as to lease. But even these trifling exceptions are not found in the *Coutume de Paris*. The law of obligations and contracts, the very centre and kernel of the whole law, was left in France to be regulated by the Roman law. The law of servitudes, of hypothec and pledge, and of suretyship, is also almost wholly Roman. Pothier, whom the French codifiers took as their guide when they drew up the Code Napoléon, and whom our commissioners cite at every turn, is in fact one of the most eminent expounders of the Roman law. The merest glance at his great work on obligations is enough to convince one of this. There is hardly a paragraph which is not supported by a citation from the Digest. A man who spent twelve years of his life in arranging the texts of the Roman law—and Pothier's edition of the Roman Pandects cost him no less—was, we may be sure, convinced of their permanent value to the world. A large part of the body of our present law is still, to a great extent, Roman law. The divisions of the field, the framework, the language, are still Roman. The old French authorities—*e.g.* Du Moulin, Cujas, Doneau, Domat, Pothier—are before everything great students of the Roman law. They are saturated with it; they speak its language, breathe its breath, and look up to Papinian and Ulpian as their great masters. It is, however, Roman law modified and adapted to suit a different state of society. In this work of stripping the Roman law of its technicalities and fitting it to be the law of modern France the great names are Domat and Pothier. It is from them and not directly from Justinian's Corpus that the compilers of the Code Napoléon drew.

The French law of obligations is the Roman law adapted by Domat and Pothier.

Nor is the belief in the excellence and value of the Roman law by any means confined to the ancients. Laurent, *e.g.*, says that for the modern lawyer no study is more necessary. He says that the works of the Roman lawyers are still the masterpieces of the art, and have no more been surpassed than Plato has been surpassed as a philosopher or Demosthenes as an orator.[1] If we were not so familiar with it, it would fill us with amazement that the Courts of Quebec and Cape Colony, of France and of Germany, should still practise and enforce a mass of legal rules formulated at Rome perhaps two thousand years ago. Why did the young countries of Western Europe adopt the Roman law instead of making a system of their own? The Roman Empire had been broken into fragments five hundred years before France and Germany and Italy began to emerge from the darkness and to assume distinct shapes as nations. Why should these young nations with one accord have said "we will be governed by the laws of Rome except in so far as we may decide to make changes"? It is a striking fact that in a considerable part of Europe the Roman law was actually a binding authority almost down to our own time. About the twelfth century France became divided into two zones called the *pays coutumiers* and the *pays de droit écrit.*[2] The line between them coincided pretty exactly with the linguistic division. In the *pays coutumiers* the language was the *Langue d'oil* which developed into modern French. In the *pays de droit écrit* it was the *Langue d'oc* which became the Provençal still spoken in southern France. The south, including Aquitaine, Gascony, Navarre, Provence, and some other small districts, was more thoroughly Romanised than the north had ever been. Great numbers of Romans had settled there. Nîmes, Arles, and other cities had been centres of Roman art and culture. The Roman law had never been forgotten. During the dark period between the sixth and

[1] *Principes*, 1, 40.

[2] Glasson, *Histoire du Droit et des Institutions de la France*, 4, 18; where a full enumeration is given of the *pays de droit écrit*. They formed about one-third of France. See the map in Brissaud, *Manuel d'Histoire du Droit Français*, i. 160.

eleventh centuries the Roman texts were almost, if not quite, unknown in the south of France. But so far as possible the people of the south followed the Roman law as it was known by tradition. When the study of the Roman law was revived by the glossarists, the *Midi* was like a country which having lost its codes for five hundred years, and in the interval practised what it could remember of them, has the good luck to find them again.[1] Now in all this country the *droit écrit*—the old Roman law—was binding. The Roman law was the common or general law of the land. They treated the compilations of Justinian as we treat the Revised Statutes. And upon the same principle the latest of Justinian's provisions upon any point was given effect to. So the Code prevailed over the Digest in cases of conflict, and the Novels over the Code. If in any district there was a fixed custom upon any matter the Courts would follow it in preference to the Roman law, and many of the towns had charters by which the Roman law was modified in some points within the municipality. But the main body of the law was the Roman law pure and simple. The most important matter not governed by Roman law was the law concerning the rights of seigneurs, the *droit féodal.*

In the north the Germanic influences were stronger, and every district was governed as to certain matters mainly by *coutumes.* So, *e.g.*, the property relations of husband and wife were those of the old Germanic community of goods instead of the dotal system, which the *pays de droit écrit* had retained from Roman days. When the custom was silent upon the point in dispute, what law was to be appealed to? This is still a moot point. Some say it was to the custom of Paris, and, failing that, to the Roman law, but only as *ratio scripta.* Others say that if the *coutume* was silent the judge had no choice but to follow the Roman law. But as regards obligations and contracts there was no difference of opinion. There

[1] Esmein, *Histoire du Droit Français*, 711.

the principles of the Roman law were to rule in the north as well as in the south.

In Germany, also, a large part of the country was governed by Roman law until 1st January 1900. The so-called Territory of the Law of the Pandects, including Holstein, Würtemberg, and Bavaria, recognised the Roman law as actually binding on the courts, except where expressly altered by local laws. The new German Code for the whole Empire came into force in 1900.

So that not only is the law of Continental Western Europe founded upon the Roman law, but to a very great extent it actually is the Roman law. And in part of Europe the Emperor Justinian's compilations were as binding as if the local legislature had re-enacted them.

What Shelley said of Greece as the mother of liberty and art, we may apply to Rome as the great lawgiver of the nations :—

> "Her citizens, imperial spirits,
> Rule the present from the past,
> On all this world of men inherits
> Their seal is set."

To a great extent Europe is still ruled by the Roman law. So are countries so remote from each other geographically, and so different in every respect, as the Island of Ceylon, the Province of Quebec, and the State of Louisiana. Why has so large a part of the world been content to take the Roman law as the basis of its own system, and in many branches to leave it on the whole very much as it was in the sixth century?

The extraordinary success of the Roman law is due, like most successes, mainly to merit, but partly to opportunity. No other nation of antiquity built up a legal system which, except in the unchanging East, would have had the least chance of surviving. Four causes among others made this possible for the Roman law :—

1. Its universal character.
2. Its fulness and refinement.
3. The prestige of Rome.
4. The support of the Church.

1. The great problem which the Roman lawyers had to solve was how to make their ancient local law applicable to a great empire. They had to examine what customs and rules were local and too peculiar to be extended, and to substitute for these, so far as possible, rules by which no reasonable and fair-minded man could object to be bound. They had to take the rude laws and customs which the Romans had inherited from their primitive ancestors, and to create out of them law which should be applied throughout the civilised world. It was a great task, and it was performed with wonderful success.

Rome had, for example, very ancient formal rules about sale. But these were not suitable for the Roman Empire or for the Roman to use in dealing with the foreign trader. They must, therefore, lay down rules as to sale which should have no local colour in them, which should be suitable for every trader to whatever country he belonged. All the law of obligations and contracts was in this way denationalised. This process was, for political reasons, so important for Rome, that her greatest statesmen gave much of their time to it. In no other country, ancient or modern, is the law so largely the work of the greatest men of the time. Papinian, Ulpian, and Paul, the main contributors to the Digest, all held in their day the post of prætorian præfect, an official who at that time combined pretty much the powers of prime minister and commander-in-chief. Like an Oriental vizier, he was the *alter ego* of the Emperor, and, in many cases, really carried on the work of government.[1] Men in such a position, and what is more, men who had risen by merit

[1] Karlowa, *Römische Rechtsgeschichte*, i. 829.

to such a position, were likely, if they had to make law, to make it, not in a pedantic spirit, but in a spirit of broad statesmanship.

When in the Middle Ages the new countries of Europe began to feel the need of laws, the Roman law struck them as free from national peculiarities and local characteristics. It was equally suitable for men of all the races from which have sprung the Frenchman, the German, and the Italian. Even looked at from the standpoint of the twentieth century, the Roman law still impresses the student with its universality. Mellish, L.J., called it "a system that more than any other exhibits the principles which ought to, and to some extent do, underlie the jurisprudence of all nations."

2. Next to its universality, it was the fulness and refinement of the Roman law which led the European peoples to adopt it. Rome had lived through centuries of refinement and civilisation, compared with which Europe in the twelfth century was as barbaric as Uganda is compared with Holland. The scanty and rude customs of the Germanic tribes were pretty much confined to rules as to the punishment of offenders, the reparation of wrongs by the blood-feud or by composition, and the law of personal status. They provided rules for the husband's rights over the property of the consorts, or the lord's rights over his vassals. But the barbarians had lived in the woods and not in cities. They had been warriors and not merchants. When town life began and commerce began it seemed to the young nations a godsend to find that the Roman law gave an answer to almost every question which could arise in these new conditions.

3. No doubt the prestige which still attached to the great fallen empire helped to win acceptance for her laws. Rome had for ages been the great centre of civilisation, and the traditions of her wonderful organisation had never died away.

4. The immense influence of the mediæval Church was at the crucial moment cast in favour of the Roman law. In the confused period when each race had its own law and a judge had to decide each case not by the territorial law, but by the personal law of the defendant, the Church found it best to adopt the Roman law. Questions affecting the property or the priests of the Church were governed by the Roman law. *Ecclesia vivit lege romana.* Among the Franks the regular clergy—the Cloisters—were under Roman law, the secular clergy under their personal law. In Lombardy all priests were under the Roman law.[1] Upon such subjects also the Roman law was much fuller than any barbarian customary law. As might be expected, there are differences as to the extent of the rule. No doubt at a later period when the canon law had itself become an important body of law, the Church claimed to be exempt from the civil law, and sometimes even showed hostility to that system. And when the conflicts between Church and State arose, the Roman law became one of the chief weapons of the secular power in its attempt to repress the power of the Church.[2] But this was after the success of the Roman law was assured. At an early stage, when it was still struggling for acceptance, if the clergy, the only educated class in the community, had set their faces against the Roman law its fate in Europe would have been very different.

To us at the present day the Roman law is valuable especially upon these grounds—(1) Its intrinsic merit. By this I mean its value as a substantive part of our knowledge of law. The discussions of the great Roman jurists will always remain models of legal reasoning. They possess in a high degree the faculty which is of all others the most important for a lawyer—viz. that of discovering the general principle

[1] Brunner, *Deutsche Rechtsgeschichte*, i. 269.

[2] Leonhard, *Institutionen*, 40.

which ought to be applied to a particular set of facts. They abound in luminous general principles which they illustrate by showing their application to different groups of circumstances. (2) As an introduction to legal terminology and method. The terms and classification of the Roman law have been retained by the modern *Droit Civil.* It is no slight advantage which the continental lawyer enjoys over his English brother that he employs a terminology which is understood over a great part of Europe. We learn in the Roman law the precise meaning of legal terms current in many countries. The Roman law, it has been said, tends to become the *lingua franca* of universal jurisprudence.. I am afraid definitions are not always very interesting, but nothing is more important for the legal student than to learn the definite and precise meaning of the terms which meet him on the pages of every law book. A considerable part of the time given to Roman law is well spent on the careful explanation of such terms as "Person," "Obligation," "Contract," "Thing," "Possession," "Prescription," "Real and Personal Rights," and many others.[1] (3) As an historical introduction to the French civil law. *Sine historia jurisprudentia cæca est.* So much of the French law has grown out of the Roman that the modern law is only fully understood when we study its roots in the ancient world and trace its development down to the present time. (4) As a study of legal history. This, though the least obvious, is, I am disposed to think, the greatest merit of the Roman law to a student of the present day. The law of the Corpus Juris is the outcome of a history of a thousand years. From B.C. 450, when the Twelve Tables were published, to A.D. 564, when the last of Justinian's Novels appeared, is more than a thousand years. During that long period we are able to follow the slow growth of the law. We can see how the

[1] See this aspect of the subject well stated by Maine in an essay republished in the volume on *Village Communities*, 330.

rude customary law of a primitive pastoral people was shaped and moulded to fit the needs of a great imperial nation whose mission it was to civilise the western world. No other study is so well calculated to teach us what legal rules are permanent and universal in their nature, and what are temporary and local.

Looked at from the practical point of view, the value of the Roman law is no doubt greater in countries whose legal system is based upon that of Rome than it is in the countries of the English common law. But the common law has been affected in a variety of ways by the Roman law, and it is altogether likely that in the future the law schools of England and of the United States will give more prominence to the study of the Roman law than they have done in the past. In these matters it is very easy to be too practical.[1]

[1] On the reception of Roman law in the sixteenth century and on its influence on the law of England, see articles by W. S. Holdsworth in *Law Quart. Rev.*, xxvii., xxviii., and the article by T. E. Scrutton in *Select Essays in Anglo-American Legal History*, i. 208. On the value of teaching Roman law in the United States, see the interesting remarks of R. Leonhard in *Harvard Law Review*, xxvi. 389. In Scotland the influence of the Roman law was much greater than in England. The Scots law was not founded to begin with upon the Roman, but after the beginning of the seventeenth century there was a marked reception of Roman law. Erskine, writing in the last quarter of the eighteenth century, said, "The Roman law continues to have great authority in all cases where it is not derogated from by statute or custom, and where the genius of our law suffers us to apply it" (*Principles of the Law of Scotland*, Book I. tit. 1, note 15). It is significant that the learned editor of the latest edition of that work has not found it necessary to qualify the author's statement (21st ed. 1913, by Prof. Rankine, p. 7). The extent to which the Roman law has affected the Scots Law is a subject which has not received the attention which it deserves (see article on "The Reception of the Roman Law in Scotland," by Prof. Dove Wilson in *Juridical Review*, ix. 361).

CHAPTER II

The Aryans

Origin of the Romans.—Latin belongs to the family of languages commonly called Aryan. The peoples who at present speak these tongues are divided into an eastern and a western branch. The eastern branch comprehends the Persians, Armenians, Afghans, and the inhabitants of Northern Hindustan. Their languages go back to Zend, old Armenian, old Persian, and Sanskrit, from which the modern Hindu dialects are derived. The western branch includes all the Europeans except the Magyars, the Turks, the Basques, the Finns, and perhaps the Albanians. All the other European tongues can be traced back to Greek, Latin, Celtic, to one or other branch of the Germanic group, or to Slavonic.

At the dawn of history in Europe we find the ancestors of these peoples occupying, broadly speaking, the same territories as at present.[1]

The Aryan languages are called by some authorities Indo-European or Indo-Germanic, and German writers prefer to employ the latter term for the whole group, and to restrict the word "Aryan" to the eastern branch alone. But the term Indo-European has the disadvantage of appearing to exclude the Persian branch of the family, and Indo-Germanic does not suggest the inclusion of Slavonic and Celtic. On the whole it is more convenient to retain the old expression "Aryan" as the designation for the group. There is no doubt that the peoples who speak one or other of these Aryan tongues have, in addition to their community of language, a certain common stock of ideas—religious, political, and legal—which go back to

---

[1] See Meyer, E., *Geschichte des Alterthums*, ii. s. 22 ; Huxley, *Man's Place in Nature*, 260 ; *infra*, p. 33.

a period before the dawn of history. For example, when the Greeks settled in Greece they brought with them a stock of ideas with regard to the worship of the gods, the division of the people into clans, the organisation of the family, the punishment of crime, and some other matters, closely similar to those of the early Romans.[1]

And the study of the early institutions of the Hindus, the Germans, the Slavs, and the Celts, clearly points to the fact that the ancestors of these peoples had, in primitive times, a civilisation very similar to that of the early Greeks and Latins. Even if we allow for a good deal of borrowing, it is difficult to avoid the conclusion that there must have been a time when the ancestors of all these peoples lived together.

Race versus Language.—We must not, however, fall into the error of assuming that the peoples who at the present day speak Aryan tongues are necessarily akin by blood. Community of language does not imply community of race. The Aryans were invaders who conquered many lands and mingled their blood with that of the peoples whom they subdued. We have abundant evidence to show that people who speak the same language are often of different races. Change of language does not mean change of race, and it is rarely, if ever, that a conquering people which brings in a new language exterminates the old possessors of the land. Thus, though the language of England is of Anglo-Saxon origin, the race of the people is by no means exclusively Teutonic. In Cornwall people largely of Celtic stock speak English, and the small dark people, sometimes called the "old dark breed," found in Ireland and the West Highlands, speaking Gaelic, are very likely not Celts at all, but belong to the same race as the primitive peoples of Southern Europe, commonly called Ligurians and Iberians.[2]

In Greece the invaders who brought the Greek language

[1] See, *e.g.*, Meyer, *Geschichte des Alterthums*, ii. s. 51 *seq.*

[2] See Ripley, *Races of Europe*, 322-330; Huxley, *Man's Place in Nature*, 253; Rhys, *The Welsh People*, 11 *seq.*

imposed it upon the inhabitants of the country. In Eastern Germany German is spoken by a large number of people of Slavonic origin, while the north-eastern third of France is probably more Teutonic than the south of Germany. Of those who speak Magyar to-day, a large proportion are not by race Magyar. Such examples might be easily multiplied, but enough has been said to prove that identity of language does not imply identity of race. According to the anthropologists the safest and most constant marks which distinguish one race from another are differences in the shape of the skull and in the colour of the skin. People can change their language but they cannot change the shape of their skulls. For racial purposes anthropologists rely largely upon what is called the cephalic index. This is the percentage which the breadth of the head above the ears bears to the length of the head from forehead to back. Taking the length as 100, the breadth is expressed by a fraction of this. If the breadth is below 75 per cent. of the length, the head is called dolichocephalic, or a long head. If the breadth is above 80 per cent. of the length it is called brachycephalic, or a broad head. Heads of which the index is between 75 and 80 are called mesocephalic, and are further subdivided into subdolichocephalic and subbrachycephalic.[1]

Other anthropologists, however, adopt another system, and regard all heads with an index of 80 or upwards as brachycephalic, and those with an index below 80 as dolichocephalic, with subdivisions of each group.[2]

It has been shown by the investigations of anthropologists that there are in Europe at least three well-defined races, namely:—

1. The Northern European dolichocephalic—blue-eyed, tall race, often termed the northern or Nordic race, and by some the Teutonic race.

---

[1] Topinard, *Anthropology*, 236; Ripley, 37.

[2] See Professor Gustav Retzius, in *Journal of Royal Anthropological Institute*, 1909, xxxix. 291.

2. The Middle European brachycephalic—dark-haired, dark-eyed, and generally short-statured race. This is also called the Alpine race, being found in strength in the Alpine regions of Southern and Central Europe, but is also found in part of France and in a large portion of Central and Northern Germany.
3. The South European dolichocephalic—dark-haired, dark-eyed, short-statured race, frequently called also the Mediterranean race.

Besides these three great races there are in Northern Europe the Lapps and the Finns, who are generally assumed to have emigrated from Asia, though this is not absolutely proved.[1]

None of these races is found in anything like purity at the present time, but the Northern race is found with the least admixture in Sweden, and with somewhat more admixture in North Germany and parts of the British Islands. The stronghold of the Middle European or the Alpine race is in the mountains of Central Europe, and that of the South European race in Spain and Southern Italy. It is by no means certain that this classification of the European races is final, and some anthropologists find as many as six races represented. One of the difficulties is to bring the very tall brachycephalic Montenegrins into the same class as the generally short-statured Alpine race; but the existence of the three principal races is universally admitted.[2]

For the present purpose all that much concerns us is the fact that we find in Europe at the present time people who belong, in the biological sense, to quite different races speaking Aryan languages which are evidently all derived from some prehistoric mother-tongue.

The Aryan Race.—It does not seem possible to explain the relationship of the European languages to one another, and the

[1] Retzius, *l.c.* 294; Ripley, 121; Huxley, *Man's Place in Nature*, 289.

[2] Retzius, *l.c.* 293.

similarity in the early institutions of the European peoples, except upon the assumption that there must have been a period when their ancestors all lived together. And it is reasonable to suppose that at this remote period there was an Aryan race in the biological sense, and that it was the people who belonged to this race who stamped their civilisation upon the whole of Europe.

Languages and institutions are of very slow growth. The Aryan tribes must have roamed together for long ages, during which the mother language was developed and the institutions were moulded which underlie the civilisation of all the so-called Aryan peoples. They came as invaders, and they imposed their language and their institutions on the various peoples whom they conquered, but in the course of their migrations they lost their own racial purity, and mingled with the peoples they subdued. The racial characteristics of the primitive Aryans can hardly be ascertained with certainty, but there is every probability in favour of the view that they were a tall, fair people, similar in type to the Scandinavians. The Achæan heroes, who are always described in the Homeric poems as fair or golden-haired—*e.g.* *ξανθὸς Μενέλαος*—may be taken as typical Aryans.[1]

What was the Primitive Home of the Aryans?—The locality of the primitive home of the Aryan race has been the subject of a long and bitter controversy. A generation ago it was regarded almost as an article of faith that they came to Europe from Asia, and lived originally in the region of the Hindu Kush, and on the Pamir Plateau, on the borders of what are now Afghanistan and Turkestan, whence the eastern branch descended into India, and the western, in successive waves of Celts, Græco-Italians, Germans, and Slavs, penetrated into Europe. The improbability of this theory was pointed out forty years ago by R. G. Latham. He maintained that it was more likely that the Aryans came from Europe, seeing that

[1] Ridgeway, *Early Age of Greece*, *passim*, Cambridge, 1901 and 1910; Huxley, *Man's Place in Nature*, 303; and authorities in the next note.

all the European languages, broadly speaking, are of Aryan origin, whereas the Hindus and the Persians are isolated peoples living among vast populations who speak non-Aryan tongues.[1] It seems more reasonable to believe that the ancestors of these peoples were Europeans, who had passed over into Asia, than to suppose that the whole of Europe had been overrun by Asiatic invaders. For some time the steppes of Southern Russia and Central Asia were regarded as the most probable seat of the early Aryans.[2]

But the opinion seems to be gaining ground among the students of this question that the primitive home of the Aryans is more probably to be found in Northern Europe, where the tall, fair race is still found in its greatest purity.[3] But the question is highly controversial, and there are many supporters of the older view.

The Civilisation of the Primitive Aryans.—Many attempts have been made to reconstruct from the scanty data which we possess the civilisation of the Aryans during the long prehistoric period when they lived together before the great migrations. These attempts are based partly upon philological and partly upon historical arguments.

Comparative Philology.—When it is found that the same name is used for an object by all the Ayran peoples, the inference is drawn that this object was known to them in their primitive home, and that they carried it with them when they

[1] See Meyer, Gustave, *Sammlung Indogermanischer Wörterbücher*, iii.; Thumb, A., in *Indogermanische Forschungen*, xxvi. 1. The European languages which are non-Aryan are Turkish, Magyar, Basque, Finnish, and Lapp. Albanian is such a mixture that it is a question whether it ought to be classed as an Aryan tongue.

[2] Meyer, *Geschichte des Alterthums*, ii. s. 28; Schrader, *Sprachvergleichung und Urgeschichte*, 632 (Southern Russia).

[3] Ridgeway, *Early Age of Greece*; Penka, *Herkunft der Arier*; Huxley, *Man's Place in Nature*, 303; Much, *Die Urheimath der Indogermanen*, 1901; Helm, K., in *Indogermanische Forschungen*, xxiv. 221; and see the references in Kuhlenbeck, *Entwicklungsgeschichte des Römischen Rechts*, 35, München, 1910.

dispersed. When we find, for example, the dog and the otter called by the same name, allowing for certain well-known phonetic changes, in Sanskrit, Zend, Greek, Latin, German, and old Slavonic, it is reasonable to infer that the ancestors of these peoples were familiar with these animals in the early period. But it must be remarked that although this reasoning is fairly safe, the converse process is very unreliable. It by no means follows that because an object is not called by the same name in a number of these languages it was unknown to the early Aryans. The life of words is exposed to many accidents, and a great many primitive words have no doubt been irretrievably lost. In many cases we can point with certainty to such losses—*e.g.* Latin must have had a word akin to "son" though we find no trace of it, and in its place the word *filius* is used, while in the same way Greek has lost the word corresponding to "sister," which almost all the Aryan languages have in common, and uses instead an entirely different word, ἀδελφή. If such losses have occurred in the case of words so familiar as these, we may well believe that many objects had the same name in all the Aryan tongues to which different appellations are now applied. The fact that the words for "servant" in many Aryan languages do not mean "slave" but merely "boy" makes it at least doubtful if slavery existed among the early Aryans.[1]

From the study of words connected with agriculture it has been suggested that the Aryans before the migrations were at that stage when the pastoral life of the nomad herdsman was beginning to be combined with a little agriculture. The European languages have the same word for ploughing, but it does not occur in Sanskrit. The word "plough" is said to be originally German, and it is suggested that the Slavs borrowed both the word and the thing from the Germans.[2]

---

[1] Greek παῖς, Latin *puer*, German *Jüngling, Knecht;* Brugmann in *Indoger. Forschungen*, xix. 390.

[2] Greek ἀρόειν, Latin *arare*, Irish *airim*, Old High German *erran*, Old English *ear*, as, *e.g.*, in Tindale's Bible, 1 Cor. ix. 10, "That he which

We have historical evidence that some of the Aryan peoples in Europe were nomads, or were, at any rate, in the transition stage, when the settlement in a particular locality is easily broken up and moved elsewhere. Thucydides, at the beginning of his history, says: "For it is evident that what is now called Hellas was not in ancient times settled in a permanent manner, but that formerly there were frequent migrations." And Strabo, writing at the beginning of the Christian era, describes the Germans as being in the habit of migrating, owing to the simplicity of their style of living, and because they had no regular agriculture.[1]

The nomad life possesses great attractions so long as pasture is abundant and the population not excessive. It is pretty safe to assume with Schrader that the Aryans did not take to agriculture, at any rate as the main means of living, until they were driven to it by the growth of the population, and perhaps by having come, in the course of their migrations, to forest tracts interspersed with meadows which were unsuitable for the pastoral life.

But fascinating as is the study of words, it must be admitted that it throws a very dim and uncertain light upon the life of the primitive Aryans. Even upon such simple matters as whether the primitive Aryans were acquainted with agriculture or with fishing the philologists are still in dispute.[2]

Many of the theories with regard to the primitive Aryans are of a highly speculative character. A recent writer argues with ingenuity that the peoples who belong to the Latin and Celtic races are not seafaring folk in the same degree as the Germanic peoples, and explains this fact, if indeed it be a fact,

eareth should ear in hope." The Sanskrit root *ar* seems to mean to put in motion. Schrader, *Sprachvergleichung*, 176; Meringer, *Indogermanische Forschungen*, xvii. 100; Jhering, *Vorgeschichte*, 26.

[1] Thuc., i. c. 2; Strabo, c. 291; Schrader, *Sprachvergleichung*, 407.

[2] See Hirt, H., in *Indogermanische Forschungen*, xxii. 63; and Helm, K., *ibid.* xxiv. 221.

by the suggestion that the primitive home of the Aryans was on the Baltic and the North Sea, and that they were fishers before they were farmers. The ancestors of the Germans went south at this stage, and never lost their maritime qualities, while the ancestors of the other Aryans became farmers before they migrated, and consequently have never become great sailors.[1] Such statements may be true, but they are neither proved nor capable of proof.

Comparative Law.—It is by combining the study of words with our other information concerning early peoples that the best results are obtained. In many cases the similarities of usages are so striking that it is natural to assume that they have a common origin, and it is frequently not difficult to disentangle those parts of the institution which are really primitive from the more modern accretions. Thus, by studying the power of the *paterfamilias*, the law of succession, and the criminal law, as we find them among the Hindus, the early Greeks and Romans, the Celts, the Germans, and the Slavs, we are able to infer with some probability the rules enforced among the primitive Aryans.[2]

The method of comparing early institutions, in which Sir Henry Maine was a pioneer, has yielded very valuable results, and the earlier attempts to reconstruct the Aryan life, such as, *e.g.*, those by Leist, are by no means without interest and importance. But in all this matter it is necessary to proceed with much caution.

[1] Helm, K., *l.c.*

[2] For the linguistic treatment, see especially *Indogermanische Forschungen*, i.-xxvii. ; Max Müller, *Lectures on the Science of Language; Biographies of Words and the Home of the Aryans, &c.* ; Schrader, O., *Sprachvergleichung und Urgeschichte*, 2nd ed., Jena, 1890. For the historical treatment, see the works of Sir Henry Maine ; Leist, B. W., *Alt-Arisches Jus Civile*, Jena, 1892 ; Bernhöft, F., *Staat und Recht der Römischen Königzeit*, Stuttgart, 1882 ; Jhering, *Vorgeschichte der Indoeuropäer*, Leipzig, 1894 ; Kuhlenbeck, L., *Entwicklungsgeschichte des Römischen Rechts*, i. 31, München, 1910 ; Dareste, R., *Études du Droit*, Paris, 1902. See for some references to earlier books, Lange, *Römische Alterthümer*, 3rd ed. l. 55 ; and for a good summary, Mommsen, *History of Rome*, i. 15-19.

The inquirer must be on his guard against two dangers. Firstly, many ideas and institutions have been considered as the peculiar property of the Aryans which have since been found to exist among peoples far removed from them in race. They are ideas which belong not to a race, as such, but to a stage of culture. The history of man in many countries exhibits a progress from the life of the savage hunter, living in caves or huts, to that of the wandering tribesman, and from that to the settled life of the farmer. Later on we have the organisation into cities and states. People living at the same stage of culture are pretty sure to have a good deal in common, to whatever race they may belong. Secondly, allowance has to be made for a good deal of borrowing. When peoples live for centuries side by side, with a constant intermingling of populations, it is to be expected that the ideas and institutions of each of them will react to a considerable extent upon those of the others. No attempt will be made here to describe the life of the early Aryans, but in speaking of some of the institutions of the early Roman law I shall try to indicate their primitive form so far as it is possible to do so, but before doing this we must turn to the early history of the Romans in Italy.

CHAPTER III

THE LITERARY SOURCES OF THE EARLY HISTORY OF ROME

MODERN scholarship has rudely shaken the foundations upon which rest the traditional accounts of the origin of Rome, and of its history during the first three centuries.

The only classical historians now extant who attempt an ordered narrative of the early period are Livy and Dionysius of Halicarnassus. Their accounts are, it is true, supplemented as to certain points by Cicero, Diodorus, and Aulus Gellius, and by occasional references of other writers, but Livy and Dionysius remain the primary sources of most of our knowledge of the early city.

Livy was born in B.C. 59 and died A.D. 17. Dionysius came to Rome about B.C. 29, and died B.C. 7. Both of them wrote after the battle of Actium, B.C. 31.

The trustworthiness of their narrative of events which happened from 500 to 750 years before their time must depend entirely upon the character of the sources from which they drew. Unfortunately, there are strong grounds for believing that these sources were in the highest degree unreliable. The narrative which they give has long been regarded with grave suspicion by historical experts, and as the evidences have gradually been more fully collected and discussed, this suspicion has deepened and darkened.[1] Here and there, it is true, a champion has arisen to defend the old historians,[2]

---

[1] See Niebuhr, *History of Rome* (translation Hare and Thirlwall), i. 3 ; Lewis, Sir George Cornwall, *Inquiry into the Credibility of the Early Roman History*, London, 1855.

[2] See, *e.g.*, Dyer, T. H., *History of the Early Kings of Rome*, London, 1868 ; B. Kuntze, in *Zeit. Sav. Stift.*, iv. 259.

but it is now agreed by the best judges that the stories told by Livy and Dionysius concerning the regal period and the early Republic are, as they stand, absolutely unworthy of belief. The narrative is a mass of falsifications and inventions, containing, no doubt, some nuggets of truth, but these can be extracted only by most careful sifting.[1] The story which Livy and Dionysius give was the "canonical version" of the history of Rome current in the first century before Christ. The authorities from whom they took it were quite uncritical and unembarrassed by any historical conscience. The traditional history was a sort of imperialistic work compiled rather with the view of painting a picture which should tend to the glorification of the Roman people, and particularly of the imperial house, than of giving an account of what actually happened during a period for which the compilers of the story had no documents at all.[2] It was in fact more like an historical novel than a genuine history. Modern historians have demonstrated that the early annalists took their facts largely from the poets, especially Ennius, who in their turn had borrowed them from the earlier poets of Greece. The annalists gleaned also from the pedigrees and family chronicles of the great houses, some of which traced their descent from Alban and Trojan ancestors. The members of wealthy and important plebeian families were often anxious to prove that their forefathers had been patricians and leaders of the state, and the invention of ancestors and of glorious events in which they played a part was a common practice not regarded with serious disapproval. Livy himself laments that

---

[1] Soltau, W., *Die Anfänge der Römischen Geschichtschreibung*, Leipzig, 1909; Pais, Ettore, *Storia di Roma*, Turin, 1898, i. alone published, see especially i. pt. ii. 716-721; Binder, J., *Die Plebs*, 176, Leipzig, 1909; Pelham, R., *Roman History*, 4th ed.

[2] For an account of the annalists, see Clark, E. C., *History of Roman Private Law*, pt. i. Sources, Cambridge, 1906; Pais, i. pt. i. 38 *seq.*; and, for Q. Fabius Pictor especially, Mommsen, *Römische Forschungen*, ii. 221-296.

in this way the genuine sources had been hopelessly polluted.[1] But by far the greater part of the familiar stories told by Livy are sheer inventions of a late period, composed to point a moral or to illustrate the virtues of the early Romans.

The story of Æneas coming to Italy after the Trojan war; the foundation of Alba Longa; Romulus and Remus with their wolf foster-mother; the rape of the Sabine women; the details of the siege of Veii, so plainly modelled on the tale of Troy; the legislation of Numa; the legends of the Horatii and the Curiatii, of Lucretia, of Horatio Cocles who kept the bridge, of Coriolanus, and many other such stories, bear on their face the mark of fiction. In many cases it is easy to point to the Greek original on which the tale has been founded. Another kind of falsification of which there are many examples is that of placing some really historical event two or three centuries before its actual date, or ascribing to some fictitious personage in the remote past the character which belongs to a real person of a much later period. Thus the account which Livy gives of Spurius Cassius and his agrarian legislation for the benefit of poor plebeians is really a description of Gaius Gracchus, put back to B.C. 484.[2] It is very possible that Professor Pais of Pisa, the most recent and one of the most sceptical of the historians, finds "anticipations" of this kind in some cases which may reasonably be explained as mere coincidences, and that some of the analogies which he traces between the Roman stories and those of the Greeks may be fanciful. But on the whole it must be admitted that his negative conclusions are supported by strong arguments, and that very little of the early history can be relied upon.[3]

It has seemed desirable to say so much by way of introduc-

---

[1] Livy, viii. 40, 4.

[2] Livy, ii. 41; Soltau, *Anfänge*, 123; Pais, *Storia di Roma*, i. 580.

[3] Pais, *Storia di Roma*. See the valuable reviews of his work by A. S. Wilkins in the *Classical Review*, xii. 419, and xiii. 456, 1899; and by Ch. Lécrivain, in *Revue Historique*, 1900, lxxiv. 156; Clarke, E. C., *History of Roman Private Law*, pt. i. Sources, Cambridge, 1906.

tion, in order to make it clear that the accounts given by the classical writers of the legal institutions of the early period have to be received with much caution. The composition of the early *populus*, the nature of the kingly office, the character of the *gentes* and of the *Comitia Curiata*, and the reforms ascribed to Servius Tullius, to mention these only, present difficult problems of which no solution can be given which is free from doubt. It is true that upon some of these matters the accounts of the historians can be supplemented by references from Cicero, and that when we reach the Twelve Tables, of which an account will be given later, we are upon comparatively firm ground.

Not only the fragments of the Tables which have survived and the references which we have to what has been lost throw great light upon many questions, but it is about the time of the decemvirs that we begin to get into touch with contemporary documents, meagre as these are. The names of the decemvirs who drew up the Tables find a place in the *fasti*. These are pontifical lists of the consuls for each year, with a few notes of the events of the year. This official list can be traced back with great confidence to this period.[1] The untrustworthy nature of the literary sources has to be admitted, and the early history of Italy must be reconstructed, as far as that is possible at all, by archæology and by the study of language and institutions, and of old ceremonies and old maxims which may fairly be regarded as "survivals" throwing light upon the period before the reliable documents.

The study of comparative law has been especially fruitful, as, from the early institutions of other kindred peoples, we can

[1] See *Corpus Inscriptionum Latinarum*, i. 486; Soltau, *Römische Chronologie*, 447. He thinks the pontifical publication began about 500 B.C. Soltau, *Anfänge der Römischen Geschichtschreibung*, 188; and the remarks of Girard in *Nouv. Rev. Hist.*, xxvi. 398. Lambert does not credit the *fasti*. See *La Fonction du Droit Civil Comparé*, i. 507, where there is a bibliography of the subject, and the same author in *Nouv. Rev. Hist.*, xxvi. 180.

often infer with reasonable safety that similar institutions must have existed among the Romans.[1] The archæologists have come to the rescue of the historians, and from a careful and scientific study of the monuments, inscriptions, frescoes, graves, and other remains of the past many facts have been placed beyond reasonable doubt.

[1] See for some good remarks on this subject, Lambert, *La Fonction du Droit Civil Comparé*, 1903, i. 538-548.

CHAPTER IV

THE EVIDENCE OF ARCHÆOLOGY

IN no country has archæology been prosecuted during the last generation with more zeal and knowledge than in Italy, and extremely valuable results have been obtained. A vast amount of archæological material has been accumulated, and the experts have long been engaged in the work of sifting this material and of explaining its bearing upon the early history. These discussions have been carried on mainly in Italian scientific journals not readily accessible to English readers. In the few pages which it is possible to devote to the subject in a work of this kind the writer has relied mainly upon two recent publications of much interest and value, which are largely based upon the researches of the Italian experts Pigorini, Brizio, Colini, and others.[1]

Periods of the Prehistory.—The periods into which the archæologists have agreed to divide the prehistory of Italy are the following:—

1. The Palæolithic Period.
2. The Neolithic Period.
3. The Early Bronze Age. This is the period which Italian archæologists call the eneolithic period. This is a hybrid word formed from the Latin *aeneus*, bronze, and the Greek λίθος, a stone, and is used to describe the period when stone is still the principal material used but when

[1] Modestov, B., *Introduction d'Histoire Romaine*, French translation from the Russian, Paris, 1907; Peet, T. E., *Stone and Bronze Ages in Italy and Sicily*, Oxford, 1909.

metal, in the form of copper, is also beginning to be employed for making weapons and implements. The earliest of the lake dwellings to be noticed later are to be assigned to this period.

4. The Bronze Age, within which falls the civilisation of the *terremare*, which will be explained later.

5. The Early Iron Age. This is generally called by Italian archæologists the Villanova period, from the fact that a large number of remains of this epoch have been found at the place of this name near Bologna.

That each of these stages represents a distinct period in the history of culture in Italy is no longer a matter of serious dispute, but their connection one with another, and the race of people to which each of them belonged, are matters with regard to which there is still much controversy. I will endeavour to indicate in a few words the character of the civilisation of each of these periods, and refer to some of the chief problems that arise from the ascertained facts.

Palæolithic Man in Italy.—It has been proved beyond a doubt that at an early date in the quaternary period man existed in Italy in company with the elephant, the hippopotamus, the rhinoceros, the cave-hyena, and the gigantic wild ox almost as large as an elephant. Palæolithic man in Italy, as elsewhere in Europe, was frequently a cave-dweller, who lived by hunting and fishing, used rude stone implements, had no metals, and was ignorant of agriculture. It has been surmised that he found his way to Italy from Africa, and flint instruments similar to those which he used have been found in the Nile Valley, in the Transvaal, and in other parts of Africa.

Neolithic Man.—At a later period are found numerous remains of men who lived in what is generally called the neolithic age—that is, the age when the art of polishing stone was understood. It is the view of many of the authorities that between palæolithic man and his neolithic successor in Italy there is a complete breach of continuity. The civilisation of neolithic man is not only higher, but is so different in character, that according to some of the experts it can only be explained by the irruption of a new race into Italy.[1] Civilisation begins in Italy with neolithic man, though it is not necessary to assume that palæolithic man was altogether exterminated. It is, on the contrary, probable that in some parts of the country he continued to exist, for at Rivoli, near Turin, and at one or two other places, flint instruments of the old type are found together with polished axes, such as were made by neolithic man, and pottery of the neolithic period.[2] The remains of neolithic man are very extensive, and it is possible to form a fair idea of his mode of life and of the degree of culture to which he attained. It has been too hastily assumed that civilisation in Europe originated with the invasion of the so-called Aryans. There is abundant evidence that during the later stone age in Western and Southern Europe an indigenous culture of no mean order was slowly evolved. Neolithic folk possessed the art of polishing stone, of which they made axes, adzes, and chisels, as well as arrow-heads and daggers; they made pottery of various kinds, some of it quite elaborately ornamented; they domesticated the ox, the sheep, and the goat, from which it is clear that they were a pastoral people; they dwelt in huts, unless there happened to be a convenient cave at hand; and they had certain well-marked burial customs, which show that they had religious ideas.[3] It is almost certain

[1] Modestov, 20; Peet, 36. See, however, Huxley's doubt as to this *hiatus* between palæolithic and neolithic man in general (*Man's Place in Nature*, 318). Professor Keith has recently advanced the opinion that Neanderthal man has been maligned, and that his skull is of considerably greater cranial capacity than he has got credit for. He is inclined to regard the Neanderthal race as really the progenitors of the long-headed part of the modern European population. Professor Gustav Retzius thinks the Neanderthal race is extinct, but that the European long-heads go back to the Cro-magnon "race" (*Journ. Anthrop. Inst.*, xxxix. 298).

[2] Peet, 73, 183; Modestov, 17.

[3] The neolithic ivory carving from the grotto of Mas d'Azil in the

that neolithic man brought into Italy the custom of building huts and of living in hut villages. They buried their dead in trenches hollowed in the earth, and laid with them funeral furniture of weapons, vases, and ornaments, probably intended for use in the future life.[1] The body is generally found either squatting in a vertical position, the so-called embryonic posture, or laid on one side with the arms and legs bent.

To what Race did Neolithic Man in Italy Belong?—It is almost universally agreed that the Italians of the later stone age belonged to the people afterwards called Ligurians. It is probable, though not as yet certain, that their original home was in Africa, from which they may have crossed over into Europe at various points, some of them passing from Egypt over to Greece, perhaps by way of the islands; others from Tunis into Sicily, not then separated by so wide a sea as at present; and still others invading Spain by way of the Straits of Gibraltar.[2] However this may have been, it may be taken as established that the primitive populations of the three southern peninsulas, Greece, Italy, and Spain, belonged originally to allied stocks, and that their occupation of all these countries goes back at least to neolithic times.[3]

If the criteria of race to which physical anthropologists attach the greatest importance are to be relied upon, there is every reason to suppose that the mass of the population of a large part of Italy, as well as that of Spain, Portugal, and Greece, still belongs to the race which came into these countries in neolithic times. Indeed it is now generally admitted that in regard to questions of race older writers attached far too much importance to political conquests. It is probably true that taking

department of Ariège in France, and the celebrated carving in bone of the reindeer from Thayngen in Switzerland, show real artistic ability. See the reproductions in Ripley, *Races of Europe*, 488.

1 Modestov, 39 ; Peet, 119.

2 Peet, 174 ; Modestov, 134.

3 Ridgeway, *Companion to Latin Studies*, n. 21 ; Ripley, 407 ; Bury, *History of Greece*, 7.

the Continent of Europe generally, in spite of numerous political changes, the geographical distribution of races has altered comparatively little since very early times. Where conquering races came in, it was frequently as military invaders, bringing with them few, if any, women and children. The invaders married the daughters of the land, and in a few generations were absorbed in the mass of the population.[1] Huxley says: "So far as history teaches us, the populations of Europe, Asia, and Africa were, thirty or forty centuries ago, just what they are now, in their broad features and general distribution."[2]

Who were the Ligurians?—This is an extremely vexed question, which can only be mentioned here. In the opinion of most modern writers they belong to what is now generally called the Mediterranean race, whose physical characteristics are those of the majority of the people of Southern Europe at the present day; that is to say, they were a rather small dark people of somewhat slender build, with decidedly long skulls and with brown or black eyes. Whether they spoke an Aryan language or belonged to the Aryan race is a matter which is still extremely controversial. According to one view they were not Aryans at all, and their language was perhaps allied to that still spoken by the Basques.[3] According to another view, however, advocated by Professor Ridgeway, the tall fair people of the North whom we associate with the name Aryan were not of a different race in the biological sense from the Ligurians and Iberians, though they had come to differ from them greatly in physical type. Professor Ridgeway's explanation of the facts

---

[1] See Ripley, *Races of Europe*, 29, 463; Huxley, *Man's Place in Nature*, 238-260; Topinard, P., *Anthropology*, 429; Ridgeway, *Who were the Romans?* 18; same author in *Companion to Latin Studies*, n. 29; Bury, *History of Greece*, 39.

[2] *Man's Place in Nature*, 238.

[3] Meyer, *Geschichte des Alterthums*, ii. n. 22; Modestov, *Introduction*, 141; Peet, 493, foot; Binder, *Die Plebs*, 304. See Bury, *History of Greece*, 7; *Companion to Latin Studies*, n. 1201; Huxley, *Man's Place in Nature*, 268.

is that colour is largely determined by climate. When the Mediterranean race first settled in Europe the greater part of Northern Europe was still clothed in ice. As the ice-sheet gradually receded man pushed further and further north from the Mediterranean until he reached Northern Europe, and he became lighter in complexion, "until, under the conditions which produced the white hare, white bears, and a tendency in the ptarmigan and the stoat to turn white in winter, and the like tendency in the dun horse, they gradually became the blond race of our time."[1] They were speaking an Aryan language when they left the Mediterranean, and when they came back at the time of the so-called Aryan invasions they rejoined their long-lost cousins the Ligurians, who were speaking a similar language to their own. Professor Ridgeway goes even further, and maintains that as the invaders were a minority, and may be assumed to have adopted the language of the mass of the people, Latin is really Ligurian.[2]

As regards the language of the Ligurians Professor Ridgeway's theory does not find universal acceptance among the philologists. A recent writer says that we know next to nothing of the language of the Ligurians, and that whether they were Indo-Europeans or not "their language contributed little, so far as we know, to the Latin vocabulary."[3]

The question whether a small dark Italian could be converted into a tall fair Scandinavian by a change of climate is one upon which I do not presume to offer any opinion. There are, however, high authorities who believe that colour is a mark of race, and has very little to do with climate, and this is still more probable with regard to the bony structure.[4]

Huxley points out that although fair Europeans living

---

[1] *Companion to Latin Studies*, n. 19; *cf.* Ripley, *Races of Europe*, 366.

[2] *Who were the Romans?* 10.

[3] Giles, P., in *Companion to Latin Studies*, n. 1202.

[4] As to the persistence of colour, see Ripley, *Races of Europe*, 119. But see *ibid.* 366.

in hot countries become tanned by the sun, there is no proof that the cutaneous change thus effected becomes hereditary. And he also points to the fact that there are no indigenous negroes in the great alluvial plains of tropical South America, or in the exposed islands of the Polynesian Archipelago, or among the populations of equatorial Borneo or Sumatra.[1] It may be added that the Samoyedes, who live in the extreme north, have jet-black hair and swarthy skins, and that the North-American Indians in Northern Canada show no tendency to become blond.

The Eneolithic Period.—The marks of this period are the first appearance of metal, and the practice of burying in rock-hewn sepulchres.[2] The culture is simply a more advanced form of that of the stone age. But there is a considerable advance in civilisation, which is, in all probability, to be ascribed to foreign trade, particularly with Crete.[3]

It is in this transition period, when metals are beginning to take the place of stone, that we first find in Italy people living under altogether new conditions. These are the lake-dwellers. In many of the lakes of Northern Italy—*e.g.* Maggiore, Varese, Como, and Garda—are found the remains of lake-dwellings. These are villages built on platforms supported on piles driven into the bed of the lake at places where the water is comparatively shallow. Similar dwellings have been found in Switzerland and elsewhere.[4] The lake-dwellers worked in bronze, cultivated corn and millet, and domesticated the cow, the sheep, and the pig.[5] Further, it is highly probable that they cremated their dead.[6]

---

[1] *Man's Place in Nature*, 245.

[2] Modestov, 70; Peet, 186.

[3] Peet, 279; Modestov, 83.

[4] See for a picture of such a lake-dwelling, *Brit. Ency. v.* "Architecture"; *Chambers's Ency. s.v.* "Lake-dwelling." They are called in Italian *palafitte*, that is, literally, palisades; in French *lacustres*, or *palafittes*; and in German *Pfahlbauten im See.*

[5] Peet, 320. [6] Peet, 327.

The Bronze Age.—In the full bronze age we have in Italy archæological remains of a unique character. These are what are called the *terremare*, which are settlements supported on piles. They resemble the lake-dwellings, but are placed on the dry land and enclosed by a rampart of earth, outside which lies a moat at one time supplied with running water. The remains of these dwellings are found underneath certain large low mounds, quite common in some parts of the Po Valley, especially in the neighbourhood of Parma and Modena, and excavations made in these mounds during the last half-century have enabled us to form a fair idea of the character of the dwellings and of the culture of the people who inhabited them. It is safe to assume that the *terremare* were constructed by people who had been used to lake-dwellings. They are "survivals," and presuppose a long previous history of dwelling in lakes and marshes. It is also proved to demonstration that the dwellers in the *terremare* cremated their dead.[1]

It is almost an axiom with archæologists that when we find a change in the manner of disposing of the dead, and especially so radical a change as that from burial to cremation, this can only be ascribed to the irruption of a new race.[2] Accordingly, the fact that cremation was practised by the people of the *terremare*, and in all probability by the people of the lake-dwellings, seeing that the *terremare* are "survivals" of lake-dwellings, strongly supports the theory that we have here the remains of an invading race, and the probabilities point to this race having been that of the Aryans. The theory of Pigorini, which is adopted in substance by Modestov and Peet, may be shortly stated as follows:—The first invasion of the Aryans came from the north over the Alps, and the newcomers planted

[1] Modestov, 195; Peet, 364. Mr. Peet says (p. 369): "Professor Ridgeway's statement that inhumation was universally practised by the people of the *terremare* culture (*Who were the Romans?* 16) is a direct reversal of the facts."

[2] Different religious ideas are associated with cremation. See Daremberg et Saglio, *s.v.* "Funus," 1393.

the first lake-dwellings in Lombardy. This was in the eneolithic period. In the full bronze age there was a second invasion of Italy by people of the same stock, who came from the East by way of the Danube Valley. The first invasion was probably between 2000 and 1000 B.C., and the second took place perhaps about 1000 B.C.[1]

From a comparison of pottery and other objects found in excavations in Latium with similar materials found in the *terremare*, Pigorini infers that it was the inhabitants of the *terremare* who gave to Latium its Aryan population.[2] According to Modestov, the fair result of the evidence is that it was the Latins who occupied the *terremare*, and afterwards descended into Latium and settled among the Alban hills, while the second invasion must be ascribed to the Oscan-Umbro-Sabellian group.[3]

The Early Iron Age.—The civilisation of the early iron age, commonly called by Italians the Villanova period, is principally known by excavations in cemeteries in the neighbourhood of Bologna. With the exception of the custom of cremation, it is said that the remains show no contact with those of the *terremare*.[4] According to Brizio, whom Modestov follows, the civilisation of Villanova is to be referred to the Umbrians.[5]

There are philological grounds for believing that between the Latins and the Umbrians, who must have belonged originally to the same stock, there had been a long separation. The Umbrian dialect, as well as its sisters Oscan and Sabine, differs somewhat widely from Latin. For example, Umbrian has P for the sound which in Latin is QU—*pis* equals *quis*.[6]

This is in favour of the view that the Latins and the Umbrians may have come into Italy at different periods. So far as one who is not an archæologist can offer any opinion on such a

[1] Modestov, 236; Peet, 495.
[2] Modestov, 231. [3] *Ibid.* 235-284.
[4] *Ibid.* 288. [5] *Ibid.* 306.
[6] See *Companion to Latin Studies*, n. 1205.

matter, I doubt if we can consider it as proved that the Villanova culture is Umbrian, though this may very well be the case. It seems, however, clear enough that it was the Aryans who introduced into Italy the lake-dwellings and the *terremare*, and very probable that they brought with them a civilisation already considerably advanced.[1]

I cannot see any probability in the theory of Brizio, which is held by Professor Ridgeway, that the lake-dwellings and the *terremare* were built by the old neolithic people of Italy.[2]

It appears impossible upon this theory to explain why the neolithic folk should have completely altered the character of their habitations, and their method of disposing of the dead. All the facts are in favour of the view that the lake-dwellings and the *terremare* were built by an invading people who brought this curious type of habitation with them from Switzerland and from the valley of the Danube. We can only suppose that the lake-dwellings and the *terremare* were erected by a people who needed to defend themselves against a hostile population; and this conclusion is supported by the evidence which shows that a people living in huts continued to inhabit the country in the neighbourhood of the *terremare*.[3] It is abundantly clear that the old neolithic people continued to live on in Italy. As a matter of fact Diodorus Siculus, who wrote towards the end of the last century B.C., described the Ligurians as living among the mountains in caves and huts, very much as their ancestors had done in neolithic times.[4]

According to another theory, which is still not without supporters, it was the Etruscans who inhabited the *terremare*.[5] But this theory is connected with the opinion that the

[1] See for the evidences of a remarkable civilisation at Hallstatt, in the region of Salzburg Ripley, *Races of Europe*, 490, and *ibid.* 502.

[2] See Peet, 496; Ridgeway, *Who were the Romans?* 1.

[3] Peet, 372-386.

[4] iv. 20; v. 39. As to his date, see Pais, i. 72.

[5] Binder, *Die Plebs*, 315.

Etruscans entered Italy from the north by way of the Alps. There are now, however, as will be shown later, the strongest grounds for believing that the Etruscans came to Italy by sea. Nothing in the character of the remains found in the *terremare* resembles Etruscan remains. The burial customs are entirely different, and if there is no ground for supposing that the Etruscans passed that way at all, the whole foundation for believing that the *terremare* belonged to the Etruscans crumbles away. This does not in any way affect the argument of those who believe that much of the early civilisation of Italy was brought there by the Etruscans and not by the Aryans. It will be shown later that this is in all probability true as regards what may be called material civilisation; but as regards the essential features of society and the elementary conceptions which meet us in the early Roman law, little, if any, trace of Etruscan influence can be found. At the time of their entry into Italy the Ayrans may have been less civilised than the Etruscans, but their legal institutions were so firmly rooted as to resist all foreign influences. The archæological evidence is very valuable, as confirming the traditional view that the population of early Rome does not belong to any single race. The expression "the Latin race," like "the Anglo-Saxon race," is a very loose one. Whether we speak with Huxley of the "wonderful ethnological hotchpot miscalled the Latin race," or with Professor Ridgeway of the "wonderful alloy from which the Romans were to develop," we must always bear in mind that we are dealing with a very mixed people.[1]

When we attempt to say that certain classes of the Romans belonged to one race, or that certain features of the early civilisation were brought in by one element of the population rather than by another, we are upon less safe ground. In recent years, for example, elaborate attempts have been made to show that the division between the Roman patricians and

[1] *Man's Place in Nature*, 295; *Who were the Romans?* 10.

plebeians, which is so striking a feature of the early city, was a race division. One modern writer maintains that the patricians were Sabines and the plebeians Latins.[1] Another writer, while agreeing that the patricians were Sabines, insists that the plebeians were Ligurians.[2] This latter view is supported partly by the fact that modern excavations in the Roman Forum have revealed graves in which bodies were interred as well as graves containing cinerary urns. Seeing that the Ligurians practised inhumation and the Aryans cremation, this fact undoubtedly goes to show that there were people in the city who belonged to various races; but this is far from proving either that those who practised these different rites were all citizens or that the urns contain patrician ashes and the graves plebeian bones. If after all the invasions the mass of the population of Italy continued to be Ligurian, as has been shown in the previous pages, there is nothing to surprise us in finding Ligurian graves at Rome, as, no doubt, there were many Ligurians there whatever may have been their political status. More will be said hereafter as to the distinction between the patricians and the plebeians. It is sufficient to say here that no sufficient proof has so far been adduced to show that it was a racial distinction.[3]

---

[1] Binder, *Die Plebs.*

[2] Ridgeway, *Who were the Romans?* same author, *Companion to Latin Studies*, n. 30.

[3] See Botsford, G. W., *The Roman Assemblies*, 38, New York, 1909; Klio, 1908, 252.

CHAPTER V

THE RELATIONS BETWEEN EARLY ROME AND THE ETRUSCANS

ONE of the most important of the facts brought out by recent researches is the extent and depth of Etruscan influence in Italy in prehistoric times. It has been said by a recent writer that the domination of the Etruscans over Italy in the fifth century B.C., followed by that of the Sabellian races, are the two facts of the early history which resist criticism.[1]

Most scholars have long been convinced that, for a time at least, Rome was subject to Etruscan lords. In a period concerning which almost everything is in dispute, the Etruscan lordship of Rome for a considerable length of time is one of the few points which are almost universally accepted.[2]

The ancient legends of Lars Porsena of Clusium, and the repulse of his host at the bridge by Horatius and his two comrades which is recounted by Livy and Plutarch, and is so familiar to us in Macaulay's *Lay*, is a pious fable.[3] It was invented to cloak the humiliating fact that Rome was conquered by the Etruscan king.[4]

Before referring further to this matter it will be well to give some account of the Etruscans themselves. Disputes have long been waged as to the origin and racial affinities of this mysterious people, whose language is still the despair

---

[1] C. Lécrivain, in *Révue Historique*, 1900, 162.

[2] Körte, in Pauly-Wissowa, *s.v.* "Etrusker," says: "*Dass sie* (i.e. *die Etrusker*), *in Rom geherrscht haben wird heute von niemand mehr bezweifelt.*"

[3] Livy, ii. 10; Plut. *Publicola*, 16.

[4] Tac., *Hist.*, iii. 72; Meyer, E., *Geschichte des Alterthums*, ii. 499; Soltau, *Röm. Geschichtschreibung*, 260; Pais, *Storia di Roma*, i. pt. i. 471, see *ibid.* 416; Binder, *Die Plebs*, 261.

of the philologists. In recent years few subjects have been worked at by scholars with greater industry than the Etruscan question, and although there is very much which still remains dark, many valuable results have been reached, and the history of the Etruscans in Italy in its main outlines is regarded by experts as fairly well established.[1]

The Etruscans appear to have called themselves Rásena,[2] but were called by the Greeks *τυρσηνοί*, or later *τύῤῥηνοί* and by the Romans Tusci.

In Egyptian inscriptions of the fourteenth or thirteenth century B.C., in the time of Menephtah and Rameses III., a people called Tursa or Turscha is mentioned as being at the head of the maritime peoples of that time and as attacking Egypt. It is agreed by most authorities that this refers to the Etruscans, and affords satisfactory evidence that they were at that date settled on the coast of the Ægean.[3]

According to Herodotus the Etruscans came from Lydia. He says that in consequence of a great famine the king of the Lydians divided the people into two portions, and drew lots which should remain and which should emigrate, and that the emigrants, headed by the king's son Tyrrhenus, went down to Smyrna and sailed thence to the territory of the Umbrici, where they erected towns wherein they were still dwelling in his time.[4]

Modern scholarship, after many wanderings, seems to be coming round again to the view as to the origin of the Etruscans which was maintained by the father of history. The remarkable similarity between the Etruscan sepulchral chambers and those found in Lydia and Phrygia affords at any rate strong evidence that this mode of burial was brought to

---

[1] See for a bibliography of Etruscology, *Jahresbericht der klass. Alterthumswissenschaft*, 1908, cxl. 79. See also Klio, 1908, 252.

[2] Dion., i. 30.

[3] Modestov, *Introduction*, 451, and references; Körte, in Pauly-Wissowa, *s.v.* "Etrusker."

[4] I. 94.

Italy from that part of Asia Minor.[1] And there are other indications which point to the same conclusion, though it cannot as yet be considered as proved. Whether the Etruscans were Lydians or not, it may be taken as an established fact that they were an Asiatic people who came to Italy by sea from the shores of Asia Minor, and settled first on the Etrurian coast from which they afterwards penetrated inland. At a later period they conquered the whole of Etruria and Umbria and the plain of the Po, and exercised lordship over Campania. They were a piratical folk who brought with them few women, and it may be assumed that in Italy they mingled with the Umbrians who were there before them, and created a mixed race. The opinion of earlier writers, who maintained that the Etruscans came into Italy by land from the Rhætian Alps, is now generally regarded as disproved by the archæological evidence which indicates in the clearest way their Asiatic origin.[2]

That a seafaring people, settled in the thirteenth century B.C. on the coast of the Ægean, should have chosen to make their way to Italy over the Alps is hardly credible. At any rate it would require very strong evidence to support it, whereas all the evidence seems to be to the contrary.[3] Still more incredible is the view that the Etruscans were part of the aboriginal population of Italy, though this opinion has been held by high authorities, and is even yet not without supporters.[4] Nor does there appear to be any ground for the belief of some writers that the Rásena or Etruscans proper were a ruling caste belonging to an Aryan race which ruled over a subject people different in origin, and largely composed of non-Aryans.[5] On the contrary, it may be taken as certain

[1] Modestov, 352.

[2] Modestov, 409, and references; Körte, in Pauly-Wissowa, *l.c.*

[3] This opinion is still held, however, by Binder, but on very unsatisfactory grounds (*Die Plebs*, 302).

[4] Meyer, E., *Geschichte des Alterthums*, ii. s. 321; Cuno, J. G., *Vorgeschichte Roms*, 1888, ii. 27.

[5] Kuhlenbeck, *Entwicklungsgeschichte*, i. 39.

that the Rásena were non-Aryans, and that the mass of the people over whom they ruled were Umbrians or other people belonging to the Latin races, whom the Oriental invaders had reduced to the position of clients and serfs, and probably also people belonging to the aboriginal race of Italy.

An inscription of some length found in 1886 on the Island of Lemnos, said to be in a dialect of Etruscan, or in a language closely similar to Etruscan, is regarded by most authorities as an important link in the chain of evidence which leads to the conclusion that the Etruscans came from Asia Minor. The ancient historians speak of the Tyrrhenians as settled on Lemnos in the seventh and sixth centuries B.C., though they often confused them with the Pelasgians.[1] The relationship of the language of the inscription on the Island of Lemnos to that of the Etruscan inscriptions in Italy is accepted by most philologists.[2]

The Etruscan Language.—Dionysius of Halicarnassus said of the Etruscans that they spoke a language unlike that of any other people—*οὐδενί ἄλλῳ γενεί ὁμόγλωσσον*;[3] and most modern philologists have come round to the same opinion. In spite of untiring efforts the language is as yet very little understood. A great number of inscriptions are already known, and others are being brought to light every year as excavations proceed, but they are almost entirely of a mortuary character, and contain little but proper names.[4] A few words

[1] Herod., 6, 137; Thuc., 4, 109. The Pelasgians were of the Greek stock, whether they were invaders like the Achæans or, as Ridgeway maintains, an Indo-European race who were aborigines in Greece. See Meyer, E., *Forschungen*, 112; Ridgeway, W., in the Cambridge *Companion to Latin Studies*, 1910, s. 22.

[2] Modestov, 400, and references. Körte, in Pauly-Wissowa, *s.v.* "Etrusker"; Meyer, *Geschichte des Alterthums*, ii. 300; and *Forschungen*, i. 27; Giles, P., in *Companion to Latin Studies*, s. 1204. Ridgeway doubts the identification of the language (*Early Age of Greece*, i. 145). Bury says the attempt to show it is Etruscan is "not quite convincing" (*Hist. of Greece*, 36, note).

[3] Dion., i. 30.

[4] Skutsch, in Pauly-Wissowa, *s.v.* "Etrusker," 803-805; Giles, P., in *Companion to Latin Studies*, n. 1204.

which have been deciphered appear to resemble Latin, but seeing that the Etruscans and the Latins were neighbours for centuries this is easily explained by the linguistic borrowing which almost invariably takes place between neighbouring peoples speaking different languages. All attempts to show affinities between the Etruscan language and that of any Aryan people appear to have failed, though one comparatively modern writer continues to assert that there is a strong connection between Etruscan and Celtic.[1] Most experts, however, now agree that the Etruscan language has to be regarded as in no way related either to any Aryan or any Semitic tongue. It has been pointed out that there is nothing in this which need surprise us. Most languages are, as a matter of fact, spoken in a very restricted area, and it is not the rule but the exception, when we find, as in the case of the Aryans and the Semites, a number of languages more or less closely related to one another spoken in different countries.[2]

Date of their Arrival in Italy.—There is no evidence which fixes with precision the time at which the Etruscans settled in Italy, and it is by no means necessary to assume that they came over all at the same time. It is, on the other hand, more probable that they came over at various periods extending over a century or more. Some writers place their entrance as early as the fourteenth century B.C., and connect their arrival with the migrations which were going on before the Trojan war.[3] But strong evidence has lately been adduced to show that the arrival of the Etruscans in Italy must not be put earlier than the ninth, or perhaps the eighth, century B.C. The grounds upon which this conclusion is reached can only be glanced at here. One reason is that in the remains of the Etruscan cities pre-Etruscan graves are found, which are

[1] Cuno, *Vorgeschichte Roms*, i. 1878, ii. 1888.

[2] Meyer, *Geschichte des Alterthums*, ii. 22.

[3] Schjott, P. O., *Die Römische Gesch. im Licht des neuesten Forschungen* Christiania, 1906.

believed by archæologists not to be older than the ninth or eighth century B.C. And another ground is that the Etruscan pictures and jewellery of the sixth century are so closely akin in character to the early art of Greece, that it is impossible to believe that when they were produced the Etruscans had been long separated from their former home in Asia Minor.[1]

From the eighth to the fifth century B.C. the Etruscans were by far the most powerful people in Italy. They held Western Italy north of the Tiber, and they were at any rate overlords in Campania. Their cities were formed into powerful confederations, and they had a markedly aristocratic form of society under their *lucumos*, who were at the same time princes and priests. They had strong cities, generally upon rocks or hills, from which these chieftains led their bands of vassals and dependants to overrun and sack neighbouring villages. Their pirate barques scoured the surrounding seas and brought back spoils from Greek and Phœnician trading ships. They carried on a lively trade with Sicily, Miletus, Corinth, and Carthage, and it is not unlikely that Greek artists were settled in Etruria.[2]

The heyday of Etruscan power was in the sixth century, and from that time they began to decline, but their power was not thoroughly broken until B.C. 396, when Veii was taken by the Romans, and when they sustained also a crushing defeat in the north at the hands of the Gauls. From that time they find themselves hemmed in between the Samnites and Romans on the south and the Gauls on the north, and their great power suffers a startlingly sudden collapse. It has been suggested that their rapid decline is due to the fact that in religion and art the Etruscans were borrowers and not originators. They "left the world no legacy worth taking up."[3]

---

[1] See on this subject generally, Modestov, 439 *seq.*; Körte, in Pauly-Wissowa, *l.c.*

[2] Körte, in Pauly-Wissowa, *s.v.* "Etrusker," 759.

[3] Fowler, W. Warde, in *Companion to Latin Studies*, s. 219. As to the

There are indications that during the later period the Etruscans became degenerated by luxury, but we have to remember that all the literary evidence which we have about them comes from their hereditary enemies the Romans, who were fond of contrasting the austere virtues of the Roman citizens with the effeminate luxury and voluptuousness of their Etruscan neighbours. There is considerable evidence to show that among the Etruscans the wife was the head of the family, and descent was counted through females and not through males. In numerous inscriptions the name of the mother of the deceased is given without that of the father, and the conclusion that the Etruscans had the form of kinship which the Germans call *Mutterrecht* seems a natural one.[1] We know from Herodotus that the Lycians followed this custom, and this is another point in confirmation of the theory of the Etruscans having come from Asia Minor.[2] The practice of counting kin through females would in itself excite the strong reprobation of the Roman patricians, who regarded the patriarchal family with the utmost veneration, and could not conceive in the early days that persons could be related except through males. They would not regard descent through females with any less horror, even if, as is quite possibly the case, the same practice was followed by their own plebeian fellow-citizens. For it has been suggested with much force that it was precisely this difference in the family organisation which kept the patricians and the plebeians so far apart from one another. This subject will be touched on later.[3]

---

essentially Greek character of Etruscan art, see the remarks of d'Hancarville in David, F. A., *Antiquités Etrusques, etc.*, iii. 41, Paris, 1785.

[1] Kohler, in *Zeit. für vergleich. Rechtswiss.*, iv. 270 ; Bernhöft, *ibid.* viii. 176 ; Binder, *Die Plebs*, 407.

[2] *Cf.* Egypt, where Diodorus says that in dotal contracts it is always stipulated that the supremacy over the husband shall belong to the wife, and the husband promises to obey her (Diod., i. 27. See Dareste, R., *Études d'Histoire du Droit*, 3).

[3] Binder, *Die Plebs*, 408 ; see Ridgeway, *Who were the Romans?* 15.

The Romans spoke of the Etruscans as fat and heavy—*pinguis Etruscus; obesus Etruscus*—and they were shocked at the fact that among the Etruscans the women joined in the banquets with the men. This may be seen from the frescoes which show the guests, both men and women, reclining on the couches round the table, while dancers of both sexes perform before them to the music of flutes and lyres.[1]

The Etruscans were short, stout, strongly built, and, as a rule, black haired. That they were a pleasure-loving people, fond of pomp and display, is abundantly shown by the monuments, and that a certain grimness, if not cruelty, was characteristic of them may be suspected, but they could not have achieved the position which they did if they had not possessed the warlike virtues. They were Orientals, and in their dress, their music, and their customs were altogether foreign to the Romans. There is abundant evidence that from the sixth century B.C., if not earlier, the Etruscans had attained to a stage of civilisation far higher than that which existed among any of the other Italian peoples. In architecture and in the laying out of cities, in medicine, in astronomy, in painting, music, engraving of gems, and in goldsmith's work they had reached a high level at an age when the Italians were rude farmers and shepherds.[2]

This foreign colony of civilised invaders held a position in Italy which bears some resemblance to that occupied in Spain by the Moors sixteen or seventeen centuries later. The most characteristic memorials which the Etruscans have left are their tombs, which are really houses for the dead, provided with chairs and other furniture, and the walls of which are decorated with elaborate paintings, which were shut up for ever when the body had been deposited in the tomb. Among the

[1] See the figure in Daremberg et Saglio, *s.v.* "Acroama," and the figure *s.v.*, "Etrusques," *ibid.* 848.

[2] See for some excellent illustrations of Etruscan art, Daremberg et Saglio, *s.v.* "Etrusques," and Baumeister, *Denkmäler*, *s.v.* "Etrurien."

subjects which the Etruscans most cultivated was the art of divination, and it is universally admitted that the Roman augurs borrowed largely from the Etruscan lore. There were three branches of these mysteries: (1) The art of predicting the future from an examination of the entrails and especially from the liver of animals which had been sacrificed. This special science, called *extispicium*, was practised in many countries, but was developed by the Etruscans with great minuteness. They divided the liver into a number of sections, each of which was designated by the name of some divinity.[1] Such a liver made of bronze, found at Piacenza, is still in existence, and a very similar one made of clay has been found in Chaldæa, where the art of divination was practised from a very early time. This connection between the Etruscan religion and that of Chaldæa is a strong argument in favour of the Asiatic origin of the Etruscans.[2] (2) The art of explaining the meaning of lightning, of averting its evil effects, and even of drawing it down from heaven; and (3) The art of interpreting portents or *prodigia* and of averting their consequences. As a recent authority has said, the science of divination "may fairly be described as the most remarkable waste of human ingenuity known to history."[3]

Debt of Rome to Etruscan Culture.—It is pretty certain that in the early times Rome must have borrowed a good deal from the Etruscan culture. When two peoples, living upon very different stages of refinement and culture, are for centuries near neighbours, it is inevitable that there should be a certain amount of filtration from the higher civilisation into the lower. It is very possible that some of the refinements of life, of which there are signs at Rome at an early date, were taken by them

[1] See the figure in Modestov, *Introd.*, 394; and in Daremberg et Saglio, *s.v.* "Haruspices."

[2] Modestov, *op. cit.* 388.

[3] Fowler, W. Warde, in *Companion to Latin Studies*, s. 219. See on the subject generally, Müller, K. O., *Die Etrusker*, i. 123 *seq.*; Daremberg et Saglio, *s.v.* "Haruspices."

from the Etruscans, who thus acted as intermediaries to carry to the Romans some of the culture of the East.[1] But it is easy to exaggerate the extent of this borrowing. The Romans were not an artistic people, and at this early period were to a great extent unable to appreciate or to profit by the art and refinement of the Etruscans. They were, however, an intensely practical people, and they did borrow the things which struck them as useful. The Romans at that time lived in huts made of woven branches smeared with clay or mud, and roofed over with branches, and it is pretty certain that they learnt from the Etruscans to build stone houses after the Etruscan type. These houses consisted of a large hall which the Romans called *atrium*, with rooms opening out of it at each side, and with an opening to the sky in the centre. The original Roman house included no other parts.[2]

From the Etruscans the Romans took also the manner of paving streets and the art of building aqueducts and sewers, such as the *Cloaca Maxima* in Rome, which is referred by tradition to the time of the Tarquins. It does not appear, however, to be the case that the Romans learnt from the Etruscans the use of the arch, though this used to be believed.[3]

The gladiatorial combats and horse races are generally assigned to Etruscan origin, and so also are some of the musical instruments used in early times, such as the *cornu* or large circular trumpet, originally of horn, later of bronze, and the *lituus*, a straight trumpet with a curve at the large end.[4]

The Roman numeral system is said to be taken from the

---

[1] See the remarks of Lenel, in *Zeit. Sav. Stift.*, xxvi. 516-571 ; Körte, in Pauly-Wissowa, *s.v.* "Etrusker," 768.

[2] Daremberg et Saglio, *s.v.* "Domus," 350 ; Pauly-Wissowa, *l.c.* ; Baumeister, *Denkmäler des Klass. Alt.*, *s.v.* "Baukunst," i. 288 ; Modestov, *Introd.*, 330 ; Gercke und Norden, *Einleitung in die Alterthumswissenschaft*, iii. 24, Leipzig, 1910.

[3] Körte, in Pauly-Wissowa, *s.v.* "Etrusker," 759.

[4] See the figures in Daremberg et Saglio, under the word "cornu" at p. 1512, and under "lituus" at p. 1278.

Etruscans, and so was the round shield of iron—*clipeus*—which the Roman soldiers used until they abandoned it for the rectangular leathern shield rimmed with iron, which they borrowed from the Samnites.[1]

It is, moreover, a significant fact that to Etruscan origin must be ascribed the marks of pomp and majesty attached by the Romans to the holders of high offices. The Roman writers describe the early king as sitting on an ivory throne clad in the purple *toga* or *trabea,* wearing red shoes with high heels—*mullei*—crowned with a laurel wreath of gold, and holding in his hand an ivory sceptre surmounted by an eagle.[2] There are even some indications which suggest that when the king sat in state upon his throne his face was rouged to give him a more striking appearance.[3] When he walked he was preceded by the twelve lictors, each bearing a *fascis* or bundle of rods containing an axe, as a sign that the king had the power of life and death, and might flog or behead a citizen at will.[4]

These *insignia* of authority, which the Roman consuls inherited from the early kings, are ascribed by the Roman writers themselves to foreign origin.[5] Their Oriental character is obvious.[6]

On the whole, there can be little doubt that the influence of Etruria upon Rome and its culture was considerable, and far exceeded what Schwegler or even Mommsen would have admitted, though I am inclined to think that a recent writer overstates the case when he says that Rome's debt to the Etruscans was "quite enormous."[7]

---

[1] *Companion to Latin Studies*, s. 431.

[2] See the figures in Rich's *Dictionary of Antiquities*, *s.v.* "Solium."

[3] See Girard, *Org. Jud.*, i. 12, n. 2.

[4] See the figure in Daremberg et Saglio, *s.v.* "Lictor."

[5] Liv., i. 8 ; Dion., iii. 61.

[6] The description of the king is a composite picture. For references to the authorities, see Mommsen, *Staatsrecht*, ii. 4 ; Müller, *Etrusker*, i. 344 ; Binder, *Die Plebs*, 578 ; *Org. Jud.*, i. 11.

[7] Binder, *Die Plebs*, 261 ; *cf.* Modestov, *Introd.*, 104.

Conquest of Rome by the Etruscans.—It is generally believed by scholars that it was in the sixth century, during the height of the Etruscan power, that they acquired lordship over Rome, which was ruled by an Etruscan dynasty until the expulsion of Tarquin the Tyrant. This event was not merely an uprising of the people to secure political liberty, but was at the same time the throwing off of a hated foreign yoke.[1] But some modern writers have adopted the much more startling hypothesis that Rome was, from its origin, an Etruscan colony, and that during the regal period the patricians or ruling caste was composed of Etruscans, while the mass of the people belonged to the Latin races. This view seems to have been put forward first by Niebuhr in the first edition of his *Roman History*, but Niebuhr at a later period abandoned it.[2] It has, however, now been revived, and it is supported by further arguments by some modern writers.[3] The argument in support of this opinion is based to a considerable extent upon philological investigations, and particularly on the work of W. Schulze on Latin Proper Names. In this work evidence is adduced to show that many of the Roman names are of Etruscan origin. The words "Rome" and "Tiber" are traced to Etruscan roots; Romulus is connected with an Etruscan *gens*, the Romilii; and the names of the kings Remus, Numa, Tullus, Ancus, Servius, and Tarquin are said to be Etruscan, and to occur in Etruscan inscriptions. It is also said that the names of the three "tribes" into which, according to the tradition, the Roman people was at first divided—the *Ramnes*, *Tities*, and *Luceres*—are Etruscan gentile names.[4] If it be the case that "Rome" and "Tiber" are Etruscan words,

[1] Meyer, E., *Geschichte des Alterthums*, ii. 435; Niese, B., *Grundriss der Römischen Geschichte*, 3rd ed. 34, München, 1906; Pais, *Storia di Roma*, i. pt. i. 471; Modestov, *Introd.*, 253, 380.

[2] *Römische Geschichte*, 1st ed. i. 181; 3rd ed. i. 426.

[3] Cuno, *Vorgeschichte Roms*, i. 1; Holzapfel, L., *Klio*, 1901, 228; Schjott, P. O., *Die Römische Geschichte im Lichte der Neuesten Forschungen*, Christiania, 1906; Ripley, *Races of Europe*, 265.

[4] Schulze's views are accepted generally by Körte, in Pauly-Wissowa, *s.v.* "Etrusker," 774; and by Soltau, *Römische Geschichtschreibung*, 144.

this is certainly calculated to arouse suspicion, but so far as a layman can judge, the suggested etymologies are far from certain. As to the names of the kings, it is quite uncertain how far they go back. It may be that the names of these very shadowy personages were invented during the time when the people still remembered the princes of the Etruscan dynasty.[1] Much has been made also of a famous wall painting, discovered in a tomb at Vulci in 1857. This shows us an Etruscan called Mastarna, who has been identified with considerable probability with King Servius Tullius, and in the same fresco a certain Tarquin is described as the "Roman."[2] The frescoes at Vulci afford undoubtedly some confirmation for the belief that Rome was at one time subject to Etruscan lords, a belief which upon other grounds is now held by almost all scholars; but so far as I can judge they are of no value as evidence that Rome was Etruscan in its origin. The frescoes, according to the opinion of experts, are probably not older than the third century B.C., and they represent figures of the heroes of the past, who were already legendary at that time if not mythical.[3]

Much more convincing evidence that Rome began its history as an Etruscan city would be the discovery there of remains of Etruscan origin of older date than those of the Latins. Professor Middleton, in a work published in 1885, declared that there had been discovered at Rome the remains of an Etruscan city older than the legendary regal period, and that this must be regarded as strong evidence against the theory of early Latin supremacy in Bome. But this statement has been challenged by Lanciani, who declares that there is no evidence that the Etruscans were the first settlers at Rome, but, on the other hand, that the explorations made there strongly corroborate

---

[1] See Soltau, *op. cit.* 145.

[2] See the reproduction of these pictures in Daremberg et Saglio, *s.v.* "Etrusques."

[3] Pais, *Storia di Roma*, i. pt. i. 338 *seq.* for full discussion; Meyer, E., *Geschichte des Alterthums*, ii. 435.

the view that Rome was founded by a colony of shepherds from the Alban hills, on ground which had never been occupied permanently before.[1]

So far as the writer can judge, the theory that Rome began as an Etruscan colony is not supported by any evidence which is at all convincing, and there appear to be strong arguments against it. If Rome had been an Etruscan city like Veii or Clusium, we should expect to find its institutions to be of an Etruscan nature, and to bear Etruscan names. Why should the Sovereign be called by the Latin word *Rex* and not by an Etruscan title like *Porsena?* And why should the great religious officials like the pontifex and the augurs bear Latin titles? If Rome had received a strong Etruscan impress from the first we should expect to find it differing in religion, in institutions, and in character from the surrounding peoples of Latin stock. But the contrary is the case. At the beginning of the period of authentic history we find Rome in close political and religious connection with the neighbouring Latins, and the Etruscans regarded as foreigners. A recent writer goes even further, and maintains that if we accept the Etruscan origin of Rome we must give an entirely new turn to our studies of the early Roman law. Much has been done in recent years to throw light upon the early legal conceptions of the Romans by a study of the primitive law of other peoples belonging to the Aryan race.[2] It is argued that no such comparison would be permissible if we were to accept the view that Rome was founded by a people who did not belong to the Aryan race at all.[3] But this argument goes too far. Whether Rome began as an Etruscan city or not, nothing is more certain than the fact that at a very early period, and in all probability not later than

[1] Lanciani, R., *Ancient Rome*, 39-43, London, 1894. *Cf.* Modestov, *Introd.*, 242, 252, 253.

[2] *E.g.* in such works as Dareste, R., *Études d'Histoire du Droit*, Paris, 1889, and *Nouvelles Études d'Histoire du Droit*, Paris, 1902.

[3] Binder, J., *Die Plebs*, 530 and 257-261-278.

the sixth century, it was essentially a Latin city.[1] Even if at one time its institutions were Etruscan, they must have been exchanged for Latin ones. The characteristic features of the early society, the patriarchal family, the State religion and the religion of the hearth, the notions about justice and the punishment of wrongs, and so forth, are unmistakably of Aryan origin. The light which can be thrown upon them by a study of comparative law is not at all affected by the fact, if it be a fact, that Etruscan institutions existed before them in the early city. But for the reasons above stated there is no need in the present state of our knowledge to accept the theory of the Etruscan origin of the city.

[1] Körte, in Pauly-Wissowa, *s.v.* "Etrusker," 473.

CHAPTER VI

The Foundation of the City and the Early Political Organisation

For the reasons which have been stated at some length in the second chapter, very little faith can be given to the accounts of the founding of the city unless they are supported by other evidence. The architectural remains corroborate the tradition that there were two separate early settlements, one on the Palatine and another on the Quirinal, and there is a good deal of evidence in support of the ancient story that the population included a Sabine and a Latin element.[1]

The date 753 B.C., assigned as that of the birth of Rome, is a purely arbitrary one. No confidence whatever can be placed in the stories told of the seven kings. The conventional account of the regal period is a mass of myth and legend, and it is not surprising, therefore, that the modern historians, who have attempted to reconstruct the history of the infant city out of such doubtful materials, should have come to very varying conclusions. There is, however, no reason to doubt that the original population of the city was divided into certain groups and classes, of which a brief account must now be given. Some of these groups and divisions are no doubt of much greater antiquity than the city itself and run back to the prehistoric age.

The Three Tribes.—According to the legend the Roman people was divided into three tribes—the *Tities*, the *Ramnes*, and the *Luceres*. The writers connected the *Ramnes* with Romulus, the *Tities* with Titus Tatius the Sabine, while various explanations

[1] See Binder, *Die Plebs*, chaps. i. and ii.; Pelham, *Roman Hist.*, 4th ed. chap. ii.

were given of the origin of the *Luceres*.[1] Many modern historians, following Niebuhr, believe that the legendary division of the people into three tribes points to the fact that these three tribes were three different races, viz. Sabines, Latins, and Etruscans, which coalesced to form the infant city. But this theory is altogether improbable, and is now generally rejected. The suggestion has recently been made that the Romans took the division into three tribes from the Etruscans, and there is some evidence that a similar division existed in some Etruscan cities.[2] If we were to accept the opinion that Rome was in its origin an Etruscan foundation, it would not be unreasonable to imagine that the Romans should have taken over from the Etruscans this threefold division of the people. But in a preceding chapter it has been argued that no sufficient grounds exist for accepting the Etruscan origin of the city, and therefore this account of the origin of the tribes must be rejected. It is much more probable that the three tribes were ancient divisions of the people which existed long before the foundation of Rome. The tribes, and the *curiae* into which they were divided, bear, in fact, a close analogy to divisions found among other Aryans, and may be compared particularly with the *phylae* and *phratries* among the Greeks, and tribes and *curiae* alike are found among the Latins and Umbrians, as well as at Rome. It is probable that the tribes, like most of the groups into which we find the Aryans divided at various periods, were, in their origin, groups of persons bound together by a political bond. It was not until the people settled down after the wanderings that the groups came to be territorial instead of personal.[3] The ancient tribes of the Latins, like the *phylae* of the Greeks, began by being associations of a number of

---

1 Dion., 2, 47, 4; Plut., *Rom.*, 13; Varro, *L. L.*, 55.

2 Holzapfel, in *Klio*, 1901, i. 228.

3 Botsford, *Roman Assemblies*, ch. i.; Meyer, *Geschichte des Alterthums*, ii. 511; Binder, *Die Plebs*, 268-395; and as to *phratries*, see Daremberg et Saglio, *s.v.* "Eupatrides"; Leist, *Alt-Arisches Jus Civile*, ii. 197.

curiae or *phratries.*[1] At Rome after the very early period the division into three tribes ceases to be of any consequence, being superseded by the later divisions, attributed to Servius, likewise called tribes.

Curiae.—Each of the three tribes was divided into ten *curiae*, so that there were in all thirty *curiae.* The *curiae*, which bear a close analogy to the Greek *phratries*, were, like them, divisions of the people originally personal, that is, based on kinship real or supposed, but which in later times became territorial. Each *curia* in all probability occupied a definite territory, and the *curia* has been not inaptly compared to a parish.[2] But there is this important difference among others, that the mere fact of residence or owning land in the territory of a *curia* would not have made a Roman a member of it. In order to be a member of the *curia* he must belong to one of the families of which the *curia* was composed. But, like a parish, the *curia* had its priest, called a *curio*, and its chapel or place of meeting, which was also called *curia.* One of the priests or *curiones* was elected at *curio maximus*, to preside over the *curiones*, who formed a college of thirty priests. The free men of full age who belonged to the *curiae*, whether they were *patresfamilias* or not, had a right to vote at the meetings of the *curiae* called *comitia curiata* held in the market-place.

The Gentes.—It is stated by many historians that each of the thirty *curiae* was divided into ten *gentes*, but this, besides being inherently improbable, rests upon a misapprehension of the language of the Latin writers. Neither of the two passages cited in its support will fairly bear this interpretation.[3] And seeing that the *gentes* or clans were natural groups and not artificial creations of the law, it is hardly credible that there should have been exactly ten for each *curia.* The divisions of

---

[1] Meyer, *op. cit.*, s. 58 and s. 192. *Cf.* Grote, *Hist. of Greece*, iii. 50.

[2] Cuq, 2nd ed. i. 22.

[3] Dion., 2, 7, 4; Gell., 15, 27, 4; Botsford, *Roman Assemblies*, 11; Mommsen, *Röm. Staatsrecht*, iii. 12; Pelham, *Roman History*, 4th ed. 21.

the people into clans is found among all the Aryans, and among some of them has continued to play an important part down to modern times. But among the Romans it decayed remarkably early, and is already far advanced in decline at the time when our knowledge of the Roman people begins. The *gens* or clan is an association of families related through males, bearing the same name, and claiming descent from a common ancestor. Among the Aryans clans existed before the formation of the State. Before any settled constitution was evolved, and when the individual families were too weak to protect themselves, it was natural that those families which were of the same blood should combine for purposes of protection against their common enemies, and for assistance to each other. At a primitive time the clans were autonomous, and their common affairs were administered by a council of elders, or, among some Aryans, by a chief of the clan exercising an unlimited power over its members. No doubt the relationship to each other between the members of the clan was often fictitious, and known to be so. Outsiders had come into the clan by adoption, and the families had spread into so many branches that the actual tie of blood had become very slight, but they still regard themselves as kinsmen, and the very name *gens* implies blood relationship, and may be compared with the Greek γένος, the members of which were called ὁμογάλακτες.[1]

Each Roman *gens* had its special religious rites and its own burial-ground, but, so far as our records go back, we find no trace of chiefs of the *gentes*, though these may very well have existed at one time. No doubt, also, in the primitive time, the clan exercised disciplinary control over the clansman, and could punish him by expulsion from the clan and exclusion from its religious rites, and we may presume, too, that at Rome, as elsewhere among the Aryans, the clan in the early period took vengeance upon anyone who had wronged one of its members, and protected the orphan children of a *gentilis*. It

[1] See Daremberg et Saglio, *s.v.* "Gens."

is probable also that at one time the land occupied by the families was assigned to them by the clans to which they belonged, but this matter will be touched upon in speaking of the early laws of property.

In historical times the most important relic of the gentile organisation at Rome consisted in the fact that, if a man left no relations on the father's side falling within the categories of *sui* or *agnati*, his succession went to his clansmen.[1]

An author whose writings have done much to elucidate the problems of the early city contends that the *gens* is not a primitive institution of the Aryans, and was not developed among the Italians till they had differentiated into races—Umbrians, Oscans, Latins, etc. He maintains that the early Aryan organisation was into families, brotherhoods or groups of near kin, and tribes.[2] It may be true that the groups of near kin are more primitive than the *gentes*, but certainly the *gentes* grew out of them at an early time. The main point is that the Roman *gentes* were natural groups, antedating the formation of the State. It is more doubtful if the *curia* is a primitive group, and I agree with Mr. Reid that it has "all the appearance of having originated in a definite act of legislation."[3] The early establishment of the city-state prevented the clan system from playing at Rome anything like so important a part as it did in the history of some of the Aryans, and especially in that of the Celts.[4]

Patricians, Clients, and Plebeians.—At a very early time the population of the city consists of these three classes. Their

[1] See Cic., *Top.*, 6, 29 ; Mommsen, *Röm. Staatsrecht*, iii. 9 *seq.*; Jhering, *Esprit du Droit Romain*, i. 184 ; Meyer, *Geschichte des Alterthums*, ii. 56 and 327 ; Launspach, *State and Family in Early Rome*, 56 ; and for a valuable discussion of many of the problems connected with the Roman *gens*, Botsford, G. W., in *Pol. Sci. Quart.*, xxii. 663.

[2] Botsford, G. W., in *Pol. Sci. Quart.*, xxii. 685.

[3] *Companion to Latin Studies*, n. 309.

[4] See Schrader, *Sprachvergleichung*, 568 ; Maine, *Ancient Law*, 15th ed. 264 ; Maine, *Village Communities*, 156 ; Vinogradoff, *Growth of the Manor*, 7 ; Brunner, *Deutsche Rechtsgeschichte*, i. 81.

origin and the relation between them, and the share enjoyed by each in the government of the city, have been for many years extremely controversial topics. It is impossible to discuss them here, except in a very summary way. According to the view of some of the highest authorities, the patricians were all the members of the clans or *gentes*. They alone had at first any political rights. Residence within the city boundary, freedom, wealth, could not enfranchise a man. He must belong to a *gens*. The clansmen alone are the *patres* or burghers. The rest are, at best, free outlanders. The assembly of the people or *comitia curiata* is an assembly of clansmen, and no one who does not belong to a *gens* can take part in its deliberations. Attached to the patricians, and dependent upon them, there grows up at a very early time the class called clients, a word which means hearers or dependants.[1] Their origin is ascribed, partly to the manumission of slaves whose descendants are clients, partly to the admission to the city of homeless wanderers who place themselves under the protection of a patrician, partly to members of neighbouring communities who were conquered, and allowed to come into the city on condition of attaching themselves as clients. When the origin of clientage was this kind of surrender, or *deditio*, the conquered peoples in some cases became clients of the commander of the army to whom they surrendered, and hereditary clients of the *gens* to which he belonged. Members of outlying communities who had made this kind of surrender were, perhaps, as a rule, allowed to remain on their own lands, no longer as owners in the strict sense of the term, but upon a precarious tenure as clients of a Roman patrician or of a Roman *gens*. The client was not a citizen, and had in law no civil rights, but was obliged to look to his patron to protect him against wrong. If he was allowed to go to the *comitia*, it was not as a member but as an attendant of his patron. He stands to his patron in a relation which, in

[1] It is, according to some authorities, the present participle of an archaic verb *cluere*, to hear, while others connect it with (in) *clinare*, to lean on.

many of its incidents, resembles that of a vassal to a feudal lord. He is bound to perform certain services for his patron, he must attend him in war, and in many cases he farms lands which belong to the patron. In return, the patron is bound to protect the client, and in the early times no duty is held more sacred. The writers who maintain the view that in the early days of Rome the only citizens were the patricians, ascribe the growth of the third class, or plebeians, to the decay of the system of clientage. In the regal period it is said that a large number of clients had been settled on public lands as clients of the king, and the downfall of the monarchy set them free. Moreover, as clans died out the clients who had belonged to them or to their members had no longer any patron, and when the gentile organisation broke up, and it was no longer membership of a clan but ownership of land which made a man liable to military service, the clients, who had possessed lands assigned to them by the *gentes*, which they held, not as owners but as dependants of the clan, were now enrolled as absolute owners.[1] But in recent times strong arguments have been brought forward against this theory of the exclusively patrician origin of the city. The classical writers speak of the *plebs* as having existed from the very beginning.[2] And it is very odd if the word *plebs*, which means the multitude or the masses, was employed to describe a class which did not exist at first. The arguments cannot be stated here, but the probabilities appear to be against the theory that the plebeians formed no part of the original population of the city.

It is more likely that the three classes, patricians, clients, and plebeians, all existed at Rome from the very beginning. Some of the ancient *gentes* had acquired at a very early time, and perhaps before the foundation of the city, a position of predominance, and had come to form a noble class. The priests

[1] Mommsen, *Röm. Forschungen*, i. 355 ; *Röm. Staatsrecht*, iii. 54 ; Pauly-Wissowa, *s.v.* "Clientes."

[2] Cic., *Rep.*, 2, 9, 16 ; Dion., 2, 9, 2.

of the State religion belonged to these privileged families, and they alone possessed the knowledge regarding auspices, portents, and days sacred and profane, on the due attention to which the safety of the community depended. It was from this privileged class that the early senate had been formed, and the name *patres* is closely associated with the senate by the classical writers. It is possible, in fact, that the word *patricii* comes from *patres* in the sense of senators, and that the first patricians were the families of those called to the original senate, as well as, of course, the senators themselves, but it seems more likely that the term patricians denoted at first the noble class from which the senators were naturally chosen.[1]

As to the clients, it is probable that they were in the beginning a semi-servile class, consisting largely of conquered aborigines, and afterwards recruited in the various manners which have been enumerated above. Such a dependent class is found in many early communities.[2]

The plebeians were, in all likelihood, of very varied origin. The nucleus consisted of the freemen who did not belong the patrician *gentes*. These were recruited by immigrants who came in from the surrounding country, by conquered Latins whose freedom had not been taken away, and by enfranchised clients, or clients attached to a *gens* which had become extinct. And it is by no means unlikely that the plebeians included also a considerable number of the conquered aborigines of the country. It seems probable, however, that most of the plebeians belonged to the same stock as the patricians, spoke the same language, and had the same customs, and it is by no means impossible that some of the plebeians were organised into *gentes*. That plebeian *gentes* existed in

[1] Pelham, *Roman History*, 4th ed. 46; Soltau, *Altröm. Volksversammlungen*, 209. Botsford thinks the adjective *patricius* applies to senators and their families (*Roman Assemblies*, 21).

[2] Compare the Penestai in Thessaly, Bury, *History of Greece*, 55; the Thetes at Athens, Grote, ii. 100; the Læti among the Germans, Brunner, i. 101; the Nativi among the Celts; Vinogradoff, *Growth of the Manor*, 25.

later times can hardly be doubted. One of the reproaches of Cicero to Clodius, who had passed by abrogation from a patrician to a plebeian *gens*, is, "You have confused the *sacra* and contaminated the *gentes*, both that which you have deserted and that which you have defiled," *i.e.* by joining it.[1] And the expression, which is quite common, *gentes patriciæ*, seems so imply the existence of plebeian *gentes*.[2] But it is generally supposed that these plebeian *gentes*, or at any rate analogous groups called *stirpes*, were of later origin, and were introduced among the plebeians on the model of the patrician *gentes*.[3]

Is the Division between the Patricians and the Plebeians a Race Division?—It has frequently been suggested that the division between the patricians and the plebeians was essentially a race division, but very different views have been put forth as to what the two races were. In a very learned and interesting work it has been argued lately that Rome originated in the amalgamation of a Sabine community, settled on the Quirinal hill, and a Latin community, settled on the Palatine. The Sabines were the patricians and the Latins were the plebeians.[4]

According to another recent writer, however, the patricians were Sabines and the plebeians were the aboriginal Ligurians whom the Sabines had conquered.[5] Other theories of the different race origins of the two orders have been propounded, but it is impossible to demonstrate the truth of any such theory, and there does not seem to be any substantial ground for believing that the division between patricians and plebeians was, primarily, a race division. It is more likely that the

[1] Cic., *Dom.*, 13, 35.

[2] See Botsford, *Pol. Sci. Quart.*, xxii. 667.

[3] Cuq, 2nd ed. i. 66; Mommsen, *Röm. Staatsrecht*, iii. 74; Binder, *Die Plebs*, 417.

[4] Binder, *Die Plebs*, 104, 134.

[5] Ridgeway, W., *Companion to Latin Studies*, n. 30; *Early Age of Greece*, i. 257.

plebeians formed a mixed multitude, partly Aryan and partly non-Aryan in origin. As a body they had not the race purity on which the patricians prided themselves, and possibly many of them belonged to families organised on the principle of relationship on the mother's side, a point to which reference is made elsewhere.[1]

Had the Plebeians the Right to Vote in the Comitia Curiata?—No question connected with the organisation of the early city has been the subject of more controversy than this. The texts of the classical writers give no precise answer to it, and in what they do say about it, it cannot be assumed that they are correct. The school of historians, of which Niebuhr may be taken as the founder, held that the *comitia curiata* was composed of *gentes*, and that as the patricians only were members of the *gentes*, though their clients belonged to it in a dependent character, it followed that the patricians alone could vote in the *comitia*.[2]

Mommsen is of opinion that the plebeians could not vote in the *comitia curiata* at first, but were admitted to it at a very early time, perhaps after the Servian scheme of division into centuries was introduced.[3] One of his main reasons is that a plebeian is known to have been elected as *curio maximus* in B.C. 209, from which he infers that the *comitia* was open to plebeians long before then. His view that the *comitia curiata* was exclusively patrician to begin with, but was thrown open to plebeians at the beginning of the really historical period, is one which is followed by many modern writers.[4] But other recent writers have advanced strong arguments in favour of the position that the *comitia* was always open to the plebeians, and that this assembly was a mass meeting of all the freemen, analogous to that which is found in most of the

[1] See the Index, *s.v. Mutterrecht; supra*, p. 39.

[2] *Hist.*, English trans., i. 162.

[3] *Röm. Forschungen*, i. 140, 147.

[4] *E.g.* Kübler, in Pauly-Wissowa, *s.v.* "Curia"; and Liebenam, *ibid.*, *s.v.* "Comitia Curiata."

Aryan communities.[1] The chief points in favour of this opinion may be summarised as follows:—(1) No ancient writer says that the plebeians were excluded from the *comitia curiata;* on the contrary, it is spoken of as an assembly of the *populus*, and this term must include the plebeians.[2] (2) The patricians must have been a small body, and the *plebs*, as its name denotes, included the mass of the population. (3) The opposite theory "assumes the existence of a community politically far advanced, yet showing no inequalities of rank among the freemen—a condition outside the range of human experience."[3]

On the other side, the most serious argument is that if the plebeians formed a majority of the people and could vote in the *comitia*, they must have had control of the government of the city, and the whole story of their long struggle for political equality becomes inexplicable. This argument would be irresistible if we were to regard the *comitia* as having legislative powers at all similar to those possessed by a free parliament in a democratic country, but any such analogy would be entirely misleading. The *comitia* was not a parliament which initiated and debated legislative proposals; it was a mass meeting of citizens to which the king or the magistrate submitted a proposal to change one of the traditional usages of the people. The *comitia* itself had no power of initiation, nor had it any power of amendment; the citizens simply vote "yes" or "no," at first by mere acclamation, and at a later time by a vote according to *curies.* If the *comitia* voted "yes," the law still required the ratification of the patrician senate. The *comitia* was presided over by the king, and after the expulsion of the kings by patrician magistrates, and the

[1] It might be compared with the Homeric ἀγορά, the Athenian ἐκκλησία, the Frankish *mallum*, or the old English *gemot* (Bryce, *Studies in Hist. and Jurisprudence*, ii. 297).

[2] Cic., *Pro. Planc.*, 3, 8; and *De Domo*, 14, 38; Mommsen, *Röm. Forsch.* i. 147; Soltau, *Altröm. Volksversamm.*, 86.

[3] Botsford, 38.

presiding officer had great control over the proceedings. If the temper of the meeting was hostile, it was easy for him to cause it to be adjourned on the plea that the auspices were unfavourable. With the king or with patrician magistrates at their head, with a senate composed of members of their own order, having the power to veto any proposal approved of by the *comitia*, with patrician priests and augurs always ready to work the machinery of the State religion in favour of their order, the mass meeting of freemen of the early city presented no terrors to the patricians. And it has always to be remembered that in such a society as that of Rome in the regal period or the early Republic there is extremely little legislation. The ancient customs of the people are too hallowed by immemorial use to be touched lightly. The family law especially is so sacred that no change in it can be contemplated. There is no commerce. The men are busy farming or fighting, and have no wish to alter the law. But for the dissatisfaction of the plebeians at their exclusion from the magistracies, and the grievances connected with their want of *conubium* with the patricians, and with the old law of debt, there would have been in the early period hardly any demand for legislation. And in such a society the primitive divisions of the people into groups, which are to a great extent autonomous, renders it unnecessary and difficult for the State frequently to intervene by legislation. So long as the *gentes* were active they controlled their own affairs and protected their own members. Within the family, again, the law was almost silent—it stopped at the door of the house. Inside it the *paterfamilias* was almost an absolute monarch, except for the restraints of public opinion. Law in early Rome, as elsewhere in communities at a similar stage of development, was almost exclusively unwritten law,—the ancient customs of the people.[1] Upon the whole, the

[1] See as to the reign of custom, Pernice, in *Zeit. Sav. Stift.*, xx. 162 and xxii. 59, 82 *seq.*; Binder, 350; Meyer, *Geschichte des Alterthums*, ii. n. 60; Botsford, 177.

probabilities are in favour of the view that the plebeians were entitled to vote in the *comitia curiata* from the earliest times, although it cannot be said that this is capable of demonstration.[1]

The King and the Senate.—Very little can be affirmed with any confidence concerning the king and the early senate. Such evidence as there is goes to show that the king was not hereditary but elective. He was not an Oriental despot but the chief citizen, and was at once the high priest, the chief-justice, and the commander-in-chief of the little community. The traditional customs of the people were in his care, and one of these customs was that he should act in consultation with his great council—the senate—though without being formally bound to follow its advice. During the period of Etruscan dominion the king was more of a despot, and a pomp and majesty were attached to his office which did not correspond with his former position as an ordinary burgess, "whom, to use Mommsen's words, merit or fortune, and above all the necessity of having one master in every house, had placed as master over his equals."[2] This kingly senate has been described earlier in speaking of the Etruscan rule.[3]

The Senate.—The primitive senate is to be compared with the council of elders or great men, common among the Aryans. Just as in the Homeric poems the over-king Agamemnon calls the minor kings together for consultation, so the Roman king called the heads of the most important clans to his council. Perhaps the Roman king chose one member from each of the distinguished clans, or possibly there was a time when the chiefs of the clans, hereditary or elective, formed the senate, but all this is in the highest degree obscure. It is, however, certain

[1] Soltau, *Altröm. Volksversamm.*, 69-105; Botsford, *Roman Assemblies*, chaps. i. and ix. Binder regards the question as still an open one (*Plebs*, especially 161, 393).

[2] *Hist.*, English trans., i. 69.

[3] For accounts of the king, necessarily to a great extent conjectural, see Girard, *Org. Jud.*, 10 *seq.*; Bernhöft, *Staat und Recht*, 115; Binder, 551.

that the original senate was exclusively patrician, and that laws approved of by the *comitia* did not go into effect unless they received the sanction of this patrician house—the *auctoritas patrum.* It may be that in the time of the Kings this constitutional safeguard was not required, but we know that it existed in the Republic.[1] And even after the senate had been increased by the admission of plebeian members, it appears probable that this right of veto, if the *auctoritas patrum* may be so called, was reserved as the special prerogative of the patrician senators.[2]

[1] Binder, 554.

[2] Karlowa, i. 46 ; Mommsen, *Staatsrecht*, i. 50 ; Bernhöft, *Staat und Recht*, 136 ; Binder, 385 *seq.* As to the nature of the *auctoritas patrum*, which will be referred to again, see the view of Mr. Strachan-Davidson in *Eng. Hist. Rev.*, 1890, v. 472.

CHAPTER VII

The Patriarchal Family

The Patria Potestas

THE central fact of the society of early Rome is the doctrine of *patria potestas*. Maine says it is "the first and greatest landmark in the course of legal history."[1] The Roman family in ancient times is an *imperium in imperio*. It is governed by the *paterfamilias*. The wife, the children, the slaves, the farm-house, the flocks and herds are in his hands. Even the word *familia* is used to include the property as well as the persons. The *paterfamilias* determines who shall belong to the family. He may decline to admit a child whom his wife bears to him. If he does not choose to take up the child—*suscipere liberos*—when it is brought to him, it is exposed, *i.e.* put out to die if nobody will take pity on it.[2] He can expel a member from the family. No member of the family but himself can own anything except upon sufferance. They cannot marry without his consent, and even if they are married he can divorce them. He has the power of life and death over wife and child and grandchild no less than over the slaves or the oxen. But custom requires him, before inflicting any punishment of great severity, to call together and consult with a council of the near relations. The family is like a corporation which never dies. The ancestors, the living, the generations to come, all belong to it. When the patriarch or *paterfamilias* dies each

---

[1] *Early Institutions*, 216.

[2] See Dion., 2, 15 ; Cic. ad. Att., 11, 9, 3 ; Marquardt, *Privatleben*, 2nd ed. 3 ; Cornil, in *Nouv. Rev. Hist.*, 1897, xxi. 419. The practice is found among most of the Aryans (Bernhöft, *Staat. und Recht*, 200).

of his sons becomes a *paterfamilias*. The original family is broken up into as many families as there are sons or male representatives of deceased sons. The early family has, as it were, three faces :—

(1) *Religious*.—It has its separate and exclusive *sacra*, communion in which is the closest link between members of the family—the dead as well as the living. The hearth is the altar of this private cult, and the *paterfamilias* is its priest.

(2) *Political*.—It has its own rules. The *paterfamilias* can make laws for it. He has the power of life and death over its members. Within the family circle he is absolute. The law of the State does not extend there. The *paterfamilias* is, in a sense, its king.

(3) *Proprietary*.—Every person and everything within the family belong to the *paterfamilias*. He is the owner of the family.[1]

The patriarchal family in early Rome as in ancient Greece and in modern India rests upon ancestor worship. This is one of the most universal forms of religion, and was common to all the Aryan peoples. It is found also among the ancient Arabs, the Chinese, the Japanese, and many races of savages. It still underlies the religion of the Hindus. The interior of India, little known to Europeans till modern times, for ages utterly uninfluenced by western thought, is a museum of customs and beliefs which were the common heritage of the Aryans, but have long disappeared in Europe. Ancestor worship has survived also among the Ossetes of the Caucasus, who, living remote from the world, have preserved much of the old Aryan life and thought.[2] Ancestor worship appeals to

[1] *Cf.* Manu, viii. 416. "A wife, a son, and a slave, these three are declared to have no property ; the wealth which they earn is acquired for him to whom they belong."

[2] Dareste, *Études d'Histoire du Droit*, 137 ; and see on ancestor worship generally, Cuq, i. 2nd ed. 44 ; Fustel de Coulanges, *La Cité Antique*, bk. i. ch. i. ; Maine, *Ancient Law*, ch. vi. ; Kovalewsky, *Coutume Contemporaine*,

human nature, for the benefits are not all on one side. The man who treats his ancestors well will not be overlooked by them, and many a stroke of apparent luck may be due to their pious care.[1]

The ancient Roman regarded the family as the great instrument for keeping up the peculiar rites upon the due observance of which depended the happiness both of the dead and of the living. To neglect them was to commit an abominable cruelty to his ancestors, and to bring down a curse upon his house. Upon the due performance of the family *sacra* by his son his own future happiness would depend. No duty was so sacred as the exact and punctilious attention to the claims of his priestly office as head of the family.[2] The extinction of the family was a thing to be regarded with horror. The duty of the young patrician was to marry as soon as possible in order to perpetuate the family, that his ancestors might not be left in misery on account of the cessation of the family *sacra*. The anxiety to prevent the extinction of the family explains the great prominence given to adoption in early law. If the *paterfamilias* is childless, or if his children predecease him, it is a sacred duty to adopt a son to keep the family alive.

The Hindus believe that if the family rites are duly performed the ancestors are advanced from stage to stage. Only a few years ago the Privy Council had to decide the question: "Is it lawful to give an only son in adoption?" The argument was to this effect: "It is abominable for a father to give his only son to another. For as a consequence of the extinction of the family, and the cessation of the family rites, the father himself, after his death, will be left in *pūt* (hell). It might be

48 *seq.*; Leist, *Alt-Arisches Jus Civile*, i. 183 *seq.*; Tylor, E. B., *Primitive Culture;* Howard, G. E., *Matrimonial Institutions*, i. 13 and 26 and references.

[1] Post, *Grundriss der Ethnologischen Jurisprudenz*, i. 130.

[2] Gide, *Condition Privée de la Femme*, 21; Post, *op. cit.*, i. 130; Hunter, *Roman Law*, 2nd ed. 745; *cf.* in Greece, Meyer, *Geschichte des Alterthums*, ii. nos. 56, 59.

replied that this was his own affair and affected nobody else. But this is not so. It affects his ancestors. If the rites had been duly performed by his son—and his action makes this impossible—he would be freed from *pūt*, his father would become immortal, and his grandfather would be raised to the solar system."[1] All this, except perhaps the rise to the solar system, would have sounded quite reasonable to a Roman in the early days of the city. And Sir H. Maine says, "It sounds like a jest to say that according to the principles of Hindoo law property is regarded as the means of paying a man's funeral expenses, but this is not so untrue of the written law, concerning which the most dignified of the Indian Courts has recently laid down, after an elaborate examination of all the authorities, that 'the right of inheritance, according to Hindoo law, is wholly regulated with reference to the spiritual benefits to be conferred on the deceased proprietor.'"[2]

Paterfamilias not a Tyrant.—It is a mistake to conceive of the Roman *paterfamilias* as a tyrant, whose wife and children are little better than slaves. As the ruler and judge of the family, his power was virtually absolute. But religion and custom compelled him to exercise that power with moderation and restraint. To the early Roman it would have seemed a profanity of the home to allow the courts to interfere in the concerns of the family. The Roman house, according to the fine description of Jhering, was "the abode of affection and morality; it escaped from the control of the dead rule of law."[3]

Such an attitude reveals, not a low but a very high state of morals. While public opinion is sound and strong little law is needed. The Roman *paterfamilias* was restrained from abuse of his powers much more effectually by fear of the

[1] *Radhamohon* v. *Hardai Bibi*, 1899, 26 Ind. Law Rep. 113. Manu says, "Through a son he conquers the worlds, through a son's son he obtains immortality, but through his son's grandson he gains the world of the sun," ix. 136.

[2] *Village Communities*, 53.

[3] *Esprit*, ii. 191.

reprobation of the censor and of his neighbours than heads of families in some modern communities are deterred from cruelty by dread of the police courts. Complaints of arbitrary conduct by a *paterfamilias* appear but rarely in the records, and when they do occur the law is able to distinguish between an act done by the father as the domestic judge, and an act done in hot blood, which even great provocation cannot elevate to the position of a legitimate exercise of parental authority.

Patria potestas in pietate debet non atrocitate consistere.[1]

Patria Potestas among other Aryans.—The Romans themselves looked upon the *patria potestas*, in the form it took at Rome, as one of their national peculiarities. Gaius says, "There are almost no other men who have so much power over their sons as we have."[2] It is however, pretty certain that the *patria potestas*, extending even to the power of life and death over the members of the family, is a primitive Aryan institution. It existed among the early Greeks, among whom in particular the practice of exposing new-born children to die of hunger, unless some charitable person adopted them, was much more common than at Rome.[3] And the sale of children in Greece is well attested.[4] The *paterfamilias* in Persia had the power of life and death over his family.[5] The German father, likewise, could expose, or sell, or kill his child, and could kill his wife, if he did so judicially. One of the old Lombard texts says: *Non licet uxorem interficere ad suum libitum sed rationabiliter.*[6] The remarkable thing is, not that the Roman *paterfamilias* at an early time should have had the power of life and death over

---

[1] *Digest*, 48, 9, 5; Liv., 7, 4; Dion., 20, 13; Jhering, *Esprit*, ii. 192 *seq.*, and especially the admirable article by M. G. Cornil, in *Nouv. Rev. Hist.*, 1897, xxi. 416, and the references there given.

[2] Gaius, i. 55.

[3] See Daremberg et Saglio, *s.v.* "Expositio."

[4] Aelian, *Var. Hist.*, 2, 7; Herod., 5, 6; Plut., *Solon*, 13; Meyer, *Geschichte des Alterthums*, ii. n. 59.

[5] Aristotle, *Eth. Nic.*, 8, 10; Esther, ch. i.; Dareste, *Études*, 107.

[6] Brunner, *Deutsche Rechtsgeschichte*, i. 75. See on *patria potestas* as a general Aryan custom, Leist, *Alt-Arisches Jus Civile*, ii. 136 *seq.*

members of his household, for this is common enough among people at a primitive stage, but that the Romans should have retained the *patria potestas* so little modified down to a late time. Among most of the Aryans the power of the *paterfamilias* over the persons of his children terminated as regards the daughters when they married, and as regards the sons when they ceased to live under the paternal roof. And over property, as will be explained in a later chapter, the power of the Roman *paterfamilias* is much greater than that of the head of the family among other Aryan peoples at an early time.

Place of Patriarchal Family in Evolution of Society.—It is not necessary here to do more than refer to the long and interesting discussions carried on for more than a generation as to the place which the patriarchal family occupies in the general history of the race. Is it a primitive institution, or does it indicate a relatively advanced stage of civilisation? One school of writers has contended that, before the patriarchal family existed, society passed through a stage when kinship was reckoned on the mother's side only. That this system, often called matriarchy, or *Mutterrecht*, has been at one time or another somewhat widely disseminated, and that it existed among many ancient peoples, are well-known facts. It is to this day in green observance in some places; for example, among some of the races of India and Sumatra.[1] In fact, the theory was at one time rather widely accepted that something like a uniform evolution in this matter could be observed. At the first stage the only relationship admitted was that on the mother's side, then followed a stage at which kinship was entirely on the father's side, and lastly the point is reached at which blood relations on both sides of the family are equally recognised.[2]

But more recently there has been a decided reaction against these views. There is much less inclination than formerly

[1] See Tylor, E. B., "Matriarchal Family System," *Nineteenth Century*, 1896, xl. 81.

[2] Post, *Grundriss der Ethnologischen Jurisprudenz*, 69.

to assume that different races of mankind, or even different branches of the Aryans, must everywhere have passed through identical stages of evolution in the institution of the family, and that matriarchy is one of these compulsory preliminary stages.[1]

It is generally admitted that there are traces of the matriarchal system in Europe.[2] According to Bede, among the Picts in Scotland, in the succession to the Crown, preference was given to maternal kin, and in Irish legends and Gaelic inscriptions there are indications which point to mother-right.[3] And upon more doubtful grounds, some scholars have believed that the matriarchal system once prevailed among the old Germans, though at the time when they first came under the observation of the Romans they had already passed through that "rude preliminary stage of culture in the law of family and succession."[4] But, upon the whole, the evidence for the practice of matriarchy in Europe is very slight, and comes far short of making it probable that it was a general custom. In some countries it may have been introduced to a limited extent through contact with aboriginal races, just as some of the Aryans who fell in with polyandrous peoples adopted their ways.[5] Nor is there any evidence that the primitive Aryan family, before the migrations, was based on kinship on the mother's side. On the contrary, the more the facts which throw light on the primitive Aryans have been sifted and examined, the less ground does there appear to be for any such belief. Some of the best authorities go so far as to think that it has now been proved affirmatively, mainly by philological evidence, that the primitive Aryans did not live

[1] See Howard, G. E., *Hist. of Matrimonial Institutions*, i. chaps. i., ii., iii., where there is an excellent bibliography.

[2] See Frazer, J. G., *Early History of Kingship*, 245.

[3] See Vinogradoff, *Growth of the Manor*, 9.

[4] Brunner, i. 80. See Tac., *Germ.*, ch. xx. *Contra*, Westermarck, *Hist. of Human Marriage*, 104.

[5] See Bernhöft, in *Zeit. für vergleich. Rechtswissenschaft*, ix. 418 and 11.

according to mother-right, but were united in joint-families, based on relationship on the father's side only, similar in character to those house-communities referred to in the following chapter, which still exist among the Southern Slavs.[1] Others are content to take up an agnostic position, and to say, with Max Müller, "Whether in unknown times the Aryans ever passed through that metrocratic stage in which the children and all the family property belonged to the mother, and fathers have no recognised position whatever in the family, we can neither assert nor deny." [2]

[1] Schrader, *Sprachvergleichung*, 568 ; Bernhöft, *Staat und Recht*, 202.

[2] *Biographies of Words*, xvii. The great storehouse of material on this subject is the *Zeitschrift für vergleich. Rechtswissenschaft.* There is a good discussion of the various theories and a full bibliography in Howard, G. E., *Matrimonial Institutions.* For a brief statement of some of the points, see an article by the present writer in *Juridical Review*, 1901, xiii. 70. Sir J. G. Frazer thinks that among the Latins the system of counting kinship through females survived in the royal family after it had been exchanged among the people generally for the system of counting kinship through males. "For royalty, like religion, is essentially conservative ; it clings to old forms and old customs which have long vanished from ordinary life."

CHAPTER VIII

EARLY THEORIES OF RELATIONSHIP—AGNATION

Wife a Quasi-Daughter

THE importance for us just now of these theories as to the evolution of society lies in the light they throw on the early view of relationship at Rome. The only relationship to which any account was paid there, in the early period, was relationship on the father's side. If a mother was considered as related to her children this was only so upon a fiction that she had altogether given up her own family, and had passed into the family of her husband. This being so, she is looked upon as a quasi-daughter of her husband.[1] She is not related to her children as a mother, but is looked upon as their sister. She takes a daughter's share in the succession of her husband. Her children are related to her only on the theory that she is their sister, and they are not related to her family at all. A paternal uncle is a near relation, a maternal uncle is a stranger in blood. This is the theory of relationship called agnation, and it is undoubtedly a very puzzling and, to us, an extremely unnatural theory.

Who are Agnates?

Let me first state who a man's agnates were before considering the theory. All persons related to him by male descents, natural or fictitious, are his agnates, unless the tie of relationship has been broken by *capitis deminutio*. By "fictitious descents" I mean that a wife *in manu*—a term to be explained later—is an agnate of her husband and of his

[1] Gaius, i. 118.

agnates, just as if she was his daughter. And, further, we must bear in mind that all adopted children are treated by the law as exactly the same as children lawfully begotten. My brother's wife *in manu*, or my brother's adopted son, are just as much my agnates as is my brother himself.

And by the tie being broken by *capitis deminutio,* I mean that if my brother had emancipated his son—*i.e.* had placed him outside his family, or if the son had been expelled from the family by suffering a penalty involving *capitis deminutio*, or "a loss of civil status," then, in either case, the son has ceased to be an agnate of his father or of me. He has become a stranger. And further, a woman when she marries, if she marries according to the *régime* of *manus*, ceases to be an agnate of her father, and becomes an agnate of her husband. His people become her people, and his gods her gods. If we assume that the agnatic bond has not been severed by the *capitis deminutio* involved in emancipation or by *capitis deminutio* as a penalty, a man's agnates will be—(1) His father, paternal grandfather, and great-grandfather; his paternal grandmother and great-grandmother, if both are *in manu;* his paternal uncles and great-uncles; his paternal aunts and great-aunts, so long as they are unmarried, or are married without *manus*. (2) His mother, if she has been brought into the agnatic circle by *manus*, and his brothers and sisters by the same father, so long as the sisters are unmarried, or are married without *manus*. (3) His wife *in manu;* his sons and his sons' wives *in manu;* descendants through sons (whether these sons survive him or not), but excluding women married with *manus;* his daughters, unless married with *manus*. (4) More remote collaterals through males—*e.g.* a paternal uncle's son or grandson.

Examples of Agnation

Among these groups group three is privileged. They are *sui heredes*, who have the first claim on the succession. They are agnates, of course, but are preferred to other agnates. And two points must be kept clearly in view:

(1) That persons who have come into the group by adoption are just in the same position as if they had been born in it; and

(2) That an agnate ceases to be an agnate if he suffers *capitis deminutio*. As it is important to have a firm grasp of the system of agnation, it may not be amiss to give a simple genealogical tree:—

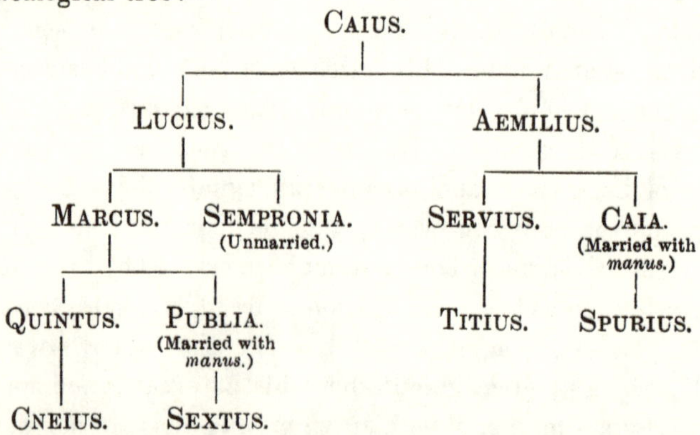

Here Caia, who is a paternal aunt of Titius, and was therefore his agnate, has ceased to be so by her marriage (assuming *manus*), and is no longer related at all to him or to her father Aemilius, or to her brother Servius.

Sempronia, being unmarried, is still an agnate of Titius or of Cneius.

Sextus and Spurius, who descend through females, are not agnatically related to Caius, or to any other members of the group. For their mothers passed altogether out of this group when they married.

Wherever in the pedigree we come to the name of a married woman, if she was *in manu mariti*, we can strike it out, as well as the names of her children. She and her descendants belong to another family altogether—viz. to the family of her husband.

At the death of the *paterfamilias* his sons and his unmarried daughters become independent, freed from the *potestas*, or, to use the technical expression, *sui juris*. And grandchildren who were in his *potestas* become *sui juris* if their own father is not living. If he is living they simply exchange the *patria potestas* of their grandfather for that of their father. But in the case of sons and of unmarried daughters, each of them becomes a *paterfamilias*, or a *materfamilias*, at the death of the head of the family. Each of them, that is to say, becomes the head of a family, because he or she ceases to be subject to any other head. If the son dies unmarried his family dies with him, as it never included anybody but himself. And in the case of a daughter her family always dies with her if she never marries, and it is extinguished during her lifetime if she marries with *manus*. For by her marriage she is, in the language of some of the jurists, born again—undergoes a regeneration—into the family of the husband. This is the explanation of the maxim *mulier familiae suae et caput et finis est.*[1] Another mode of explaining agnatic relationship is this: Suppose we frame a genealogical table of the descendants of some celebrated man, let us say of Oliver Cromwell. All of these descendants will be cognates of each other. But it would only be those who are Cromwells whom the Romans would have reckoned as agnates. The married daughters have changed their name and their children are not Cromwells.[2]

Agnates and Gentiles.—But if agnates are all those persons related by male descent from a common ancestor, what is the difference between agnates and *gentiles?* For a *gens* is just a

[1] D. 50, 16, 195, 5.

[2] It is interesting to compare the Hindu joint family at the present time. It is composed of the "male descendants of a common ancestor, any males who have been adopted by members of the family, and the wives, widows, and unmarried daughters of the male members ; all of whom are living as a joint Hindu family, and none of whom have separated from the others." (See art. by Sir W. C. Petheram in *Law Quart. Rev.*, 1899, 175.) All of these persons are joint owners of the family property.

clan composed of persons bearing the same name and claiming common descent in the male line. That a difference was made in pretty early times is shown by the law of the Twelve Tables. The succession of an intestate is to go—(1) to *sui*, (2) to agnates, and (3) to *gentiles*.

Now at what degree of relationship do we say that the class of agnates is to close, and the class of *gentiles* to open? This is a vexed question. According to many writers anyone who was able to prove his relationship in the male line with the deceased could claim as an agnate.[1] Failing any such person the estate went to the *gens* or clan to which the deceased belonged. Agnation and *gentilitas* were the same thing. All agnates were *gentiles*, and all *gentiles* were agnates. But many of the *gentiles* were so far removed in blood from the deceased that the relationship was impossible to trace. The common name and the common religious rites showed that it must exist. But the kinship was so distant that it was impossible to prove it. For purposes of succession a line had to be drawn. If a *gentilis* could prove his relationship he was preferred to the *gentiles* who were unable to bring such evidence. He was an agnate in a narrower sense. I think this is the more probable view.

According to another theory the line was drawn at a fixed degree of relationship. Agnates were all relations on the father's side up to and including the sixth degree. This is supported by an analogy from India where a similar line is drawn between *Sapindas* relations through males up to the sixth degree inclusive, and *Samanodocas*, or all those persons who bear the same family name.[2]

---

[1] Mommsen, *Staatsrecht*, iii. pt. i. 16; Fustel de Coulanges, *La Cité Antique*, liv. ii. ch. x.; Girard, *Manuel*, 4th ed. 144.

[2] See Hearn, *Aryan Household*, 168; Starcke, *Primitive Family*, 96; Muirhead, 2nd ed. 164. Karlowa, ii. 884, compares the right of the agnates to come before the clansmen with the right given by the old German law to the *Sippe*. Among the Salian Franks a man's land descended to his sons. Failing sons it went to the village community

What happened in the early Roman law when the *gens* succeeded is by no means clear. Did the *gens* succeed as a corporation and hold property for the general use of its members, or did the *gentiles* divide the estate? We have no information upon this point, and in fact the gentile organisation altogether is full of obscurity.

Some writers think that in the regal period no distinction was drawn between agnation and *gentilitas*. If a man had no widow and children his estate went to his *gens*.[1] When the plebeians were admitted to equal rights by the Twelve Tables the difficulty at once presented itself that they had no *gentes*. If a plebeian died unmarried, let us say, upon whom was his estate to devolve? To get over this difficulty the separate class of agnates was created, and according to some of these authorities a line was drawn at the sixth degree—*i.e.* at second cousins. All relations through males within the sixth degree inclusive were agnates. Those of the seventh degree or more remote were *gentiles*. And having made this rule they applied it to the patricians as well as to the plebeians. There is no textual authority for this, and it strikes me as a somewhat improbable assumption. Even before the Twelve Tables if a man left, let us suppose, brothers and sisters surviving him, one would hardly expect them to be excluded from his succession in favour of a body so vaguely connected with him as the *gens*. And it is rather curious that a rule introduced, *ex hypothesi*, to place patricians and plebeians upon the same footing should first alter the order of succession to a patrician by introducing

which at that time was composed of persons related or supposed to be related to each other. King Chilperic by an edict decreed that if a man left no sons his lands should go to his daughters, and failing these to brothers and sisters. It was only failing all these that the succession opened to the village community. (See Brunner, *Deutsche Rechtsgeschichte*, i. 90.) This, so far as it goes, would support the theory that only near agnates had a preference. The whole question is obscure, because the Roman *gentes* disappeared early.

[1] Muirhead, 2nd ed. 43.

this new class of agnates, and should after all leave the patrician and plebeian subject to a different law. For if the patrician died and had no *sui* or agnates his succession devolved on his *gens;* whereas if a plebeian left no *sui* nor agnates his succession was vacant.[1] It seems to me more likely that persons able to prove their agnatic relationship were from a very early time preferred to the *gens.*[2]

Upon what does the Theory of Agnation rest?—The commonly accepted view is that agnation is a principle of relationship based on the Roman *patria potestas.* The best-known English exponent of this view is Sir Henry Maine. "The foundation of agnation is not the marriage of father and mother, but the authority of the father. In truth, in the primitive view, relationship is exactly limited by *patria potestas.* Where the *potestas* begins kinship begins, and, therefore, adoptive relatives are among the kindred. Where the *potestas* ends kinship ends, so that a son emancipated by his father loses all rights of agnation. And here we have the reason why the descendants of females are outside the limits of archaic kinship."[3] But there are many difficulties about this theory.

If agnation rests on *patria potestas* why does it not cease when the *potestas* ceases? If a *paterfamilias* dies leaving two sons, and afterwards each of these sons has a son, why are the cousins agnates? They are not, and have not ever been, in the same *potestas.* In the case of a large household with children, grandchildren, and great-grandchildren, why might it not happen that a woman-descendant married within the *potestas?* And if she did so, why should her children not be agnates? Yet we know that the children of women were always excluded.[4] This last difficulty may, perhaps, be ex-

[1] Muirhead, 2nd ed. 164.
[2] See Voigt, *Jus Naturale*, iii. 1163 *seq.*
[3] *Ancient Law*, 15th ed. 149.
[4] See M'Lennan, *Patriarchal Theory*, 192.

plained by assuming that marriage within the *potestas* was forbidden.[1] Schulin says, founding on Tac., *Ann.*, 12, 6, that from the earliest time the marriage of relations within the sixth degree was forbidden.[2] The theory of Mr. M'Lennan, as opposed to that of Sir H. Maine, is that agnation as a principle of relationship rests on the *gentile* organisation. In early times all the members of a *gens* were kin, and no member of one *gens* could be related to a member of another *gens*. They were mutually exclusive circles of kindred.

The *gens* was exogamous. A woman if she married passed into another *gens*, and therefore she and her descendants are lost to the *gens* of her birth. A male member of the *gens*, if he marries, brings his wife into his *gens*.

I am inclined to think this is a more probable theory than the other.[3]

Cognatio.—In opposition to this ancient Roman conception of the agnatic family came later that of relationship by blood, whether on the father's or the mother's side. This is *cognatio*. In the course of the development of the law of succession, by slow degrees, the cognatic rule—*i.e.* relationship as we now understand it—finally supplanted the agnatic rule of relationship on the father's side only. In the law as it was finally settled by Justinian, everything depends upon cognation.

---

[1] *Cf.* M'Lennan, *Patriarchal Theory*, 207.

[2] *Lehrbuch*, 176, 204.

[3] See M'Lennan, *Patriarchal Theory*, especially 205 *seq.*, and *cf.* Post, *Grundriss*, 121 *seq.*; Howard, G. E., *Matrimonial Institutions*, i. 30. "This ancient idea of relationship still survives in High Albania, where exogamy is still practised, and relationship through the female line is hardly recognised." Durham, M. E., *High Albania*, 22.

CHAPTER IX

THE SERVIAN REFORMS

The Census.—To the end of the Regal Period, according to the tradition, belong the important constitutional reforms which are attributed to Servius Tullius—the last but one of the kings.[1] Servius reorganised the army, and this new organisation was, afterwards, made use of for two purposes—the military divisions, with important modifications, were employed as voting units in an assembly of the people, and the tribes or wards into which those liable to military service had been enrolled were used as census areas for purposes of taxation. In order to arrive at a basis for a rearrangement of the taxes, a census was established. Every independent citizen was compelled, on pain of loss of freedom, to declare the situation and value of his real estate with all its appurtenances.[2]

Comitia Centuriata.—Servius, for military purposes, had divided the citizens, patricians and plebeians alike, into five classes.

According to the tradition—

Class	I. consisted of those who had			100,000	*asses;*
„	II. „	„	„	75,000	„
„	III. „	„	„	50,000	„
„	IV. „	„	„	25,000	„
„	V. „	„	„	11,000	„

according to Livy, or 12,500 according to Dionysius.[3]

[1] Livy, 1, 43; Dion., 4, 16; 7, 59; Cic., *Rep.*, 2, 22; Mommsen, *Röm. Staatsrecht*, iii. pt. i. 245; Karlowa, i. 67; Botsford, 66. They were probably of considerably later date. Pais, i. pt. i. 320.

[2] See Gaius, 1, 160; Cic., *De Leg.*, 3, 3; Dion., 4, 14.

[3] As to many problems connected with these ratings, see Botsford, 84 *seq.*

The classes were divided into centuries. The first class had 80 centuries; the second, third, and fourth classes 20 centuries each; and the fifth 30 centuries. With some additional centuries of musicians and craftsmen, and 18 centuries of knights or cavalry, there were in all 193 centuries. The values given by the historians in *asses* or money represent in all probability an older valuation in land. Possibly the scale was twenty acres or more for Class I., fifteen acres for Class II., and so on. When these divisions came to be used for voting purposes they gave the rich man a higher voting power than the poor man. Cicero says the idea was *ut suffragia non in multitudinis, sed in locupletium potestate essent,* and *is valebat in suffragio plurimum cuius plurimum intererat esse in optimo statu civitatem.*[1] As we might put it in modern phraseology, a man's political weight was to be in proportion to his "stake in the country." Class I. so much overshadowed the other classes that it was called the "class" *par excellence;* the members of the others being described as *infra classem.* With its 80 centuries and the 18 centuries of the cavalry, Class I. had a majority of the 193 centuries. In the voting the Knights voted first, and then Class I. If they agreed there was a majority, and it was unnecessary for the other classes to vote at all. It is clear that the rich had a preponderating weight, but the exact way in which this was secured is one of the most obscure problems of Roman history. If the centuries were equal in size, it is hard to see how the richest class should have had the most centuries. And Cicero expressly says that every century in one of the lower classes contained almost as many citizens as the whole of Class I. So that there is some plausibility in the theory of Niebuhr that we must assume that the value of a man's vote varied in some way in proportion to his property qualification.[2] The vote of the man with a hundred acres in his view must have

[1] *De Republica,* ii. 22, 39, 40; Karlowa, i. 74.
[2] Karlowa, i. 74.

counted for more than the vote of the man with five acres. But this difficulty has been exaggerated. It may be that the twenty acres which formed the original qualification for Class I. was the normal holding of a freeman. Class I. would be composed then of the great mass of peasant-proprietors. It was when the land qualification was exchanged for one in money that the rich acquired an advantage.[1]

This division of the people into classes and centuries came to be used for both purposes—military and political. The classes and the centuries formed the army, and when they met for political purposes they are called sometimes *exercitus urbanus.* As a political assembly, this new assembly—the *Comitia Centuriata*—was the nation in arms met to vote. It became the great constitutional body, and the old meeting of the *curies* ceased to have any real importance. The *Comitia Centuriata* was called together to pass laws, to elect magistrates, to decide on peace and war, and to act as the supreme court of appeal in questions involving the civil death or loss of *caput* of a Roman citizen. Every citizen had by the *Lex Valeria*, which is said to have been passed in 509 B.C., in the first year of the Republic, and to have been the first statute enacted by the *Comitia Centuriata*, the right of appeal against a capital sentence to the assembly—*provocatio ad populum.*[2]

When the *Comitia Centuriata* met to exercise its legislative functions, it was summoned by a magistrate who had the authority to command the army, and so usually by a consul. An announcement of the law to be proposed—*promulgatio rogationis*—was made seventeen days (*trinundinum*) before the day fixed for the *comitia.* On the morning of the appointed day the magistrate who was to preside had to take the auspices. If there was a thunderstorm, or if the auspices were otherwise unfavourable, the assembly was deferred. If they were favourable, it was supposed that the gods favoured the measure to be

[1] Girard, *Manuel*, 4th ed. 16; Botsford, 79.

[2] Cic., *Rep.*, 2, 31, 53; Botsford, 201; Cuq, i. 116.

proposed. The subsequent vote was both *vox populi* and *vox dei.*[1] If the *Comitia* was to go on, there was a new summons by trumpet call—*vox tubae*—and the *Comitia* came out usually under arms; for it was still regarded as the army. A flag was hoisted on the Janiculum. When the order was given *Ad Comitia*, the army marched out to the *Campus Martius*, it being illegal to meet within the city. Even when assembled, the *Comitia* would break up if a thunderstorm came on, or if anyone was seized with an epileptic fit—*morbus comitialis.* There was no discussion in the *Comitia.* This must be done first in preliminary and less formal meetings called *contiones.* The presiding magistrate at the *Comitia* merely put the question, *Velitis, jubeatis Quirites?* If a majority of centuries voted for the bill it became *populi jussum* but not yet *lex.* For a long time it needed the *auctoritas patrum*, which, probably, means the ratification of the patrician part of the Senate.[2] But, to anticipate on this point, it was enacted by one of the *Leges Publiliae* in B.C. 339, that for the future the *patres* should give their *auctoritas* in advance—*i.e.* give *carte blanche* to the *Comitia.*[3] After this the *populi jussum* was at once *lex.* And the *Comitia* itself is not to be compared with a modern Parliament. It was not an administrative body, nor even a debating chamber. It was only a way of getting a popular vote upon a question already decided upon by the Senate. The *Comitia* very rarely refused to pass a measure duly proposed. The magistrate who wished to propose a bill first introduced it into the Senate, where it was fully discussed. The right of the Senate to be first consulted was admitted by constant practice. As a matter of theory, the magistrate might bring a bill

[1] Livy, 8, 23, 15; 10, 40, 2; Botsford, 110.

[2] Karlowa, i. 46; Mommsen, *Abriss*, 325; Soltau, *Altröm. Volksversamm.*, 208; Botsford, 235.

[3] The Senate, or rather its patrician members, before the measure was voted upon in the *Comitia*, gave their *auctoritas*, *i.e.* perhaps a sort of certificate that the procedure had been regular. See the discussion by Mr. Strachan Davidson in *Eng. Hist. Rev.*, 1890, v. 472, and *infra*, p. 118.

directly before the *Comitia*. But this hardly seems to have occurred.[1] The law passed usually took its name from the magistrate who presided—*e.g. Lex Publilia, Lex Sempronia, Lex Servilia*. Sometimes it was called after the two consuls for the year—*e.g. Leges Valeriae Horatiae*. Occasionally a further descriptive title was given to it, especially when the presiding magistrate had already given his name to previous leges—*e.g. Lex Sempronia judiciaria, lex Calpurnia repetundarum*.

The Servian Tribes.—According to the tradition, the division of the city into four tribes—*tribus*—was also the work of Servius. These tribes were local areas like municipal wards. There were four city wards and a varying number of suburban wards—*tribus rusticae*. All real property—*res mancipi*—had to be enrolled for purposes of taxation in one or other of the tribes.[2] At a later period the tribal organisation came also to be used politically, and out of it grew the *Comitia Tributa*.

The Servian Constitution bristles with difficulties which cannot be discussed here, and for the lawyer are not of special interest. They are dealt with fully and excellently in a recent work.[3]

Custom Main Source of Law in Regal Period.—During the period of the kings it is doubtful if there was any enacted law of a general character. The *Comitia* passed laws, it is true, but they were laws analogous to our private Acts, such as to permit a citizen to make a will or to allow a *paterfamilias* to become by arrogation the *filius familias* of another. We hear, also, of certain "royal laws"—*leges regiae*—which were afterwards collected by Papirius and were known under the name of *Jus Papirianum*. But it is now agreed on all hands that the compilation of Papirius was not made until somewhere

[1] Mommsen, *Abriss des römischen Staatsrechts*, 330; *Hist.* (Eng. trans.), i. 325.

[2] Dion., 4, 14, 1; Mommsen, *Hist.* (English trans.), i. 94; Bruns-Pernice in Holtzendorff's *Encyclopädie*, 12; Botsford, 48, for a full discussion.

[3] Botsford, G. W., *The Roman Assemblies*.

about the end of the Republic, and that the so-called *leges regiae* are mainly regulations of a religious or ceremonial character, perhaps taken from the archives of the pontiffs. Some of the fragments which have come down to us are evidently of great antiquity, but they hardly touch the private law, and their ascription to particular kings is quite unreliable. Nor were they ever laws in the sense of statutes enacted by a legislature. In fact the proper title of the work of Papirius was *de ritu sacrorum*.[1]

[1] Serv., in *Aen.*, 12, 836. On the *leges regiae* see Girard, *Textes*, 3 and references; Krüger, *Rechtsquellen*, 4; Ferrini, *Storia delle Fonti*, 2; Costa, *Storia delle Fonti*, 2; Girard, *Org. Jud.*, i. 27, n. i.; Pernice, in *Zeit. Sav. Stift.*, 1886, vii. 153; Lambert, *Études de Droit Commun*, i. 575.

CHAPTER X

SECOND PERIOD—THE REPUBLIC

The Consuls and the Senate.—After the expulsion of the kings, the regal power—*imperium regium*—was placed in the hands of two consuls elected by the centuries for one year. Their position differed widely from that of a modern president of a republic, who is intrusted with a certain number of powers carefully limited and defined. The Roman consuls held, so to speak, the royal power in commission. They were joint-kings. But their abuse of their theoretically absolute powers was checked, first, by their short tenure of office, and, second, by the fact that each of them could block by his veto—*intercessio*—any official act of the other. *Melior est causa prohibentis.* And as time went on the power of the consuls came to be greatly limited also by the increased strength of the Senate. The Senate, in theory a mere body of advisers who might counsel but not compel, came to get the complete control of the public finances, and by their power over the purse-strings obtained a commanding control over all the magistrates. A permanent body like the Senate could exert much more authority over the annually elected consuls than it had possessed over the kings who held office for life, and were hedged about with a sanctity which did not belong to the consuls.[1] The Senate itself had gradually undergone a change. The clans or *gentes* had ceased to feel their separate political existence. They had merged together. It was no longer felt to be necessary that each senator should represent a particular *gens*. Even before the end of the regal period, the king was not tied strictly to this rule in filling up vacancies in the Senate.[2]

[1] Cic., *De Rep.*, 2,32, and Mommsen, *Hist.* (English trans.), i. 257; *Abriss*, 84; Karlowa, i. 207. [2] Mommsen, *Hist.*, i. 71; Karlowa, i. 41.

Consuls as Judges.—Moreover there were certain of the royal powers which were not carried over to the consuls. The king's powers as head of the Church passed to the *pontifex maximus*. And although the consuls remained vested with the royal judicial powers, it seems that they never had like the kings the right to hear and decide cases, or that if they ever had such a power it was given up almost at the beginning. Their right was limited to that of deciding if a relevant case had been stated, and if the necessary formalities had been complied with. This being so, they were bound to adjust the issue and send it for trial to a private citizen, chosen by the parties, and called the *judex*.[1] This was the famous distinction between *jus* and *judicium*. The preliminary proceedings before the magistrate were said to be *in jure*. The final trial of the issue was *in judicio*. It remained for ages a characteristic of Roman practice that the judge should be in principle a private citizen, not a State official, and should be chosen by the parties, though from a limited panel. Cicero says: *Neminem voluerunt majores nostri esse judicem nisi qui inter adversarios convenisset.*[2]

The Struggle for Equality.—In the early part of the Republic is witnessed the long struggle of the *plebs* for political equality. They were citizens entitled to vote, and the consuls who had now the right of choosing senators might and did choose plebeians as well as patricians. But according to most authorities the plebeian senators did not enjoy the same rights as their patrician colleagues. In the ratification or sanction which was required to give validity to a law voted by the *Comitia*—the *patrum auctoritas* as it was called—plebeian senators took no part. They were not *patres* but *conscripti*.[3] And the better opinion

[1] Girard, *Org. Jud.*, 77.

[2] *Pro Cluentio*, 43, 120. Possibly the *judex* or arbiter was a primitive Roman institution—a "legacy from the life of the clan," as Mr. Greenidge suggests, and remits to him *might* be made even in the time of the kings. Greenidge, *Legal Procedure*, 17.

[3] See Cic., *Pro domo*, 14, 38; Livy, 6, 42, 14; Mommsen, *Röm. Forsch.*, i. 234 *seq.*; Lambert, *Fonction du Droit Civil Comparé*, i. 649; Binder, *Die Plebs*, 387. See *infra*, p. 118.

appears to be that the plebeian senators could not deliver their individual opinions in the senate but could only take part in the voting, for only senators who had filled a curule office were called upon to speak.[1] And for a long time the plebeians were ineligible for any of the magistracies. These officials frequently exercised their powers in a despotic way, and showed class spirit. The *Comitia* had no initiative, and could not even amend a bill sent down to it. It could only vote Aye or No. The senate was the *probouleutic* body, and in it the patricians were the great majority. The patricians kept more than their share of the public lands to themselves, and had great tracts which they farmed by gangs of slaves, many of them prisoners of war. The plebeian yeomen were continually being called out to fight. They had to leave their little farms untilled, or let the crops rot on the ground. Most of them were reduced to borrow at high rates from the patrician money-lenders, and under the harsh law of *nexum* found themselves prisoners for debt in the private prisons of their creditors. The sufferings of these *nexi*,—Roman citizens who had fought the battles of their country,—inflamed the passions of the *plebs* to fever heat.[2]

The First Secession. — At length, on returning from a campaign, the plebeian part of the army withdrew to a hill outside the city, afterwards known as *Mons Sacer*, and were joined there by many of their fellows from inside the city. They threatened to march away and found another city unless their grievances were redressed. This was the First Secession, 494 B.C.[3] The patricians had to make terms. The most important concession was that the *plebs* should have representatives called Tribunes. They were to be sacrosanct, a great protection, for it made anyone who

[1] Gell., 3, 18; Mommsen, *op. cit.*, 257. *Contra*, Willems, *Le Sénat*, 140.

[2] See the chapter on the Law of Debtor and Creditor.

[3] Pais is very sceptical about the First Secession, i. pt. i. 425. But see Soltau, *Röm. Geschichtschreibung*, 166.

injured them an outlaw—*sacer*.[1] They were not magistrates in the strict sense, for no *imperium* was delegated to them. Their most important power lay in their right of veto. If the tribunes agreed with each other, they could block the official act of any magistrate, even of a consul.

The Concilium Plebis.—The *plebs* had so far been an unorganised rabble, which occasionally made itself felt when driven to desperation, but when the temporary end had been achieved lost all its cohesion. The tribunes organised this rabble into a political party. They began to call the plebeians together to public meetings—*concilia plebis*—at which the grievances of their order were discussed, and resolutions passed determining the policy of the plebeians as a party. For purposes of voting it seemed convenient to take the Servian division into tribes or wards. The resolutions passed at these *concilia plebis* were known as *plebiscita*. They were at first only binding on the plebeians themselves. But, by the *Lex Hortensia*, 287 B.C., it was enacted that their resolutions should be of the same efficacy as those of the centuriate assembly—*i.e.* should bind the whole people—*ut quod tributim plebs jussisset populum teneret*. After that time the *concilium plebis* became in fact another assembly, and the *plebiscita* were commonly called *leges*. This subject will be referred to later.[2]

Could Patricians Vote in the Tribes?—Seeing that the division of the people was by wards, it is difficult to resist the conclusion that a patrician freeholder must have been entitled to vote in his ward. On the other hand some of the texts, including the *Institutes*, speak as if the *Comitia Tributa* consisted of plebeians only.[3] Perhaps the explanation is that for a long time the patricians were too proud to exercise their right of voting in an assembly where their

---

[1] See Festus, 318; Livy, iii. 55, 6; Mommsen, *Röm. Staatsrecht*, ii. 286; Botsford, 264, 274.

[2] *Infra*, p. 118.

[3] *Inst.*, i. 2, 4.

order was in a great minority. At a later date, when the rivalry between the two orders had died down, they consented to take part in the tribal assemblies. But there was always a distinction between a meeting of the *plebs* as a class and a political assembly of the tribes.

The first was called a *Concilium Plebis.* It was convoked by a tribune, and a patrician could not take part in it.

The second was the *Comitia Tributa,* an assembly of the whole people, convoked and presided over by a consul or other patrician magistrate. At this meeting patricians could be present.[1]

[1] See Botsford, 275 ; Mommsen, *Röm. Forschungen,* i. 177.

CHAPTER XI

THE TWELVE TABLES

The Decemvirs.—The reforms wrested from the patricians at the First Secession were regarded by the plebeians as an instalment of their rights. Many grievances still remained. In particular it was a hardship for them to be at the mercy of patrician magistrates who were restrained by no written law to which the plebeians could appeal. There rose a strong agitation among the plebeians for a codification of the customary law, or, at any rate, of so much of it as was necessary to protect them against arbitrary injustice at the hands of the magistrates. The leader of the plebeian party was C. Terentilius Arsa, a tribune. After eight years of struggle, in 454 B.C., a beginning was made, according to the traditional account, by sending commissioners to Greece to examine and report on the laws in force there.[1] Upon their return in 451 B.C., ten commissioners, called *Decemviri legibus scribundis*, were appointed.[2] The patricians agreed to allow the constitution to be suspended, and the consular power to be vested for the time in the decemvirs; the plebeians for their part agreeing that the tribunate should

---

[1] Livy, 3, 31, 8; 32, 6; 33, 3; Dion., 10, 52, 54, 56.

[2] The story of the embassy to Greece is now thoroughly discredited. It grew out of the desire to connect the Greek civilisation with that of Rome, and out of the mistaken belief that such resemblances as were noticed between the early laws of Greece and Rome could be explained only on the theory that the Romans borrowed them directly from the Greeks. See the very searching criticism of Pais, *Storia*, i. pt. i. 392, and *cf.* Lambert, *Études de Droit Commun Législatif*, i. 601; Girard in *Nouv. Rev. Hist.*, xxvi. 396.

be in abeyance. The whole power of the State was therefore vested in the decemvirs. They did their work with great rapidity, and by the end of the year 451 B.C. they had codified a great part of the law. Statutory effect was at once given by the *Comitia Centuriata*, and the new code was carved upon ten tables, either of wood or of brass, which were set up for all to see in the forum.

Source of Law of Tables.—The work was, however, not complete, and the decemvirs were reappointed with some changes in the membership. In the following year they brought in a supplementary work which was confirmed as before, and set up on two additional tables. The Twelve Tables were for centuries regarded by the Romans with peculiar reverence. Livy calls them *fons omnis publici privatique juris*, and even in Cicero's boyhood, 400 years after their promulgation, the Roman schoolboys learnt to repeat the Twelve Tables by heart: *a parvis, Quinte, didicimus "si in jus vocat" atque alias ejus modi leges nominare.*[1] And the Twelve Tables through all the changes of the law retained their statutory authority for nearly 1000 years. They were never repealed until Justinian's codification 948 years later. It is quite a mistake to infer that the decemvirs imported, to any considerable extent, Greek, or any other foreign laws. It is foolish to infer this from a few similarities which have been noticed between Greek and Roman law. Such similarities are only to be expected in the laws of two peoples so closely allied. As Puchta says, the similarities in the Greek and Latin languages are far more striking, yet no one suggests that commissioners were sent to Rome to bring in Greek words.[2] The Twelve Tables have not come down to us, and from the few fragments which we possess it is impossible to know exactly how far they were intended to form a complete code. It is probable that they took a great deal of the customary

[1] *De Leg.*, 2, 4, 9.

[2] *Inst.*, 10th ed. i. s. 54.

law for granted without re-enacting it, and only made declarations of the law upon points as to which questions were likely to arise. From the relative fulness with which certain subjects are dealt with we can form some idea of the state of society at the date of the Twelve Tables, and of the matters as to which disputes were possible. We possess only about 100 fragments, most of which are quoted by Cicero, Aulus Gellius, or Festus the grammarian. Of these some forty purport to be in the original words of the Tables, the others only giving the effect of a provision said to be there contained.[1]

Reconstruction of Tables.—Many attempts have been made to present from these scanty materials a reconstruction of the Twelve Tables. Some writers, and especially Voigt, have even formed a number of ingenious and archaic words and expressions in which to state the rules in those cases where the classical writers have given the sense but not the words of the Tables. There may almost be said to be an arrangement of the fragments which has become traditional. But it is extremely uncertain, and it rests upon two premises both of which are doubtful.

1. It is known that Gaius wrote a work on the Twelve Tables which consisted of six books. Of this we have some fragments. It is assumed that he followed the order of the Tables, and that each of his six books took in two tables, so that if Gaius speaks of divorce in his third book, we should infer that this subject was in the fifth Table.[2] But this assumption is quite gratuitous and in fact would lead to inconsistencies.

2. Of a few matters we are told that they were treated of in some particular table. It is assumed that the subject will be begun and ended on that table. But the Romans

[1] The fragments are collected and arranged with notes in Bruns, *Fontes*, and in Girard, *Textes de Droit Romain.*

[2] D. 48, 5, 54 ; Bruns-Pernice, s. 16.

thought nothing of ending a table even in the middle of a sentence, as we know from other ancient tables which are preserved. In fact all these reconstructions of the Tables, from that of Jacobus Gothofredus in 1616 to that of M. Voigt in 1883, are made up largely of guesses.[1]

Illustrations of the Law of the Twelve Tables.—The following are illustrations taken from some of the fragments which have come down to us, and are selected to give an idea of the character of this primitive code. For the reasons stated above the assignment of the fragments to particular tables is, in most cases, far from certain :—

Table I., which dealt with the private summons by which the plaintiff called the defendant into court — the *in jus vocatio* — says : "If you call anyone before the magistrate and he refuses to go, take witnesses and arrest him. If he shirks the summons or runs away, seize him by force. If he is hindered by sickness or age, let the plaintiff who calls him before the magistrate furnish him with the means of conveyance, but not with a covered carriage, unless the plaintiff chooses."

Table II. seems to have laid down the procedure in court. We have only a few words of it.

Table III. states the right of a creditor over a debtor who admits the debt or has been found liable by a judgment. This will be discussed in the chapter on the Early Law of Debtor and Creditor.

Table IV. treated, probably, of *patria potestas*. It contained, perhaps, a passage referred to by Dionysius of Halicarnassus, declaring that the father had *potestas* over his children, and had the right to throw his son into prison, to scourge him, to make him work in chains on the farm, to sell or to kill him, and that even though the son might hold high official rank in the Republic.[2] To this Table is assigned the well-known fragment,

[1] See Karlowa, i. 114 ; Muirhead, 2nd ed. 98.

[2] Archaeol., 2, 26, 27.

"If a father should sell his son three times, the son shall be free from his father"—*Si pater filium ter venum duuit, filius a patre liber esto*—which was at a later period made use of to render it possible for a father to emancipate a child, though this was never thought of by the decemvirs.

Table V. treated of succession and tutory, and stated in the briefest possible terms the principle that a man should be free to bequeath his estate, and named the persons to whom his succession would go if he failed to make a will:—*Uti legassit super pecunia tutelave suae rei, ita jus esto. Si intestato moritur, cui suus heres nec escit agnatus proximus familiam habeto. Si agnatus nec escit, gentiles familiam habento.* "As a man shall have made a bequest of his estate, *res sua*, so let the law be." The words *super pecunia tutelave* are very likely an interpolation of later date. Gaius cites the passage as *uti legassit suae rei* (ii. 224), and the word generally used in the Tables for an intestate succession is not *pecunia* but *familia*.[1]

"If a man dies intestate, leaving no *suus heris*, let the nearest agnate take his family estate." It is worth noting that the Code does not find it necessary to declare that if there is a *suus heres*, the estate will go to him. That elementary rule is left to rest as before upon custom. "If there is no agnate, let the clansmen take the estate."

Table VI.—It is perhaps to this Table that we should refer the famous passage dealing with mancipation—*cum nexum faciet mancipiumque, uti lingua nuncupassit, ita jus esto.* "When a man shall enter into a contract of *nexum* or mancipation, as he shall declare with his tongue, so let the law be." The necessity for this provision was, in all probability, created by the introduction of coined money.

[1] See Muirhead, *Roman Law*, 2nd ed. 158, note; Appleton, C., *Le Testament Romain*, 59. What is meant by *res sua* will be discussed under the head of the Law of Property and Wills, *infra*, p. 158.

In the earlier period the weighing which formed a part of the ceremony of mancipation had nothing fictitious about it. The price consisted of a certain weight of metal which was weighed off like any other commodity.

When coined money was introduced, which was of course counted and not weighed, the weighing in the ceremony of mancipation became merely a form; and in the Twelve Tables it is here declared that the operation is to be valid although there has not been any actual weighing, the parties being bound by their declarations.[1]

This is one of the passages which throw light upon the date of the Twelve Tables, a matter to be noticed presently. It is generally believed that coined money came into use about the same time as that ascribed by tradition to the Twelve Tables themselves, that is about the year 450 B.C., and it is indeed very probable that it was the decemvirs who introduced the first coinage.[2] If this is so, one can understand why the Tables should declare that weighing was no longer to be necessary. But if the Tables belonged, as some say, to a period two hundred years or more after the introduction of coined money, we should hardly expect to find in them a provision of this kind. Many cases would inevitably have arisen before then in which a party wishing to escape from the consequences of a mancipation had taken the technical objection that there had been no weighing, and that this was essential to the ceremony. Some way of meeting this objection would have been devised by the lawyers. It is incredible that no provision to meet so serious a difficulty should have been made before the Twelve Tables if they belonged to a date so long after the introduction of coined money.[3]

Table VII. perhaps gave the rules about the duties of

---

[1] Girard, *Manuel*, 5th ed. 287.

[2] Girard, *Manuel*, 5th ed. 246, note 4.

[3] See the remarks of M. Girard in *Nouv. Rev. Hist.*, xxvi. 426.

neighbouring owners. We know that the Twelve Tables contained provisions prescribing the space to be left between buildings, the width of roads, the right of an owner of land to gather the fruits which have fallen from his tree on to his neighbour's property, and some other matters relating to the law of land and buildings, but with the exception of a few words the declarations of the Tables on these subjects have not come down to us, and we have merely the statements of later writers as to their effect.

Table VIII. contained the provisions as to crimes and delicts. It will be convenient to deal with this subject separately in the chapter on the Early Law of Crime and Punishment. To this Table also is usually assigned the provision, *patronus si clienti fraudem fecerit, sacer esto*, that is, "if a patron shall commit a breach of his duties to his client the patron shall be accursed." It is not by any means certain that this provision formed a part of the Twelve Tables; if it did, by *fraus* we are probably to understand not failure on the part of the patron to protect his client, but something in the shape of actual abuse.[1] Perhaps it refers specially to a failure on the part of the patron to lend the client his assistance when the client has a lawsuit.[2]

Table IX. contained provisions of public law. It made it unconstitutional to propose a law inflicting pains and penalties or disabilities upon a particular person only—a *privilegium*.[3] Its intention is to prevent *ex post facto* legislation of the kind forbidden by section 9 of the Constitution of the United States. This Table also declared that no citizen should be condemned on a capital charge, that is a charge involving loss of life, freedom, or citizenship, without a right of appeal to the great assembly of the people—the *comitia centuriata*.[4] It enacted

1 Mommsen, *Röm. Strafrecht*, 566; *cf.* Voigt, *XII. Tafeln*, ii. 814.

2 See Bréal, M., in *Nouv. Rev. Hist.*, xxvi. 147.

3 Cic., *De Leg.*, 3, 4, 11; 3, 19, 44. See Greenidge, *Legal Procedure of Cicero's Time*, 312.

4 Cic., *De Leg.*, 3, 9; *De Rep.*, 2, 31, 53; Girard, *Org. Jud.*, 105.

the penalty of death against a judge or official arbitrator convicted of taking a bribe.[1] And the same penalty was provided against anyone who should provoke an enemy to attack the Roman people, or should betray a citizen to the enemy.[2]

Table X. contained some sumptuary and funeral regulations, forbidding burial or cremation within the city, the immoderate wailing or tearing of their faces by women at funerals, or the burial of gold ornaments with the dead. But this last prohibition was not to apply to the bridges or fastenings of gold by which the teeth of the deceased might have been connected during his life.[3]

Table XI. and Table XII.—Of the contents of these Tables we know very little, but in one of them was contained the famous provision forbidding the intermarriage of patricians and plebeians, giving effect to the old principle that there was no *conubium* or possibility of a lawful Roman marriage in the sense explained in the chapter on Marriage between members of the two orders.[4] And one of these titles also contained the rule that if a slave had committed a theft or some other delict which had caused damage, the person injured should have what was called a noxal action against the slave's master, in which the latter might be condemned to pay the damages or give up the offending slave.[5]

The Authenticity of the Twelve Tables.—In the last few years a serious attack has been made upon the authenticity of the Twelve Tables as being a code of law promulgated in the middle of the fifth century B.C. According to the later Roman historians, the first work upon civil procedure, giving the forms in which actions might be brought, was the book which got the name of the *Jus Flavianum*, published in the year 304 B.C. by Cn. Flavius, secretary of Appius Claudius Caecus. This work was understood by the

[1] Gell., 20, 1, 7. [2] *Dig.*, 48, 4, 3. [3] Cic., 2, 24, 60.
[4] Cic., *De Rep.*, 2, 36, 37. See *infra*, p. 164, and index, *s.v. conubium*.
[5] *Dig.*, 9, 4, 2, 1.

historians to have been a publication of the forms of actions which up to that date had been jealously preserved by the College of Pontiffs, and the intention of Flavius was to make the law of the Twelve Tables practically available for the people.[1]

It is now maintained by Professor Pais that this *Jus Flavianum* was not a work of interpretation of the Twelve Tables, but was the Twelve Tables themselves.[2] And a more recent writer, Professor Lambert, of Lyons, carries this scepticism a stage further, and argues that the Twelve Tables were compiled by Sextus Aelius Paetus Catus. Aelus was consul in 198 B.C., and the author of a book called the *Jus Aelianum*, containing new forms of action, and bringing the *Jus Flavianum* down to date, and also of a commentary on the Tables called the *Tripertita*.[3]

The arguments of these writers are too long to be fully stated here, but among the grounds upon which they chiefly rely are:—

1. That the Twelve Tables are not referred to by writers who might have been expected to mention them if they had been in existence.

2. That the language of the Twelve Tables is much too modern for its traditional date.

3. That the accounts given by the historians of the compilations of the Twelve Tables are mixed up with stories, such as that of Virginia and of the embassy to Greece, which are obviously fables.

4. That the Tables contain laws which belong to different stages of culture, and could not therefore have originated at the same date. For example, it is argued that the law of

[1] Pomponius, in *Dig.*, 1, 2, 3, 5; Livy, 9, 46, 5; Muirhead, 246; Krüger, *Röm. Rechtsquellen*, 29.

[2] *Storia di Roma*, i. pt. i. 579; i. pt. ii. 627.

[3] *La Fonction du Droit Civil Comparé* and *Nouv. Rev. Hist.*, 1902, 52. See for an account of S. Aelius Paetus Catus, Jörs, *Röm. Rechtswissenchaft*, 99-112.

talio and the right of creditors to divide the body of their debtor, which will be explained later, clearly belong to a primitive age, whereas such laws as those which forbid luxury and extravagance in connection with burials bear the mark of a much later time. It is not suggested that the author, whether Flavius or Aelius, who is credited with the authorship of the Tables, invented the laws which he put forth, but rather that he took a number of old rules and legal maxims which had been preserved by the pontiffs, and ascribed them to the fictitious decemvirs. These arguments have given rise to a spirited discussion, and in my opinion the authenticity of the Twelve Tables, as an official code, published by the decemvirs about the year 451 B.C., has been triumphantly vindicated by Professor Girard.[1]

It has been shown in a very convincing manner that there is no such suspicious silence on the part of early Latin writers in regard to the Twelve Tables, as is suggested by Pais and Lambert. On the contrary, we find allusions to them as soon as there is a Latin literature, and they are referred to by name from the period at which we have texts in which such reference might reasonably be expected. It is not surprising that Plautus does not expressly refer to the Twelve Tables; the poets are not expected to cite statutes, and it is possible, as Mr. Greenidge suggests, that the Twelve Tables were not called by that name till S. Aelius Paetus published his commentary. Before then they may have been spoken of simply as the *Jus Civile.* As regards the language of the Tables, there is no doubt that in some respects it has been modernised, and does not give the orthography of 450 B.C. But this is not in the least surprising. The Tables were issued for practical purposes,

[1] Girard, P., in *Nouv. Rev. Hist.*, 1902, 381. See also Erman, H., in *Zeit. Sav. Stift.*, 1902, xxiii. 450; Lenel, O., in *Zeit. Sav. Stift.*, 1905, xxvi. 498; Greenidge, A. H. J., *Eng. Hist. Rev.*, 1905, xx. 1; Goudy, H., *Jurid. Rev.*, 1905, xvii. 93; Binder, J., *Die Plebs*, 1909, 522; Costa, E., *Storia delle Fonti*, 1909, 6; *Jahresbuch fur klass. Altwiss.*, 1907, cxxxiv. 17.

and it is natural that copyists in later times should have modernised the spelling of words to suit the fashion of their day.[1] And on the other side is to be set the fact, established by the philologists, that the Twelve Tables contain archaic words and grammatical constructions clearly of great antiquity, and, further, that the character of many of the provisions themselves affords strong evidence that they belong to a period long before that assigned to them by these modern critics. *E.g.* the defendant who is old or ill has the right to be conveyed to the court at the expense of the plaintiff by a *jumentum*, a word which, according to Gellius, is used here in the sense of a carriage of some kind, whereas in later times it means a beast of burthen. But he cannot claim to be taken in an *arcera*, which the same writer explains as a large covered carriage used for old or sick people—a kind of primitive ambulance. Both the rule itself and the words in which it is expressed are of a very archaic character.[2]

Nor could the right of the creditor to put the debtor to death or to sell him across the Tiber, or the right of the creditors, if more than one, to divide the body of the debtor, have been invented in the age of Flavius or Aelius. They belong to a ruder age. And the right to sell the debtor "across the Tiber" clearly means to the enemy, and must belong to the period when the bank of the river opposite Rome was still occupied by the Etruscans. One of the strongest arguments in favour of the early date of the Twelve Tables is the prominence which they give to rural matters. A code prepared for the citizens of a large town would hardly have contained so much relating to country matters. The Tables are full of provisions as to the maintenance of roads, as to boundaries between fields and damage caused by straying animals, and as to penalties against one who cuts down his

[1] See Schoell, R., *Legis Duodecim Tabularum Reliquiae*, 5 ; Wordsworth, *Fragments and Specimens of Early Latin*, 509.

[2] Gell., 20, 1, 27.

neighbour's tree, or steals his neighbour's crops. This is quite natural if we suppose that the code was prepared when the Roman population consisted of peasant proprietors, but we should expect these rural regulations to take a much less prominent place in a code promulgated in the second or even in the third century B.C.[1] Moreover, in the *Fasti*, which give a chronological list of the consuls from the beginning of the Republic, we find in the year 450 B.C. decemvirs along with consuls, and in 449 B.C. decemvirs only.[2] And, after the most searching criticism, the best judges are convinced of the substantial accuracy of the *Fasti*.[3] The probabilities are altogether in favour of the traditional view that the decemvirs whose names occur in the *Fasti* were appointed, as the historians tell us, to prepare and publish a code of law, and that the Twelve Tables is the work which they promulgated. In accepting the authenticity of the Twelve Tables it is by no means necessary to believe all the stories which the early writers have associated with the decemvirs. The story of the embassy to Greece to study the laws in force there rests upon no safe foundation, and may, like the legend of Virginia, be relegated to the region of fable.[4] The history of early times is full of such interpolations and accretions, and the removal of these legends in no way affects the reasons for believing that the Twelve Tables are genuine, and belong to the date customarily ascribed to them.

Value of Tables.—The great and permanent value of the Twelve Tables was by no means the introduction of any great body of new law. Some new doctrines, no doubt, there were, but most of the law was declared and not made

---

[1] Voigt, *XII. Tafeln*, i. 17; Girard, in *Nouv. Rev. Hist.*, xxvi. 422.

[2] *Corp. Inscript. Lat.*, i. pt. i. 16, 106.

[3] Pauly-Wissowa, *s.v.* "Annales"; *Companion to Latin Studies*, Nos. 130 *seq.*; Girard, in *Nouv. Rev. Hist.*, xxvi. 399 *seq.* See, however, Lambert, *Etudes de Droit Commun Législatif*, 507, and the bibliography.

[4] Pais, i. pt. i. 592; Girard, *op cit.*, 396. See *supra*, p. 97.

by the decemvirs. And the old and thoroughly settled rules, such as that a man's first heirs are his *sui*, are not stated. Much of the law remained common law, even after the codification. The great service the Tables rendered was to make it clear that all citizens were equal before the law. There is no longer to be one law for the patrician and another for the plebeian. They created a certainty of equal justice for all citizens, which till then had never existed at Rome. Moreover, the Tables did much to remove the ground of the complaint on the part of the *plebs*, that the law was an affair of mystery, the knowledge of which was kept from them by the pontiffs. This grievance was to some extent a fanciful one, for the general customary law of a country must be largely matter of common knowledge. The law has grown out of the usage. But at the same time the pontiffs were, as a fact, the exclusive possessors of certain knowledge, such as the days on which it was lawful to sue, and of the various steps of procedure without which the knowledge of the law itself was of no great service. But, even after the Twelve Tables had become law, the pontiffs for a long time retained a position of great influence. An ordinary citizen, as some one has said, no more knew how to make use of the Twelve Tables, than a modern peasant knows how to use a table of logarithms. The language of the Tables was very abstract and brief. A great many points were not dealt with, or only dealt with by implication. The Tables had to be interpreted, and the pontiffs supplied this legal construction or *interpretatio*. They had also to frame actions in accordance with the Tables. The forms of actions were most narrowly scrutinised, and if there was any want of precision a defendant would plead that no relevant averment was made of any breach of law. These forms of actions were afterwards known as *Legis Actiones*, where the word *lex* perhaps means the Twelve Tables—a use not uncommon. Before the Twelve Tables there was no considerable body of law to which the term *lex* could be applied. The Twelve Tables were a *lex, par excellence,* and these actions were "actions at law in this special sense."[1]

Interpretation of Tables a Source of Law.—The Tables satisfied for a long time the demand for general legislation in the sphere of private law. For centuries the chief advance was by the method of *interpretatio,* or construction of the Tables. Instead of repealing a provision of the Tables, or of setting up customary laws alongside of it, legal ingenuity busied itself in making the text of the Tables apply to new circumstances. During the 1000 years in which the Twelve Tables was nominally the Roman Code, Rome had advanced from the position of a little town to that of the mistress of the world. Commerce had grown up to a degree unparalleled in history. The law had to fit itself to these new exigencies. And in the early period this business of interpreting and thus slowly developing the law fell upon the pontiffs. It was they who gave legal advice, not only to the magistrates to help them in the exercise of their jurisdiction, but also to private persons as to how they should make a contract or conduct an action. To take an example. The Tables said *si pater filium ter venumduit, filius a patre liber esto.* "If the father sell his son three times, let the son go free." This was meant most likely as a check on harsh fathers who made a practice of selling their children to their creditors to serve as security until a loan was repaid.[2] But when a method was wanted to enable a *paterfamilias* to set free his son, this rule of the Tables was ingeniously twisted into another sense. The father might sell his son by a purely imaginary sale to a friend, thrice repeated, into the bondage of another. The buyer every time manumits the son by *in jure cessio.*[3] The letter of the Tables has now been satisfied. The father has thrice sold his son. Accordingly he is free from the *patria potestas.*

This resort to forced constructions of the Twelve Tables is

[1] See Gaius, 4, 11 ; Greenidge, *Legal Procedure,* 50.

[2] Muirhead, 2nd ed. 114.

[3] Gaius, *Inst.,* i. 132.

due in part to a strong unwillingness to repeal any part of the Tables themselves. Some changes were made, but it is easy to see how reluctant the Romans are to alter a word of the Twelve Tables, though they are quite willing to read it in a very unnatural sense. Perhaps this devotion to the letter is because the Tables were looked upon as of the nature of a constitutional compact between the patricians and the plebeians.[1]

[1] Bruns-Pernice, s. 19 ; Cuq, 2nd ed. i. 35 ; Jhering, *Esprit*, ii. 64.

CHAPTER XII

Plebeian Grievances

Conubium and Praetor Urbanus.—There were two grievances of the plebeians which the Twelve Tables had not redressed :—

1. Their intermarriage with the patricians was still unlawful.

2. The plebeians were still ineligible for the magistracies.

No time was lost in attacking these fortresses of the *ancien régime.* C. Canuleius, a tribune, moved in 445 B.C., only five years after the Tables—

First, That there should be *conubium* between the two orders; and

Second, That the plebeians should be eligible for the consulship.

He carried the first reform, and his name is perpetuated in the *Lex Canuleia,* an important instance of a *Plebiscitum* which received the *auctoritas* of the Senate. The admission to the consulship was staved off for a time. It was not until B.C. 367 that it was enacted by one of the *Leges Liciniae* that in future one of the consuls should be a plebeian.[1] The patricians attempted to deprive the concession of some of its value by taking away from the consuls their judicial functions, and by entrusting them to a new magistrate to be called the *praetor urbanus.* It may be that he was to be a patrician, so that they hoped in this way to retain in their own hands the

[1] Livy, 6, 42 ; Gell., *N. A.*, 5, 4, 3. The date and the connection with the Licinian law are by no means free from doubt. Pais, i. pt. i. 559 ; Binder, 363. See Girard, *Org. Jud.*, 168.

administration of justice.[1] Livy describes the chief duty of the prætor as *qui jus in urbe diceret.* He was a colleague of the consuls, though inferior to them in dignity,[2] and, in their absence from the city, might, in some matters, act as their substitute. Like them he possessed the *imperium* or state authority. But, as the *imperium* of the consuls was military, and gave them the supreme command of the citizen army, so that of the prætor was civil, and gave him the supreme judicial power. The word prætor means, primarily, a general, and is a title of honour which was accorded to the consuls in the first centuries of the Republic. He was really a third consul specially intrusted with the administration of justice, and in principle his power was consular, though from the civil nature of his functions he took rank after the consuls. During his year of office the prætor, like the consuls before him, was invested with the judicial power which had belonged to the ancient kings. That is to say, in administering justice he was authorised to exercise his sovereign judicial discretion, being bound only by the letter of the *leges* or popular enactments which had then been passed, and by such ancient customs as tradition had invested with the force of law. The *leges* which affected the private law were few in number. I shall explain presently how the prætor came to exercise a great influence in moulding the law.

The Praetor Peregrinus.—As the city grew, and as foreign commerce became important, it was found necessary later on to appoint a second prætor whose duty was to administer justice in cases between foreigners at Rome litigating *inter se*, or cases between a Roman and a foreigner. This prætor was called, from his special duties, the *praetor peregrinus.*[3] This office dates from 242 B.C., and after that

[1] Muirhead, 2nd ed. 228 ; Girard, *Org. Jud.*, 167. Mommsen thinks this unlikely, *Abriss*, 166.

[2] Gell., 13, 15, 4 ; Karlowa, i. 218.

[3] D. 1, 2, 2, 28.

the judicial work at Rome, so long as the Republic lasted, was divided between the prætor *urbanus* and the prætor *peregrinus.* Later on other prætors were created with special duties. *E.g.* six of them presided over different *quaestiones publicae.* These were kinds of grand-juries, competent each to deal exclusively with particular crimes, and will be noticed later in speaking of the law of crimes.

Other Offices.—Other magistracies were also created—the censors, with their charge of the census, of the valuation roll, and of the preparation of the annual budget, and their *regimen morum;* the curule ediles, who looked after public health, sanitation, management of streets and public buildings, ordering of markets, &c., the quæstors, with their *custodia pecuniae publicae*—their duties as treasury officials—and their curiously different duties as public prosecutors in capital charges. All of these offices, except that of the curule ediles, were at first confined to patricians. But with the exception of the quæstorship, they were all created at a period when the plebeians had already become conscious of their power, and were determined to vindicate for themselves the full enjoyment of political equality. In no long time they were all thrown open to plebeians. The last citadel to fall was, naturally, the pontificate. This also was thrown open by the Ogulnian law of 300 B.C., although it was fifty years later—252 B.C.—before a plebeian was actually made *pontifex maximus.*[1]

[1] See for the dates at which the offices were thrown open, Mommsen, *Hist.* (Eng. trans.), i. 306.

CHAPTER XIII

The Comitia

The Comitial System.—During the Republic we are presented with the extremely curious phenomenon of the co-existence of three, if not four, distinct and co-ordinate legislative bodies.

In theory the legislative power lies with the people. They exercise their power not as with us in electing representatives. The people themselves vote directly upon the question proposed. But the method of voting is never the simple counting of the suffrages of individuals. It is always a vote of the people arranged into groups of some kind. The groups may consist of persons of the same stock, as in the curies; of persons of a certain wealth, as in the centuries; of freeholders in a certain ward, as in the tribes. But it is always a majority of groups, whether curies, or centuries, or tribes, which carries the day. It is not a majority of the voters present. And it might therefore happen that a majority of actual voters was so distributed as to carry only a minority of groups.

What strikes the modern student as odd is that various assemblies continued to exist at one and the same time in which the people were grouped according to different principles.

The Curies.—There is—(1) the old *Comitia Curiata.* This it is true is a mere shadow of its former self. After the *Comitia* of the Centuries got its full power, the *Comitia* of the *Curies* fades into insignificance, and is kept in existence mainly for certain religious and ceremonial reasons. It continues to meet under the presidency of the pontiffs to pass the *lex curiata de imperio,* by which the higher magistrates, such as the consuls and prætors, were formally invested with the state-authority after their election by the centuries. And the *Curies* met twice a year for what we might call private business. When so assembled it was called *Comitia Calata*. Its chief duties were first to inquire into all proposed arrogations, these being transactions by which a *paterfamilias* puts an end to his *patria potestas*, and is adopted by another *paterfamilias*, and, second, to ratify the wills made by citizens.[1]

Business was first laid before the pontiffs, and by them submitted to the *Curies*. As the assembly became a mere form the members ceased to attend. In the time of Cicero the pontiffs still used to summon the *Curies*, but no one came except the thirty lictors or beadles, one for each *curia*. The *Curies*, therefore, were not during the Republic a genuine legislative body which passed laws of a public nature.

The Centuries and the Tribes.—But the centuries, the tribes, and perhaps the *concilium plebis* were all in a sense legislative bodies. It depended on chance or on the magistrate who proposed a measure whether it was introduced in one assembly or another. If the magistrate was a consul he would introduce it into the centuries; a prætor preferred the *Comitia Tributa;* and a tribune generally summoned the *concilium plebis*. About 241 B.C. a change took place by which the centuries and the tribes were in some way amalgamated. The records are too meagre for us to know exactly what was done.[2] It appears that some uniform franchise was adopted, so that every voter in the centuries was also a voter in the tribes, and *vice versâ*.

But the two assemblies continued to meet separately, the same electorate being convened for certain purposes to the

[1] Gaius, *Inst.*, ii. 101. See *infra*, p. 147.

[2] Livy, i. 43; Karlowa, i. 385. Mommsen's solution in his *Staatsrecht* is so complicated that it has been called, not unfairly, a "counsel of despair," *Companion to Latin Studies*, n. 337. The best and most recent review of the subject is by Mr. Botsford in his *Roman Assemblies*, 215 *seq.* All the solutions are very conjectural.

centuriate assembly, and for other purposes to the tribal assembly. The centuries were convoked for the election of consuls, censors, &c., for making constitutional changes, and for state trials.

The tribes met to pass ordinary measures of domestic legislation.

The Concilium Plebis.—As time went on, the less formal body—the *concilium plebis*—or, at any rate, the *Comitia Tributa* under the presidency of a tribune, became the most active legislative body. It was easier to convoke; discussions were allowed in the meeting itself; there was less technicality about its proceedings; and *de facto* it consisted of the same members as the *Comitia Tributa.* During the later Republic this is the active legislative body. The so-called *leges* of the last two hundred years of the Republic were really *plebiscita,* and even measures of finance and provincial government were introduced in the *concilium plebis.* There has been much discussion of the question whether the *concilium plebis* is a term correctly applied to the meeting which actually voted upon legislative proposals. The better opinion seems to be that when the voting took place the *concilium* where the bill had been discussed resolved itself into the *Comitia Tributa.* When this body was presided over by a tribune it was called *Comitia Tributa Plebis,* because the plebeians had the preponderance in voting strength. If this is the correct view there were not four but only three legislative assemblies in the strict sense, even if we reckon the *Comitia Curiata* as one.[1]

Extensive emancipation converted the *concilium* into a rabble of freedmen. Many of these were practically paupers, and ready for any intrigue or faction.

Hence under the early Empire the legislative power was transferred from the Comitia to the Senate, and *senatus-consulta* took the place of *leges.*

[1] Botsford, 138, 275, 465; Costa, *Storia delle Fonti,* 18; *contra,* Mommsen, *Röm. Forschungen,* i. 155 *seq.*

Legislation as to Plebiscita.—The course of legislation by which the *plebiscita* were placed upon the same footing as laws passed in the formal *comitia* is one of the riddles of Roman constitutional history. According to Livy, one of the *Leges Valeriae Horatiae*, 449 B.C., enacted *ut quod tributim plebis jussissit populum teneret.*[1] This can only mean that the resolutions passed by the plebeians according to tribes shall be binding upon the whole people, patricians and plebeians alike. But the same authority, in a subsequent book, describing the events of the year 339 B.C., says that among them was the passing of a *Lex Publilia* which provided *ut plebiscita omnes Quirites tenerent.*[2] Notwithstanding these two enactments, the second of which seems to be identical in meaning with the first, we find a number of the classical writers attributing the legislative force of *plebiscita* entirely to a third law, the *Lex Hortensia* of 287 B.C.[3] There is an obvious difficulty in reconciling these three enactments, which at first sight appear to be merely repetitions one of another. It is natural to suppose that it was only the latest of them by which complete and unrestricted validity was given to the *plebiscita*, and that the earlier ones must have contained some restrictions which had to be removed. According to some authorities, the *Lex Valeria Horatia*, while it declared that the resolutions of the plebs were to have the same efficacy as those of the centuriate assembly, made this subject to the condition that the *plebiscitum*, before being brought before the people, should have first been discussed and approved of by the Senate. This is not stated by Livy in this place, but there are several passages in the historians describing the passage of *plebiscita*, which lend it some support.[4] The Senate at the time of the *Lex Valeria*

[1] Liv., 3, 55, 3. [2] Liv., 8, 12, 15.

[3] Pliny, *N. H.*, 16, 10, 37 ; Gaius, 1, 3—*ut plebiscita universum populum tenerent : itaque eo modo legibus exaequata sunt;* Gell., 15, 27, 4 ; Pomponius in *Dig.*, 1, 2, 2, 8.

[4] Liv., 4, 49, 6 ; 4, 6, 3 ; 3, 55, 15 ; and, esp., Appian, *Bell. Civ.*, i. 59 ; Mommsen, *Röm. Forschungen*, i. 211 ; *Röm. Staatsrecht*, iii. pt. i. 159 ; Botsford, 277.

was composed wholly of patricians, and the requirement that the Senate should approve of *plebiscita* before their introduction gave them even more control over the *plebiscita* than they had had over the comitial *leges* in virtue of their *patrum auctoritas.* The other article of the *Lex Publilia* of 339 B.C. made the *patrum auctoritas* a mere formality as regards legislation in the centuriate assembly, because the Senate was thereby required to grant the *auctoritas* in advance. This provision, however, did not apply to *plebiscita,* and the article of the *Lex Publilia* referring to them, while it put *plebiscita* on the same level as *leges,* did this only subject to the condition that the *plebiscita* received the *patrum auctoritas.* At any rate, if this was not stated in the law, it was asserted by the patricians in the period between 339 and 287 B.C. that this was the intention of the statute. It was this claim which was negatived by the *Lex Hortensia.*[1] But the passages from which the necessity for this *probouleuma* of the Senate has been inferred are by no means conclusive, and in particular the statement of Appian probably refers to a later period. During the century after the equalisation of the two orders from 367 B.C. on, during the time of the wars with Pyrrhus, Carthage, and Macedon, it is well known that the Senate had acquired the right, as a matter of constitutional custom, to be consulted by the magistrate before he brought a measure either before the *populus* or the plebs. And it is most likely to this period that Appian refers. The account given by the historians of the progress of certain pieces of legislation, and more particularly the description given

[1] This is the explanation of Mr. Botsford in his elaborate work on the *Roman Assemblies.* See esp. 235 and 314. Solutions differing to some extent from this and from each other are given by Mommsen, *Röm. Forschungen,* i., esp. 208 *seq.*; and Soltau, *Gültigkeit der Plebiscita.* Pais regards Livy's story of this *Lex Valeria Horatia* as undeserving of credit. It is a "doublet" of the *Lex Publilia,* and both accounts refer to the same law (i. pt. i. 563; i. pt. ii. 279). Binder is inclined to take the same view (*Plebs,* 371, 485).

by Dionysius of the course of the *Lex Icilia*, 456 B.C., has suggested another theory.[1]

The practice seems to have been as follows: — If the plebeians desired the passing of a measure they would discuss it in their *concilium* and pass a resolution recommending it. Their tribunes would then petition the consuls to bring the matter before the Senate. If the Senate was against it it might be dropped, but if the Senate was persuaded that public opinion was so strongly in favour of the measure as to make resistance dangerous, they would recommend the consuls to bring it before the *Comitia* for acceptance or rejection. And the tribunes could put a good deal of pressure upon the Senate by using their veto in such a way as to paralyse public business. If the Senate was persuaded or coerced into recommending the measure, its acceptance by the *Comitia* was pretty much a matter of form, because the voters in the *Comitia* will be practically the same persons as had already voted for the resolution in the *concilium plebis.* The fact that in the *Comitia* a few patricians were also present could make little difference. If the above is a correct account of the way in which the plebeians secured such legislation as they desired before the passing of the *Lex Valeria,* that law and the later laws of Publilius Philo and Hortensius must have been directed to removing all possible obstacles from the path. The first of these obstacles was that the consul might not accede to the demand of the tribune to lay the petition of the plebeians before the Senate, and a reasonable explanation of the *Lex Valeria* would be that it deprived him of the power to block the measure in this way and made it obligatory upon him to bring the petition before the Senate without delay. The Publilian law, a century afterwards, may have gone a step further, and ordered the consul to bring such a petition at once before the *Comitia* for acceptance or rejection, thus striking out altogether the preliminary stage in the Senate. Lastly, the

[1] Dion., 10, 52.

Hortensian law enacted that the *plebiscitum* itself should have all the validity of a comitial enactment, and did away with the necessity for bringing the measure before the *Comitia*, which had always been little more than a matter of form. This theory, which is that of Mr. Strachan-Davidson, makes the whole sequence of laws natural and intelligible and it seems to me by far the most plausible solution of the problem.[1]

One reason why there was a tendency for the assembly of the tribes to gain power at the expense of that of the centuries must have been that a tribune who wanted to introduce a bill before the tribes could not be stopped by any veto of a consul or a prætor, whereas, on the other hand, if a consul wanted to submit a bill to the centuries, a tribune could block it by his veto.[2]

[1] *Eng. Hist. Rev.*, 1886, i. 209, and 1890, v. 462.
[2] See Karlowa, i. 223.

CHAPTER XIV

The Senate

Importance of Senate.—The popular meetings I have just described were quite unsuited for performing the work of administration. They met, voted, and dispersed. A permanent body to carry on the government of the country, or at least to keep a check on and supervision over the magistrates, was absolutely necessary, and this want was supplied by the Senate. Nor are we surprised to find that the Senate gradually drew to itself the chief power in the state. As the affairs of Rome changed from municipal politics to world politics, the man in the street, the ordinary voter, became more and more unable to understand the issues involved. The conquest bit by bit of the civilised world; the conduct of long and anxious campaigns by land and sea; the management of an intricate foreign policy; the raising of an enormous revenue, and the supervision over its expenditure, were not things which could be decided upon in mass meetings, or left to the judgment of an ignorant electorate. More and more the Senate became the centre of government. Except the British Parliament, no deliberative assembly in the world has had to deal with such difficult questions of government, and especially government of foreign races, as the Roman Senate.

The composition of the Senate was completely changed during the Republic. The old Senate of the kings had consisted of representatives of the patrician *gentes*, who may have been selected from the *gens* on the ground of their experience and reputation for wisdom, but very possibly were chosen rather on the ground of birth as the hereditary chiefs of the clans. After the downfall of the kings, the consuls acquired the *lectio senatus*, or right to nominate senators. This was natural enough, as the Senate was in theory the council or advisory body which the consuls were bound to consult. At an early date, if not from the beginning of the Republic, the consuls began to choose from the plebeians as well as from the patricians.[1] And early, too, the practice grew up of choosing as a matter of course the ex-magistrates. After their year of office, the consuls, prætors, ædiles, and in later times the tribunes and quæstors, were virtually entitled to a seat in the Senate. In this way the Senate became a representative assembly. The people chose the magistrates, and the magistrates after their term of office became senators. They took their place in the Senate after their year of office, and could speak and vote, but were still not full senators until they had been chosen by the censors at the next revision.[2] By the *Lex Ovinia*, a plebiscite of about 312 B.C., the right of choosing senators was transferred from the consuls to the censors.[3] The censors also were empowered to remove from the Senate any member whose conduct was unworthy. For this purpose they held a revision of the list of senators every five years. After that time a senator, though chosen for life, had an absolutely safe seat for five years only—*i.e.* until the next revision. The censors then filled up the vacancies, taking first ex-magistrates. But they might reject an ex-magistrate on the ground of unworthiness (*praeterire*). They seem to have exercised this very important function with great discretion, and a senator whose conduct was good was not removed. The number of senators was about three hundred until the

[1] See Karlowa, i. 357 ; Willems, *Le Droit Public Romain*, 188; and *Le Sénat Romain*, 63 (end of fifth century B.C.).

[2] Karlowa, i. 358 ; Mommsen, *Abriss des römischen Staatsrechts*, 309.

[3] Festus, *s.v. Praeteriti Senatores*, 246; Willems, *Le Sénat*, 156; Mommsen, *Staatsrecht*, ii. 413.

changes made by Sulla in the last century of the Republic. He raised it to about twice that number.[1]

The Choice of Senators.—The censors could, as a rule, only fill up vacancies as they occurred, and there were more ex-magistrates than vacancies. As they had a recognised right to sit in the Senate, the nominal number of 300 was somewhat exceeded. But this was only permitted so far as necessary, so that in practice the censors' choice of senators became inoperative. They must take the ex-magistrates, and the ex-magistrates more than filled up the vacancies. As the magistrates were more often plebeians than patricians—at least in the later Republic—the Senate lost its old patrician character. It became a chamber of ex-officials.

The Senate was the great Roman Parliament. Like our Parliaments it was the body which controlled the administration. To the Senate the Roman magistrates were responsible for the discharge of their duties. The Senate had supreme control over the public peace, and could take such measures as were necessary to preserve order, to suppress insurrection, and so on. It organised the government of the provinces, and when a new country was conquered decided what amount of self-government should be left to it. It divided among the magistrates the provincial governships and other important offices, and in this way exercised a great deal of patronage. It had the general management of the public domain and of public buildings. It discussed the budget and voted taxes.

It considered all negotiations with foreign peoples, and could virtually make peace or war, though there had to be a vote in the *Comitia* before the last step was taken. But as a modern Cabinet can so conduct negotiations as to leave to Parliament no escape from a war, so could the Roman

[1] There was no fixed number, but Sulla, by admitting ex-quæstors to the Senate, and by other modifications of the law, seems to have about doubled the size of the Senate. See Mommsen, *Hist.*, iii. 360.

Senate. The great point of distinction between the Senate and a modern Parliament was that during the Republic the Roman Senate was not a legislative body. Its resolutions were not, strictly speaking, laws.

Senatus-Consulta.—The Senate was convoked by a consul, prætor, or, in later times, by a tribune. The magistrate who convoked it presided.[1] If it passed a formal resolution, this was called a *senatus-consultum*. It was really a direction to the magistrates, and couched in the form of advice. The Senate *censuere* so and so. The magistrate is to carry it out *si ei videbitur*. And the Senate in the later period of the Republic by usage established the right to suspend laws on grounds of urgency.[2] In practice, the influence of the Senate was so great that its resolutions were sometimes treated as equivalent to laws, and, in any case, there was generally no difficulty in obtaining the formal consent of the *Comitia* to what the Senate had agreed upon.[3]

[1] The *jus agendi cum patribus* was given to the tribunes, perhaps, as a consequence of the *Lex Publilia* of 339 B.C., which has been explained in the previous chapter. See Willems, *Le Sénat*, ii. 139.

[2] Willems, *Le Sénat*, ii. 116.

[3] Mommsen, *Hist.* (Eng. trans.), i. 324 *seq.*; Karlowa, i. 373 *seq.*; Willems, *Le Sénat*, 223 *seq.*; Krüger, *Röm. Rechtsquellen*, 24.

CHAPTER XV

PROCESS OF LEGISLATION

Illustrations of Laws of Republic.—The usual course of legislation was as follows:—

The bill must be initiated and drafted by a magistrate. Here is a great difference from our system. But it is more theoretical than practical. A private member can introduce a bill in our parliaments; but his chance of getting it carried is in most cases a slight one.

The Roman magistrate who has prepared his bill then brings it before the Senate. There it is discussed and voted upon. If the Senate is in favour of it, it is published, and a day fixed for proposing it to the *Comitia*. Before that date it may be discussed in informal *contiones* or public meetings. At the *Comitia* it is voted upon "Aye" or "No" without discussion.[1] This probouleutic power of the Senate was, however, as we have seen, greatly restricted by the *Lex Publilia* and the *Lex Hortensia*.[2] But even after the preliminary discussion in the Senate had ceased to be indispensable in point of law, it did not cease to be common. Broadly speaking, the volume of legislation upon matters of private law is not so great as might be expected.

Most of the laws recorded during this period are in character constitutional, fiscal, sumptuary, or criminal. There are not a large number which make alterations in the private law, and few of these are of great importance. I may mention some of the chief *leges* of the Republic.[3]

---

1 See Costa, *Storia delle Fonti*, 40; Krüger, *Röm. Rechtsquellen*, 18.

2 *Supra*, p. 118.

3 See the list in Bruns-Pernice, s. 25; Girard, *Manuel*, 5th ed. 34 *seq.*; Muirhead, 2nd ed. 237.

The *Lex Aquilia*—the great statute dealing with damages for injury to property, which is referred to under the law of crimes and delicts.

The *Lex Falcidia*, which entitled the instituted heir to a clear fourth of the succession, and cut down legacies so far as inconsistent with this.

The *Lex Voconia*, which for a time limited the freedom of bequeathing large fortunes to women.

The *Lex Cincia de donis*, to restrain lavish donations.

The *Lex Plaetoria*, which introduced remedies for the protection of minors against people who had taken advantage of their inexperience (*circumscriptio adolescentium*).

The *Lex Aebutia*, which revolutionised the ancient forms of civil process, and introduced the formulary system.

These may serve as examples. If we consider the long duration of the Republic, we cannot but be struck with the small amount of legislation upon private law. One great reason for this is that there were other ways of introducing necessary or desirable changes. The private law underwent, as a matter of fact, profound modification during the Republic. But the changes were made by custom, and by the prætor's edict, rather than by comitial legislation or by *senatus-consulta.*

CHAPTER XVI

Early Legal Procedure—The Old Legis Actiones

Legis Actio Sacramento.—The earliest form of legal procedure and the parent of the revendication of the modern civil law is the action which came to bear this name. It did not begin with any summons except an oral one. The plaintiff had to find his man, and by word of mouth solemnly call upon him to accompany him before the judge—in the earliest time the king, later the consul, and still later the prætor. This oral summons was called *in jus vocatio.* If the defendant declines to come, the plaintiff can call witnesses to take note of his refusal, and then hale him by force to the Court. This was called *manus injectio.* If no witness is available, he may, after calling on the defendant and being refused, put a notice on the door of his house. He is then entitled as before to proceed to *manus injectio.* But the defendant may, if he cannot conveniently go in person, produce a satisfactory representative—*vindex*—who takes his place in the proceedings and binds him. At a later period, if the defendant could be got hold of, the prætor would give the plaintiff the right to seize his goods.[1] When they get before the judge, the plaintiff states orally the nature of his complaint. This is *editio actionis.* The defendant will, probably, require time to prepare his defence, and the judge fixes a future day for further proceedings, and makes the parties solemnly engage to appear on the day fixed. In general the defendant had to find sureties—*vades*—for his appearance. From this the engagement to appear got the name *vadimonium.* On the day of trial the parties appear together

[1] See Gaius, iii. 78 ; iv. 46 ; D. 42, 4, 7, 1 ; Cuq, i. 138 ; Maynz, *Cours de Droit Romain*, 5th ed. i. 506.

before the judge. Each of them carries a *festuca* or rod, which stands for a spear—*quir* or *hasta*. This was itself, Gaius tells us, the symbol of ownership. To take the instance Gaius gives: suppose the action is one to recover from the defendant a man who is alleged to belong to the plaintiff. The plaintiff taps the man on the shoulder with his *festuca*, and repeats the following form of words: *Hunc ego hominem, ex jure Quiritium, meum esse aio (secundum suam causam) sicut dixi, ecce tibi vindictam imposui.*[1] By *secundum suam causam* Gaius means that the plaintiff must here state in what character he claims the man—*e.g.* must say the man is his *filiusfamilias* or his slave, &c., as the case may be. This claim made in this set form of words is the *vindicatio*. If the defendant makes no reply, judgment—*addictio*—is given forthwith for the plaintiff. If, however, the defendant contests the ownership he likewise touches the man with his *festuca*, and makes the *vindicatio*. When the *contra-vindicatio* is made there is *manus consertio, litis-contestation*—joinder of issue.[2] Then comes the stage of the *sacramentum*, from which the action takes its name. *Sacramentum* means, primarily, an oath,[3] and is in fact the word from which *serment* is derived. It is very likely that at first the parties swore by the gods that their contentions were just, and that the money forfeited by the loser was a peace-offering to the offended deity. At the period about which we have information, the plaintiff says, "Why have you vindicated?" The defendant rejoins, "Because it was my right." The plaintiff (*i.e.* the original vindicant)

[1] This formal seizing of the thing to which a legal claim is being made is common in the early laws of the Aryans. See Manu, 8, 31; *Lex Ripuaria*, 33, 1, pr.; Grimm, *Rechtsalterthümer*, 588; Bernhöft, *Staat und Recht*, 248; Leist, *Alt-Arisches Jus Civile*, ii. 266.

[2] See *Nouv. Rev. Hist.*, xxvi. 529. It is essentially, as its name denotes, a solemn attestation that there is a certain matter in controversy between the parties.

[3] "Mr. Strachan-Davidson, however, points out that there is no trace of an oath as a step in the procedure, and he argues that *sacramentum* here means the money stake, and was so called because it was to be spent on sacrifices" (*Problems of Roman Criminal Law*, i. 58).

retorts, "Your vindication is unjust. I challenge you with 500 *asses* (*i.e.* pounds of copper) to make good your claim"—"*D aeris te provoco.*" The defendant replies, "*Similiter ego te.*"[1] The stake is then deposited *in sacro* under the charge of the pontiffs. It remains there pending the trial. At the end the winner got back his stake, while that of the loser was forfeited, originally to the pontiffs for religious uses, later to the treasury. If the value of the object in dispute was below 1000 *asses* a *sacramentum* of 50 *asses* was sufficient, and, out of that care for the personal freedom of a citizen which is a mark of the Roman law, in a controversy concerning a man's freedom there was no question as to the man's value to his alleged owner. The minimum deposit of 50 *asses* was always enough.[2] Jhering points out what a hardship to a poor litigant such a system was.[3] A poor plebeian comes back from the war and finds that his father has died during his absence, and that the little paternal farm has been seized by his patrician neighbour. He has not 500 *asses* in the world. How can he raise the *sacramentum*? He cannot borrow it, for the only security he could offer is precisely the few acres in dispute. This obvious grievance was partly met by the *Lex Papiria* (*circa* 246 B.C.). This made it enough for the plaintiff to find sureties—*praedes sacramenti*—for the payment of the *sacramentum* in the event of want of success. But this was long past the early period, as to which Jhering's criticism seems very just. When the *sacramentum* had been handed over, the magistrate gave interim possession—*vindicias dicere*—to one of the two, making him find sureties—*praedes litis et vindiciarum*—to restore it with the fruits for the interim period, if he were ultimately unsuccessful.[4] Owing to a lacuna in the MS. of

[1] See the reconstruction from passages in Cicero and Gaius given by Greenidge, *Legal Proc.*, 58.

[2] Gaius, 4, 14.

[3] *Scherz und Ernst in der Jurisprudenz*, 175; and see Muirhead, App., note D.

[4] Gaius, 4, 16. *Vindiciae* means the thing vindicated and its fruits.

Gaius, the subsequent procedure is very doubtful. The magistrate before whom the ceremony I have been describing took place did not decide on the merits of the dispute. He remitted it to another Court. It must be tried according to its nature either by a *judex* or arbiter agreed on by the parties or by special large juries—the centumviral and decemviral Courts which had jurisdiction in certain classes of cases or by the *tres viri capitales.* The details as to the collegiate jurisdiction are obscure. Possibly in very early times the remit was made to the pontiffs, but this is doubtful.[1] The formal question for trial was, "Is the sacrament of A. just?" but its answer, of course, involved the merits. Before the magistrate the proceedings were said to be *in jure.* Before the arbiter they were *in judicio.* The act of remit was called the *litis contestatio*—the calling to witness of the cause,—because originally the parties called on those present to witness what was the issue which was being sent to trial.

When the subject in dispute was not a thing which could be brought into Court—*e.g.* was a field, the plaintiff's *vindicatio* was, "I say that such and such a field is mine, and I call upon you to go there and join issue with me before the magistrate" —*in jure manum conserere.* The parties then repaired with the magistrate and with their backers to the ground, and there went through the ceremony of the *vindicatio* and the *contra-vindicatio.* They then returned to the Court, and went through the ceremony of the *sacramentum.* At a later period they obviated the inconvenience of this procession to the land which might be a great distance away, by bringing a turf from the land in dispute.[2] This was accepted as a symbol of the land, and when the magistrate ordered the parties to go to the land they produced the turf, and each of them laid his *festuca*

---

[1] See Pauly-Wissowa, *s.v.* "Centumviri"; Girard, *Org. Jud.*, 173; *Manuel*, 4th ed. 974 and 994; Cuq, 2nd ed. i. 147; Greenidge, *Legal Proc.*, 1S3.

[2] Gell., 20, 10, 19; Cic., *Pro Mur.*, 12, 26; Greenidge, *Legal Proc.*, 55.

upon it instead of upon the actual field. Perhaps they had other similar symbols, such as a tile for a house. As time went on, as Muirhead suggests, the convenience of this plan would commend itself, and probably no particular inquiry would be made as to where the turf came from. A few sods and tiles would be kept at the Court to do duty when required.[1] The character of the ceremony suggests that it was invented for moveables which could be produced in the Court, and was extended at a later time by rather clumsy artifices to claims as to immoveables. And this is the more probable if there was a period during which private property in land did not exist.[2]

The whole procedure of the *actio sacramento*, primitive as it is, is a symbol of a procedure still more primitive which it had replaced. Behind it we see a period when the appeal was made not to the civil magistrate but to the gods, whose will had to be interpreted by the pontiffs. Still earlier we see that the appeal was to the strong hand. The vindicant and the counter-vindicant, who now lay their rods upon a symbolical turf as part of an antique ceremonial, decided in a simpler age their right to the land by single combat. They now go through certain ceremonial acts, and when the proper time for the combat has arrived the officer of the State intervenes to prevent the threatened violence and to appoint a means for a peaceful settlement.[3]

The *actio sacramento* was the general form, and was applicable in all cases where no other was prescribed—*e.g.* in claims to property, to recover a wife *in manu* or a *filiusfamilias* from a person who wrongfully detains them, to a servitude, and to personal claims which result in the payment of a definite sum of money or of a particular specific thing—*certa pecunia* and

[1] Muirhead, 2nd ed. 179.

[2] See Girard, *Manuel*, 5th ed. 989, note 6, and *infra*, chapter on Law of Property and Wills, p. 151.

[3] See Maine, *Ancient Law*, ch. x.; Bernhöft, *Staat und Recht*, 232. See also on the development from "self-help" to legal process the chapter on the Early Law of Crimes.

certa res. The judge had no discretion to award less than was claimed. If the plaintiff sued for 1000 *asses*, and a debt of 500 *asses* was proved, the judgment was for the defendant. It is possible that when the plaintiff's claim was not for *certa pecunia* or *certa res*, but was a claim uncertain as to its amount, such as, *e.g.*, a claim for damages, the question of liability or non-liability could be decided by the sacramental action, and the question of amount then remitted to an arbitrator—*arbiter liti aestimandae.* Some such machinery appears indispensable, but we have no reliable information about it.[1] In certain cases other forms of action are appropriate, but, unfortunately, little can be said with confidence about them. These other forms were the following:—

Per Judicis Postulationem.—This seems to have applied to small cases when the sum in dispute was less than 50 *asses*, which was the minimum *sacramentum.* The scale was 500 *asses* if the value of the thing claimed exceeded 1000 *asses*; if less it was 50 *asses.* Now if a man claimed 25 *asses*, say, as a fine for an assault, it would be absurd to make him advance twice as much as a stake.

Perhaps the *actio per judicis postulationem* applied also to other personal claims in which the sum to be awarded had to be assessed by the Court. And it has been suggested, with some probability, that in divisory actions in which the Court divides property previously held jointly, so that neither party loses, it would be grossly unjust to make either of them forfeit a sacrament, and that therefore the *postulatio judicis* was applicable in such cases. Where it was available, the plaintiff had the right to ask for a remit to a judge, without going through the preliminary sacramental procedure.[2]

---

[1] See Greenidge, *Legal Proc.*, 62; Muirhead, 2nd ed. 186; Girard, *Manuel*, 5th ed. 989; Karlowa, ii. 440.

[2] See Gaius, 4, 12; Greenidge, *Legal Proc.*, 63; Cuq, 2nd ed. i. 148; Muirhead, 2nd ed. 187; Schmidt, A., in *Zeit. Sav. Stift.*, 1881, ii. 145; Girard, *Manuel*, 5th ed. 991.

Legis Actio per Condictionem.—This is of later date. It was introduced as to *pecunia certa* by the *Lex Silia* of uncertain date.[1] It was a right given to the plaintiff who sued for a fixed and definite sum of money to give formal notice—*condictio*—to his opponent to appear on the 30th day thereafter for the appointment of a judge. It was a peculiarity of this action that when the sum claimed was *pecunia certa* the plaintiff might call on the defendant who disputed liability to pay one-third more than the debt if judgment went against him. He himself had to undertake to pay the same penalty if he lost his action. These engagements were called *sponsio et restipulatio tertiae partis.* The same procedure was extended later, by a *Lex Calpurnia*, to debts having for their object some definite thing other than money—*res certa.* The *condictio* in that case was called *condictio triticaria.* Whether the one-third penalty applied to this kind of *condictio* is doubtful.[2] One great peculiarity of the *condictio* was that the plaintiff had the right to refer the matter to the oath of the defendant. The defendant was bound to declare on oath whether he owed the debt or not. If he denied liability there was an end of the matter. If he admitted liability or refused to swear, the plaintiff gained his suit.[3]

The other two so-called actions of the law are really forms of execution, one against the person and the other against the property of the debtor.

Per Manus Injectionem.—This was a right of summary execution against the person of a debtor whose debt was indisputable. It applied specially to debtors who by the old contract called *nexum* had given their creditors the right, if the debt was not paid, to seize them and keep

---

[1] Gaius, 4, 17a-20.

[2] Cuq; 2nd ed. i. 213 ; Girard, *Manual*, 5th ed. 992 ; Muirhead, 2nd ed. 220. Jobbé-Duval thinks the penalty applied here also (*Etudes sur l'histoire de la Procédure*, i. 196).

[3] See *Dig.*, 12, 2, 34, pr. ; Cuq, 2nd ed. i. 213 ; Girard, *Manuel*, 5th ed. 992 and 610.

them in bondage. This matter will be dealt with in the chapter on the Law of Debtor and Creditor. A debtor of a sum of money against whom his creditor has obtained a judgment, or a debtor who has made a formal admission in Court of his liability, may be seized by the creditor and held as a bondsman. His position is that which will be described in speaking of the debtor under a *nexum*.

Per Pignoris Capionem.—This was a right of summary execution without judgment against the property of a debtor in certain cases. *E.g.* the publicans who farmed the taxes had the right to seize the property of persons who were in arrears with their taxes, and by the Twelve Tables one who had sold on credit an animal for sacrifice and could not get the buyer to pay him, was entitled to *pignoris capio.* And a soldier had his right against the official who was responsible to him for his pay—the *tribunus aerarius.* The case of the publican and that of the soldier may, perhaps, be explained most naturally as cases in which upon public grounds the State delegates to an individual its own exceptional power of enforcing payment from its debtors. But the case of the seller of the sacrificial animal seems to be an example of the primitive right of self-help which is still tolerated here as an exception to the rule. There are interesting analogies in other laws of such extra-judicial seizure by a creditor accompanied by the use of some formal declaration of his right.[1]

About all these old forms of procedure, except that of the *sacramentum*, our information is very scanty from the defective state of the MS. of Gaius, who is, practically, the only authority.

[1] See Pernice, in *Zeit. Sav. Stift.*, v. 128; Maine, *Early Institutions*, 275; Cuq, 2nd ed. i. 143; Greenidge, *Legal Proc.*, 67; Girard, *Manuel*, 5th ed. 981.

CHAPTER XVII

Early Forms of Conveyance—Mancipatio and In Jure Cessio

Mancipatio.—The characteristic and most important form of conveyance in the old law was mancipation. Everything about it bears the mark of antiquity, and there is no reason to doubt that it goes back to a remote period. For a thousand years its quaint ritual was practised in transactions between Roman citizens in every part of the Empire.[1] *Mancipatio* is a curious and picturesque little ceremonial. When it was desired to make a transfer of certain kinds of property—*res mancipi*—the parties must call a weigher—*libripens*—who brings with him his scales and copper weights. *Mancipatio* is often called the ceremony of the copper and the scales, *quod per aes et libram geritur.* They must also summon five witnesses—adult male citizens. The *libripens* was a private citizen merely acting like the five witnesses to oblige the parties. Some writers think that he was a public official whose duty it was to lend his services and his scales when called upon, but there does not seem to be any ground for this supposition.[2] The buyer, in the presence of the *libripens,* the seller, and the five witnesses, lifts the thing if it is a moveable in his hand or seizes it—*rem tenens*—and pronounces a formula called the *nuncupatio.* The words

[1] See Kuntze, *Excurse,* 168, and for an example in 355 A.D. see *Cod. Theod.*, 8, 12, 7.

[2] Gaius, 2, 108; Karlowa, ii. 371; Kuntze, *Excurse,* 172, *Contra,* Danz, *Geschichte des Röm. Rechts,* s. 143, note 6; Muirhead, 57.

are not preserved in their entirety. He says, *Hunc hominem ex jure Quiritium meum esse aio isque mihi emptus sit hoc aere, aeneaque libra.* Here he states the price. He then struck the scales with a piece of copper—*raudusculum*—and handed the bit of copper to the seller. The transaction was then complete. But the property did not pass unless the price was paid or the seller accepted some equivalent.[1] If the thing sold was a piece of land, or a thing like a ship which could not be taken up by the hand, it was sufficient to describe it. It was not necessary in mancipating land to go to the spot, nor were symbols used as in the *vindicatio.* And from this and other indications it seems highly probable that mancipation was invented first for moveables alone. It applied originally only to things which could be seized, and it was used long before immoveables could be alienated at all.[2] Where, however, moveables were transferred, it was only as many as could be seized at once which could be mancipated together. From a document found lately at Pompeii we find that even in the first century A.D. it was necessary in mancipating several slaves to go through the ceremony separately for each.[3] Even as early as the Twelve Tables *mancipatio* was in some respects antiquated. The weighing, which is its chief feature, had no longer any reality, and the Tables recognise this in declaring *cum nexum faciet mancipiumque, uti lingua nuncupassit ita jus esto.* That is, the weighing is not to be essential, but the verbal declaration is to have full effect whether there was any weighing or not. It is probable that the reason for the necessity of this declaration was the introduction of coined money. After that the price was counted, not weighed, and the weighing became merely

[1] Girard, *Manuel,* 5th ed. 286.

[2] Cuq, i. 129 and 124; Karlowa, ii. 352; Pais, i. pt. i. 574; Girard, *Manuel,* 5th ed. 286, note 2.

[3] See Girard, *Textes de Droit Romain,* 2nd ed. 738.

a piece of ritual.[1] Gaius calls mancipation *imaginaria venditio*, and in his time, and for many centuries before, the ceremony of the weighing was a mere piece of formality.[2] But originally it was the actual weighing of the price in bars of raw metal. It must have come into use when bars of metal were the medium of exchange. Earlier still cattle had been the medium at Rome, as in so many early states.[3] When coined money was introduced it was not necessary to weigh the price, but to count it. But the old form of sale was retained. It had peculiar effects which made it valuable.

(1) If the buyer was evicted because it turned out that the seller was not the owner, he had an action *en garantie* called the *actio auctoritatis* by which he could compel the seller to restore to him double the price stated at the mancipation.

And (2) if land had been mancipated and declared to be of a greater extent than it actually was, the buyer had an action *de modo agri* for twice the value of the extent wanting.[4] When mancipation was employed as a form of donation, or when it was not intended that the seller should assume this warranty, the price stated in the mancipation was a nominal one—*nummus unus*. A clause excluding warranty was not valid, but by this device the liability was made nominal, being restricted to twice the nominal price mentioned. This in no way

[1] Muirhead, 2nd ed. 129; Girard, *Manuel*, 5th ed. 287 and 479, note 2. See another view in Cuq, i. 83, note 4.

[2] Gaius, i. 119.

[3] *Pecunia* is from *pecus*, "cattle." *Cf.* Eng. *fee* from A.S. *feoh*, "cattle." "Rupee" is said to have originally meant "cattle." Professor Ridgeway says, "Wherever the cow has been domesticated it has always been the chief unit of barter amongst primitive communities" (*Comp. Latin Studies*, n. 685).

[4] Paul, *Sent.*, 2, 17, 1-4; Girard, *Manuel*, 5th ed. 288 and 555. See the examples in Bruns, *Fontes*, 6th ed. 288, 289, and article by Girard, in *Nouv. Rev. Hist.*, vii. 280.

prevented the actual price paid from being a substantial sum.[1]

Mancipation belongs to the old civil law, and it was confined to Roman citizens and to Latins or peregrins who enjoyed the *commercium* in virtue of a treaty.[2] And certain things could be validly transferred only by *mancipatio*. These were the *res mancipi*, or mancipation-things. *Res nec mancipi* might be alienated without mancipation. Many authorities think that the five witnesses symbolise or represent the five classes into which Servius divided the people.[3] Mancipation would thus be an act performed before the whole people through their representatives. But this theory is almost certainly erroneous, for (1) we find mancipation employed by the Latins who had not the Servian classification, and (2) Gaius says that there must be not fewer than five witnesses—*non minus quam quinque testibus*.[4] He could hardly have expressed himself thus if there had been any magic about the number 5. It seems a large number of witnesses to require, but we must remember that mancipation goes back to a period before writing. Out of five witnesses there was a likelihood that enough would survive to bear testimony in the event of the sale being challenged before the buyer's title had by prescription become unassailable. It may be looked on as a kind of primitive registration. Like the law of registration in countries which register titles to immoveable property, it applied only to certain property which was regarded as the most important kind, and like registration it attempted to secure that the ownership of this property shall be publicly known.[5] Things which fall into this category are called *res mancipi*.

[1] Karlowa, ii. 377; Girard, *Manuel*, 5th ed. 556.

[2] Ulp., xix. 4.

[3] Muirhead, 2nd ed. 58.

[4] Gaius, i. 119.

[5] Against the theory that the witnesses represent the fivefold division of the people (Karlowa, ii. 370; Girard, *Manuel*, 5th ed. 287, note 2),

What Things were Res Mancipi?—1. Real property in Italy, whether houses or farms—*praedia urbana vel rustica.*

2. Slaves.

3. Native beasts of draught or burden—*quadrupedes quae dorso collove domantur;* horses, oxen, mules, asses.[1]

Camels and elephants which were imported into Italy at a later date were not *res mancipi.* There was an old controversy as to whether a beast of burden such as an ox was a *res mancipi* from its birth, or only from the time when it was broken in.[2] The former theory, supported by the Sabinians, was that which ultimately prevailed.

4. *Servitutes praediorum rusticorum;* such as rights of way of carrying water, &c.

All other things were *res nec mancipi.* We see that the *res mancipi* were practically the homesteads and the instruments—slaves and cattle—by which the farm was worked. The reason provincial land was not included was, that it did not belong to private citizens. Theoretically, it was owned by the State, although this came to be little more than a fiction.

Origin of Distinction between Res Mancipi and Res Nec Mancipi.—There has been much discussion with regard to the origin of this distinction. That it is an ancient division is clear. The use of *nec* for *non* is, in itself, a proof of this,

Bruns thinks the classes may have *suggested* the number 5, though the witnesses were in no way representatives (*Kleinere Schriften*, i. 119). But this is fanciful. The numbers 3, 5, 10 were favourites. See Goudy, *Trichotomy in Roman Law*, for an interesting discussion of the charm which the number 3 exercised.

[1] Gaius, i. 120; Ulp., xix. 1. One German theorist—Huschke—thinks each of the Servian classes may have had a special animal of this kind. As unfortunately only these four animals are mentioned, he boldly invents a fifth—the *bovigus*—from his inner consciousness. Huschke thought first that the *bovigus* guided the plough by its tail, but, in a later work, he comes to the conclusion that it was by its proboscis. As the animal never existed except in the mind of Huschke, there is a wide field for speculation. See Jhering, *Scherz und Ernst*, 191.

[2] Gaius, iii. 15.

but there are many others. It belongs to a time when the Romans were yeomen-farmers, cultivating small plots of land and the *res mancipi* were those things which formed the essential wealth of a peasant-proprietor. The introduction of coined money and the rise of pasture-farms changed the economic situation, but flocks and herds were never *res mancipi*.

Fictional Uses of Mancipation.—Mancipation was employed for various purposes besides that of genuine sales. As I shall explain later, it was resorted to as a way of contracting marriage. In *coemptio* the husband went through a fictitious ceremony by which he bought the wife by mancipation. It was employed for emancipating a son, or for giving him in adoption, and for contracting a nexal loan in which the borrower became bound to become a bond-servant of the lender, if the loan was not duly repaid, as is explained in the chapter on the Law of Debtor and Creditor. And lastly it was employed for making a will. The testator went through the form of selling his estate to a friend who was charged with the trust of dividing it after the testator's death according to his instructions.[1] So that to the enumeration of *res mancipi* we might add,

5. A freeman or freewoman who, if they can be sold at all, are to be sold by *mancipatio;* and,

6. The *familia* or estate sold *en bloc* for the purpose of making a will.

But (5) and (6) are fictional *res mancipi*, not thought of when the division was first made.

Res mancipi could be alienated in the early law only by *mancipatio* or by *in jure cessio.* And mancipation continued to be the normal mode of conveyance of such things down to a late period. But in the later law, when a *res mancipi* had been transferred by delivery to a purchaser who acquired it in good

[1] See *infra*, chapter on Early Law of Property and Wills, p. 148.

faith and on a just title, the prætor protected him in his possession, and prevented the seller from taking fraudulent advantage of the want of *mancipatio*. Gradually the distinction between *res mancipi* and *res nec mancipi* became of less importance. Protected by the prætorian equity, the buyer who had got his *res mancipi* was secure, though it had been sold to him without the old ceremonial. Finally Justinian abolished the distinction altogether, as it had no longer any practical utility.

Mancipation of a Res Nec Mancipi.—There is an old and not very profitable controversy as to the effect of mancipating a *res nec mancipi*. It was not necessary. The thing could be sold and validly transferred by mere delivery. But if the seller chose to go through the ceremony, was the sale a good sale? In other words, was *mancipatio* incompetent except as to *res mancipi*? Some authorities think that it was.[1] And this is probably the correct view in the sense that if a *res nec mancipi* was mancipated — and instances of this certainly occurred—the seller was not liable in the warranty of twice the price. But when the mancipation of a moveable *res mancipi* was accompanied by delivery and payment of the price it is hardly doubtful that there was a valid transfer of the property. For why should the *libripens* and the witnesses impede the legal effect of the delivery and the payment of the price? It seems unreasonable to maintain that the property was not transferred because something more was done than the law required. The rule *superflua non nocent* would seem to apply.[2] The other early form of conveyance applies to *res mancipi* and to *res nec mancipi* alike.

In Jure Cessio.—The early forms of conveyance are as cumbrous and ceremonial as the legal process. In fact this one is a simulated action.[3] The seller agrees to allow a judgment

[1] Girard, *Manuel*, 5th ed. 291. [2] *Ibid.*, note 2; Muirhead, 2nd ed. 137.

[3] Gaius, ii. 24; Ulp., xix. 9-11; Karlowa, i. 381; Girard, *Manuel*, 5th ed. 292.

to be pronounced by the Court in which it is found that the buyer is the owner. The *in jure cessio* was just the sacramental action cut short. The two parties, having come to an agreement as to the transfer, go before the magistrate ; the plaintiff takes hold of the thing, if it is a moveable, and declares in formal terms that it belongs to him—*hunc ego hominem ex jure Quiritium meum esse aio.* The magistrate asks the defendant if he makes claim to the thing *an contra vindicet.* The defendant says he makes no counter-claim, or is silent. Whereupon the magistrate applying the rule *confessus pro judicato habetur* pronounces the thing to belong to the plaintiff. The whole procedure is fictitious and known to be such. The magistrate is quite aware that though in form he is declaring the plaintiff to have come into Court as the owner of the thing in question, he is in reality making him the owner of a thing which before the judgment belonged to the defendant. The mock trial is merely a way of getting a legal title. Such an employment of legal machinery for an indirect purpose can hardly be primitive, and it was probably invented as a means of transferring something for which no other mode of conveyance was available. It is possible that it may have arisen when lands first became alienable, and before mancipation, which was used for moveable *res mancipi*, had been made to apply to immoveables also.[1] It had one great drawback, that in it no warranty of any kind was implied. The plaintiff got a judgment that the thing was his, but the defendant had kept mute and had given no guarantee against eviction or otherwise.[2] *In jure cessio* was less used for conveyance of property than for the transfer of incorporeal rights. It could be employed only by citizens. The simulated action was found so convenient that it was used :—

1. For transfer of property.

[1] Karlowa, ii. 383.

[2] Karlowa, *l.c.* ; Muirhead, 2nd ed. 138.

2. For manumitting a slave.

3. For emancipating a son.

4. For adopting a son.

5. For assigning a *hereditas en bloc* before entry (see Gaius, ii. 35).

6. For assigning the tutory over a woman.

7. For creating a servitude.

The old English law made a somewhat similar use of fictitious actions as a mode of acquiring a title to property in what were called fines and recoveries.[1]

[1] See Blackstone, *Com.*, ii. 349, 357.

CHAPTER XVIII

The Early Law of Property and Wills

One of the most striking and singular characteristics of the Roman law is that in the earliest times of which we have any record we find the *paterfamilias* as the absolute owner of the family estate, with unrestricted powers of alienation *inter vivos*, and according to the common interpretation of the passage in the Twelve Tables—*uti legassit suae rei, ita jus esto*—with full power of bequeathing his estate by will to anyone whom he shall choose. And, what is hardly less remarkable, if the *paterfamilias* dies intestate his succession is to be divided equally among the children who were in his *potestas*, daughters as well as sons, with representation to the descendants of children who have predeceased him; the widow, if she had been *in manu*, taking a child's share. These rules of the Roman law differ widely from those found among most of the Aryan peoples at an early stage, nor do they bear the marks of a primitive state of society. In particular the absolute freedom of disposition by will is so extremely unusual that some writers find in the provision of the Twelve Tables, which appears to confer that power, one of the strongest arguments against the authenticity of the Tables as a document of the fifth century B.C.;[1] and other writers who cannot believe that absolute freedom of willing existed at Rome at the time of the Twelve Tables interpret the passage which seems to declare that right in a sense which greatly restricts its application.[2] Before discussing

[1] Pais, i. pt. i. 574.

[2] Cuq, 2nd ed. 124-131; Lambert, E., *Études de Droit Commun Législatif*, i. 411 *seq.*

this subject it will be convenient to explain the early forms of wills and then to show in what respects the Roman law presents such singularities.

Early Forms of Wills.—The chief source of our information as to the early forms of wills is a passage in Gaius, which is supplemented by a few references in other writers. Gaius says: In the beginning there were two kinds of wills, for people made a will, either *in calatis comitiis*—*comitia* which were fixed twice a year for that purpose—or *in procinctu*, that is, when they were arming for battle, for *procinctus* is an army equipped and under arms. The one kind of will, therefore, they made in time of peace and leisure, the other when they were going out to battle. A third kind of will came afterwards, namely, that made *per aes et libram*, for a testator who had not made his will either *calatis comitiis* or *in procinctu*, if he was driven thereto by imminent peril of death, conveyed his *familia*, that is, his patrimony, to a friend by mancipation, and instructed him what he wished to have given to each of his beneficiaries after his death. This is called the will made by the copper and the scales, because it is executed by mancipation. The two former kinds of wills have fallen into disuse, and only the one made by the copper and the scales is still retained in practice.[1] It is significant that Gaius speaks of the two earlier forms of wills as going back to the beginning, and it is pretty certain that the *testamentum calatis comitiis* was in existence before the time of the Twelve Tables. The *testamentum calatis comitiis*, as its name implies, was made in the presence of the citizens assembled according to *Curies* in the *Comitia Calata*, a term which means merely the *Comitia* formally convoked.[2]

The fixed dates on which it met for testamentary purposes are not certain. In the Calendar of Numa the dates, 24th March and 24th May, are followed by the letters Q. R. C. F.—*quando rex comitiavit fas*, and Mommsen understands this as meaning that

[1] Gaius, ii. 101, 102.
[2] See Botsford, 154.

these were the days appointed for the meetings of the *Comitia Curiatia*.[1] But, apart from the fact that it seems unlikely that two dates so near together should be fixed for this purpose, there are other reasons which make this interpretation doubtful.[2]

However this may have been, the citizen declared his will before the assembled people. It was no doubt an oral declaration, and it is safe to assume that only very simple wills were possible in this form. Probably in most cases it was not much more than the naming of a particular person as heir. There has been much controversy as to the *rôle* which the assembled people played in the transaction. Were they merely witnesses, or were they called upon to give their consent to the proposed will? Most modern authorities are of the opinion that in order to answer this question a distinction must be made between two periods. In the earliest period the actual consent and approval of the people was necessary, and the will was, in effect, analogous to what is now called a private Act of Parliament, but at a later stage the position of the *Curies* became merely passive, and they were simply called upon to witness a will without having power to interfere with it. There are strong reasons for accepting this view. If it is merely a question of procuring witnesses it is extremely unlikely that the law should have required the testator to call the whole people to witness his deed, whereas, if legislation was necessary, the assembly was the place for it. Moreover, if the theory which will be explained later in this chapter is correct, namely, that the *pater-familias* had not originally the right to defeat the claims of his natural heirs, it is easy to see why the transaction should be before the assembly. Special legislation was necessary to give the testator exceptional power, and, according to the general view, it was the Twelve Tables which did away with the necessity for legislation of this special kind, and declared in the passage, *uti legassit*, that without such legislation the *pater-*

[1] *Röm. Staatsrecht*, iii. pt. i. 319.
[2] Karlowa, ii. 848; Botsford, 159.

familias could dispose of his estate as he chose. That the *Curies* at first required to give a legislative sanction is now the opinion of most writers, and this seems to be supported by all the probabilities, though there is not quite so much agreement as to whether the second stage, which reduced them to the position of witnesses, was introduced by the Twelve Tables.[1]

The Testamentum in Procinctu.—When the army was drawn up in battle array after the auspices had been taken it was competent for a soldier to make a declaration of his will before the army, that is in practice, before those of his comrades who stood near him in the ranks. Seeing that in this case there can never have been any question of giving legislative sanction, and the testator's comrades must always have been merely witnesses, it seems probable that the right of making a will in this way did not exist until the Twelve Tables had reduced the curiate assembly to the position of witnesses and not makers of wills.[2]

It has recently been suggested, however, that the *testamentum in procinctu* is earlier in date than the *testamentum calatis comitiis.* The right of making a will was first granted as a favour to soldiers, and it was afterwards extended to the citizens in general.[3] But it hardly seems likely that, at a time when there was no general freedom of willing, this right should have been given wholesale to all the citizens who happened to be in the ranks of the army. It is more natural to suppose that there was a time when the *Comitia* had control of the situation, and allowed a citizen to make a will only upon sufficient cause shown.

Testamentum per aes et Libram.—Gaius expressly says that this form was later than the two others, and, even if we had

[1] Mommsen, *Staatsrecht,* iii. pt. i. 318; Jhering, *L'Esprit du Droit Romain,* i. 147; Lambert, *Études de Droit Commun Législatif,* 421; Appleton, *Le Testament Romain,* 75; Girard, *Manuel,* 5th ed. 802; Kuhlenbeck, *Entwickelungsgeschichte,* 55, 169. *Contra,* Karlowa, ii. 849.

[2] Girard, *Manuel,* 5th ed. 806.

[3] Appleton, *Le Testament Romain,* 78 *seq.*

not his testimony, the character of the transaction itself seems to denote a later period. It is one of those artificial uses of the ancient ceremonial of the copper and the scales which was probably due to the ingenuity of the lawyers. But the old formula employed by the testator, which is preserved by Gaius, contains a word *endo* which, except in the Twelve Tables, is not found elsewhere, and there are various reasons which make it probable that this form of willing, if it was not in existence at the date of the Twelve Tables, which is by no means impossible, cannot be at any rate much later than that time.[1]

The reason of its introduction has been much discussed. One view is that it was introduced for the benefit of the plebeians, seeing that they could not make a will in the *Comitia Curiata*, not being members of that body.[2] But apart from the consideration that, as has been explained earlier, it is probable that the plebeians were members of the *Comitia Curiata*, there does not seem to be any difficulty in a man getting a private bill passed by an assembly of which he is not a member.[3]

The reason given by Gaius appears quite sufficient. The citizen who was at the point of death could not wait for the next meeting of the *Comitia*, which might be more than six months hence. The *mancipatio familiae* was at first a very rude contrivance. The testator had to convey his whole estate *inter vivos* to his friend, and had to trust to the friend's honour to distribute it among the beneficiaries in the terms directed, or to restore it to the testator if, contrary to expectation, he recovered. It says much for the Roman character that there is no evidence to show frequent abuse of such trusts. Their execution was secured by a stern and active public opinion, and by the possibility of the censor branding with infamy the trustee who was guilty of a breach of his trust. The advan-

[1] See Appleton, 107; Karlowa, ii. 855; Lambert, 440; Girard, *Manuel*, 5th ed. 809.

[2] Mommsen, *Staatsrecht*, iii. pt. i. 78, 93; Muirhead, 64.

[3] Karlowa, ii. 853.

tages, however, of the new method of making a will were considerable. In the first place, it was less public; the testator did not need to declare to everybody his testamentary intentions; in the second place, it was more easily revoked. If the testator changes his mind he can call upon the *familiae emptor* to remancipate the estate, which has never passed into his actual possession, and the testator can then make a new will, or die intestate if he so prefers. If the will had been made in the *Comitia* or *in procinctu* the testator could not have revoked it until the opportunity of making a new will in one of these forms presented itself.[1] But above all the mancipation of the estate to a friend was a method which was capable of great development and improvement. The ingenuity of the lawyers, through the agency of the prætor, was able to turn it at a later period into a genuine will. Instead of an *inter vivos* conveyance, it became a conveyance taking effect only at death. Instead of the testator having to trust to the good faith of a friend, the estate is allowed to vest at once in the heir. Instead of an oral declaration, necessarily of a very simple nature, the testator is allowed to write down his will, and without reading it, to show it to the witnesses. The great virtues of revocability and secrecy are thus secured. This later development, however, of the primitive *mancipatio familiae* does not belong to this place.

Exceptional Character of Power of Willing of Roman Paterfamilias.—The study of comparative institutions, especially as prosecuted during the last generation, has brought into much clearer light the unusual position of the Roman *paterfamilias.* It has made it appear extremely probable that his absolute power of disposition, at any rate of immoveables, cannot be primitive, and that if he possessed this power at the time of the Twelve Tables, we must assume that the Roman law on this subject had undergone considerable development. Indi-

[1] Appleton, 114.

vidual ownership of land, unless it be of very small lots, and unrestricted powers of alienation of land are not primitive institutions, and the power to leave land to persons outside the family is in most countries of late introduction.

Tribal Occupation of Land.—So long as the Aryans were in the nomad stage individual property in land was not thought of. The flocks and herds of the tribe pastured in common, and neither the tribe nor its members had more than a temporary occupation of the soil. When the tribes settled down in a definite territory, and formed the settlements out of which the European nations have grown, no sharp distinction was drawn between the conceptions of sovereignty and ownership. The tribe acquired sovereignty over a territory by occupation, and assigned the use of subdivisions of the territory to the clans of which the tribe was composed. The clans in their turn portioned the land out to individual families. It is not necessary to assume, nor is it probable, that this subdivision among the families was made on the same conditions at all times and in all places. On the contrary, there are reasons for believing that in some cases the arable lands were portioned out to the families for a limited time only, when a new distribution took place, the pastures or forest lands remaining common to the whole group.[1]

Another method was to assign the lands to a family, giving it the right to retain them so long as the family existed, but subject to the provision that the lands are to return to the *gens* if the family dies out. This is, in fact, corroborated by the rule of the Roman law enshrined in the Twelve Tables, but going back to a much earlier time, that if the citizen has no *sui heredes* and no agnates his succession is to go to the clansmen. It came from the clan, and, as the family has died out, it returns to the clan.[2]

---

[1] See Cæsar, *Comm.*, 6, 22; Tac., *Germ.*, 16; Viollet, *Hist. du Droit Français*, 556; Glasson, *Hist. du Droit et des Institutions de la France*, ii. 60.

[2] *Cf.* Kovalewsky, *Coutume Contemporaine*, 70, 87.

It is easy to see how, under such a system, it is a long time before it becomes necessary to evolve any precise theory of property in land. The tribe occupies a territory, and through the *gentes,* the lands or parts of them over which the sovereignty of the tribe extends, are divided among families for periods, sometimes very short and sometimes of indefinite duration. As Maitland says: "The question as to the whereabouts of ownership might go unanswered and unasked for a long time." [1]

The Paterfamilias as Administrator.—If we conceive the history to have been something in the manner above sketched, it becomes clear that the *paterfamilias* was not at first an absolute owner of the land which was occupied by the household over which he presided. He was the administrator, not the owner, of the family property, and his sons were co-owners even during his lifetime, though they might be subject to the personal authority of the *paterfamilias.* It is a faint echo of this state of things which makes the jurist Paul, in the third century A.D., in explaining the term *sui heredes,* say that they are looked upon in a sense as owners even while their father is alive —*qui etiam vivo patre quodammodo domini existimantur.*[2]

In his day this was the merest fiction, but there had been a time when it had been a reality. Everything points to the conclusion that there must have been a time among the Romans, as among other Aryans, when the *paterfamilias* was not an absolute owner, and could neither alienate the family estate *inter vivos* nor dispose of it by will, at any rate without the special authorisation of the community. The study of the Aryan family in other countries would in itself make this almost certain, and it is confirmed also by many traces in the language of the Roman law. In addition to the expres-

[1] *Domesday Book and Beyond,* 340 *seq.* See Jenks, E., *Law and Politics in the Middle Ages.*

[2] *Digest,* 28, 2, 11. See Cuq, i. 75 ; Lambert, *Études du Droit Commun,* i. 432 ; Appleton, *Le Testament Romain,* 91 ; Girard, *Manuel,* 5th ed. 260 ; Botsford, *Roman Assemblies,* 48. *Contra,* Hölder, in *Zeit. Sav. Stift.,* 1882, iii. 211.

sion *sui heredes*, already mentioned, the strongest evidence perhaps is the undisputed tradition that every *paterfamilias* had a lot of two *jugera*, which was called the *heredium*, assigned to him by Romulus.[1]

The ascription to Romulus of this division is a mere fable, but it points to the tradition that the *heredia* go back to the beginning of the city. Whether, as Mommsen thinks, the *heredium* was merely the garden round the farmhouse, or whether it may have been an arable field or two, as Karlowa maintains, it is equally clear that the citizen could not have lived on the produce of two *jugera*—about an acre and a quarter—and that the tradition represents the bulk of the land as not divided among the burghers.[2]

This undivided common land must have remained in the possession either of the State or of the *gentes*, and the latter is the more probable of the two, as it explains the right of succession which the *gentiles* enjoyed when a family died out.[3]

Other reasons which go to show that land was inalienable to begin with are—(1) that wealth is described by words—*pecunia*, *familia*—which primarily refer to cattle and slaves; and (2) that mancipation, the earliest form of acquiring property, was evidently devised originally, as its name shows, for things which could be seized by the hand—*manu capere*—*i.e.* moveables, and was adapted only at a later date to the transfer of immoveables.[4] That family ownership of land preceded the

[1] Varro, *R. R.*, 1. 10 ; Cuq, ii. 174 ; Mommsen, *Hist.* (English trans.), i. 194.

[2] *Röm. Staatsrecht*, iii. pt. i. 23 ; Karlowa, *R. R.*, ii. 350. As to the size of a *jugerum* see Mommsen, *Hist.* (English trans.), i. 194 ; *Companion to Latin Studies*, n. 678. Originally it meant an oblong strip of ground, such as could be ploughed in an average day's work by a yoke of oxen ; *cf.* English *ploughgate*, German *Morgen*.

[3] Mommsen, *loc. cit.* ; Pais, i. pt. i. 574 ; Girard, *Manuel*, 5th ed. 261 ; Cuq, 2nd ed. i. 75. *Contra*, Karlowa, who prefers to put the ownership with the State, ii. 346. For another view see Botsford, in *Pol. Sci. Quart.*, xxii. 685.

[4] Mommsen, *Hist.* (English trans.), i. 194 ; Girard, *Manuel*, 5th ed. 260 ; Karlowa, ii. 352 ; Cuq, i. 81.

absolute ownership of it by the *paterfamilias* at Rome, as elsewhere in the Aryan world, may be regarded as certain, though but faint traces remain of it in the records.

Inalienability of the Family Estate among other Aryans.—So long as family ownership of land is in full vigour the head of the family, being merely the administrator for the time being of the property which belongs to the whole family, cannot alienate the land either *inter vivos* or by will except with the consent of the co-owners or by the special authorisation of the State. Or, if such power exists at all, it is subject to great restrictions. Such family ownership of land is found in the history of all the Aryans, and among some of them it exists to the present day. Thus Sir Henry Maine, speaking of the collective holding of property in certain parts of India, says: "That system is one of common enjoyment by village communities, and inside these communities by families. The individual here has almost no power of disposing of his property: even if he be chief of his household the utmost he can do, as a rule, is to regulate the disposition of his property among his children within certain very narrow limits."[1]

In Greece at an early time the territory of the tribe was marked out by the king into parcels according to the number of families in the community, and the families then cast lots for the separate shares. The head of each family administered this separate estate, but had no power to alienate it. This explains why a farm or piece of land is called by a word meaning "lot"—κλῆρος—long after family ownership in Greece has given place to private ownership.[2]

Among the Ossetes of the Caucasus, where much of the old Aryan law still survives in singular purity, family ownership of land still prevails, and the head of the family cannot alienate

[1] *Village Communities*, 41, London, 1871.

[2] Meyer, *Geschichte des Alterthums*, ii. notes 194, 196; Dareste, *Nouv. Études*, 77; Bury, *Hist. of Greece*, 70.

it without the consent of all the adult males of the family.[1] A like state of matters is found in the history of the old Slavs, and it still exists in a more developed form among the Servians.[2] And in like manner family ownership of land is the conspicuous feature of the old German and Celtic laws. In various ways collective ownership gradually gave way to private ownership, leaving in many countries curious traces, such as the old German law, that alienations of land require the consent of the heirs—*Beispruchsrecht*—and the rule of the old French law up to 1790, that if a man sold lands which had come to him by succession—*propres*—his nearest kinsman had the right of repurchasing them from the buyer at the same price—*le rétrait lignager.*[3]

The Joint Family or House Community.—Among some of the Aryans the patriarchal family in many cases did not break up on the death of the *paterfamilias,* but continued to live together for several generations, so that families of as many as a hundred persons are found living together under one roof and eating at the same table, without claiming to take out their several shares of the common property. Such a system still survives among the Ossetes and the Southern Slavs, and it formerly existed among the Welsh.[4] Traces of the same thing exist among the Greeks and the Romans.[5] And in France similar groups have existed in rare instances down to modern

---

[1] Kovalewsky, *Coutume Contemporaine*, 97.

[2] Dareste, *Études*, 189, 241.

[3] See Schröder, R., *Deutsche Rechtsgeschichte*, 4th ed. 336; Viollet, *Hist. du Droit Civil Français*, 555-565 and the bibliography; Maine's Works; Vinogradoff, *Growth of the Manor*, 18.

[4] Dareste, *Études*, 136; *Nouv. Études*, 347; Kovalewsky, *Modern Customs and Ancient Laws*, 47; Vinogradoff, *Growth of the Manor*, 15; Bernhöft, in *Zeit. für vergleich. Rechtwissenschaft*, ix. 412.

[5] The family of Nestor, in *Iliad*, i. 247; other Greek examples in Jevons, "Kin and Custom," *Journal of Philology*, xvi. 102. At Rome the family of M. Crassus, who was brought up in a small house with his two brothers. These married while their parents were living, and they all ate at the same table. Plut., *M. Crassus*, i.; see Schrader, *Sprachvergleichung*, 570.

times, and perhaps still exist.[1] Or, without living under the same roof, the family may continue to be undivided for several generations, the kinsmen not taking out their shares and living together in a village.[2]

No Wills.—It is this collective ownership of property which explains the fact, otherwise very puzzling, that among most of the Aryans the will is of such late introduction. Wills did not exist among the Athenians until the right of willing was given by Solon, and then only when the testator had no children.[3] There was no testamentary freedom in the old Hindu law or in the old law of the Germans or Slavs.[4] Among the Ossetes the right to make a will was given only in 1859, and the principle of the inalienability of the family property is so rooted in the customs of the people that a writer who describes them in 1893 says they have hardly made any use of their testamentary power.[5]

No Right of Primogeniture.—The principle that lands should descend exclusively to the eldest son would be altogether irreconcilable with family ownership, and it does not in fact exist in the early law of any of the Aryans, nor was it ever introduced at any time into the Roman law. Where the family remained undivided after the death of the *paterfamilias* it was the custom in some countries for the eldest son to take the father's place as head of the family and administrator of the family estate, and it is perhaps in consideration of his trouble and responsibility as chief of the family that under some laws he was entitled to a share greater than that

[1] Viollet, 562.

[2] See Maine, *Village Communities*, *passim*; *cf.* article by Sir W. C. Petheram in *Law Quart. Rev.*, 1899, 175.

[3] Plut., *Solon*, 21.

[4] See Maine, *Village Communities*, 40; *Ancient Law*, 15th ed. 196; Leist, *Alt-Arisches Jus Civile*, ii. 176 *seq.*; Dareste, *Études*, 291; Grimm, *Rechtsalterthümer*, 482; Brunner, i. 79; Lambert, *Études de Droit Commun Législatif*, 411 *seq.*

[5] Kovalewsky, *Coutume Contemporaine*, 220.

of his brothers;[1] but of this there is no trace in the Roman law.[2]

Succession of Daughters.—Under the system of family ownership it is also natural to find that a preference in successions should be given to males. If a daughter marries she goes out of the family, and if she carries her share with her the family estate will be thereby diminished. It is characteristic of all the early Aryan laws that the daughters are either excluded altogether from the succession, and dependent upon portions provided for them by their father or brothers, or that, where the rule is not carried to this extent, or has been relaxed, they receive a smaller share than their brothers.[3] Where there are daughters only it may be a part of the custom that one of them should be appointed to marry, subject to the provision that her son shall succeed to the estate of his maternal grandfather, a custom found among the Hindus, Greeks, and Slavs.[4]

Peculiarity of the Roman Law.—From the preceding account of Aryan customs in general it will be sufficiently clear that the position of the Roman *paterfamilias* is one which is very unusual. He is an absolute owner with full power of disposition by will, and if he dies intestate his daughters share equally with his sons. It is not surprising that a learned writer should say that if this is a correct statement of the facts the Roman law on this subject must be regarded as a monstrosity.[5] The study of comparative law has led several writers to attempt to show that the Roman law at the time of the Twelve Tables cannot have been as above described. I will touch first on the succession of daughters, and then on the question of testamentary freedom.

[1] Manu, ix. 112; Kovalewsky, *op. cit.*, 221.

[2] As to the history of primogeniture in modern law, see Maine, *Early Institutions*, 199; *Ancient Law*, c. 7.

[3] This was so among the Hindus, Armenians, Ossetes, Czechs, Poles, Slavs, Scandinavians, and Franks. Dareste, *Études*, 74, 121, 144, 168, 198, 227, 287, 314, 331, 349, 414.

[4] Manu, ix. 131; Plut., *Solon*, 20; Meyer, *Geschichte des Alt.*, ii. s. 59 and s. 196; Leist, *Alt-Arisches Jus Civile*, ii. 136 and 154.

[5] Lambert, *op. cit.*, 415.

Succession of Daughters.—Although by the early Roman law daughters succeed equally with sons, this did not at first carry with it any great risk of diminishing the family estate, and it certainly did not arise from any prematurely "advanced" views as to the equality of the sexes. If the daughter had married with *manus* she was not an heir of her father. If she was *in potestate* and became *sui juris* by his death she was an heir, but it was easy for him during his lifetime to make a will disinheriting her, and it is probable that fathers frequently deprived the daughters of an equal share with the sons, and gave them a portion of less amount to serve as a dowry if they married.[1] But if the *paterfamilias* had not disinherited his daughter, and she took, accordingly, her equal share, there was no great risk. She was in tutory, and could not marry with *manus* without her tutors' consent. She could not, without their consent, alienate her lands, they being *res mancipi*, and she could not make a will at all, even though the tutors did consent. The woman's agnatic tutors had the power and the duty of keeping the lands in the family.[2] And if she married without *manus* her children had, by the early law, no right of succession to her.[3] It is this want of testamentary capacity in women which makes the position intelligible. Keeping this in mind we realise that, as regards the equality of daughters with sons, the difference between the Roman law and the other Aryan laws is more nominal than substantial.

Testamentary Freedom.—The passage in the Twelve Tables comes to us in several forms differing slightly from one another. *Uti paterfamilias legassit de re sua*, or *super familia pecuniaque sua*, or *super pecunia tutelave rei suae*, or *uti legassit suae rei-ita jus esto.*[4] The probability is that the original text was *uti*

---

[1] See Appleton, *Le Testament Romain*, 97.

[2] See *infra*, p. 171.

[3] Ulp., xxvi. 7; Gaius, i. 115a; Cic., *Top.*, 4; Muirhead, 44; Gide, *Cond. Privée de la Femme*, 109.

[4] *Twelve Tables*, v. 3; Gaius, ii. 224; *Inst.*, ii. 22, pr.; *Nov.*, 22, c. 2, pr.; Ulp., xi. 14.

legassit suae rei, ita jus esto, and that the words *super pecunia tutelave* are later additions.[1] The question is, Does this provision of the Twelve Tables give to the citizen the unrestricted power to dispose of his estate by will? It is certain that Pomponius, writing in the second century A.D., understood it in this sense,[2] and this opinion was shared by the lawyers of the classical period.[3] But it is quite possible that they should have assigned to the text of the Twelve Tables a meaning which it did not originally bear. According to Cuq, what the passage in the Twelve Tables did was to give power to a testator to dispose by legacy of his *pecunia,* that is of moveables, but not of the lands which were *res mancipi* and belonged to the family. The power to make a disposition *mortis causa* of these did not exist at the time of the Twelve Tables, and when the right of testation was created the will required the approval of the pontiffs and the consent of the assembled people.[4] If, however, the word *pecunia* did not originally form any part of the passage in the Twelve Tables, but is a gloss or explanation interpolated at a later time, the foundation of this argument is struck away. And it is further open to the very serious objection that there is nothing whatever to indicate the possibility at any time in the Roman law of making a legacy which did not form part of a will.[5] A learned writer, who does not agree with M. Cuq that it is possible to divide the estate of a citizen in this way, and say that he could dispose by legacy of his *res nec mancipi* but could not test on his *res mancipi,* nevertheless maintains, upon quite different grounds, that the Twelve Tables cannot have introduced or declared the unrestricted freedom of willing. According to him the study of comparative law makes this

1 See Appleton, *Le Testament Romain,* 59; Muirhead, 158; *Suae rei* is the dative, *legare = legem dicere;* Schöll, *R. Legis Duodecim Tabularum Reliquiae,* 127.

2 *Dig.,* l. 16, 120.

3 Gaius, ii. 224; *Inst.,* ii. 22.

4 Cuq, 2nd ed. i. 124 and 129.

5 Girard, *Manuel,* 5th ed. 805.

incredible. Absolute freedom of willing could not have existed among a people at the stage of culture of the Romans in 450 B.C., as is shown by the fact that wills are of such late introduction elsewhere, and especially among the Germans.[1] In a very learned and interesting argument he maintains that the passage in the Twelve Tables *uti legassit* does not refer at all to a genuine will in the modern sense. It is a kind of contract by which a man gives to another an irrevocable right to the whole or part of his succession. The heir, if he may be so called, acquires an indefeasible right there and then, and becomes, as it were, a joint-owner of the property, and it was only a citizen who had no *sui heredes* who could make a contract of this kind.[2] Plausible as some of M. Lambert's arguments are, I think that they have been triumphantly answered by his colleague in the University of Lyon, M. Appleton.[3] His reasons for rejecting the new theory may be summarised as follows :— 1. It is dangerous to argue that, because the Germans had no wills in early times, this must have been the case among the Romans also, for in many respects the Romans, even at the beginning of the Republic, were much more advanced in legal ideas than the Germans at the time when their codes were compiled. Both in its form and contents the Twelve Tables is a document of much more refined character than, for example, the *Lex Salica*, more than a thousand years later in date. 2. In the Roman law the power of the *paterfamilias* was clearly much greater than it was under the German law, as is shown by the fact that the Roman *paterfamilias* was perfectly free to alienate the property *inter vivos* without requiring the consent of his heirs, which the German father could not do.[4] 3. If the early Roman will was not a will at all but a contract, it is incredible

[1] Lambert, E., *Études de Droit Commun Législatif*, i. 411 *seq.*

[2] P. 433 ; Binder accepts this view, *Plebs*, 507.

[3] *Le Testament Romain*, Paris, 1903.

[4] See Pernice, *Labeo*, i. 187. The right of the heirs in the old German law was called *Beispruchsrecht*.

that there should not be some trace of the necessity for the presence of the other party to the contract. The transaction would not be represented in the sources as purely unilateral. 4. If the "heir" or other party to the contract acquired an indefeasible right at the date of the transaction, this can only have been because he accepted it at the time, and if so, no subsequent acceptance would have been necessary. But we know that the Roman heir, unless he was an *heres suus et necessarius* or an *heres necessarius*, had to make a formal acceptance of the succession. 5. It is not necessary to assume that the Romans reached at once the modern conception of a will as a disposition which the testator was perfectly free to revoke at any time before his death. On the contrary, the early Roman will could not be revoked except by a subsequent will. A mere change of intention on the testator's part was not sufficient, and even after the time when wills were generally put into a written form the testator could not revoke his will merely by destroying the document.[1] 6. One main reason why it is natural that the Roman law should have been led to permit the making of wills at an early period in its history is the vital importance, for religious reasons, of leaving an heir. "Let him be the last of his line" was a familiar imprecation. The *paterfamilias* who wants to insure his repose in the world of the *manes* must leave an heir who can be trusted to perform the sacred rites. The last argument alone does not seem to me very convincing, for the Hindus, with whom the religious reasons weighed certainly as much as with the Romans, found in the practice of adoption sufficient means for securing the performance of the family rites, but on the whole there does not seem to be any necessity to accept the new theories. There is no insuperable difficulty in believing that the clause *uti legassit* in the Twelve Tables did in fact confer complete freedom of willing. It may be necessary to assume that the previous law had been different, and that the

[1] Gaius, ii. 151. See *Zeit. Sav. Stift.*, 1886, vii. pt. i. 1; 1886, vii. pt. ii. 91; and 1887, viii. 109; Girard, *Manuel*, 5th ed. 836.

Roman law had passed through a stage in which some of the other Aryans are still found at a much later date ; but such an assumption is quite consistent with the exceptional genius for law which is a marked characteristic of the Romans. For one reason or another the Roman *paterfamilias* acquired at a very early time powers greater than those enjoyed by the head of the family among other Aryan peoples. At Rome family ownership gave place at an exceptionally early period to the private ownership of the *paterfamilias*. Intensely conservative as the Romans were, and animated as they were in the early period by a profound belief in the ancestral religion, it may well be imagined that the disherison of a son was altogether rare,[1] but there appears to be no sufficient reason for refusing to believe that the power to make a will by which the *sui* might be excluded is given in the Twelve Tables in the passage under discussion. In this case, as in so many others in the Roman law, there is a *de jure* absolutism which *de facto* is restricted within narrow limits by the influences of religion, tradition, and public opinion.

[1] Appleton, 102. In a paper read to the Historical Congress of 1913, Prof. Lenel has argued that the comitial will was purely a legacy will, and that *institutio heredis* is no older than the fully-developed mancipatory will. But the reasons which he advances do not appear by any means conclusive, and they are criticised with much force by Prof. Buckland in *Law Quart. Rev.*, xxxii. 97.

CHAPTER XIX

The Early Law of Marriage

In the *Institutes* of Justinian marriage is defined as the union of the male and the female, involving an unbroken intimacy for life—*viri et mulieris conjunctio individuam vitae consuetudinem continens.* This is perhaps a modification of the definition by the jurist Modestinus given in the *Digest*, which is as follows:—Marriage is the union of the male and the female and "a partnership in the whole of life, a sharing of rights both sacred and secular"—*nuptiae sunt coniunctio maris et feminae, et consortium omnis vitae, divini et humani juris communicatio.*[1] The definition of Modestinus is very likely a traditional one. At any rate it brings out clearly the religious character of marriage which is so prominent in the earlier law.

Pre-Requisites to Marriage.—Three conditions must be fulfilled before a lawful marriage can come into existence—(1) the necessary consents must be given; (2) the parties must be of lawful age; and (3) in the Roman phrase there must be *conubium* between them. Even when all these conditions are satisfied there is not necessarily a marriage which gives to the husband the *potestas* over the children. If, for example, the parties are both foreigners, the Romans recognised the marriage as lawful, but its legal consequences were determined by the foreign law, and such a marriage is described as *matrimonium juris gentium.* The Roman marriage, from which the *patria potestas* flowed, was called *justum matrimonium* or *justae nuptiae.*[2]

[1] *Inst.*, i. 9; *Dig.*, xxiii. 2, i. I have borrowed the translation of Lord Bryce, *Studies in History, &c.*, ii. 400.

[2] Ulp., 5, 2; Gaius, i. 56; *Inst.* i. 10; Rossbach, 390.

The three conditions of marriage must be briefly explained.

1. In the early law the authority of the *paterfamilias* is so absolute that if the *paterfamilias* of the bridegroom and that of the bride agreed to the marriage the consent of the young people was not required. Marriages were made usually when the bride and bridegroom were little more than children, and the marriage was a family arrangement between the respective *patresfamilias;* but in the later law, when the *patria potestas* became much restricted, the *paterfamilias* could not marry his son without the latter's express consent, and the daughter had a legal right to object to being married to a man of disgraceful character or very unsuitable position.[1] In the early law, also, the *paterfamilias* had the absolute right to refuse his consent, and without it the marriage was impossible; but in the later law there was a right of appeal to the magistrate against an unreasonable refusal.[2] When the marriage was that of a grandson, who was in the *potestas* of his grandfather, it was necessary that the father as well as the grandfather should consent to the marriage. This was because the children of the marriage, when the husband's grandfather died, would fall into the *potestas* of the husband's father, and it was a principle that no one should be bound without his consent to have a child brought into his *potestas*, and thereby made one of his heirs. This reason did not apply when it is a granddaughter who is being married; it is sufficient in that case that her grandfather, as her *paterfamilias*, gives his consent, for her children will never fall into the *potestas* of her father.

2. *The Required Age.*—At an early period the earliest age at which a girl could be married was fixed at twelve years. In the case of boys the age of puberty was a question of fact to be determined in the particular case, and it was not until the later law that fourteen was fixed as the uniform age.[3]

---

[1] *Dig.*, xxiii. i. 11, 12.

[2] *Dig.*, xviii. 2, 19.

[3] *Inst.*, i. 22; Rossbach, 404.

3. *Conubium.*—*Conubium* has two meanings which must be clearly distinguished. It means (1) the right of intermarriage between Roman citizens and non-Romans, or, in the early period, between patricians and plebeians; and (2) the absence of any special impediment, such as relationship within certain degrees, between the two parties. Want of *conubium* in the first sense prevents the marriage from being a Roman marriage, but does not prevent its being a legal union; want of *conubium* in the second sense prevents the possibility of any legal union at all.

A Roman marriage in the strict sense of the term, *justum matrimonium*, can take place only between two Roman citizens, or between a male Roman citizen and a foreign woman belonging to a community to which *conubium* with Roman citizens has been granted. Other marriages may be lawful, but they are not Roman marriages. There could be no *conubium* except between free persons. With slaves *conubium* was impossible, and with anyone but a Roman citizen there is no *conubium* except by express grant. But by international treaties and otherwise such grants of *conubium* were made to the citizens of many foreign communities, and the right was gradually extended to the whole of Italy, and in the later law to all free subjects of the Empire. It is not necessary to give this history in detail. During the earlier period, if a Roman citizen married a foreign woman who had not *conubium*, the children were foreigners, and did not fall under the *potestas* of the father. If a Roman woman married a *peregrinus*, with whom she had *conubium*, the children by the old law were Roman citizens. But in order to preserve the purity of the Roman citizenship the *Lex Minicia*, a law probably passed in the second half of the sixth century of the city, provided that even in this case the children should follow the condition of the father, that is, should remain peregrins or foreigners.[1] And if a Roman woman married a foreigner, between whom

[1] Gaius, i. 78; Karlowa, i. 182.

and herself there was no *conubium*, the children were peregrins, and there was no *potestas*.[1]

From what has been said it will be seen that the term *conubium* is an ambiguous one. The marriage between a Roman citizen and a citizen of another community was a valid marriage, although there might be no *conubium* between the parties. Probably in the early law this was not so, but such marriages came to be recognised as valid by the *jus gentium*. It was a *matrimonium ex jure gentium*, to be distinguished on the one hand from concubinage, and on the other from a Roman marriage, *justae nuptiae*, the children of which would fall into the *potestas* of the husband.[2] And the doctrine had no application to barbarians. It applied to peregrins who belonged to communities with which friendly relations existed if there was no more definite bond.[3]

Conubium between Patricians and Plebeians.—In the early law there was no *conubium* between the patricians and the plebeians, and this was one of the main grievances under which the plebeians suffered. The Twelve Tables did not remove this barrier between the two orders, but on the contrary contained an express declaration enforcing it, *conubia ut ne plebi cum patribus essent*.[4] But almost as soon as the Twelve Tables had come into force an agitation arose among the plebeians for the abolition of a law which, it was felt, placed their order in a position of inferiority; and in the year 445 B.C., at the instance of the tribune C. Canuleius, a law was passed enacting that a marriage between a patrician and

---

[1] Rossbach, 465. At Athens also there might be a valid marriage without *conubium*, but it did not produce all the legal effects of a marriage between two Athenians. When the Athenians made a grant of ἐπιγαμία to a people this did not authorise mixed marriages, which were already valid, but it gave to such marriages all the legal consequences of marriage between Athenians.—Dareste, *Nouv. Études*, 62.

[2] Ulp., iii. 3 ; Rossbach, 464 ; Meyer, *Röm. Konkubinat*, 15.

[3] See Leonhard, *Inst.*, 186.

[4] Cic., *De Rep.*, 2, 36, 37 ; Dion., 10, 60 ; Liv., iv. 4, 5.

a plebeian should be a Roman marriage, and that the children should follow the rank of the father and be subject to his *potestas.* Livy gives a dramatic account of the debates upon the *Lex Canuleia*, and represents the horror with which some, at least, of the patricians regarded the introduction of *conubium* between the two orders.[1] The consuls declared in the Senate that to admit such unions would be to bring about such confusion that no one would know who he was or who were his relations. The marriage of a patrician and a plebeian, instead of bringing about that union in religion which was the mark of a true Roman marriage, could only be a promiscuous intercourse like that of wild animals.[2]

It is difficult, at first, to see why the intermarriage of a patrician with a plebeian should bring about such a confusion in family relations. Many authorities are now inclined to think that the explanation is that there was a radical difference between the two orders in the organisation of the family. Among the patricians the patriarchal family was the foundation of society—the keystone of the arch. Children followed the rank and were in the *potestas* of the father or of his *paterfamilias.* The only relationship known to the law was that on the father's side; but among many nations of antiquity we know that an entirely different system prevailed. Instead of the children bearing the name and following the rank of the father they took their mother's name, and followed her condition; and the kinship of which the law takes account is kinship in the female line. This was so, for example, among the Egyptians, among the Lycians, and others,[3] and there are good grounds for believing that kinship and succession were reckoned through the mother among the Illyrio-

[1] Liv., iv. 2, 3.

[2] *Quam enim aliam vim conubia promiscua habere, nisi ut ferarum prope ritu vulgentur concubitus plebis Patrumque? Ut, qui natus sit, ignoret, cujus sanguinis, quorum sacrorum sit; dimidius Patrum sit, dimidius plebis, ne secum quidem ipse concors.*—Livy, iv. 2.

[3] Herod., i. 173; Mitteis, *Reichsrecht und Volksrecht*, 57.

Thracian tribes and among the aboriginal peoples of Southern Europe.[1]

If the early Roman plebeians lived according to this system, it is easy to understand how the patricians should have regarded intermarriage with them with horror. It cannot be affirmed with certainty that among the plebeians kinship by females, or *Mutterrecht*, as the Germans call it, prevailed, but the probabilities seem to be in favour of that supposition. In another of the speeches which Livy invents, the orator describes the patricians as being those who were able to name their father, *qui patrem ciere possent*.[2] And in the worship of Ceres, a special protector of the plebeians, it was an ancient usage that no one was to name his father or his son.[3] The plebeians were of mixed race, and included, in all probability, many people who belonged to the aboriginal Ligurians. It is likely enough that among the plebeians kinship by females prevailed, if not universally, at least among some sections of the people.[4]

Absence of Legal Impediment.—When two persons are within certain degrees of relationship to each other marriage between them is impossible, and for this purpose there is no difference between kinship on the father's side and on the mother's side, although in succession there is in the early law a great

---

[1] Some writers believe that kinship through females preceded kinship through males among the primitive Germans and Slavs. See Tac., *Germ.*, c. 20; Brunner, *Deutsche Rechtsgeschichte*, i. 80; M'Lennan, *Primitive Marriage*, 53; Kovalewsky, *Modern Customs*, 19. But the supposed evidences for this are very slight, and it is doubtful if any of the Aryans passed through a period when mother-right was the general custom of the people. See Leist, *Alt-Arisches Jus Civile*, ii. 95 and 117; Westermarck, *Hist. of Human Marriage*, 104; Bernhöft in *Zeit. für vergleich. Rechtswissenschaft*, ix. 418; Kohler, *Shakespeare, &c.*, 223. See *supra*, p. 75.

[2] Liv., x. 8.

[3] Serv., iv. 58.

[4] Bernhöft, *Staat und Recht*, 138, 204; Binder, *Die Plebs*, 356, 409; Costa, E., *Storia delle Fonti*, 10; Ridgeway, *Who were the Romans?* 15. See on mother-right generally, Westermarck, *History of Human Marriage;* M'Lennan, *Primitive Marriage;* Howard, G. E., *History of Matrimonial Institutions*. See *supra*, p. 63.

distinction between these two sets of relations. Marriage is also impossible between certain persons who are not related to each other in blood but are connected through marriage. And a relationship created by adoption is also a bar to marriage so long as the adoption lasts. The forbidden degrees varied considerably at different times, and it is not necessary to give them here in detail. In the early period it seems that even second cousins were forbidden to marry each other;[1] but before the end of the Republic not only second cousins but even first cousins were allowed to marry each other.[2] Certain other impediments introduced at a later period, such as that between a man and the sister of his deceased wife, or between a tutor and his ward, do not need to be explained here.

Sponsalia.—Marriage was usually preceded by a formal betrothal, *sponsalia*, and in the early period the principal parties were the respective *patresfamilias* of the bride and bridegroom, unless the bridegroom happened to be *sui juris*. It was the *paterfamilias* or the tutors of the bride who promised to give the bride in marriage to the bridegroom, and this promise was made by the formal contract of *sponsio*. The father of the bridegroom put the question to the father of the bride if he would give her in marriage—*spondesne*—and the father answered *spondeo*. But as the *patria potestas* becomes weaker, the *sponsalia* required the consents of the bride and bridegroom as well as of their parents and guardians. The man usually gave the woman a pledge, *arra*, generally in the form of a betrothal ring.[3]

In the early period there was an action for breach of promise of marriage among the Latins and perhaps among the

---

[1] Tac., *Ann.*, xii. 6; Rossbach, 430; Girard, *Manuel*, 5th ed. 159; Roby, i. 128.

[2] The first case of which we hear seems to be in 171 B.C. (Liv., xlii. 34, 3).

[3] The betrothal ring as well as the bridal wreath and veil seem to have been borrowed from the Romans by the Germans, so that we have inherited them from the Romans. See Howard, *Matrimonial Institutions*, i. 278; Grimm, *Deutsche Rechtsalterthümer*, 4th ed. i. 245.

Romans, but after the time when the Latins all became Roman citizens it became a fixed rule that either party to the contract of *sponsalia* was free to break it at any time, and that no damages could be given for the breach, and even a special provision for the payment of a penalty in that event was held to be against public policy.[1]

Marriage with Manus and Marriage without Manus.—From a very early period, perhaps even from the date of the Twelve Tables, down to the time of Gaius, who wrote on this subject probably in the reign of Antoninus Pius, 138-161 A.D., we find two forms of marriage co-existing, widely different in their effect upon the position and property of the wife. In one case the wife is said to be in the hand, *manus,* of the husband, while in the other she remains independent of his "hand" or power.

If a rough analogy may be used, the wife *in manu* is, as regards her property, somewhat in the position of a French wife, married according to the system or *régime* of community, while the wife married without *manus* is somewhat in the position of the wife married under the system or *régime* of separation of property. I do not mean to imply that there is the slightest historical connection between the Roman and the French law upon this matter, or that important differences do not exist, but speaking broadly, when the wife was *in manu,* whatever fortune she had at the time of the marriage or acquired afterwards went to the husband or to his *paterfamilias,* if he had one, by a universal assignation, whereas if she was not *in manu* the wife's property remained her own. But it would be odd indeed if, in the early history of Rome, we found married women enjoying the complete management of their own property, and having the power to dispose of it as they chose during their lifetime or by will. This was far from being the case. The wife married without *manus*, if she was a *filiafamilias,* remained after her marriage in the *potestas*

[1] D., xxiii. 1, 4; Gell., iv. 4; Leist, *Alt-Arisches Jus Civile,* 157, 180.

of her *paterfamilias;* and if, when she was married, she had no *paterfamilias*, or if she ceased to have one during the marriage, she fell by law under the tutory of her agnates, that is, of her brothers or paternal uncles, or failing them, of her more distant heirs-presumptive. And these tutors were there, not to protect the wife herself, but to protect the property which should come to them at her death from being dissipated. This tutory of the agnates lasted all through the Republic, and was only abolished by a *Lex Claudia*, 41-54 A.D.[1]

The Effects of Manus.—When a woman was married in such a way as to pass into *manus*, the legal tie by which she had previously been bound to her *paterfamilias* and his family was broken, and she became, legally speaking, no longer related to her father or mother, sister or brother. She suffered a complete change of legal status of the kind which the Romans called *capitis deminutio.*[2] She ceased to be one of the heirs of her *paterfamilias*, and if he dies intestate she will not be entitled to share with her brothers and sisters; but when the *paterfamilias* had property the practice was for him to give his daughter a portion—*dos*—when she married. And as the wife passes entirely out of her original family, so likewise she passes entirely into the family of her husband. If his *paterfamilias* is living she becomes subject to his *potestas*, though probably the custom was for the *paterfamilias* not to interfere, except on rare occasions, with the marital authority of his son. Even when the son had a *paterfamilias* he was still said to have *manus* over his wife.[3] The wife's property, of whatever kind,

---

[1] See *infra*, p. 180. Married women who had borne a certain number of children were free from tutelage by the *Lex Julia et Papia Poppaea*, 9 A.D. On the tutory of women, see Gaius, i. 190; Gide, P., *Condition Privée de la Femme*, 103; Savigny, *Vermischte Schriften*, i. chap. 10. *Cf.* Manu, who says of women, "Her father protects (her) in childhood, her husband protects (her) in youth, and her sons protect (her) in old age; a woman is never fit for independence," ix. 3.

[2] Ulp., xi. 13.

[3] Gaius, iii. 3; Ulp., xxii. 14; Rossbach, *Römische Ehe*, 11.

passes to the husband if he is a *paterfamilias*, or if he is in *potestas* to his *paterfamilias*. Whatever she acquires thereafter she acquires for him. As regards her rights of property she is in the same position as one of her own children, and we are expressly told that she stands to her husband in the position of a daughter—*filiae loco*—and in accordance with this idea she is entitled to a daughter's share in her husband's property at his death.[1]

In this change of status the most prominent feature to the early Romans was that the wife passed from one religious communion to another. The most sacred duty of the *paterfamilias* was to offer the prayers and sacrifices at his own hearth on which depended the happiness not only of the living members of the household but of the ancestors. Every family is a separate communion with its own gods. The daughter has taken part from her infancy in the religion of her father's house. Every day she has poured libations and prayed for the protection of her father's gods. If she marries with *manus* this means abandoning the gods of her childhood for gods whom she does not know. She must be prepared to say to the husband, "Thy people shall be my people and thy gods my gods." It is this consideration which makes the early Romans regard marriage as an act of the greatest religious significance. To pass safely from one religious community to another the intervention of the gods themselves is necessary, and so the Greeks, whose marriage ceremonies in the early times bear a striking resemblance to those of the Romans, called marriage by the word τέλος, which signifies simply the sacred rite, as being the rite *par excellence*.[2]

---

[1] Servius, in *Georg.*, i. 31 ; Gaius, i. 111.

[2] F. de Coulanges, *Cité Antique*, 43. As to the religious character of the marriage ceremony among the Aryans in general, see Leist, *Alt-Arisches Jus Civile*, ii. 119 ; Westermarck, *Hist. of Human Marriage*, 425. The same feature still characterises country weddings among the Southern Slavs : "Before becoming a member of her husband's family the bride must sever all the ties which have hitherto bound her to the house spirits

Marriage without Manus.—Marriage without *manus* is just as much lawful marriage as marriage with *manus*, but its effects as regards the legal position and the property of the wife are widely different. When the wife is married without *manus* she does not pass out of her original family, but retains her position as one of the heirs of her *paterfamilias*. She remains in the *potestas* of her *paterfamilias*, and he can, if he choose, take her away from her husband and put an end to the marriage.[1] If she has no *paterfamilias* when she marries, or if her *paterfamilias* dies during the marriage, she is in the tutory of her agnates. If she has any property at the time of the marriage it does not pass to the husband unless her *paterfamilias* chooses to provide her with a *dos* or dowry. Whatever she acquires during the marriage belongs to the wife herself, and her husband has no control even over the administration of her separate property. She acquires no rights of succession to her husband, though at a later period in the history the prætor gave her a right to succeed to the husband's estate if he left no relations.[2]

Personal Authority of the Husband over the Wife.—Except for the fact that the *patria potestas* over the wife belonged to her original *paterfamilias* if she was married without *manus*, whereas if she were married with *manus* she became subject to the *patria potestas* of her husband's *paterfamilias* if he had one, the authority of the husband over the wife was the same under the two systems. The husband, in his mere quality as such, had wide powers over the person of the wife irrespective altogether of the question of *manus*. The husband as such had the right to chastise the wife, and for grave offences might even put her to death, but custom, as strong as law, forbade

under whose protection she has passed her youth, and must solemnly adopt the worship of those of the family into which she is about to enter" (Kovalewsky, *Modern Customs*, 33).

[1] Ulp., 6, 10; Rossbach, *Röm. Ehe*, 56; Gide, *Condition Privée de la Femme*, 115; Esmein, *Mélanges*, 19; *Cic. ad Heren*, ii. 24, 38.

[2] D., 38, 11.

his inflicting any severe punishment upon her without first calling together a family council.[1] In the very early period it is also possible that the husband had the right to sell the wife or to give her over as a *mancipium* or bond-servant, but these powers, if they ever existed, disappeared before the date of our documents.[2]

Co-Existence of the Two Forms of Marriage.—For many centuries marriage with *manus* and marriage without *manus* continued to exist side by side, and it was only by very slow degrees that marriage with *manus* became more and more uncommon, until at last it disappeared altogether. The higher classes of society, among whom family traditions were stronger, continued to give their daughters in marriage with *manus* after this had become unusual among the lower orders. The origin of marriage without *manus* will be discussed later, but probably it did not become common, at any rate among the upper classes, till after the Punic wars, when the old religion began to lose its power, and there are signs of a growing laxity of morals. By the end of the Republic marriage without *manus* has become the rule, and in the time of Tiberius it is evident that marriage with *manus* has become rare even in the highest classes.[3] The *senatus-consultum* of 23 A.D. in his reign provided that the wives of the Flamens of Jupiter should be *in manu* only for religious purposes. From the early Empire downwards *manus* is in decay, though it may have existed in this rather shadowy form among the priests until the abolition of the old Pagan religion.[4]

How Manus was Created.—There were three ways in which *manus* might be created, namely, *usus*, *confarreatio*, and *coemptio*. In the first of them the wife is not brought into *manus* by the

---

[1] Rossbach, 19-54; Gide, 116; see Tac., *Ann.*, 13, 32. The wife in question there cannot have been in *manus*, for *manus* had by that time fallen into desuetude.

[2] Karlowa, *R. R.*, ii. 153; Rossbach, 49-134; Cuq, *Inst. Jur.*, 2nd ed. 66, note 5.

[3] Tac., *Ann.*, 4, 6.

[4] Gaius, i. 112, 136; Rossbach, 57.

celebration of the marriage, but comes into *manus* at a subsequent date. In the other two ways, *confarreatio* and *coemptio,* the celebration of the marriage itself brings the woman into *manus.* I will defer what I have to say about *usus* until after explaining the two forms of celebration by which *manus* was created. *Confarreatio* was a religious ceremony performed in the presence of the high priests of the State religion, and accompanied by usages which are manifestly of great antiquity. The resemblance which it bears to one of the forms of marriage employed by the Hindus and to the marriage rites of the early Greeks is much too close to be accidental. It is evident that they are all derived from a primitive Aryan custom. *Confarreatio,* in the strict sense of the term, appears to have been at all times confined to the patricians. The three high officers of religion, called the *flamines maiores,* and probably also the high priest, called the *rex sacrorum,* were bound to be patricians and the children of marriages celebrated by *confarreatio,* and also to be married themselves according to this rite, while no such restrictions applied to the *flamines minores* who were plebeians.[1] It is generally believed that in the earlier period all the priests required to be born of confarreate marriages, and that this requirement was at a later time exacted only in the case of the four just mentioned, and it is certain that confarreation was not a form of marriage confined to the marriage of priests. It was open to all patricians, but was confined to their order.[2]

Ceremonies Peculiar to Confarreatio.—The peculiarity of *confarreatio* in contrast with *coemptio* is that it is a religious ceremony performed in the presence of two of the officials of the Roman religion, the *pontifex maximus* and the *Flamen* of Jupiter, in which certain formal words—*certa et solemnia verba*—are used. It is necessary also that ten witnesses should

[1] Gaius, i. 112.

[2] Rossbach, 97 ; Karlowa, *R. R.*, ii. 165 ; Binder, *Die Plebs*, 414 ; F. de Coulanges, *Cité Antique*, 369 ; Esmein, *Melanges*, 7 ; Mommsen, *Staatsverwalt*, iii. 221.

be present, and it has been surmised that these represent either the ten *curiae* or the ten *gentes* into which accordingly the *curia* was divided.[1] It is very possible that the ceremony took place in the public hall of the *curia* before the assembled people. Part of the ceremony of *confarreatio* consists in the employment of a cake made from a grain called spelt—*panis farreus*—which was probably thrown into the sacrificial fire, though it is possible that it was eaten by the bride and bridegroom, which we know was done in Athens with the bride-cake made of sesame.[2] Part of the ceremony consisted also in the bride and bridegroom sitting with their heads veiled upon two seats over which had been stretched the fleece of a sheep slain as a marriage sacrifice. The veiling of the head was a common feature of sacrifice, and the spreading of the fleece over the two seats was a symbol of the union into which the parties were entering. The other marriage customs, which will be explained presently, were not peculiar to confarreation.

The Ceremonies of Coemptio.—*Coemptio* is a symbolic sale of the wife to the husband, performed by the *libripens* before the five witnesses in the ordinary mode of mancipation, though a somewhat different form of words was employed. What the precise words were we do not know, and the suggestion that it may have been *Te ego ex jure Quiritium matrem-familias meam esse ajo, estoque mihi emta hoc aere aeneaque libra* is a mere guess.[3] The term *coemptio* was understood by late writers to imply a mutual sale in which the wife sold herself to the husband and the husband sold himself to the wife;[4] but the notion of a wife who was going to pass into the power of the husband purchasing him is in the highest degree improbable, and the idea of a mutual sale, unsupported as it is

[1] See *supra*, p. 58.

[2] Gaius, i. 112; Ulp., 9; Rossbach, 106.

[3] Huschke, *Studien*, 186; see Rossbach, 71.

[4] Serv., *Aen.*, iv. 103, and in *Georg.*, i. 31; Bruns., ii. 79 and 81; Lewis and Short, *s.v.*

by any analogy, may be dismissed.[1] The origin of *coemptio* as a marriage ceremony will be referred to later.

Usus.—The third form in which *manus* was created was by *usus*, that is by a sort of usucapion or prescription. Our information about it is scanty, because it had altogether passed out of use before the time of the classical jurists. Gaius says: "A woman passed into *manus* by use who, being married, lived with her husband a whole year, for she was acquired, so to speak, by prescription based on a year's possession, and passed over into the family of her husband and took the place of a daughter." Accordingly provision was made by the Twelve Tables that if any woman was unwilling in this way to fall into the *manus* of her husband she should every year absent herself for three nights, and in this way interrupt the prescription of that year.[2] By the old law the period of prescription, in the case of moveables, was one year, and Gaius evidently understands that just as the possessor of a moveable article becomes its owner by continuous possession for a year, so the husband, by possessing the wife for the same period, acquires *manus* over her. No particular form for the celebration of the marriage itself is required. The origin of *usus* in this connection will be spoken of presently.

Ceremonies usually Practised at all Marriages.—Whether the marriage was by *confarreatio* or *coemptio*, or whether it was a free marriage, as the marriage without *manus* is often called, there were certain matrimonial usages which were required by inveterate custom. These usages bear upon their face the mark of great antiquity, and are, for the most part at any rate, part of the common Aryan traditions. Among a conservative people like the Romans such ancient customs are preserved with jealous care long after their original significance has been lost. It is doubtful if any of these usages was,

[1] See Girard, *Manuel*, 5th ed. 155; Roby, i. 70; Goudy's note to Muirhead, 2nd ed. 415.

[2] Gaius, i. 111.

even in the early times, essential to the validity of the marriage, and in the later law it became an accepted principle that, apart from one or two special cases, no form of marriage at all was prescribed. All that was essential was that the necessary consents should have been given, and that there was no legal impediment to the union, but in the early period it may be taken for granted that at all marriages the traditional usages would be followed. On the day before the wedding the bride laid aside her childish dress—the *toga praetexta*—and dedicated it with her toys to the *lares* of her paternal home.

On the wedding-day she wore a white tunic woven vertically after an ancient manner, called the *tunica recta*. Her head was covered with a red veil—the *flammeum*—and from this veiling of the head—*nubere*—that term came to be used for the marriage of a woman. Her hair was parted into six locks by a comb in the form of a spear called a *hasta caelibaris*. She wore on her head a wreath of flowers gathered by herself. The company assembled in the morning at the house of the bride's father, and the ceremony began by taking the auspices. If they were unfavourable the wedding was postponed, if not altogether abandoned. A thunderstorm or an earthquake was likewise ground for breaking off the ceremony. If the auspices were favourable the next ceremony was the joining of the hands of the bride and bridegroom—*dextrarum junctio*. The *pronuba*, a matron friend of the bride, led her over to the bridegroom and placed her hand in his. Then followed the sacrifice of an animal, in the earliest times of a pig, but later generally of a sheep. A libation is poured by the bridegroom over the sacrificial fire, and prayers are offered to the gods. The bride and bridegroom solemnly walk round the altar from right to left. At the end of the ceremonies the guests raise a shout wishing prosperity—*feliciter*—and then join in a banquet—*cena*. In the evening the bride is borne in a solemn procession to her new home. This is called the *in domum deductio*. This is a symbol of the carrying off of the bride by force, and was so understood by the Roman writers themselves.[1] The bride fled to her mother's arms, and had to be torn away from her with a show of force. At the door is a crowd, partly of guests and partly of the uninvited populace, with lighted torches. A procession is formed, headed by a boy bearing a torch of white thorn. Then follows the bride, a boy holding her on either side. Flutes are played, and certain ancient verses called *fescennines* of a not very decent character are sung by the crowd.[2] Every now and then the crowd raises a shout—*talas io*—probably the name of the god of marriage.[3] When the procession reaches the house of the bridegroom the bride anoints the door-posts with oil and binds woollen fillets upon them. The bridegroom meets her at the door and asks her who she is, to which she replies, *Ubi tu Gaius ibi ego Gaia*, which means probably, "Where thou art there am I," though more fanciful interpretations have been suggested. The bridegroom then lifts the bride over the threshold, which she is not allowed to touch with her foot, and in the house presents her with fire and water, symbolical of their union in domestic life and in religion.[4]

Comparative Law.—Many of these marriage customs are part of the common stock of the Aryan peoples, and appear with comparatively slight variations among Hindus, Greeks, Germans, and Slavs. The *in domum deductio* in particular, with its symbols of marriage by capture, the joining of the hands of the bride and bridegroom, and the carrying of fire from the house of the bride to that of the bridegroom, are ceremonies which go back to a period before the great migrations.[5]

[1] Festus, 289; Bruns, *Fontes*, ii. 31; Catull., 62.

[2] *Joci veteres obscaenaque dicta canuntur;* Ovid., *Fast.*, 3, 535, 675, 695.

[3] Cf. *hymen io* in Greece.

[4] For the ceremonies see Rossbach, 275, 371; Marquardt and Mau, *Privatleben*, 28 *seq.*; Baumeister, *Denkmäler*, *s.v.* "Hochzeit"; *Companion to Latin Studies*, note 226.

[5] Leist, *Alt-Arisches Jus Civile*, ii. 108; Rossbach, 198 *seq.*; Daremberg et Saglio, *s.v.* "Matrimonium"; Grimm, *Deutsche Rechtsalterthümer*, 4th ed. i. 600.

Origin of Confarreatio, Coemptio, and Usus.—The origin of the three ways of creating *manus* and the reasons which led to the introduction of free marriage are still remarkably obscure. The theory which has the support of the greatest number of modern writers is that *confarreatio* was the ancient religious ceremonial confined to the patrician order, and that when the right of intermarriage between patricians and plebeians was created it was necessary to introduce a form of marriage ceremony which could be employed at a marriage between a patrician and a plebeian. *Confarreatio* was excluded upon religious grounds, and the form of an imaginary sale or mancipation was adopted, just as a similar ceremony was employed for adoption, for making a will, and for other purposes.[1] If this is the true explanation the marriage of a patrician and a plebeian did not at first create *manus*. Before the device of *coemptio* was thought of, when a plebeian and a patrician were married the marriage ceremonies above described were employed, but these did not create *manus*, the special form of *confarreatio* not being available. But the rule came to be accepted that cohabitation for a year without interruption created *manus*. But this was not always desired. The interruption of this *usus* by the wife absenting herself for the *trinoctium* was found very convenient in many cases. In the first place a *paterfamilias* might prefer to keep his daughter in his *potestas* until he was satisfied by experience that the son-in-law was to be trusted. So long as the *manus* had not been created the *paterfamilias* could claim back his daughter and practically dissolve the marriage, whereas if the wife was *in manu* her father had no such right.[2] Secondly, when the wife had no *paterfamilias*, but was in the tutory of her agnates, these tutors had a strong

---

[1] Karlowa, *R. R.*, ii., 164 ; Bernhöft, *Staat und Recht*, 188 ; Binder, *Die Plebs*, 412 ; Esmein, *Mélanges*, 5 ; Leonhard in Pauly-Wissowa, *s.v.* "Coemptio."

[2] Esmein, *Mélanges*, 19 ; Jhering, *Esprit*, ii. 187 ; Gide, *Condition Privée de la Femme*, 115.

interest to prevent her passing into *manus*, which would involve the carrying away of her fortune into another family. If she had children it might not be unfair that her estate should go to them, but if she had no children why should her share of her paternal succession pass away into an altogether different family? The agnates were her next heirs, and had every interest to prevent this result. The annual interruption of the *usus* will preserve the property in their control. Thirdly, the growth of a feeling in favour of the greater independence of women inclined them to avoid a form of marriage which put their property absolutely at the disposal of the husband.[1] After a time *coemptio* was devised as a means of creating *manus* instantaneously when this was desired, and gradually where there had not been any *coemptio* the necessity for annual interruption of the *usus* by the absence for the three nights came to be regarded as unnecessary, and the *manus* did not supervene if it was omitted. Another theory of the history of this matter, and one which I prefer, is that *coemptio* and *usus* were old forms of marriage among the plebeians, and that *coemptio* is a survival of the form of marriage by purchase which is found among all the Aryans. The main argument against this is that in the form of *coemptio*, as described by Gaius and other late writers, it is not represented as a sale by the *paterfamilias* of his daughter, but as a sale of herself by the wife with the authority of father or guardians.[2] But it does not seem safe to lay so much stress on expressions used by writers of a period when *coemptio* was altogether in decay. The change from sale by the father to self-betrothal in the form of self-sale is just what we should expect to find, and has a close parallel in the old German law.[3] When we find, as will be noticed later, bride-purchase among Hindus, Greeks, Germans, and Slavs, as well as among other

[1] See Karlowa, *R. R.*, ii. 168; Labbé in *Nouv. Rev. Hist.*, 1887, xi. 6.

[2] Gaius, i. 113, 195; Coll., 4, 2, 3; Girard, *Textes*, 503; Karlowa, *R. R.*, ii. 159; Binder, *Die Plebs*, 412.

[3] See Howard, *Matrimonial Institutions*, 258 and 277.

Aryan peoples, it is hardly possible to doubt that there was a time when it was practised among the Romans. It may be, of course, that it passed out of use at a very early time, and that *coemptio* was a subsequent invention by the lawyers, unconnected with the primitive custom of bride-purchase. Our information is too slight to enable us to arrive at certainty, but on the whole the probabilities seem to be in favour of the older theory that *coemptio*, though entirely symbolic during the period of which we have any knowledge, is a survival of an actual sale. It seems to be an instance, by no means singular, of a custom belonging to the lower classes of the people—for it may be assumed that *confarreatio* was invariably practised by the aristocratic and conservative patricians—gradually winning its way and gaining acceptance as a legal institution. That there should have been several forms of marriage existing at the same time is in no way surprising. Among the Hindus there were no less than eight forms, including a specially religious ceremony which was essential for members of the priestly caste.[1] It has been urged as an objection to the theory that *coemptio* was an ancient form of marriage among the plebeians that we cannot suppose them to have been married without any religious ceremony.[2] Religion, it is said, belongs not to a class but to the whole people. But the sufficient answer is that whether the knot was tied by *confarreatio* or *coemptio* the religious rites such as taking the auspices, offering the sacrifice, and so on, were duly performed.

If *coemptio* is to be considered as a form of marriage traditional among the plebeians and going back to primitive times, it is still more probable that this is the case with *usus*. The conventional explanation of *usus* is, in fact, singularly unsatisfactory. According to Gaius it was the Twelve Tables, which gave a wife

[1] Rossbach, 87 and 202; M'Lennan, *Primitive Marriage*, 8; Ridgeway, in *Companion to Latin Studies*, note 32; see Schrader, *Sprachvergleichung und Urgeschichte*, 551; Howard, *Matrimonial Institutions*, i. 199.

[2] Launspach, *State and Family in Early Rome*, 149.

the right of escaping *manus* by absenting herself every year for three nights,[1] but this was before the *Lex Canuleia* had given to the plebeians *conubium* with the patricians. Free marriages, therefore, in his view existed at least as early as the Twelve Tables, and perhaps earlier, if the provision in the Tables merely consecrated the traditional custom. But it certainly seems unlikely that at such an extremely early time the conservative patricians should have approved of any marriages except those in which the wife was *in manus*. If *usus* marriages existed at all it must have been among the plebeians. It is not surprising that the writers who are sceptical as to the early date of the Twelve Tables point to this provision as to *usus* as one which it is impossible to ascribe to such an early date as 450 B.C.[2] If *usus* was the first way of creating *manus* which was applied to the mixed marriages between patricians and plebeians, why should it be found before such unions were possible? Its invention would naturally be placed at some date after the *conubium* between the orders existed. To meet this difficulty it has been suggested that Gaius is wrong in ascribing the provision concerning the *trinoctium* to the Twelve Tables, and that we must assume that this rule was introduced by the lawyers at a later time.[3]

I venture to suggest the following as the most probable explanation of a very obscure matter. In the early period the patricians recognised no marriages except those which created *manus*, but among the plebeians free marriages were customary. Among the marriage customs of the plebeians was also that of trial-marriages. It might be agreed by the man and the woman that they should enter into a conjugal relation which should become binding after a year of cohabitation. Within that time either party should be free to break up the union. All marriages were not begun in this way, but trial-marriages were tolerated. To secure the privilege of *conubium* with the patricians the plebeians agreed to give up

[1] Gaius, i. 111. [2] Pais, i. pt. 574. [3] Binder, *Die Plebs*, 415.

their free marriages and to come under the universal rule of marriage with *manus*. After the *Lex Canuleia* the trial-marriage created *manus* if the cohabitation was continued for a year, just as *confarreatio* or *coemptio* did. But traditional ideas about marriage and its effects were too deeply rooted among the plebeians to make them satisfied with this state of things. Their women were used to retaining control of their own property, or at any rate to having it in the hands of their *patresfamilias* or tutors, over whom they had naturally much influence. It was unwelcome to them to see their property pass completely under the control of the husband or of his *paterfamilias*. Accordingly means were sought to evade the creation of *manus*, and the lawyers devised the *trinoctium* as a method of interrupting the prescription. Free marriage was thus brought back, and in course of time its advantages began to appeal even to patricians, and the necessity for the *trinoctium* gradually disappeared. This explanation involves the assignment of a *trinoctium* to a date later than the Twelve Tables, contrary to the statement of Gaius; but there does not seem to be any insuperable difficulty about this, as when Gaius wrote, the history of the whole matter had been forgotten.[1]

[1] Trial-marriages were found among many peoples, ancient and modern, and were common among the Egyptians (Mitteis, *Reichsrecht und Volksrecht*, 223). Under the name of handfasting they were prevalent in Scotland down to the eighteenth century (Howard, *Hist. of Matrimonial Institutions*, i. 49 and 235, and references; Brissaud, *Hist. du Droit Français*, i. 420; Brand, *Popular Antiquities*, 1870, ii. 46; Pennant's *Tour in Scotland in* 1772, i. 91; Scott, *Monastery*, xxv.). The old law of some of the French customs that the community of property between the consorts should not take effect until after they had lived together for a year and a day, or, as in some customs, until a child was born, is perhaps to be referred to the same order of ideas (Viollet, P., *Histoire du Droit Civil Français*, 2nd ed. 780); and by the law of Scotland until 1855, if a marriage was dissolved within a year and a day and without the birth of a living child neither consort had any right in the property of the other, and as regards the pecuniary rights of the consorts there was a *restitutio in integrum* (Stair, *Institutions*, i. 4, 18; Fraser, *Husband and Wife*, ii. 963). By the law of Jutland a concubine became a lawful wife by being a partner at bed and

The supposition that trial-marriages existed among the plebeians explains a fact otherwise puzzling. The creation of *manus* by *usus* is hardly credible except upon the assumption that there was a form of conjugal relation which was not complete marriage and yet was not mere concubinage. Continued cohabitation with a woman without any thought of marriage and without giving her the rank and position of a wife could not have created marriage; there must be the *affectio maritalis.* If it were otherwise we should expect to find some device by which the man, instead of the woman, could break the prescription. But the *trinoctium* is for the benefit of the woman, and one can hardly suppose that a concubine should need to be protected against the risk of becoming a wife.[1]

Social Position of the Roman Wife.—From what has been said concerning the legal rights of a married woman, and especially of the wife *in manu*, it might be supposed that her position was one of social inferiority. Subject to the almost despotic power of a *paterfamilias* or a husband, having no property of her own, described as being in the place of a daughter to her own husband, there is little to suggest that the Roman wife enjoyed a position of exceptional dignity and influence. And yet this is undoubtedly the case. Legal texts would frequently mislead us as to the character of social institutions if we had no other sources of information. Social position and influence depend much more upon custom and public opinion than upon statutes or rules of law. Even the slave, in law a mere chattel, was in practice, in many cases, the confidential friend of the family. The *paterfamilias* did not treat his children tyrannically as a rule, though his legal powers of doing so were great. So it was with the wife; although her legal guarantees were slight she enjoyed at Rome, and especially in the early period, a position of great influence. She was not, as

board for three years and carrying the keys of the house (Dareste, *Études*, 309). See Brissaud, *Manuel d'Histoire du Droit Français*, ii. 1650.

[1] See Meyer, P., *Röm. Konkubinat*, 15; Bernhöft, *Staat und Recht*, 187.

in Greece, relegated to the semi-oriental seclusion of the *gynaeceum* or women's apartments, but had the place of honour in the *atrium*, the centre of the life of the house, where she directed the work of the slaves and guided the education of the young children. Custom, it is true, did not approve of the Roman wife taking part with men in public meetings, and the most frequent eulogy of a wife in the mortuary inscriptions is that she stayed at home and span—*domum servavit, lanam fecit.*[1] As Mr. Bryce says, "Roman law begins with two phenomena which seem at first sight inconsistent. One is the complete subjection of the wife to the husband on the legal side as regards both person and property, the other is her complete equality on the social and moral side as regards her status and the respect paid to her."[2] Perhaps among no other Aryan people was the *materfamilias* held in such honour as among the Romans, and it is generally considered as one of the characteristics of the Aryans that among them the position of the wife was exceptionally high, and greatly superior to that which she held among other races, even at a time when some of these were in other respects much more civilised than the primitive Aryans.[3] The fundamental equality of the sexes has been said to be an old Aryan notion. The dignity of the Aryan wife rested mainly on the fact that she was a partner with her husband in the family religion and a priestess at the domestic altar.[4] The respect paid to the wife must, no doubt, be ascribed also largely to the fact that the Aryans were, on the whole, monogamous. The Roman law at no time gave any recognition to polygamy. Among the early Aryans, even after

[1] Gide, *Condition Privée de la Femme*, 98.

[2] *Studies in Hist. and Jurisprudence*, ii. 386.

[3] See Lecky, *European Morals*, i. 104; Jhering, *Vorgeschichte*, 45; Launspach, *State and Family in Early Rome*, 49 and 195.

[4] See Leist, *Alt-Arisches Jus Civile*, i. 75, 165, and 176; Rossbach, 200; Howard, *Matrimonial Inst.*, i. 26. Manu says, "Among all (twice-born men) the wife of equal caste alone, not a wife of a different caste by any means, shall personally attend her husband and assist him in his daily sacred rites" (ix. 86).

the migrations, there are traces of polygamy, mainly among the kings and chiefs. It probably existed among the ancestors of the Romans, but it had disappeared and left no traces behind it.[1] Probably, however, the position of the primitive Aryan wife has been a good deal idealised. When women were procured by capture and purchase and not by ceremonies, which merely symbolise these rude methods, it does not seem probable that the position of the wife can have been a very high one.[2] Pais says that in the first period of the Roman history the wife was little better than a slave.[3] But this stage, if it ever existed at Rome, cannot have been of very long duration.

Divorce.—It is probable that a marriage celebrated by *confarreatio* was in the early period absolutely indissoluble. At a later time, indeed, the priests invented a ceremony called *diffarreatio*, but this consisted in rites of a frightful nature, and was very rarely resorted to.[4]

When the *manus* had been created by *coemptio* or *usus* the husband could put away his wife, but he must act judicially, and was required by custom to call together the *judicium domesticum*, of which in this case the wife's relatives were members. The wife, however, had no right to divorce the husband. In this respect there is a great difference between marriage with *manus* and marriage without *manus*. In the free marriage the wife, if she is *sui juris*, or her *paterfamilias*, if she has one, can at any time put an end to the marriage, although a frivolous divorce may entail penalties.[5] It is no

---

[1] See for polygamy among the Persians, Herod., i. c. 115; among the Germans, Tac., *Germ.*, c. 18; Grimm, *Deutsche Rechtsalterthümer*, 4th ed. i. 608; among the Gauls, Cæsar, *De Bell. Gall.*, vi. c. 19; among the Hindus, Westermarck, *Hist. Human Marriage*, 442; Bernhöft, *Staat und Recht*, 175. Among some of the Aryans, *e.g.* the Hindus, polyandry is also met with, but this was probably borrowed from polyandrous peoples among whom the Aryans came. See Bernhöft, *Zeit. für vergleich. Recht.*, ix. 11.

[2] See Schrader, *Sprachvergleichung und Urgeschichte*, 559.

[3] *Storia di Roma*, i. 575.

[4] Plut., *Q. R.*, 50; Karlowa, *R. R.*, ii. 186.

[5] Ulp., 6, 10; Rossbach, 56; Karlowa, ii. 188.

doubt due to the greater permanence of marriage with *manus* that it was long regarded by the Romans as the normal and more honourable type of marriage. Cicero says the wife *in manu* was called *materfamilias*, while the wife not *in manu* was designated as merely *uxor*.[1] Divorce in the earlier period was rare, and frowned upon by public opinion. The domestic council, which custom required of the husband to call together when the marriage was accompanied by *manus*, would not approve of the husband putting away the wife except for some grave offence, and even when marriage without *manus* became common divorce seems for a long time to have been by no means frequent. But before the end of the Republic the decline of *manus*, the loss of belief in the old religion, and the growing laxity of morals led to an extraordinary freedom of divorce.

Forms of Marriage among other Aryans.—Among many of the Aryan peoples the carrying off of the bride with an assumption of force and a mock resistance is found as an early form of marriage, or as a custom observed at weddings, and at the dawn of history among almost all the Aryans the most usual marriage ceremony is a symbolic purchase of the wife. It cannot be doubted that these symbolise actual capture or actual purchase. Neither form is peculiar to the Aryans, but, on the contrary, both forms occur in all quarters of the world, and may be observed among savage races at the present time. It has been assumed too hastily that they mark successive stages through which all the Aryans, and perhaps all civilised peoples, have passed. It is not necessary to believe, nor indeed is it probable, that the capture of women was at an early stage of civilisation the only recognised way of procuring wives, and that in more peaceful times this mode was superseded by wife purchase. Actual capture as the more violent form no doubt belongs to a

[1] See on the use of the term *materfamilias* the interesting collection of examples by Labbé, in *Nouv. Rev. Hist.*, 1887, 13 ; *cf.* Esmein, *Mélanges*, 26.

rude age, and would disappear as life became more settled and orderly. But marriage by purchase is probably as old as marriage itself. Its evolution can be traced with great clearness among some of the Aryans, best of all perhaps among the Germans. Beginning with an actual sale by the father of his daughter, in which her consent is pretty much taken for granted, it gradually becomes a symbolic sale of herself by the bride for a sum of money which is not to be retained by her father, but is to be settled upon her as a dowry.[1]

[1] See Manu, iii. 33; Schrader, *Sprachvergleichung und Urgeschichte*, 2nd ed. 550; Leist, *Alt-Arisches Jus Civile*, ii. 106; Rossbach, 198; Dareste, *Études*, 72-108-142-348-388; Brunner, *Deutsche Rechtsgeschichte*, i. 72; Grimm, *Deutsche Rechtsalterthümer*, 4th ed. i. 585; Westermarck, *Hist. of Human Marriage*; Howard, *Hist. of Matrimonial Institutions*, ch. 4. For an interesting account of bride-purchase, as it still exists in High Albania, see Durham, M. E., *High Albania*, 126.

CHAPTER XX

THE EARLY LAW OF DEBTOR AND CREDITOR

ONE of the most striking features of the old law is the harshness with which it proceeds against a debtor who is unable to pay his debts. At Rome the rigorous enforcement of a cruel law of debt came very near to breaking up the State. According to the conventional account the sufferings of the plebeian debtors almost led to their leaving Rome and forming a new city by themselves. What was called the first secession to the Sacred Mount in 494 B.C. was a revolt on the part of the farmers against an economic situation which had become intolerable.[1] Capital was at that time very scarce in proportion to land, and was lodged in few hands. The farmer who needed oxen to plough his land, and other instruments of tillage, and was obliged to borrow money, had in early times to consent to exorbitant terms. There is much evidence of a similar state of affairs in the old law of other countries.[2] The early city was engaged in continual wars against its neighbours, and the yeomen-farmers, who formed the army, had to leave their little farms uncultivated, as they could not afford to pay others to do this for them. When they came back from the wars they found their fields run wild, and they were driven to raise loans in order to pay the taxes and to restore the land to

[1] The accounts of the three secessions are very confused, and it is even maintained by some writers that the events described as having occurred in 494 B.C. and called the first secession did not take place till much later. What Livy calls the first secession is merely the second secession ante-dated. See Pais, i. pt. i. 425 and 492. *Contra* Soltau, *Röm. Geschichtschreibung*, 166.

[2] See Maine, *Early History of Institutions*, 108; Bury, *History of Greece*, 181.

cultivation. They had no security to offer, and must submit to the terms of the patrician money-lenders and bind themselves by the ancient contract of *nexum*.

The social conditions, which made such loans a necessity for enormous numbers of the plebeians, likewise made it impossible in many cases for the loan to be repaid, and the creditor was then in the position of being entitled to put into execution the exorbitant powers which the old contract of *nexum* permitted to him. *Nexum*, which is probably the oldest contract known to the Roman law, was contracted with the same ceremonial as the mancipation, and, like that ancient form of conveyance, originated at a period before the use of coined money. In its original form the bars of metal which did the duty of money were weighed out by the official *libripens* in the presence of five witnesses, and were at the same time handed by the lender to the borrower. After the introduction of coined money the lender merely touched the scales with a coin and the weighing becomes symbolic, and after the famous declaration of the Twelve Tables, *cum nexum faciet, uti lingua nuncupassit ita jus esto*, if the sacramental words are pronounced, there does not need to be any actual weighing, but there was probably a rapid gesture with the scales.[1]

What is important now is the *nuncupatio*, or formal declaration which the lender makes in passing over the amount of the loan. The exact terms of this declaration in the *nexum* have not been preserved, but from the words used in the discharge of the obligation, and from other facts which we have, we are able to infer with some certainty what the declaration must have contained. It must have included words of which the effect was that the debtor, if he failed to pay the debt, was to be in the same position as if a judgment had been obtained against him. In the form of liberation the debtor speaks of

[1] Girard, *Manuel*, 5th ed. 287 ; Senn, in *Nouv. Rev. Hist.*, xxii. 59, note 2.

having been "condemned" when he became bound, and it is probable that the declaration made by the creditor in the *nexum* was called the *damnatio*. Several attempts have been made to reconstruct it; it was, probably in some such terms as the following, which are given by a recent writer:—"Whereas I hereby weigh out to thee so many thousand sesterces (or, originally, so many pounds of copper) be thou therefore bound, and indebted to me in that amount with the interest, by this ceremony of the copper and the brazen scales." *Quod ego tibi tot milia* (originally *tot libras aeris*) *adpendo, tu mihi eo nomine* (*et ob foenus unciarium*) *nexus obaeratusque esto hoc aere aeneaque libra.*[1]

Effect of Failure to Pay the Debt.—After a delay of thirty days from the date on which the debt should have been paid the creditor has the right to seize the debtor by force and carry him off to his private prison without any formality whatever. He can keep him there in prison till he works off the debt, or if he choose to do so he can kill the debtor, or sell him as a slave beyond the Tiber. This forcible seizure or *manus injectio* can be stayed only by the debtor paying the debt, or producing a satisfactory *vindex* who undertakes to be responsible for the payment.

The law with regard to debtors upon the contract of *nexum* as well as those against whom a judgment had been obtained is dealt with in Table III. of the Twelve Tables. This is one of the most complete of the fragments of the Tables which we possess, but its interpretation has been much disputed. It runs somewhat as follows:—"For the payment of a debt of money admitted to be due, or of an award made by judgment, let the debtor have a legal delay of thirty days. In default of payment after the thirty days he may be arrested and brought before the magistrates—*manus injectio*. Unless he shall then pay the debt, or unless someone offers himself in

[1] Kretshmar, in *Zeit. Sav. Stift.*, xxix. 261. *Cf.* the reconstruction of Huschke, *quod ego nexi sum damnas. Nexum*, 231.

Court to guarantee payment—*vindex*—the creditor may take the debtor away with him, and bind him with thongs or with fetters, but the fetters shall not weigh more than fifteen pounds, and may be less if the creditor chooses. The debtor may, if he choose, live at his own charges, but, if not, the creditor who keeps him in prison shall give him a pound of coarse meal a day, or more if the creditor chooses." The debtor who had become bound by a *nexum* is in the position of one who has admitted his liability to pay a sum of money and to whom the maxim would apply *confessus pro judicato habetur.*[1]

The Twelve Tables made it necessary for the creditor to take the debtor before the magistrate in order to get a formal authority to lead him away to prison, but this change in the old law did not imply the necessity of a trial of the cause. The production of the debtor in court is merely a formality, and the magistrate has no discretion to refuse to the creditor the right of imprisoning his debtor. The debtor has agreed by the original contract to be in the position of an *addictus* or judgment debtor if he cannot pay the debt or find a *vindex*, and there is no necessity therefore for any judgment or *addictio.*[2] The *vindex* is not the same thing as a surety. He is a person who challenges the validity of the arrest and cries "hands off" to the creditor. Festus, the old grammarian, explains the term thus: *vindex ab eo, quod vindicat, quo minus is, qui prensus est ab aliquo, teneatur.*[3] If the intervention of the *vindex* is found to be unfounded, it is pretty certain that he had not only

---

[1] See for the effects of *confessio in jure*, Collinet, P., in *Nouv. Rev. Hist.*, 1905, xxix. 171; Girard, *Manuel*, 5th ed. 978, note 1. See, however, Kretshmar, in *Zeit. Sav. Stift.*, xxix. 236.

[2] See Livy, 2, 27; Bethmann-Hollweg, *Civil Prozess*, i. 160; Senn, F., in *Nouv. Rev. Hist.*, 1905, xxix. 82; Girard, *Manuel*, 5th ed. 985, note 4; Jobbé-Duval, *Histoire de la Procédure Civ. chèz les Romains*, Paris, 1896, 9; Lécrivain, in Daremberg et Saglio, *s.v.* "Manus Injectio."

[3] Bruns, *Fontes*, pt. ii. 48.

13

to pay the debt but also to pay an additional amount by way of penalty—the *poena dupli.*[1]

By a statute of uncertain date, perhaps not earlier than the third century B.C.—the *Lex Vallia*—the debtor is for the first time given the right himself to challenge the *manus injectio* or arrest, without the necessity of having to furnish a *vindex*—*manum sibi depellere.*[2] For the subsequent procedure we have not the words of the Tables but have to rely upon the account of them which is vouched for by Aulus Gellius.[3] In default of settlement of the claim the debtor may be kept in bonds for sixty days. During that period he is to be brought before the magistrate in the *comitium* on three successive market days held at intervals of nine days—*nundinae*—and the amount of the sum for which he is held is publicly proclaimed. After the third market day, if no one comes forward to pay the debt, the debtor may be put to death, or may be sold abroad beyond the Tiber, or may be kept indefinitely in the creditor's prison.[4]

The Right of Sectio.—The case of the debtor who has several creditors is dealt with in a fragment still extant, of which the interpretation has been much disputed. The words which we have are *Tertiis nundinis partis secanto. Si plus minusve secuerunt, se fraude esto.* Literally translated this would mean: "After the third market day the creditors may cut him in pieces and anyone who cuts more or less than his share shall be guiltless."

Are we to believe that the creditors had the right to take their dividend in this way out of the body of their debtor, so

---

[1] See Gaius, 4, 9, and 4, 171. Bethmann-Hollweg, *Civil Prozess*, i. 156 and 157 ; Gaukler, E., in *Nouv. Rev. Hist.*, 1889, xiii. 615 ; Girard, *Manuel*, 5th ed. 986, note 4, and 1021, note 4 ; Krüger, H., *Capitis Deminutio*, 195.

[2] Gaius, 4, 25 ; Gaukler, E., *l.c.* ; Cuq, 2nd ed. i. 248 ; Girard, *Manuel*, 5th ed. 986.

[3] Gell., 20, 1, 46.

[4] See a curiously close analogy in the old German law in the case of an offender who cannot pay the *wergeld* or ransom (Lex Sal., 58 ; Brunner, *Deutsche Rechtsgeschichte*, ii. 477).

that one creditor was entitled to his pound of flesh and another to his two pounds, if the second creditor's claim was twice as large as the first? Such a bankruptcy proceeding is certainly picturesque, but is it credible that it was ever put into force? Gellius, who has preserved the passage for us, says: "For my part I never read or heard of anyone being dissected in this way in ancient times," but Gellius wrote about 169 A.D. and his testimony as to what happened in 450 B.C. has to be received with caution.[1] Other classical writers, like Quintilian and Tertullian, speak as if the division of the debtor's body among his creditors had at one time been lawful, but had come to be so reprobated by public opinion as to have fallen into disuse.[2] Many writers try to explain the passage as referring to a cutting up or *sectio* of the debtor's property and not of his person, though the law does not explain how the division is to be made.[3] Some of those who support this view do not admit that when there was only one creditor he had a right to put the debtor to death if he failed to satisfy the debt within sixty days. They understand the expression *capite poenas dabat* to mean, not that the debtor must suffer death, but that he is to make amends with his person instead of with his property. The creditor is to have the right of detaining the debtor as a free bondman, and of making him work for him as if he were a slave. But the great objection to this view is that the passage was understood by the old writers such as Gellius to refer to a literal division of the debtor's body, and, as Professor Goudy points out in his notes to Muirhead, "Africanus, whose words are given by Gellius, is quite distinct, and he must have known the construction put upon the law by the jurists of the Republic, as, for instance, by Sextus Aelius

---

[1] Gell., 20, 1, 52.

[2] Bruns, *Fontes*, 21, note 6.

[3] See, *e.g.*, Lenel, in *Zeit. Sav. Stift.*, xxvi. 507; Muirhead, 2nd ed. 196; Kleineidam, F., *Die Personalexecution der Zwölftafeln*, Breslau, 1904; Erman, H., in *Zeit. Sav. Stift.*, xxvi. 560.

in his *Tripertitum.* There is nothing more astonishing in a creditor being allowed to kill his debtor than in a father being allowed to kill his son."[1]

I am inclined to agree with those who think that we have here in the Twelve Tables a vestige of the law which belonged to a far more primitive age than that at which the Tables were composed. The decemvirs preserved it in the Tables, though in their day no creditor would have ventured to exact his literal rights to his pound of flesh. The right of a creditor to kill or mutilate his debtor is found among other peoples at a primitive stage.[2] The knowledge on the part of the debtor that if the worst came to the worst his creditor might insist on obtaining satisfaction in this way would stimulate the debtor and his friends to raise all the money they could to prevent this form of execution. Probably, as Jhering suggests, what actually happened in practice was that as the creditors did not wish to destroy their only asset, and as public opinion would not in any case have permitted them to do so, the debtor was sold to that one of the creditors who offered to pay the highest price for him. This creditor, having now become the sole owner of the debtor, could sell him abroad as a slave, though the law did not allow the creditor to keep his debtor as his slave in Rome.[3]

A curious parallel has been found in the old Scandinavian law. By the law of Gulating, chapter lxxi., if a debtor could not pay his debts he was bound to go to the *ting* or assembly, and there offer himself in sale to his relations for the amount of his debts, beginning with his nearest relative. If none of his relatives consents to buy him at this price then he belongs

[1] Muirhead, 200, note.

[2] See Savigny, *Vermischte Schriften*, ii. 420; Mommsen, *Roman Hist.* (Eng. trans.), i. 164; Cuq, *Institutions Juridiques*, Paris, 1904, 2nd ed. i. 116; Kohler, *Shakespeare vor dem Forum der Jurisprudenz*, 1883, 7; *Das Recht als Culturerscheinung*, 1885, 17; Dareste, *Études*, 334; Puchta, *Inst.*, 10th ed. s. 179, note (*n*); Kretshmar in *Zeit. Sav. Stift.*, xxix. 262.

[3] *Scherz und Ernst in der Jurisprudenz*, 6th ed. 232.

to his creditor until he has paid his debt. The conditions upon which he passes into this state of servitude are stated before witnesses. The debtor in this way becomes the temporary slave of his creditor or of the relative who has paid for him, but as regards third parties he is a free man—he is *in mancipio.* The provision which so closely resembles that of the Twelve Tables is that if the debtor is not willing to work for his master the latter has the right of taking him before the assembly and giving the debtor's relatives the opportunity of liberating him by payment of the debt. If they will not do so the creditor has the right to kill or to mutilate the debtor. The common idea in both these early laws is that the threat of killing or mutilating the debtor is employed to put pressure upon his friends to pay the debt. But the old Norwegian law is less harsh than the Twelve Tables, because, under its provisions, it is only a recalcitrant debtor who is not willing to work who can be treated in this way.[1]

The miserable condition of these *nexi*, as the prisoners for debt were called, to distinguish them from the *addicti*, against whom a judgment had been pronounced, is graphically described in many passages by Livy and Dionysius.[2] Kept in loathsome dungeons, loaded with fetters, and half starved, many of them dragged out a hopeless existence. In a famous passage Livy narrates how an old soldier escaped from his prison into the forum, dressed in filthy rags, worn to a skeleton, and with shaggy beard and hair, so that he looked like a wild man. He described how his house had been burned by the enemy and his cattle driven off, how he had had to borrow money to pay taxes, and how his debts had grown, swollen by usury, until in the end he had been compelled to surrender himself to his creditor, who had carried him off to a dungeon and tortured him with scourges.[3] Many of the bystanders recognised in

[1] Dareste, *Études d'Histoire du Droit*, 333.

[2] Livy, 2, 23 ; 2, 34 ; 7, 19, 5 ; 7, 21, 8 ; Dionysius, 4, 11 ; 6, 26 ; 6, 79.

[3] Livy, 2, 23.

him an old comrade, and cried out with rage that the men who had fought for the freedom and sovereignty of Rome were at home the prisoners and captives of their fellow-citizens, and that it was safer for a plebeian to face the enemy in war than his own countrymen in time of peace. According to the view of many writers, the security at Rome, as at Athens, included the children of the debtor as well as himself, so that they likewise might be reduced to slavery.[1] But in other passages of the historians we hear of sons who became *nexi* in order to pay their fathers' debts, which could not have happened if they had been in that position under the contract made by the father himself.[2] On the whole it cannot be considered as established that, by the Roman law, the children of the debtor were included in the *nexum*.[3]

The Lex Poetelia Papiria.—Some alleviation of the condition of the *nexi* was introduced by the *Lex Poetelia*, which is probably to be assigned to the year 428 B.C. Livy's account of this law has led many to suppose that it abolished imprisonment for debt, and instead gave to the creditor the right to seize the goods of the debtor. *Pecuniae creditae bona debitoris non corpus obnoxium esset.*[4] But it certainly cannot be the case that it abolished imprisonment for debt, because there is abundant evidence that this continued to be practised even down to the time of Justinian, although by the Julian law of the time of Augustus a debtor who gave up his whole estate to his creditors,—*cessio bonorum*,—could not be kept in prison. The *Lex Poetelia* seems to have liberated

---

1 Huschke, *Nexum*, 71; Kohler, *Shakespeare von dem Forum der Jurisprudenz*, 9; Livy, 2, 24; Dion., vi. 26, 29, 37. *Cf.* in Athens, Plutarch, *Solon*, 13; and among the Frisians, Tacit., *Annal.*, iv. 72.

2 Livy, 8, 28, 2; Val. Max., 6, 1, 9.

3 Mitteis, in *Zeit. Sav. Stift.*, xxii. 109; Kretshmar, in *Zeit. Sav. Stift.*, xxix. 240; Krüger, *Capitis Deminutio*, 298.

4 Livy, 8, 28. As to the date of the *Lex Poetelia*, see Girard, *Manuel*, 4th ed. 482, note 2. Huvelin thinks it must have been later than 428 B.C. (Daremberg et Saglio, *s.v.* "Nexum," 83).

the existing *nexi*, to have prohibited the use of fetters in the case of prisoners for debt, and very likely it abolished the right of putting the debtor to death or selling him across the Tiber. It did away also with the right of summary execution by the creditor, and made it necessary for him to obtain a judgment against his debtor before he could make him prisoner. This led to *nexum* going out of common use because it presented no practical advantages, as the same end could be obtained by getting the debtor to bind himself in a simpler way—*e.g.* by a stipulation.[1]

Was Nexum a Sale by the Debtor of Himself?—The theory has lately been advanced that *nexum* was not a contract of loan of the character above described by which the debtor pledged his body in security of the debt if he was not able to pay his creditor, but was, on the other hand, an actual sale by the debtor of his body to the creditor, which was to take effect if a debt already existing was not duly paid. This theory, propounded by Mitteis in 1901, has led to a long controversy.[2] The supporters of this view argue that no obligation creating a personal right existed at the time of the Twelve Tables.[3]

According to this theory *nexum* is a general word for every transaction performed by the ceremony of the copper and the scales, and when the Twelve Tables speak of *nexum mancipiumque* this expression merely means mancipation. *Nexum* is merely another word for mancipation when the mancipation is of the debtor himself, and that it was the debtor himself and

---

1 As to the survival of imprisonment for debt, see *Dig.*, 43, 1, 34; *Code*, 7, 71, 1; Mitteis, *Reichsrecht und Volksrecht*, 444; and as to the *Lex Poetelia*, Girard, *Org. Jud.*, 191; Muirhead, 153; Bethmann-Hollweg, *Civil Prozess*, ii. 661; Pais, *Storia di Roma*, i. pt. ii. 281; Binder, *Die Plebs*, 178. *Nexum* existed nominally at any rate in the time of Gaius (3, 173).

2 Mitteis, *Über das Nexum*, in *Zeit. Sav. Stift.*, 1901, xxii. 96. See art. by F. de Zuleta in *Law Quart. Rev.*, xxix. 137.

3 See on this point Krüger, *Capitis Deminutio*, 296, and the review of that work by Kipp, in *Zeit. Sav. Stift.*, ix. 173.

not a sum of money which formed the object of the conveyance is confirmed by the common expression that the debtor gave himself bound, *se nexum dare*.[1] But the expression *se nexum dare* will not bear this weight. It is quite natural to speak of the debtor as bound, without implying thereby that he has sold his body. Further, a definition by the grammarian Festus indicates clearly that he regarded the money lent and not the debtor as the object of an obligation created by *nexum*. *Nexum aes apud antiquos dicebatur pecunia, quae per nexum obligatur*.[2] Moreover, the evidence that the contract of *nexum* contained a clause of *damnatio* is very strong. Gaius expressly tells us that when the debt was paid the debtor had to be liberated by employing the ceremony *per aes et libram*, and by the debtor saying: "Whereas I have been condemned to you in so many thousand sesterces, in respect thereof I now release and free myself from you with this copper and these copper scales."[3] And the form of this *nexi liberatio* is much against the theory that *nexum* was a sale of the debtor by himself. There are many grounds for supposing that the *damnatio* in the contract of *nexum* had the same effect as a judgment in authorising the creditor to proceed to the *manus injectio*. Although the texts are some of them difficult to reconcile one with another, there does not appear to be sufficient reason for adopting the new theory. There is no evidence in the Roman law of the possibility of the sale of the free man by himself, and there are many arguments, too long to be stated here, in favour of the view that *nexum* was not such a sale.

In some of the old Teutonic laws the sale of a debtor by himself into the slavery of the creditor is recognised. Later the law refuses to admit the possibility of more than a pledge of freedom instead of an out-and-out sale, and, finally, all such

[1] Livy, 8, 28, 2.
[2] Bruns, *Fontes*, pt. ii. 17.
[3] Gaius, 3, 174.

clauses are made ineffectual.[1] But the evidence for any such self-sale in the Roman law is entirely wanting.[2]

Did Nexum involve a Change of the Debtor s Status?—Those who maintain that *nexum* was a sale of the debtor by himself are obliged to assume that he became in law the slave, or at any rate the legal bondsman—the *mancipium*—of the creditor.[3] But we nowhere find these debtors given in the enumeration of persons *in mancipio*.[4]

From the passages in Livy it is clear that these debtors were not slaves, or otherwise they could not have served in the army. Nor does it seem that they had undergone the minor change of status, generally called *capitis deminutio minima*, which would have given the creditor a *potestas* over them, such as that which he had over persons who were *in mancipio*, for such persons cannot enter into a contract with their masters, and we know from the form of *nexi liberatio* preserved by Gaius that in it the debtor is represented as contracting in his own name with the creditor. There are, therefore, strong grounds for believing that the debtor who had become bound by the contract of *nexum* remained *de jure* a free man who had suffered no loss of legal status, although he was *de facto* detained in captivity according to the terms of the bond.[5]

Slavery for Debt among other Aryan Peoples.—In early times it appeared natural enough that a debtor who could not pay his debts should become the slave of his creditor,

---

1 Brunner, *Deutsche Rechtsgeschichte*, ii. 442, 477; Kohler, *Shakespeare, &c.*, 65 *seq.* See for examples the documents given by him at pp. 271 and 277.

2 See Senn, F., in *Nouv. Rev. Hist.*, 1905, xxix. 49; Jhering, *Esprit du Droit Rom.*, ii. 216; Kohler, *Shakespeare vor dem Forum der Jurisprudenz*, 58; Kipp, in *Zeit. Sav. Stift.*, ix. 178; Girard, *Manuel*, 5th ed. 482, note 2; Kretshmar, in *Zeit. Sav. Stift.*, xxix. 331, and the literature there referred to.

3 Mitteis, *Zeit. Sav. Stift.*, xxii. 125.

4 See Gaius, i. 138, and i. 123; Cuq. 2nd ed. i. 55.

5 Livy, ii. 23, ii. 24; Kretshmar, in *Zeit. Sav. Stift.*, xxix. 257.

and we find evidence of such a practice among many of the Aryan peoples. By the Hindu law the creditor could reduce the debtor to bondage till he worked out the debt.[1] At Athens, before the time of Solon, the debtor used to borrow on the security of his body, *ἐπί σώματι*, as the Greeks called it, and if he could not pay his debt in money he had to pay it with his person. Indeed the description given of the sufferings of the peasant farmers in Attica in consequence of the law of debt bears so close an analogy to the account of the Roman historians as to make it very probable that some of the picturesque features in the Roman history were taken from Greek sources. But there is no reason to doubt the substantial accuracy of both. Plutarch says that in Attica the *thetes* or peasant farmers were so weighed down with debt that they had been obliged to engage their persons to their creditors, and on failure of payment many of them had been made slaves in Attica itself, while others had been sold by their creditors to foreigners. At Athens, as at Rome, the law of debt almost led to civil war. But the famous law of Solon, called the *seisachtheia* or "shaking off of burdens," improved this state of matters in that city as early as about 592 B.C., nearly a century and a half before the date of the Twelve Tables. Solon's law, which was perhaps inspired by Egyptian influence, not only cancelled past contracts of this kind but deprived the creditor in future of all power to enslave his debtor, and left him entitled only to obtain a judgment for the seizure of his property.[2]

[1] Manu, viii. 49; Leist, *Alt-Arisches Jus Civile*, ii. 304; Dareste, *Études d'Histoire*, 83. The creditor could also enforce payment by "sitting dharna"—*i.e.* by sitting down at the debtor's door and taking no food till the debt is paid. If he starves to death this brings a curse on the debtor. This is an old Aryan custom, found also in Persia and in the old Irish law (Maine, *Early Inst.*, 39, 297). See the illustrations from various laws collected in Bernhöft, *Staat und Recht*, 241.

[2] Plutarch, *Solon*, c. 13; Grote's *History of Greece*, iii. 95; Bury, *History of Greece*, 182; Meyer, *Gesch. des Alt.*, ii. 406; Kohler, *Shakespeare vor dem Forum der Jurisprudenz*, 13. Solon's law did not abolish imprison-

We find slavery of debtors also in the old Scandinavian law and among the Ossetes of the Caucasus.[1] But the fullest information which we have of a condition of the law of debt analogous to the Roman *nexum* is in the old German law. By some of the German customs there was a regular form by which the debtor sold himself to the creditor in security for the debt. The debtor laid his hand and head in the hand of the creditor, let the creditor seize him by the hair and set the arm of the creditor on his neck. In one of the forms the debtor says that the creditor is to have the power of dealing with him as he chooses—*Quicquid de memetipso facere volueritis . . . habeatis potestatem faciendi*, a clause which suggests the *damnatio* in the *nexum*. The effect was to make the debtor the slave of the creditor, who could sell him to a third party, and was not obliged to release him from his servitude even if the debt was subsequently paid. At a later date, under the influence of the Church, this absolute sale was forbidden, and the debtor was allowed only to pledge himself instead of to sell himself, so that he was bound merely to render services until he had worked out the payment of the debt.[2] In France also the imprisonment of a debtor in the private prison of his creditor was common until the second half of the thirteenth century. In 1256 St. Louis, by an ordinance similar to the Julian law at Rome, allowed debtors who made a cession of their goods to be free from liability to imprisonment.[3] But this did not apply to Crown debtors. Among almost all the European

ment for debt, though he forbade the enslavement of the debtor, which, however, continued to exist in other Greek states. For evidences of its survival in other Greek states, see Pais, *Storia di Roma*, ii. pt. ii. 285, note 2; as to Egypt, see *infra*, 204. Solon's archonship was either 594-3 or 592-1 B.C.

[1] Dareste, *Études*, 333 and 141.

[2] Brunner, *Deutsche Rechtsgeschichte*, ii. 442.

[3] Viollet, *Établissements de St. Louis*, i. 927: and *Histoire du Droit Civil Français*, 2nd ed. 593.

nations at an early period the enslavement of a debtor was recognised, though in time it came to be a mere imprisonment, first in the private prison of the creditor, and, at a later period, in the public prison. It is by no means confined to the Aryan peoples. The servitude of debtors was admitted by the Jewish law.[1] It still exists among the Malays and among many African tribes, and was found among the Aztecs in the New World.[2]

It was noted as a peculiarity of the ancient Egyptians that they did not allow the enslavement of debtors, and it has been suggested with some plausibility that the legislation of Solon was inspired by Egyptian influence.[3] The Egyptians had instead the curious practice of pledging the bodies of their parents, which deprived them of honourable burial and rendered the heir infamous who neglected to redeem them.[4]

---

[1] 2 Kings, iv. 1; Joshua, l. 1; Nehemiah, v. 8; Matthew, xxv. 30.

[2] Kohler, *Shakespeare, &c.*, 17.

[3] Diodor., i. 79; Kohler, *Shakespeare, &c.*, 19.

[4] Kohler, *l.c.* With this it is interesting to compare the ancient usage of the creditor seizing the dead body of his debtor in order to force the heirs to pay the debt at once or to find security for its payment. This practice is found in the late Roman law and is prohibited by Julian (*Cod.*, 9, 19, 6), and we find creditors employing this form of pressure in the old German law and in Belgium as late as 1600. See Kohler, *Shakespeare, &c.*, 20; Voet., *Comm. ad Pand.*, 47, 12, note 4; Esmein, *Mélanges*, 245.

CHAPTER XXI

Crimes, Wrongs, and Punishments in the Early Law

Criminal law in the sense of an ordered body of rules administered by regular courts of justice does not exist in the early period, and many acts now considered as crimes are not yet regarded in that light. They are still merely delicts which cause injury to the individual, but which the State has no duty to punish, though the injured person may invoke its aid in obtaining satisfaction. These delicts will be spoken of later. Primitive society recognises, it is true, two kinds of offences which require to be stamped out by collective action—

1. The State must protect itself against offences which endanger its own existence or are directed against the constituted authorities. Acts, such as stirring up a foreign enemy to attack, or delivering a fellow-citizen to the enemy, must be severely dealt with if the existence of the State is to be maintained, and in the Roman law, at a very early period, the slaying of a citizen, unless justified upon some special ground, such as self-defence, is treated as a public matter and punished as an offence against the community. The word *perduellio* is used to cover all acts of a treasonable character, while *parricidium* is the technical term for the unlawful slaying of a free man.[1] These are the great crimes of the early law in the sense of acts which

[1] The etymology is doubtful, but it is unlikely that the word is a contraction of *patricidium*. Mommsen suggests that the first part of the word is "per," a pejorative prefix meaning "evil," as in *perduellio*, *perjurus*. (*Strafrecht*, 922. See Strachan-Davidson, *Problems of Roman Criminal Law*, 1, 22.)

are punished by the community itself in its own interest. They are too important to be atoned for by any pecuniary compensation, or, in fact, by any penalty short of death. The man convicted of *perduellio* is hung upon the *arbor infelix* and put to death by being beaten with rods.[1] The parricide was beaten with rods and then put into a leather sack (*culleus*) together with snakes and cast into the river. In later times the term parricide was restricted to the murder of a near kinsman, and the old form of punishment was retained in these cases.[2]

2. In addition to such wrongs as those just mentioned, which seem to strike at the existence of the body politic, the early law takes account of acts which are an outrage to the gods, and unless expiated would bring down the wrath of Heaven upon the community. Here it is not the law of the city but the divine law which has been violated, and it is for the pontiffs, as guardians and ministers of the State religion, to exact the penalty. Here, too, there is a class of deadly sins which can only be atoned for by the death of the offender. He is sacrificed to the god against whom he has sinned, and his property is forfeited as well as his life. This punishment is designated as *consecratio capitis*. The patron who wrongs the client whom he is bound to protect, the child who ill-treats the parent whom he is bound in duty to revere, the man who removes his

[1] See Cic., *pro Rab.*, 2, 10; Livy, 1, 26, 6; Mommsen, *Röm. Strafrecht*, 918; Girard, *Org. Jud.*, 28, note 2; Daremberg et Saglio, *s.v.* "Crux." After the early period crucifixion was reserved for slaves, with rare exceptions. Our information is scanty, and it is possible that a distinction was made between this form of crucifixion and that in which the sufferer was left to die by exhaustion (see Pernice, *Zeit. Sav. Stift.*, xvii. 211).

[2] We hear in later times of a dog, a cock, and an ape being put into the sack as well as the snake. It is not certain whether the cock and the dog were thus used in the early period, but certainly the ape is an innovation (Plutarch, *Ti. Gracch.*, 20; *Inst.*, 4, 18, 6; *Cod. Theod.*, 9, 15, 1; *Digest*, 48, 9, 9, pr.; Mommsen, *Röm. Strafrecht*, 922); Strachan-Davidson, *Problems of Roman Criminal Law*, 1, 21.

neighbour's landmark or destroys his corn by night, commits a sin which must be expiated it this way.[1] But in the early days of the Republic, and perhaps, indeed, before the end of the regal period, this sacrifice of the life of the offender, according to a prescribed ritual, gives place to a milder penalty of outlawry and confiscation of goods. When in the Twelve Tables we find it said of certain classes of offenders *sacer esto*, this no longer means that his life is to be forfeit, but that he is to be excommunicated or outlawed, and his goods confiscated for religious uses—he is an exile, cut off from communion of fire and water with his people, and anyone may kill him with impunity.[2] It is by no means clear that in the early period any judgment was necessary to make a man *sacer*. The man who had committed the heinous sin was *ipso facto* accursed; but if anyone slew him the slayer must justify himself by proving that the victim had incurred the penalty. It is a disputed question whether, when a man had become *sacer*, it was a part of the king's duty, as protector of the religion of the State, to have him put to death. I am inclined to think that this was not the case, but that the law, and the king as its chief executive officer, left the outlaw to his fate.[3]

Prohibition of Witchcraft and Incantations.—Among the public crimes punishable under the Twelve Tables with death are the use of witchcraft and incantations. There has been a good deal of discussion as to the interpretation of the fragments, but the best view seems to be that the words *qui malum carmen incantassit* refer to the use of

[1] Dion., 2, 10; Serv. ad. Verg., *Aen.*, vi. 609; in Bruns, *Fontes*, pt. ii. 79; Festus, *s.v.* "Plorare."

[2] See Dion., 2, 10; Festus, *s.v.* "Sacer," *si quis eum occiderit, parricida ne sit;* Voigt, *XII. Tafeln*, i. 493; Rein, *Criminalrecht der Römer*, 30; Strachan-Davidson, *Problems of Roman Criminal Law*, 1, 3 *seq.* An instructive comparison may be made between the position of the *sacer* and the outlaw in the old German and Scandinavian laws (see Dareste, *Études*, 351; Jhering, *Esprit du Droit*, i. 282; *infra*, 215).

[3] See in this sense Jhering, *l.c.*; Pernice, in *Zeit. Sav. Stift.*, 1896, xvii. 183; and for the opposite opinion, Girard, *Org. Jud.*, 29, note 1.

charms or incantations, and that this is regarded as a crime against the gods — *scelus* — punishable with death. Some authorities think the *malum carmen* is an insulting song or satire directed against a person. But it is difficult to believe that at the time of the Twelve Tables such an offence can have been regarded as so serious as to merit the penalty of death, and it seems much more probable that the *malum carmen* is a charm or incantation procured and sung in order to bring about the death of an enemy or to injure his health.[1]

In another passage, said by Cicero to occur in the Twelve Tables, and frequently assigned to the same place as the *malum carmen*, there is the famous prohibition, *si quis occentavisset sive carmen condidisset, quod infamiam faceret flagitiumque alteri.* It seems likely that this prohibition strikes at the singing of satirical songs or pasquinades directed against a particular person. The offences *carmen condere et occentare* would, in this view, be private delicts punishable with a small penalty, and quite distinct from the crime *mali carminis incantatio*, which is the use of witchcraft. The private delicts will be spoken of later.

It has been doubted, however, if in so rude an age as that at which the Twelve Tables were promulgated people could have been so senitive about insulting remarks, or if such things as lampoons or pasquinades had been dreamt of. And it is not impossible that *occentare* was an obsolete word which Cicero misunderstood, and that it meant chanting charms.[2] To bewitch a man's harvest or to attract his crop by witchcraft into one's own field was likewise forbidden by the Tables, and was,

[1] See Voigt, *XII. Tafeln*, ii. 800 ; Cuq, *Institutions Juridiques*, 2nd ed. i. 108 ; and in Daremberg et Saglio, *s.v.* " Injure " ; Esmein, *Nouv. Rev. Hist.*, 1902, 352 ; Huvelin, P., *La Notion de l'Injuria dans le très ancien Droit Romain*, Lyon, 1903 ; Kübler, B., in *Zeit. Sav. Stift.*, xxv. 420 ; Girard, in *Nouv. Rev. Hist.*, 1902, xxvi. 434. Mommsen, on the contrary, takes the *malum carmen* to mean an insulting song (*Röm. Strafrecht*, 794).

[2] See Esmein, in *Nouv. Rev. Hist.*, 1902, xxvi. 352 ; Girard's *Manuel*, 4th ed. 399, note 1 ; *infra*, 234.

probably, punishable by death.[1] One kind of theft of private property, and one only, is in the Twelve Tables treated as a public crime. This is when a man, by night, furtively cuts his neighbour's crop. The offender was offered as a sacrifice to Ceres, the goddess who protected crops, and was put to death by hanging, or, according to Mommsen, by crucifixion—*suspensum Cereri*. If he was below the age of puberty he was beaten with rods at the discretion of the magistrate, and condemned to pay twice the amount of the damage.[2] No doubt capital punishment for such crimes became obsolete at an early period.[3] The severity of the penalty was, probably, because in cases of this kind the owner of the property could not protect himself. In a rural community such offences are regarded as particularly heinous, and this is one of the provisions which show that the Tables belong to an age when Rome was a community of farmers.

The public crime, the offence against the community, is in the early law regarded always as something which has to be expiated. It is not so much that the offender must be punished as that the community must be purified from the stain of his guilt. Unavenged blood cries to Heaven and brings down the wrath of the gods upon the land. But as time goes on, and as the advantages of preserving order within the community become more evident, the expiatory character of the punishment becomes less emphasised, and is superseded by the modern view, which regards it as the means by which the State maintains order and security within its bounds.[4]

[1] Mommsen, *op. cit.*, 639, 643. It is interesting to notice that in some countries the necessity for legislation against the use of charms and witchcraft still exists. See for modern instances of such laws in Rhodesia, Nigeria, and elsewhere, *Legislation of the Empire*, in Index, *s.v.* "Witch-craft."

[2] Plin., *Nat. Hist.*, 18, 3 ; Mommsen, *Röm. Strafrecht*, 772, 918.

[3] Mommsen, *op. cit.*, 773.

[4] See Mommsen, *Röm. Strafrecht*, 36 and 900 ; *cf.* Meyer, *Gesch. des Alt.*, 2, note, 363 *seq.* It has frequently been pointed out that the Roman form of execution by decapitation was carried out in a way which strikingly resembles the slaying of an animal as a sacrifice (Marquardt, *Staatsverwaltung*, 3, 181 ; Mommsen, *Röm. Strafrecht*, 918).

Procedure for the Trial of Public Crimes.—During the period of the kings it is entirely probable that the trial of the few offences regarded as being of a public character was left to the king. Crimes committed by a subordinate member of a family were dealt with by the *paterfamilias* in his judicial character, as has been explained earlier in speaking of the *patria potestas.* And the king, as father of the whole people, has naturally the right and the duty of punishing those offences which affect the safety of the community, or might bring down upon it the wrath of the gods. As commander-in-chief it is for him to deal with acts of treason ; and as the head of the State religion he must see that heinous offences against the gods are duly expiated. The king conducts the inquiry—*quaestio*—but custom requires him to have the assistance of a council of assessors—*concilium.* It is one of the charges made by Livy against Tarquinius Superbus that he was wont to try capital charges without the assistance of this council.[1]

The Provocatio.—Where the king pronounced the sentence, he might, before putting it into execution, consult the assembly of the people, and might take their judgment as to whether the criminal should be put to death or should be allowed to go free. And it is thought by some writers that the accused himself had a right to demand such a reference to the assembly—the *provocatio ad populum*—but there is strong evidence to show that this right of appeal to the people was first given by the *Lex Valeria* after the beginning of the Republic.[2] We know that when a dictator held office instead of the consuls there was no such right of appeal, and this was because the dictator had the power of the old kings.[3]

After the introduction of the Republic the consuls, as succeeding to the supreme office, were naturally entrusted with the judicial authority. But the jurisdiction to try criminal charges

[1] Livy, 1, 49.

[2] Cic., *De Rep.*, 2, 31, 54 ; see Strachan-Davidson, *Problems of Roman Criminal Law*, 1, 126, 144, note 1.

[3] Livy, 8, 32-35 ; Mommsen, *Röm. Strafrecht*, 42 and 474 ; Girard, *Org. Jud.*, 23.

involving the life or liberty of a Roman citizen was taken from the consuls and given to other officials. If a case of *perduellio* arose, the consuls nominated two delegates called *duumviri perduellionis* to conduct the inquiry and pronounce the sentence. And in cases of murder, and also of sacrilege, and of such other crimes, not falling under the name of *perduellio*, as came to be regarded in the light of public offences, the two *quaestors* acted as judges, and were called in this capacity *quaestores parricidii.*[1]

Trials for high treason, if that term may be used as roughly corresponding to *perduellio*, were unusual, and the *duumviri* were appointed specially in each case. But parricide was a much more common crime, and the *quaestors* were permanent officials, and at an early period the practice of appealing against a capital sentence to the assembly of the people, which, under the kings, had been merely a matter of grace, became a constitutional right which the accused was entitled to claim. According to the traditional account it was the *Lex Valeria* of 509 B.C. which first laid it down as a matter of law that no Roman citizen was to be put to death by sentence of a magistrate without a right of appeal to the people.[2] This right of *provocatio*, or appeal to the people, applied only to sentences pronounced on charges of public crimes, and not then unless the sentence was one of death. All the Roman magistrates who possessed the *imperium* had wide powers of coercion to enforce their decrees by means of imprisonment, fining, and, perhaps, even scourging offenders when the scourging was not accessory to the capital sentence, and the right of appeal did not exist here. The abuse of such power had to be checked by the veto

[1] The dual character of these offices and the fact that in the account of the trial of Horatius, which is one of the chief sources of our information on this matter, the *quaestores parricidii* are not mentioned, makes it almost certain that the *duumviri perduellionis* and the *quaestores parricidii* do not go back to the time of the kings (Livy, i. 26 ; Mommsen, *Röm. Staatsrecht*, 2, 523 ; *Röm. Strafrecht*, 155 ; Girard, *Org. Jud.*, 24).

[2] Cic., *De Rep.*, ii. 31, 53 ; Liv., 2, 8 ; Dion., 5, 19 ; Plut., *Publ.*, 11. See Binder, *Die Plebs*, 467.

of the Tribunes or by other constitutional means, nor was there any *provocatio* when the sentence was against persons not Roman citizens, such as foreigners, or slaves, or, apparently, women. It was only the citizen voter who had the right of appeal.[1] Nor was there any right of appeal if the sentence had been pronounced by a dictator. The assembly to which the right of appeal existed must in the earliest period have been the ancient assembly of the people by *curiae*, the *comitia curiata;* but, after the constitutional change had been made which introduced the assembly of the people according to centuries, it was to the *comitia centuriata* that the citizen made his appeal, and the Twelve Tables contained an express provision that no capital sentence should be pronounced except by this assembly —*per maximum comitiatum.*

Another *Lex Valeria* of 300 B.C. is said to have amended the law relating to the *provocatio* by extending it to sentences rendered by a dictator and by making it apply to a sentence of scourging as well as death. This later *Lex Valeria* also said that the magistrate who did not bring an appeal which was claimed by the accused before the assembly should be guilty of an *improbe factum*, which would involve certainly a moral stigma, and might lead to his official disgrace.[2]

It is by no means impossible that the historians who tell us about these two Valerian laws are merely giving varying accounts of one and the same piece of legislation, and that the only authentic Valerian law is that of 300 B.C.[3] By certain laws of a later time, called the Porcian laws, the date of which is unknown, the magistrate who refused the *provocatio* was probably made liable to a charge of treason—*perduellio.*[4]

The fact that no Roman citizen could be deprived of life or citizenship for any political or public crime until the sentence

[1] See Mommsen, *Röm. Strafrecht*, 37 and 143.

[2] Livy, 10, 9.

[3] Pais, *Storia di Roma*, i. pt. i. 489 ; *cf.* Binder, *Die Plebs*, 470.

[4] Cic. in *Verr.*, l. 5, 12, 14 ; Greenidge, 320 ; Mommsen, *Röm. Strafrecht*, 31, 47, 163.

had been confirmed by the vote of the sovereign people was always regarded as a great mark of Roman freedom; but when the absolute right to the appeal had been secured under severe sanctions, its actual exercise became uncommon. After the magistrate had inquired into the offence, and was satisfied that it was one to which the right of appeal extended, he thought it unnecessary to pronounce any sentence of his own, but, instead of so doing, brought the charge directly before the people. During the greater part of the Republic criminal jurisdiction is exercised by the Roman people itself, and the magistrate is not the judge but the public prosecutor; and with the rise in power of the plebeian assemblies and of the tribune of the plebs a large part of the criminal jurisdiction was transferred to them. The tribunes, like the regular magistrates, acquired the right of acting as public prosecutors, and, in the earlier Republic, brought even capital cases before the plebs; but later the rule came to be that whether a tribune or one of the magistrates was stating the case, it should come before the plebeians if a monetary penalty was proposed, but prosecutions in which the capital penalty was sought were to be brought before the centuries. The procedure is only known to us from the descriptions of trials by writers of a much later date, and there is a good deal in it which remains obscure.[1]

The *judicium populi*, as it was called, begins with an investigation conducted by the magistrate in the presence of an informal meeting—*contio*—which he has called together. The magistrate is either a *quaestor* or a tribune. This investigation is known as the *anquisitio*, and evidence for the prosecution and defence is produced.[2] The inquiry must be prolonged for three days, and the accusation made on the first day may be amended or modified to suit the facts which have been brought out. On the third day the *accusatio* is definitely formulated. After the magisterial inquiry there must be an interval of at

[1] The fullest account of such a trial is that by Livy, 25, 3 4.

[2] See Livy, 26, 3, 5; Cicero, 17, 45.

least three market days, that is, of twenty-four days, and the proposal may then be brought by the magistrate before the *comitia.* This is called his *quarta accusatio.* It is put in the form of a bill or *rogatio,* and has to be passed or rejected in the ordinary form.[1] The accused can defend himself before the assembly either personally or by his friends, and in the later Republic is generally assisted by *oratores*—pleaders of experience in criminal trials. After the speeches the witnesses on both sides are examined.[2] If a majority in the *comitia* is in favour of condemnation the presiding magistrate pronounces the sentence.[3]

One singular feature of Roman criminal procedure has not been mentioned; that is, that at any time before the final vote of the assembly the accused has the right to flee the country as a voluntary exile. It does not seem to have been the practice for the criminal to have been arrested pending the trial, and if before its conclusion he became afraid to abide the result, and was able to get away from Rome to one of the allied states, which by treaty had the right of receiving Roman exiles, and there became a citizen, he escaped the death sentence of the Roman *comitia.*[4]

In the assembly at Rome the plea was generally put in that the offender had changed his country and become an exile, and proof of this was followed by a sentence of *aquae et ignis interdictio.* This practice made the execution of the death penalty in the case of citizens very uncommon, except when the regular laws were suspended, as in the proscriptions of Sulla. The exile

---

[1] If the magistrate declares for death, the appeal is to the centuries; if he pronounces for a fine, it is to the tribal assembly if the magistrate is a tribune, and to the *populus* if he is a *quaestor.* See Strachan-Davidson, *Problems of Roman Criminal Law,* 1, 155.

[2] Livy, 25, 3.

[3] On the subject see, especially, Mommsen, *Röm. Strafrecht,* 163 *seq.*; Greenidge, *Legal Procedure,* 345 ; Maynz, C. H., in *Nouv. Rev. Hist.,* 1881, v. 587.

[4] Polyb., 6, 14, 7 ; Cic., *pro Caec.,* 34 ; Liv., 26, 3.

against whom the sentence of outlawry had been pronounced could not return to Rome, and, after the social war, was excluded from Italy. If he returned he might be killed with impunity, as one who is accursed—*sacer*.[1]

The criminal procedure which has just been sketched was superseded at Rome not long before the beginning of the last century of the Republic by a new process; this was the institution of standing courts or commissions—*quaestiones*—to each of which was assigned by statute the duty of trying certain crimes. These *quaestiones perpetuae* are also called *judicia publica*. Their creation marks the commencement of the trial of crimes by ordinary tribunals instead of dealing with them by a legislative process. The multiplication, however, of the *quaestiones*, each of which is strictly tied down by the law which creates it to certain special forms of crime, led in the later period to great confusion and abuse; but this is a subject which cannot be dealt with here.[2]

Criminal Law among other Aryan Peoples.—It is difficult for us to realise that the administration of criminal justice by regular tribunals should be so late a growth, but the history of this matter at Rome is in no way singular, and a parallel development can be observed in the history of other members of the Aryan family. In Greece, also, in the early period, there is no idea that the community has the duty of preserving the peace, or of punishing the murderer or the thief. For private wrongs the injured man or his kinsman will take vengeance. In the rare cases where the existence of the State itself has been threatened, or a wrong has been done to the gods, the king and the council of the elders may take action, while at a later date the small number of offences which were regarded as public crimes were tried before the assembly of the people, afterwards divided for convenience into ten panels of

1 Mommsen, *Röm. Strafrecht*, 70; Greenidge, *Legal Procedure*, 511.

2 See Maine's *Ancient Law*, 15th ed. 385; and the criticism by Strachan-Davidson, *Problems of Roman Criminal Law*, 2, 16.

five hundred each, called the *heliaea*;[1] and at Athens and in other Greek cities the murderer in early times had the right to flee the country, and must never return on pain of becoming liable to death.[2] In the old German and Scandinavian law it is the *ting* or assembly which tries the public offender, the assembly being, as at Rome, guided and assisted by a presiding magistrate.[3]

The Outlaw.—The form of punishment which consists in declaring the offender accursed and cut off from all rights is a marked feature of the early German and Scandinavian laws. The Roman *sacer* and the Icelandic outlaw are very likely survivals of an Aryan institution, which belongs to the primitive home.[4] In Scandinavia the accused was generally allowed to take refuge in flight after he had been pronounced an outlaw. The outlaw may be killed by anyone with impunity. He is excommunicated and cut off from the society, his goods are confiscated, and his marriage dissolved. It is forbidden to anyone to give him food or shelter—even his wife or child cannot receive him. He is not allowed to live in any community, but must flee to the forest or the mountain, from which fact he gets the name of the man of the woods—*Waldgänger*—or of the wolf. The Icelandic saga of Gretti the Strong, written between 1010 and 1030 A.D., describes the story of one of these outlaws, who lived this life of wandering misery for nineteen years, and died just at the moment when the assembly was about to restore him to his rights. And among these northern peoples, as among the Greeks and the Romans, we find traces of the still earlier conception that the *consecratio*, or sentence of outlawry, is the sacrifice of the life of the victim to the gods whom he

---

[1] Grote, iv. 68; Meyer, *Gesch. des Alt.*, note, 53, 60, 409. See *Nouv. Rev. Hist.*, xxxi. 177, article by M. Huvelin.

[2] Demosth., *Arist.*, 643; *Il.*, 9, 632; 24, 480; Kohler, *Shakespeare, &c.* 155; Dareste, *Nouv. Études*, 3.

[3] Brunner, *Deutsche Rechtsgeschichte*, i. 148.

[4] Jhering, *Esprit du Droit*, i. 282.

has offended, the main idea being still expiation, not punishment.[1]

Private Delicts

In the early law many acts which are now regarded as crimes and punishable by the State are treated merely as personal wrongs, for which the individual must exact such satisfaction as he can. And at Rome, as in many other countries, it is not difficult to trace the gradual development by which the State assumes more and more control in the repression of delicts or private wrongs. According to the primitive conception, if a man is wrongfully slain, his kinsmen are entitled, and indeed bound by custom, to exact vengeance from the offender and his kindred. Every death by private violence gives rise to the blood-feud between two families or kindreds. The outrage can only be appeased by blood, and, as there is no way of fixing the point at which an exact balance of injury has been reached, the blood-feud may go on until the two families are exterminated. Similarly, when a man is assaulted or insulted, or when his property is stolen, it is his business by himself and his friends to exact satisfaction and compensation from the wrongdoer. The stage of *talio* or self-help may still be witnessed among many savages, and there is abundant evidence of its existence in the early history of almost all the civilised peoples. As society becomes more organised the practice of the blood-feud begins to be frowned upon, and the kinsmen of a murdered man are expected to submit their claim for satisfaction to the judgment of the king or the assembly of the people, who will fix a blood-price, or compensation in money, in place of the right to a life for a life. The reference to arbitration and the acceptance of the compensation fixed are at first not compulsory, but in time the custom hardens, and it becomes compulsory to abandon the blood-feud and to take the compensation awarded or agreed upon. Where

[1] Brunner, *op. cit.*, 166-175, and ii. 587 ; Mommsen, *Röm. Strafrecht*, 901-918 ; Meyer, *Gesch. des Alt.*, ii. note, 63, 365, 377.

the injury has been specially atrocious, as, *e.g.*, where the murder is aggravated by treachery, the right to the blood-feud continues. For wrongs less than death the law gradually provides a fixed tariff, varying in amount according to the nature of the injury itself, the rank of the victim, the relation between him and the offender, and other circumstances. Many early codes of law contain the most minute provisions for fitting the punishment to the crime, and for assigning to every injury its appropriate price. The pecuniary payment is not to be looked upon merely as compensation for the wrong; it is the price which the sufferer is allowed for sacrificing his right to private vengeance. This is illustrated by the fact that a large sum can be claimed if the offender is caught red-handed. In the earliest time a thief caught red-handed may be slain by the owner of the stolen goods, and if money is to paid instead, it will be the price of blood rather than mere reparation for the damage. Accordingly a higher penalty will be given than if the thief had been detected at a later period. Both among the Romans and the Greeks the blood-feud has disappeared before the historial period, though the right to kill the nocturnal thief still remains, and for some forms of injury less than death retaliation can be claimed even under the Twelve Tables.[1] It is indeed significant of a high state of civilisation among the Romans, even at the earliest time of which we have historical knowledge, that murder or *parricidium* is treated as a public crime and not as a private wrong. Among the Germans, the Celts, and others of the Aryan peoples we find the blood-feud in full operation many centuries after it had become obsolete at Rome.

Universal Prevalence of Talio.—The idea involved in *talio*, that the man who has committed a wrong must make reparation in kind—the rule of life for life, eye for eye, tooth for tooth—is by no means peculiar to the Aryan peoples. It is found among almost all races and at all periods in the world's history. It

[1] See the traces of "self-help" noted in Rein, *Criminalrecht der Römer*, 36. As to the Greeks, see Meyer, E., *Gesch. des Alt.*, ii. note, 364.

is laid down in the earliest codes of law which we possess, such as the laws of Hamurabi,[1] in the Mosaic law,[2] and in the ancient code of the Magyars, who were neither Aryans nor Semites.[3] It still exists among the Ossetes of the Caucasus,[4] and it lasted in Russia down to the seventeenth century;[5] and in every quarter of the world where the laws and institutions of people living under primitive conditions can be studied, we find *talio* still in green observance. For example, a recent writer, describing the Araucanos, or Indians of Southern Chile, says: "Every injury had its price, which varied with the importance of the offended."[6] And another writer, describing the Bangala of the Upper Congo, says: "Retaliation in kind, when possible, was the essence of justice among the natives—an eye for an eye, a cut for a cut, a bump for a bump, and a life for a life." When retaliation was impossible, compensation by fines was imposed.[7] Some other illustrations will be given later, but for the present these will be sufficient to indicate the universality of the rule of *talio*.

Symbolic Punishments.—Even when punishment is exacted by the State upon public offenders, instead of by the victim himself or by his kinsmen, we frequently find indications of the idea that the mode of punishment is to indicate in a visible way the nature of the crime. Thus, by the Twelve Tables, the man convicted of setting fire to a building is to be burnt alive.[8]

In the old German laws there are many illustrations of this tendency. The tongue of the blasphemer or slanderer is cut out, the right hand held up by the perjurer in taking the false oath is cut off, the man who refuses to accept in payment a

1 Ss. 116, 196, 197, 200, 210, 230, &c.

2 Ex. xxi. 23-25; Lev. xxiv. 19-21; Deut. xix. 16-21.

3 Dareste, *Études*, 253.

4 Dareste, *op. cit.*, 146.

5 See Lenel, in *Zeit. Sav. Stift.*, xxvi. 509.

6 R. E. Latcham, in *Journ. Roy. Anthrop. Inst.*, 1909, xxxix. 356.

7 *Ibid.*, 433, by Rev. J. H. Weeks.

8 *Digest*, 47, 9, 9.

coin of full weight is branded with a red-hot coin upon the forehead, and so on.[1]

Talio in the Twelve Tables.—The passage in the Twelve Tables in which the rule of *talio* is laid down has occasioned much controversy. The whole passage, which is usually assigned to Table VIII., reads as follows:—*Si membrum rup(s)it, ni cum eo pacit, talio esto. Manu fustive si os fregit libero, ccc, (si) servo, cl poenam subito. Si iniuriam faxsit, viginti quinque poenae sunto.* That is to say, "If one have broken the limb of another and have not come to terms with him, let there be *talio.* If he have broken a bone of a freeman with his hand or with a club, let the penalty be three hundred *asses;* if the bone be that of a slave, let it be one hundred and fifty *asses.* If one have committed an *iniuria,* let the penalty be twenty-five *asses.*" We see that a tariff is here fixed for the breaking of a bone, and that it varies according to the status of the victim, but that for the wrong described as the "breaking of a limb"—*membrum rupere*—no pecuniary penalty is stated, but the code says simply, let there be *talio.* We have to consider, therefore, the meaning of this wrong, for which the primitive remedy seems to be preserved. It is clear that the expression *membrum rupere* refers to an injury graver than the mere fracture of a bone, and, according to a plausible theory, it means the destruction of a limb, as by being amputated or rendered permanently useless. It is probable also that the word *membrum* covers such parts of the body as the eyes, the nose and the ears.[2] Muirhead suggests as an analogy the *mayhem* of the old English law, which Blackstone explains as "a battery attended with this aggravated circumstance that

[1] See Grimm, *Rechtsalterthümer,* 740; Brunner, *Deutsche Rechtsgeschichte,* ii. 589. The Germans said, "*Wodurch man sündigt, büsst man.*" So in the laws of Manu the tongue of a slanderer may be cut out, and "with whatever limb a thief in any way commits (an offence) against men, even of that (the king) shall deprive him in order to prevent (a repetition of the crime)."—viii. 270, 334.

[2] See Girard, *Manuel,* 5th ed. 401, note 3.

thereby the party injured is for ever disabled from making so good a defence against future external injuries as he otherwise might have done. Among the members important for self-defence are reckoned not only arms and legs, but a finger, an eye, and a fore-tooth, and also some others."[1] And Blackstone says in another passage: "By the ancient law of England he that maimed any man whereby he lost any part of his body was sentenced to lose the like part—*membrum pro membro*—which is still the law of Sweden."[2]

A learned French writer has recently put forward another theory as to the meaning of *si membrum rup(s)it*. He maintains that the law of the Twelve Tables fixes a tariff for two kinds of injuries to the person, one of them very serious, the fracture of a bone, which is to be 300 *asses* for a free man, and 150 for a slave; the other a very slight injury, where there is no physical lesion, for which the penalty is twenty-five *asses*. Between these two extremes come all other lesions, wounds and contusions. The law did not wish to fix a tariff proportionate to the gravity of each case, for this would have involved an interminable enumeration. It preferred to leave to the parties the fixing of the penalty, and if they did not agree, the *talio* or right of private vengeance came into force, though even in this case he thinks if the defender refused to submit to the *talio* the judge would fix a pecuniary penalty.[3]

This theory is ingenious, but it does not seem possible to think that the *membrum ruptum* refers to a less serious injury than the fracture of a bone.[4] If we are to reject this theory, as I think we must, and follow the traditional opinion that the Twelve Tables preserve the *talio* for the most serious bodily injuries, we see that the law is in a period of transition.

---

[1] Muirhead, 2nd ed. 439, note 3; Blackstone, *Com.*, 3, 121.

[2] *Ibid.*, 4, 206.

[3] Appleton, Ch., *Le Testament Romain et l'Authenticité des XII. Tables*, Paris, 1903, 23, note 3.

[4] See Girard, *l.c.*

The old right of private vengeance still exists for certain grave delicts, but before it can be exercised there must be a judgment of the magistrate authorising it. The law contemplates the probability of the parties coming to an agreement as to the compensation, and it is only failing this that there is a claim to *talio.* At a later period in the history the magistrate will refuse to order the *talio* in any case, but, even when the parties cannot agree, will fix the amount of compensation which is to be paid.[1]

It is possible that the words *ni cum eo pacit* mean that the injured person or his kindred, who are not satisfied with the compensation offered; are entitled, on their own authority, to *passer outre* and take personal vengeance. But I am inclined to think that the correct interpretation of the words is that, before this ultimate course can be taken, the matter must at any rate be submitted to the court. The *pactum* contemplated is not a private agreement but the compromise of an action at law.[2]

We may compare this stage with that described by Homer in his account of the trial scene which forms one of the pictures on the shield of Achilles. There the kinsman of a murdered man and the murderer are disputing before an arbiter, and in the presence of the assembled people, as to the amount of the blood-price. The murderer offers a certain sum, but the avenger refuses to take it, either because it is insufficient or because the murder was premeditated, and, therefore, not to be redeemed by a money payment. The heralds compel order, and bring the parties and their backers to silence, and the matter is referred for judgment to the elders, who sit round in a half-circle upon seats of polished stone. In the Homeric times we may assume that the reference to the assembly or to any tribunal has not

[1] Gell., 20, 1, 38; Lenel, in *Zeit. Sav. Stift.*, xxvi. 509; Jhering, *L'Esprit du Droit Romain*, i. 139; Cuq, i. 105; Beaudouin, in *Nouv. Rev. Hist.*, ii. 641.

[2] Authorities in preceding note.

become compulsory. The right of private vengeance still exists, and no judicial authority is required for its exercise, but probably the point has been reached at which a reference to the assembly is regarded as the normal and the right procedure. The man who stands out for his absolute right to take vengeance at his own hand is looked upon with some disapproval. It will not be long before public opinion compels the avenger to obtain judicial sanction, unless the murder has been aggravated by special circumstances.[1]

The Special Delicts of the Twelve Tables.—The delicts to which the Twelve Tables specially refer are—

1. *Furtum* or theft.

2. *Iniuria*, which includes, roughly, damages to the person, including the *membri ruptio* and the *ossis fractio*, and also certain special cases of damage to property. I will speak later of theft, and of *iniuria* in the sense of a wrong done to the body, and, as some think, to the reputation, and will first refer briefly to the special cases in which the law provides remedy for damage to property. It is significant of the antique character of the Twelve Tables that in them no general rule is laid down, such as that found in modern codes, that every person shall be responsible for the damage caused to another by his fault.[2] The Tables proceed by enumerating certain special cases of injury to property for which reparation must be made, but do not grant any remedy at all unless the damage can be brought under one of these heads.[3] The general rule for liability for wrongful damage was not introduced until much

---

[1] See *Iliad*, xviii. 497 *seq.*, and the notes in Leaf's *Iliad*, 2nd ed., and the Appendix I. to vol. ii.; Dareste, R., *Nouv. Études*, 1.

[2] See *Code Civil Français*, 1382; *German Code*, 823; *Egyptian Native Civil Code*, 151. On the question whether such a general rule forms part of the English law, see Salmond, *Torts*, 3rd ed. 9, against that view, and Pollock, *Torts*, 10th ed. 1, in favour of it. Cf. *Law Quarterly Review*, 1919, 287, note on *Janvier* v. *Sweeney*, 1919, 2 K.B. 316.

[3] See Girard, *Manuel*, 5th ed. 414; Saleilles, *Théorie Générale de l'Obligation*, 3rd ed. p. 355. *Contra*, Leonhard, *Institutionen des Römischen Rechts*, 446.

later by the *Lex Aquilia*, the date of which is commonly assigned, though not upon very conclusive grounds, to about the year 286 B.C.[1]

The particular kinds of property protected by the Twelve Tables are houses, slaves, quadrupeds, crops and trees. The man who has set fire to a house or to a stack of corn near a dwelling-place, if he has done it intentionally—*sciens prudensque*—is to be scourged and then burnt to death. If he has done it negligently he is to make good the injury—*noxiam sarcire*—or, if he has no money, is to suffer a moderate beating.[2] Where the liability is civil there is a special action—*de aedibus incensis*. If a man has wrongfully killed a slave or a quadruped which belongs to another, he must make compensation, and may be sued by the *actio de servo quadrupedeve occiso*.[3] It is true that we have no actual textual evidence for this, but we know that the Twelve Tables gave damages for breaking the bone of a slave, and they cannot have done less for killing him. The man who allows his cattle to enter his neighbour's field on which the crop has already come up—*laeta seges*—and there to graze, is liable under the action—*de pastu pecoris*.[4] The man who unlawfully cuts down his neighbour's tree may be sued by the *actio de arboribus succisis*. But there are many kinds of damage done to property with which the Twelve Tables did not deal, and for which in the early law no legal remedy was provided. The delict which is the most instructive for us in throwing light upon early legal conceptions is that of *furtum* or theft, which must now be described.

Furtum.—It is generally agreed by philologists that the word *fur*—a thief—is from the same root as the Greek word φώρ, and that both of them come from a root *bher*—φώρ—*fer*—which

[1] See Grueber, *Lex Aquilia*, 174; Girard, *Manuel*, 5th ed. 413, note 1.

[2] *Digest*, 47, 9, 9.

[3] Voigt, *XII. Tafeln*, ii. 528; Grueber, *Lex Aquilia*, 188.

[4] Voigt, ii. 537.

means to carry away.[1] It has been suggested, however, that if this were so, instead of *fur* the Latin would be *fer*, and that the explanation of the form *fur* is that the Latin word is borrowed directly from the Greek.[2] In any case, the primary meaning of *fur* seems to be "one who carries away." As a matter of law, notwithstanding, it was not necessary, in order to constitute the delict of *furtum*, that the object should be removed. It was sufficient that the thief should have touched it or seized it with the intention of carrying it away feloniously—*attrectare, contrectare, attingere.*[3] It is possible that this is a later refinement, and that in the time of the Twelve Tables there was no theft without an actual carrying off of the object. Theft was only possible of moveable objects, perhaps, as Mommsen suggests, because the law was fixed at a time before there was such a thing as private property in immoveables.[4] The essential elements of theft consist in the laying hands on, or carrying away of, a moveable object which belongs to another with the intention of appropriating it, and without the consent of its owner. The Twelve Tables do not contain any definition. In the classical period it was recognised that there might be such a thing as a man stealing his own property, and there might be a theft of the use or possession of a thing. If a man has given his property to another in pledge, and then furtively takes it away from him, this is theft. And so it is if a depositary, with whom a thing is left to take care of it, makes any use of the thing unless he has the express or implied consent of the depositor. In like manner one may steal from a possessor the thing which he possesses.[5] But these are later refinements. The old law distinguishes theft into *furtum manifestum*, that is, speaking roughly, the case where the thief is caught red-handed, and *furtum nec manifestum*, when

[1] Lindsay, *Latin Language*, 1894, 233 ; Mommsen, *Röm. Strafrecht*, 733.
[2] Conway, *Indogerman. Forschungen*, iv. 215.
[3] *Dig.*, 47, 2, 21 pr.
[4] *Röm. Strafrecht*, 741 ; *Röm. Staatsrecht*, iii. 22.
[5] *Dig.*, 47, 1, 3. See Schirmer, in *Zeit. Sav. Stift.*, v. 207.

the theft is discovered later. Manifest theft is regarded as an offence for which a much higher penalty is due than for non-manifest theft. This is an interesting distinction on which much emphasis is laid in the early law of other Aryan peoples, and some illustrations of it will be given later. The manifest thief was liable to the capital penalty, though, if he was a free man, he was not sentenced to death, but was adjudged to become the slave of the person whose property he had stolen. If the thief was a slave he was sentenced to be scourged and put to death by being hurled down from the top of a rock. Offenders under the age of puberty were to make the damage good, and to be beaten at the discretion of the prætor.[1] The non-manifest thief was exposed to the much lighter penalty of paying twice the value of what he had stolen.

The traditional opinion is that this distinction was brought in by the Twelve Tables, and that before them theft, whether manifest or not, was a capital crime.[2] But there is no proof that this was so, and it does not seem probable. Before the time when the manifest thief could be adjudged as a slave, there was no doubt a more primitive stage during which he might be killed without any form of trial, if caught red-handed. There are many parallels for this in the early law of other peoples; *e.g.*, in Greece, before the legislation of Draco, the thief caught *ἐπ' αὐτοφώρῳ*, that is the manifest thief, might be killed without any judgment, and the same was the case among the Saxons.[3] In fact, in the early law of all the Aryans, a sharp distinction is drawn between offenders caught in the act, or in a hot pursuit after the act, and other wrongdoers. Long after a regular form of criminal procedure has become necessary for dealing with ordinary crimes, the primitive right of

---

[1] Gaius, 3, 189; Gell., 11, 18, 8.

[2] Mommsen, *Röm. Strafrecht*, 750.

[3] Glotz, *s.v.* *κλοπή*, in Daremberg et Saglio; "Laws of Ina," c. 12 and c. 35, in Schmid, R., *Gesetze der Angelsachsen*, 2nd ed., Leipzig, 1858; Pollock and Maitland, *Hist. of Eng. Law*, i. 36.

private vengeance persists as to the offender who is caught red-handed. The rough old rule still applies to the flagrant delict, or the *handhafte That*, as the Germans call it.[1]

Two cases of the right to kill an offender caught in the act are especially prominent in the early law, namely, those of the adulterer and the manifest thief. By the Roman law the husband or the father can kill the man whom he finds in the act of adultery with his wife or daughter, and the right of killing in this case is recognised among many peoples, *e.g.* by the old Norse law a man can kill one caught in adultery with the wife, mother, daughter, sister, mother-in-law, sister-in-law, or daughter-in-law of the slayer.[2] A similar rule is found among the Greeks and the Germans.[3] In like manner the thief caught red-handed can be killed. In many of these laws before the slayer is entitled to kill the offender he must raise a hue and cry, in order that the neighbours or the friends of the pursued may have an opportunity to interpose if they think fit, or otherwise may help to "lynch" the offender. This primitive practice is mentioned in the Twelve Tables in the case of the manifest thief caught in daylight who defends himself with a weapon. He may be slain, but the hue and cry must be raised —*endoplorato*.[4] The right to kill a manifest thief is found among almost all the European peoples at an early stage, and may safely be regarded as one of the rules which belonged to the primitive

1 Brissaud, *Manuel d'Histoire du Droit Français*, 1203, 1208, 1244, 1362; Brunner, *Deutsche Rechtsgeschichte*, ii. 481.

2 *Dig.*, 48, 5, 24, and 20; Gell., 10, 23; Dareste, *Études*, 337.

3 See the passages collected in Bernhöft, *Staat und Recht*, 239; Demosth., in *Aristoc.*, 53; Esmein, *Mélanges*, 80; Pernice, in *Zeit Sav. Stift.*, xvii. 189; *Law of Gortyn* (ed. Bücheler), 104.

4 Our expression "hue and cry" and the term in the old French law—*clameur de haro*—are connected with a similar usage. In the Channel Islands some actions are still commenced by the plaintiff kneeling down in the presence of two witnesses, and crying *haro haro haro, à l'aide mon prince, on me fait tort* (Brissaud, *Hist. du Droit Français*, ii. 1244; Brunner, ii. 481; Pernice, in *Zeit. Sav. Stift.*, xvii. 189; E. Glasson, in *Nouv. Rev. Hist.*, vi. 397).

Aryans. We know that it existed among the Czechs, the Anglo-Saxons, the Danes, the Icelanders, the Swedes, and the Germans.[1]

It is likely enough that among the ancient Romans, as among some other primitive peoples, there was a period when, unless an offender was caught in the act, the law did not touch him at all. If he was caught *in flagranti delicto* he might be slain. That was the only case in which the guilt was certain and undeniable. The next step was to make the sentence of a Court necessary even when the offender was caught red-handed. The Court may give the offender over to the mercy of the man whom he has wronged, or may order *talio*, or, at a later stage, a pecuniary composition. It is not until society has made a further advance that punishments are created for theft and for some other private delicts, although the defender has not been caught in the act. There is a good deal of plausibility in the view that before the Twelve Tables non-manifest theft was not punished at all, and that the double penalty for that delict was first introduced by the Tables.[2] At any rate it is improbable that by the primitive Roman law a thief, not caught in the act, could be slain in cold blood. Under the Twelve Tables the primitive right of killing the manifest thief is reserved only in two cases—when he is caught by night in the act, or when he is caught by day and defends himself with a weapon. In all other cases there must be the judgment of a Court, but the penalty is still capital, and the manifest thief is adjudged as a slave. The thief could, of course, try to come to terms, and pay a ransom instead of going into slavery, but the other party was not obliged to accept any fixed sum.

When is the Theft Manifest?—In the classical period there was a good deal of discussion as to the definition of manifest theft. Some lawyers said the theft was manifest when the thief

---

[1] See Dareste, *Études*, 167, 299, 315, 355, 398, 401 ; Brunner, ii. 483.

[2] Esmein, in *Nouv. Rev. Hist.*, xxvi. 321, and *Mélanges d'Histoire du Droit*, 84, following Leist, in *Græco-Italische Rechtsgeschichte*, 298 ; Hitsig, in *Zeit. Sav. Stift.*, 1902, xxiii. 320. *Cf.* Brunner, ii. 481.

was caught, and not merely seen in the act; others, when the thief was caught while still on the spot, *e.g.* in the house; while others, again, said the theft was manifest if he was caught before he had brought the stolen thing to the place where he intended to put it. A fourth opinion that the theft was manifest if the thief was found at any time in possession of the thing—*rem tenens*—was rejected by high authorities.[1] Judging from the analogies in the other laws it seems safe to assume that in the early period the theft was manifest if the thief was caught in the act, or, if having been detected, he was pursued and caught in a hot pursuit. So long as the capital penalty for manifest theft continued to exist, the tendency would be to give a strict interpretation to the word "manifest." There was, however, one case where the penalty for manifest theft was incurred though the thief was not caught in the act—this was when the stolen thing was found by the exercise of a formal search.

Furtum Conceptum Lance et Licio.—The person from whom the thing has been stolen, who suspects that it is concealed in a house, can claim the right of making a search, but the right can only be exercised according to certain forms. He must go to the house naked, or, at least, wearing nothing but a loin-cloth—*licium*—and he must carry a platter. If this ritual is observed, and the stolen thing is found in the house, the theft is manifest, and the occupier of the house is liable to the penalty for that delict. If the householder refuses to allow the search he renders himself liable also to the penalty for manifest theft.[2] Gaius, who describes this ancient ceremony, is evidently much puzzled by it, for he says: "The whole thing is ridiculous, for he who would prevent a man wearing his ordinary dress from making a search would equally prevent him when naked, especially as the discovery of a thing when sought for would subject the prohibitor to a heavier penalty. And as for the platter, whether it was to be used in order to prevent the searcher from surreptitiously introducing

[1] Gaius, iii. 183, 184; *Dig.*, 47, 2, 3.

[2] Hitsig, in *Zeit. Sav. Stift.*, xxiii. 331.

the thing sought for, his hands being occupied in holding the platter, or, if he was to place the thing found on the platter, neither reason is valid when the article sought for is of such a size or nature that it could not be brought in surreptitiously nor yet laid upon the platter. There is no doubt that the law was satisfied whatever might be the material of which the platter was made."[1] Jhering thinks that the loin-cloth, which is still the ordinary dress of the poorer Hindus, must have been the old Aryan costume which has survived in this old ceremony. But he wrote when the Asiatic origin of the Aryans was generally accepted. If they came from the shores of the Baltic they must have worn more than this.[2] This search of a house by a naked man is undoubtedly a bit of old Aryan law, and is found among the Greeks, Germans, Scandinavians, and Slavs, as well as among the Romans.[3] In some of these laws, *e.g.* among the Greeks and the Germans, we do not hear anything of the platter or *lanx*, and there has been a good deal of dispute with regard to the part which it played among the Romans. As early as the time of Festus it was suggested that the searcher held the platter before his eyes out of regard for the modesty of women who might be present.[4] This has been adopted by later writers in spite of its evident absurdity. The *licium* was there for the sake of modesty, and it is not explained how a man could make a search who was holding a dish before his eyes.[5] Another explanation is that the search was an infringement of the inviolability of the house, and to justify it it was necessary to

[1] Gaius, iii. 193.

[2] *Vorgeschichte der Indo-europäer*, 14.

[3] Aristophanes, *Nubes*, 497 ; Plato, *De Leg.*, xii. 7 ; Grimm, *Rechtsalterthümer*, 640 ; Leist, *Alt-Arisches Jus Civile*, ii. 241, 276, 282 ; Bernhöft, *Staat und Recht*, 223-247 ; Pernice, in *Zeit. Sav. Stift.*, xvii. 181 ; Dareste, *Études*, 299 (Swedes), 316 (Danes) ; Brunner, *Deutsche Rechtsgeschichte*, 496 ; Goudy's note to Muirhead, 2nd ed. 428. Among the Scandinavians this search for stolen property had a special name, *ransaka*, connected with our word *ransack*.

[4] Festus, *s.v.* "Lance et licio."

[5] Rein, *Criminalrecht der Römer*, 299, note.

appease the gods of the hearth. The platter was carried to make a libation to propitiate the domestic gods.[1] Perhaps the most plausible view is that the platter, which was the kind of vessel used for sacrificial purposes, is employed here that the searcher may lay the thing found upon it in symbol of gratitude to the gods.[2] Besides the solemn search, according to this ancient ritual, Gaius refers to a search conducted without any ceremony, and says that a man is liable in the *actio furti concepti,* when stolen things are sought for and found on his premises in the presence of witnesses, and the liability was a penalty of three times the value of the stolen property. Moreover, he says that if stolen property has been found in a man's house but has not been put there with his knowledge or consent, although the householder is liable in the triple penalty, he has an action in recourse against the person who has wrongfully put the stolen goods in the house. And this action of recourse bears the name of the *actio furti oblati.*[3] And Gaius goes on to say that a man who prevents the search for stolen property being made on his premises is liable in a penalty of four times the value, by the *actio furti prohibiti,* an action which he says did not exist under the Tables, but was introduced later by the prætor. It is not easy to understand how there can have been two forms of search, one with the curious ritual of the *lanx* and *licium,* and the other of an informal nature, and that in the one case the penalty, if the thing was found in the house, should be capital, whereas in the other case the owner of the house should be liable only to a money penalty. It is thought by some writers that the explanation is that no one could be compelled to allow any search except that with the old ceremonial, but if he chose to allow an informal search he exposed himself to less risk.[4] If

[1] Leist, *Græco-Italische Rechtsgeschichte,* 246; Esmein, *Mélanges,* 240.

[2] Pernice, in *Zeit. Sav. Stift.,* xvii. 182. *Lanx* was a deep hollow dish (see *Aen.,* viii. 284, *cumulantque oneratis lancibus aras*).

[3] Gaius, iii. 187.

[4] Jhering, *L'Esprit du Droit Romain* (translation, Meulenaere), ii. 154; Girard, *Manuel,* 5th ed. 408.

the two forms of search were really contemporaneous, it is difficult to see why a man who knew that stolen property was in his house should ever insist on the searcher employing the *lanx et licium*, if the only consequence of that course would be to increase the penalty if the thing was found. It seems to me much more probable that under the Twelve Tables there was only one kind of search, that conducted in the form *lance et licio*, and only one consequence of the search if the thing was found, namely, the penalty as a *fur manifestus*. It was after the Tables that the informal search with the money penalty came in, and at the same time that the action in recourse was enacted against one who had introduced stolen property into a house. Both these actions were due to the consciousness which was not at first felt, that the mere fact of finding stolen property in a man's house was not conclusive proof that he had stolen it.[1] We hear also of an old action, *furti non exhibiti*, but it does not seem to have been a part of the law of the Twelve Tables. According to a passage in Justinian's *Institutes*, which is the only place in which this action is referred to, it was introduced by the prætor as a remedy against a man who refused to give up a stolen article sought for and found in his house. The penalty is the same as for manifest theft.[2] These old actions went out of use at an early period, and our information about them is more or less scanty.

---

[1] Hitsig, in *Zeit. Sav. Stift.*, xxiii. 330; Krüger, in *Zeit. Sav. Stift.*, v. 219.

[2] *Inst.*, 4, 1, 4; Mommsen, *Röm. Strafrecht*, 749; Hitsig, in *Zeit. Sav. Stift.*, xxiii. 331. Other explanations of this action have been suggested, such as that if the searcher suspected that an article in the house had been stolen from him but was not certain of its identity, he might, instead of making the search, call upon the householder to produce—*exhibere*—the thing in question, so as to determine whose it was, and that if the householder refused to make this production, he was liable in this *actio furti non exhibiti* (Kuntze, *Excurse*, 565). According to another view still, the penalty for *furti non exhibiti* was a penalty, not against the householder at all, but against the searcher if the thing was not found in the house (Krüger, in *Zeit. Sav. Stift.*, v. 219. But these explanations are probably to be rejected.

Penalties for Manifest and for Non-Manifest Theft.—By the old law, as has been explained, the penalty for manifest theft was very severe, while that for non-manifest theft was limited to repayment of twice the value of the thing stolen. At a later time it was felt that to hand over the manifest thief as a slave, and that irrespective of the value of the thing stolen, was too severe a penalty, and one which was no longer supported by public opinion. To a primitive people there was nothing shocking in the fact that the life of the manifest thief should be forfeited, but with a change of manners the possibility of such a thing became revolting. In Greece, by the laws of Draco, a man who stole a few apples or pot-herbs was liable to the death penalty likewise.[1] And by the old Scandinavian law, if a thief was caught in the act and the property stolen was worth more than half a mark, his hands were tied behind his back and he was taken before the assembled people. The complainant and twelve co-jurors swore to the theft, and thereupon the offender was hanged without any other form of process.[2] The severity, therefore, of the Twelve Tables in regard to manifest theft is in no way unique. In a gentler age, when the capital penalty was felt to be altogether too harsh, the prætor substituted for it a penalty of four times the value of the thing stolen, so that when the theft was manifest the penalty was a fourfold one, and when it was non-manifest it was a twofold one. These private actions for theft continued to be available throughout the history of the Roman law, but were not much employed in the later period. By the imperial legislation the thief was liable to a criminal prosecution, and if found guilty was punished in his person instead of in his purse. The prosecution was at the instance of the victim of the theft, and he had the right to

[1] Plutarch, *Solon*, ch. 19; Daremberg et Saglio, *s.v.* κλοπή; Grote, *Hist.*, 3, 76.

[2] Dareste, *Études*, 298. *Cf.* among the Anglo-Saxons "Ina," chaps. xii. and xxxv., in Schmid, R., *Gesetze der Angelsachen*. See Pollock and Maitland, *Hist. of Eng. Law*, i. 30.

elect whether he would bring this criminal action, or would proceed by the old civil action for a penalty. No doubt his choice would be determined to a considerable extent by the pecuniary position of the offender, and the probability of obtaining the twofold or fourfold penalty.[1]

Condictio Furtiva.—In addition to the civil action for the double or for the fourfold penalty, according as the theft has been manifest or non-manifest, the owner of the stolen property had, by the old law, an action against the thief for the recovery of the thing itself. And this *vindicatio* or real action might be brought against a third party into whose hands the stolen property had come. But in some cases the real action might be impracticable. The thing might have perished and could not therefore be vindicated, or it might be untraceable. And if the thief had died and the thing stolen was not in the possession of the heirs, there was, by the old law, no remedy at all, for the penal action was a strictly personal one against the thief, and could not be brought against his heirs. To remedy these defects at a later date than the Twelve Tables, a new action, called the *condictio furtiva,* was introduced, by which the owner of the stolen property could sue either the thief or his heirs for its value. This action, like the old revendication, which was still available if required, was quite independent of the action against the thief for the penalty.[2]

Iniuria.—The other special delict dealt with in the Twelve Tables is that to which this name is applied. In a wide sense the word *iniuria* means everything that is unlawful, but in the more technical sense with which we are now concerned it means a delict against the person. As the term is used in the Twelve Tables it covers the more serious outrages described as *membrum ruptum* and *os fractum* and minor offences which now fall under the designation of assaults. The question as to whether the

[1] *Dig.*, 47, 2, 93 (92); *ibid.* 57 (56).

[2] Gaius, 4, 4; Mommsen, *Röm. Strafrecht*, 757; Pauly-Wissowa, *s.v.* "Condictio furtiva."

term covers also slander and the use of witchcraft is discussed later. The more serious offences, described as the breaking of a limb or a bone, have already been referred to, and it remains only to explain the less grave cases of *iniuria*. It is pretty clear that in the early law the term always denoted an act of violence against the body, such as a blow or a beating. And it is generally agreed that, at any rate at the time of the Twelve Tables, the expression *iniuria* did not involve the idea of an offence or injury to the dignity or feelings of the victim, though at a later date this was a prominent feature of the wrong. Nor was it essential to the delict of *iniuria* in the early period that there should have been any intention to injure.[1] In the early days, if the bodily injury was caused by wrongful negligence this was a case of *iniuria*, though at a later time *dolus* or wrongful intention was required. The penalty fixed by the Twelve Tables for the cases of *iniuria* other than the *membrum ruptum* or the *ossis fractio* was twenty-five *asses*, which in a simple age may have been an adequate penalty, but from the fall in the value of the *as* and the growth of wealth became altogether insufficient. Gellius preserves an anecdote of a man who for mere amusement went about striking people on the face, followed by a slave with a bag full of copper *asses*, whose business was to pay each of the persons thus insulted the statutory penalty of twenty-five small coins.[2]

Did Iniuria Include Slander or Insult?—Until recently it was generally believed that by the Twelve Tables penalties were laid down for slander or libel as well as for assaults. *Iniuria* covered an attack upon the reputation as well as an attack upon the body, and a famous passage in the Twelve Tables has been understood to mean that the slanderer was to be liable to the punishment of death. It is very doubtful, however, if this is not a misinterpretation. Such sensitiveness with regard to

[1] Cuq, *Institutions Juridiques*, 2nd ed. i. 107; Mommsen, *Röm. Strafrecht*, 790.

[2] 20, 1, 13.

reputation is hardly characteristic of primitive people. In an early stage of society slanderers are punished by rough and ready means, but to put them on a level with murderers and make them liable to a capital penalty is not what one would expect.[1] In the later law one familiar form of *iniuria* is the singing of a defamatory or satirical song or pasquinade, to bring opprobrium or ridicule upon another. It may be that it is this offence which is prohibited in the fragment of the Twelve Tables, *si quis occentavisset sive carmen condidisset quod infamiam faceret flagitiumve alteri.*[2] It has long been suggested that there is a distinction between *carmen condere* and *occentare,* the former being a singing of a defamatory song, while *occentare* is the particular kind of injurious conduct which is now called a *charivari,* and from which the Latin word at a later time was *convicium.* It is said that the offence prohibited by the Twelve Tables under the term *occentare* consisted in wrongfully exciting the anger of the populace against a man by making a din before his door to show disapprobation of his conduct. There is no doubt that this practice of beating pans and kettles before the door of a man who has incurred the disapproval of his neighbours is a very ancient one. In the modern law it is naturally treated as a form of insult for which damages can be awarded,[3] but it is difficult to believe that at the time of the Twelve Tables such offences should have been thought of, and

[1] The laws of Manu have graduated penalties for defamation varying according to the relative rank of the slanderer and the slandered. A once-born man (a Sudra) who insults a twice-born man (an Aryan) with gross invective shall have his tongue cut out (viii. 270).

[2] Cic., *De Rep.*, 4, 10, 12.

[3] See a recent case in the Province of Quebec, *Duquette* v. *Pesant*, 1892, R. J. Q. I. S. C. 465. And on the subject generally, see Voigt, *XII. Tafeln*, ii. 800 ; Cuq, *Institutions Juridiques*, 2nd ed. i. 108 ; Esmein, *Nouv. Rev. Hist.*, 1902, 352 ; Huvelin, P., *La Notion de l'Injuria dans le très ancien Droit Romain*, Lyons, 1903 ; Kübler, B., in *Zeit. Sav. Stift.*, xxv. 420 ; Girard, in *Nouv. Rev. Hist.*, 1902, xxvi. 434, and *Manuel*, 5th ed. 401, note 1. Mommsen, on the contrary, takes the prohibitions to refer to insulting songs (Mommsen, *Röm. Strafrecht*, 794) ; Strachan-Davidson, *Problems of Roman Criminal Law*, i. 107, note 3.

most unlikely that they could have been regarded as so serious as to merit the penalty of death. It seems to me much more probable that *occentare* as well as *malum carmen* referred to charms and incantations sung to injure the health or bring about the death of an enemy, and that, as has been stated earlier, this wrongful use of witchcraft was a public crime.[1]

Iniuria in the Later Law.—After the Twelve Tables the law of *iniuria* was greatly developed by the prætors. The delict was extended to all cases of injury to reputation as well as to the body. The *paterfamilias* was allowed to bring the action of his *filiusfamilias* had been assaulted or insulted, and the husband in the same way was allowed to protect the wife. An aggravated assault on a slave came to be regarded as an insult to the master, for which he could sue; and a distinction came to be made between an *atrox iniuria,* or what we might call an aggravated assault, and an ordinary assault. Whether the outrage was *atrox* or not depended on various considerations, such as the outrageous character of the act itself, as if a man is wounded or beaten with clubs; the place where the wrong is done, which from its publicity may add to the indignity, as if a man is assaulted or slandered in the theatre or the market-place; the rank of the person injured, as if a magistrate or senator is outraged by a person of low condition; or the relation between the parties, as if a parent is beaten by his child or a patron by his freedman. In place of the old penalty of twenty-five *asses*, which had now become illusory, the prætor allowed the plaintiff to fix the damages to which he considered himself entitled, and the judge had the power to award him this amount or such a lower one as seemed to meet the justice of the case. This prætorian action was called the *actio iniuriarum aestimatoria.* But if the injury was *atrox*, the prætor himself fixed the amount of damages to be given if the case was proved; and although it was in the power of the

---

[1] *Supra*, 207.

judge who tried the case to reduce the damages so fixed by the prætor, the practice was to defer to the prætor's authority, and if the defendant was found liable, to accept the amount at which the prætor had estimated the damages.[1]

Lex Cornelia de Iniuriis.—Among the courts or *quaestiones* established by Sulla and his commissioners, each of which was to deal with a certain group of crimes or offences, was one which was to deal with *iniuria.* This court was set up by the *Lex Cornelia de iniuriis,* B.C. 82. By this law three kinds of aggravated assaults, blows, beatings, and forcible invasion of a man's house, were made public delicts and must be tried criminally if committed in such circumstances as to make them *atrox.* Severe penalties, varying according to the nature of the offence and the position of the offender, might be inflicted. Death, penal servitude, exile, and, in the case of a slave, beating, are among the punishments mentioned.[2] In the latest period the person wronged had, even in the case of these aggravated assaults, always an option between bringing the civil action and proceeding by way of the criminal indictment; but where the injury was very serious the prætor discouraged proceeding civilly.[3] But it appears that the option to proceed civilly in such cases was an innovation not introduced until the time of Caracalla.[4]

Latest Law.—Under the emperors the principle of the *Lex Cornelia* was extended, and in assaults or other wrongs covered

---

[1] Gaius, iii. 224. [2] Paul, *Sentences*, 5, 4. [3] *Dig.*, 47, 10, 7, 1.

[4] *Dig.*, 47, 10, 7, 6 ; D., 47, 10, 37, 1 ; Puchta, *Cursus*, 2, s. 277 ; Cuq, in Daremberg et Saglio, *s.v.* "Injures." The text of the *Lex Cornelia de iniuriis* has not been preserved, and the references to it leave many points doubtful. See Mommsen, *Röm. Strafrecht*, 785. Some writers think that the *Lex Cornelia* abolished the civil remedy in every case when the offence was one of the three kinds—*pulsare, verberare, vi domum introire* (Girard, *Manuel*, 5th ed., 403 ; Costa, *Storia del Diritto*, 311). But it is hard to reconcile this with the texts above cited from the *Digest*. Others think the *Lex Cornelia* left the civil remedy optional in all cases (Rein, *Criminalrecht*, 273). But this is in direct conflict with Ulpian in D., 47, 10, 7, 6. On the whole, the view stated in the text seems the most plausible.

by the term *iniuria*, whether they were aggravated or not, the victim had always the choice between the civil remedy and the criminal indictment.[1]

The Blood-Feud and Composition for Wrongs among other Peoples.—The instinct of the Romans for law and order is illustrated by the fact that the right of the injured individual to take vengeance by his own hand or with the help of his kinsmen is cut down to very small proportions, even so early as the date of the Twelve Tables. As we have seen, in all quarters of the world and among almost all races of mankind the same process of evolution as regards the punishment of wrongs can be observed. In the beginning there is no attempt on the part of the State to protect the life or property of the citizen. Offences against the public authority itself or sins against the gods, which may bring down the wrath of Heaven upon the community, are punished in the common interest by the king or the rulers of the people. They are public crimes, and may be dealt with by those whose duty it is to protect the public interest. But wrongs committed against a private citizen are not regarded as public affairs at all, and it is left to the victim or his kinsmen to take vengeance for them at discretion. At a later stage among some peoples the State takes up the duty of punishing the murderer, but among other peoples the blood-feud continues to be exercised by the kinsmen, though the right of public prosecution is open.[2] The victim of less serious wrongs, such as theft or assault, is first encouraged and then compelled to take a money compensation as a substitute for his right to exact vengeance, though where the offender is caught red-handed the old right of private vengeance may be preserved. In course of time there comes

[1] *Institutes*, 4, 4, 10.

[2] In Scotland, until comparatively modern times, the sovereign could not remit the sentence of death unless the murderer produced "letters of slains" signed by the four principal branches of the kindred of the deceased, showing that they had received the assythment or blood-money (see Green's *Encyclopædia of Scots Law*, *s.v.* "Assythment").

to be a fixed tariff for many of these minor offences. Finally, wilful injuries to persons and property come to be looked upon as public offences endangering the order of the State, and are punished by the State itself, while the victim of the wrong is left in some cases with a pecuniary claim for damages in addition, but with no right to exact a penalty. Among the Romans the blood-feud for murder has disappeared before the Twelve Tables, though the right to kill an offender caught in the act is still retained in some cases.[1] Personal vengeance may still be taken for the serious mutilation of the body described as *membrum ruptum*, the nature of which has been previously explained, but for the breaking of a bone and for less serious assaults a tariff has been fixed of a very simple character. It is characteristic of the practical good sense of the Romans that the law does not attempt to graduate the composition payable with the particularity which is found in so many of the early laws, and that at a comparatively early period the claim for a penalty resolves itself into a right to such damages as the judge shall award. We do not find among the Romans a minute scale of compensation by which, for example, sixty shillings is to be paid for cutting off a nose, thirty shillings for an ear, fifteen shillings for a forefinger, twelve shillings for a middle finger, as in the laws of the Saxon King Alfred.[2] Attempts of this kind to fix with minute particularity the penalty for various wrongs are common enough in the early laws of other Aryan peoples, but they point to a rather primitive stage in the development of legal ideas. There can be no doubt that the blood-feud existed at one time among all the Aryan peoples, though it disappeared very early among the Romans and among the

[1] Traces of the blood-feud are not wanting, such as the duty of the heir to prosecute the murderer. *Honestati enim heredis convenit, qualemcumque mortem testatoris inultam non praetermittere* (Paul, *Sentences*, 3, 5, 2 ; C. 6, 35, 1 ; Leist-Glück, *Serie der B.*, 37 and 38, S. 64 *seq.* ; Kohler, *Shakespeare, &c.*, 156).

[2] Schmid, R., *Gesetze der Angelsachsen*, "Aelf.," cc. 47, 48, 57, 58.

Hindus, whereas among the Persians it lasted down to modern times, while in some parts of Europe, such as Albania and Corsica, it is still in operation. The history of the blood-feud, superseded by a money composition, may be studied alike in the early laws of the Celts, the Slavs, the Germans, and the Scandinavians.[1] But although the blood-feud is found among all the Aryans, we must not fall into the error of assuming that it is in any way their peculiar property. On the contrary, it is one of those few institutions which belong, not to any particular race, but to a stage of civilisation through which the Aryan peoples, with many others, have passed, while many savage peoples still remain in it.

[1] See a particularly valuable collection of illustrations in Kohler, *Shakespeare vor dem Forum der Jurisprudenz*, 131 *seq.* *Cf.* Dareste, *Études d'Histoire du Droit;* Brunner, *Deutsche Rechtsgeschichte*, i. 156, and ii. 585; Bernhöft, *Staat und Recht*, 208; Kovalewsky, M., *Coutume Contemporaine et Loi Ancienne*, Paris, 1893 (Ossetes); *Nouv. Rev. Hist.*, 1907, xxxi. 177 (Greece). In High Albania the blood-feud is still in full use (Durham, M. E., *High Albania*, 32).

CHAPTER XXII

Edicta Magistratuum

The Checks on Magistrates. — The political insight of the Romans is nowhere seen to greater advantage than in the degree of power which they gave to the magistrates. They perceived that a jealous limitation of the authority of these great officials would hinder the progress of the community, and that individual freedom was not to be bought at the expense of strong government. Rather was it only by strong government that it could be secured. Against the danger which might arise from a too arbitrary use of the power of the magistrates they sought to guard, not by narrow limitations of the authority committed to them, but by other checks. Such checks were:—

1. The limitation of the magistrate's power to a definite period — generally of one year — at the expiration of which he was responsible for his conduct to the Senate, and liable to a process resembling impeachment for abuse of his official position.[1]

2. The having two or more magistrates holding the same office with co-ordinate powers, each of whom has the right of *intercessio*—*i.e.* of blocking any act of his colleague, *par majorve potestas plus valeto.*

3. A graduation of rank by which a higher magistrate could check any abuse of power by a lower.

4. The *tribunicia potestas*, one of the chief functions of which was the *intercessio* upon acts of all magistrates, except those of a dictator.

[1] Karlowa, i. 204; Mommsen, *Abriss des römischen Staatsrechts*, 135.

Theoretical Absolutism.—This theoretical absolutism is very characteristic of Roman ideas. Thus the *paterfamilias* in early times had absolute power over those in his *patria potestas.* No doubt it was checked by the supervision of the *gens*, which in an extreme case might exclude an offender from his gentile rights. And the fear of the censor's note was a restraint. But in theory the *pater* is absolute. So with the early kings. The Senate was merely a council of advisers which could counsel but could not restrain. And the idea was not lost when the Republic came in. Instead of one life-king we have two year-kings, subject to the two checks—(1) that one of them could veto the orders of the other; and (2) that they were liable to "impeachment" on leaving office.

In considering the great powers possessed by the Roman magistrates it must not be forgotten that the whole constitution was bound up with the State religion, and the sacred character which attached to the office of the magistrate generated a feeling of moral restraint. Every magistrate was to administer his office according to the will of the gods, and to ascertain this will he had the right of taking the auspices. The right to take the *maxima auspicia* belonged to consuls, prætors, censors, and dictators, and these were the *magistratus majores.* Minor magistrates were the ædiles, the *tribuni plebis*, the quæstors, and the *tribuni militum.*

Religious Character of Office.—It was this auspicate character of office, this necessity for the holder of it to commune with the gods, which made the patricians regard the admission of the plebeians to the magistracies as impossible. The *patres* for a long time had the idea that it was one of the prerogatives of their order to be able to discover the will of the gods. If magistrates were elected without this power—and the plebeians did not possess it—how was the State to be safely governed? This made them appoint censors to guard the sanctity of the Senate when, by the *Lex Canuleia*, the *plebs* at last got the *conubium.* This made them institute prætors and curule ædiles when the plebs were admitted to the consulship.

All the higher magistrates had *imperium et auspicium.* The *imperium* involved the *jus vocationis*—the right of issuing a summons to parties to appear before him—and the *jus decernendi*—the right of pronouncing a *decretum* or judicial sentence. The magistrate could compel obedience to his orders by taking security or by fine and imprisonment—*jus pignoris capionis, jus multae dictionis.* Even some of the minor magistrates—*e.g.* the tribunes, had the *jus prensionis* or *prendendi praesentem* —*i.e.* the right of arresting a man who was before them, and of keeping him in detention. But the Roman's house, like the Englishman's, was his castle, and he could not be dragged thence; and a tribune had no *vocatio*, but he enjoyed an exemption from the *vocatio* of other magistrates.

The *imperium* also included the *jus edicendi*—the right to issue an edict or proclamation, and, as we shall see, this right became in the hands of the prætors a most powerful engine for the development of the law. Like the *jus decernendi,* it was one of the attributes of the ancient kings which had descended to the magistrates, who held, so to say, the royal authority in commission.

Widening of Power of Prætor.—The first edicts were probably of special, and not of general, application. When the office of prætor was created in 367 B.C., the new official was invested with the supreme judicial power which had formerly belonged to the kings, and afterwards to the consuls. When a person appeared before him alleging a civil wrong for which no remedy had been provided by the Twelve Tables, the prætor in those early days ordered the defendant to make a wager—*sponsio*—with the plaintiff that he would pay a certain sum if the plaintiff's averments were proved to be true. The *sponsio* grounding a *legis actio*, the matter was sent to a *judex* to ascertain the facts. Or, if two parties disputed the ownership of a thing, the prætor decided who should have the possession *ad interim*, on giving security, thus introducing the most important legal conception of possession, as distinct from ownership. But the excessive rigidity of the old procedure made it necessary by hook or by crook to get an action relevantly laid upon the express terms of the Twelve Tables. And the old forms of conveyance and of contract—the *mancipatio*, the *in jure cessio*, the *stipulatio*—were so formal that equitable considerations or questions of intention of parties were altogether excluded. The plaintiff either had a clear right because all the forms had been complied with, or he had no right at all because some formality had been neglected. The prætor's hands were tied, and his power of disposing of cases in an equitable manner was very restricted.[1] His powers were, however, greatly widened by the *Lex Aebutia* and by the *Leges Juliae*. The date of the *Lex Aebutia* is uncertain, but it seems to have been passed between 148 B.C. and 125 B.C.[2] It would seem that the *Lex Aebutia* gave the parties an option to apply to the magistrates for a *formula* or to employ the old procedure. The *Leges Juliae* rather more than a century later (16 B.C.) abolished, except in two special cases, the old system of procedure—the *legis actiones*—and substituted for it the new one called the formulary procedure, which had long been optional. Instead of presiding at the antiquated ceremonial of the vindication and the oath, the magistrate is to formulate in a simple way the issue which the juryman or *judex* is to try.[3]

---

[1] Some writers think the prætor must have had some discretion, even under the *legis actiones*, to give an action for which no express authority could be found in the Tables, and to refuse one when the plaintiff could show a right of action by the words of the Tables, but had no just claim. But the arguments in favour of the existence of this discretionary power, except in the sphere of administration, are not very convincing. See Girard, *Org. Jud.*, 69, note 2. *Contra*, Lenel, in *Zeit. Sav. Stift.*, xxx. 329, and references; Costa, *Storia delle Fonti*, 57, note 1.

[2] See article by Girard, in *Nouvelle Revue Historique de Droit Français*, 1897, 249, 294; and Girard, *Manuel*, 5th ed. 998.

[3] See Wlassak, *Römische Processgesetze*, i. 62-72, and 85-103; and *Nouv.*

The Lex Aebutia and the Leges Juliae.—Probably the *Lex Aebutia* and the *Leges Juliae* did not give any cut and dry scheme. They provided, generally, that actions should be brought in the first instance before the prætor. If it appeared to him in his discretion that a relevant case was presented, he must set down the issue in writing—*formula*—*verba concepta*—and remit it to a *judex*—*i.e.* to a private citizen taken from a panel, to be tried. The *formula* began with the appointment of a *judex*—if possible one agreed upon by the parties—*Titius judex esto.* It then went on, "If you (*judex*) are satisfied that such and such a right exists, or that such and such a fact is true (*intentio*), condemn the defendant (*condemnatio*); if not, acquit him"—*si paret, condemna; si non paret, absolve.*[1]

The immense step marked by the *Lex Aebutia* and the Julian laws was that it was no longer necessary to frame an issue out of the Twelve Tables. The prætor had not to draw up the pleadings or *formula* himself, but merely to decide that there was a relevant case presented, and that the pleadings were in proper shape; that there was, as we should say, a joinder of issue, or, in the Roman phrase which the French law has retained, that there was *litis contestatio.* The plaintiff had to see that everything material to his case was stated, and the defendant had to see that every defence or exception upon which he relied was duly set down. Thus the formula generally contained, as pleadings do to-day, a number of statements drawn up by the plaintiff, and a number of other statements in defence drawn up by the defendant.

Perpetual Edicts.—After the *Lex Aebutia* the prætors began

Rev. Hist., 1889, 298. The two special cases in which the *legis actiones* continued to be used were in proceedings as to *damnum infectum*, and in actions before the centumviral court. Cf. Strachan.Davidson, *Problems of Roman Criminal Law*, 1, 70; and Greenidge, *Legal Procedure*, p. 170. There is much that is doubtful about the *Lex Aebutia.*

[1] Observe the division is not between "law" and "fact," as in the English jury-system. The *prætor* may, and does, ask the *judex* to pronounce on questions of law.

to find the importance of following some general rules, and the advantages which would ensue to the community if these rules were generally known. Accordingly they took to publishing edicts of a different nature from the special and private ones to which I have referred. These edicts, limited to special cases, came to be called *edicta repentina.* The new kind were called *edicta perpetua* or *perpetuae jurisdictionis causa proposita.* This was a publication by the prætor at the commencement of his year, that if certain facts were averred he would grant a case for a *judex* to try. *E.g.* the old law regarded an obligation as binding, although one of the parties had been coerced into it. If a man had undertaken to pay money he was bound, although in fact he had never willingly consented, but had yielded to the fear of violence. This was obviously unjust, and the prætor declared that he would not treat an obligation as binding if it was shown to have been extorted by violence or threats of violence. *Quod metus causa gestum erit ratum non habebo.* Again it was a too common experience of travellers to find that their horses or goods had disappeared mysteriously without its being possible to fix anyone with liability. The prætor declared that he would hold the innkeeper or the carrier liable, unless he could show that the things had been destroyed by *vis major*—the act of God or the king's enemies, as English lawyers say. Innkeepers and carriers were by this rule to guarantee the honesty of their servants, *nautae caupones stabularii quod cuiusque salvum fore receperint, nisi restituent in eos judicium dabo.* The rules of the modern civil law as to the liability of common carriers and hotelkeepers are derived from this edict.

The Traditionary Edict.—In declarations of this kind the incoming prætor indicated the principles by which he intended to be guided during his tenure of office. At first these proclamations were not binding, even upon the prætor who issued them. One of the charges against Verres was that he had shown gross partiality by not adhering to the rules which he had declared in his edict. And, without such gross breach of trust, it was common enough for a prætor who thought he could improve on his original edict to vary it by *edicta repentina*, or subsidiary edicts issued during the year. As this led to a want of certainty in the administration of justice, it was enacted by the *Lex Cornelia*, 67 B.C., that the prætors should abide by their first edict, *ut praetores ex edictis suis perpetuis jus dicerent*. But the new prætor who succeeded was, in theory, entirely free to disregard the edict of his predecessor, and to publish a new one, containing, perhaps, rules directly opposed to those which had been in operation the year before. In practice little mischief seems to have resulted from this freedom. The common course seems to have been for the new prætor to get some jurists in whom he had confidence to go over the edict of the retiring prætor, making minor alterations which experience had shown to be desirable, embodying the *edicta repentina* of his predecessor, if these contained any valuable principle, and sometimes inserting a few new rules which commended themselves to the new prætor and his advisers. In time, the profession and the public felt the importance of adhering to settled rules, and the convenience of making gradual emendations. Novelties were seldom introduced unless they had been called for by this public opinion. The edicts were published upon boards or tables of wood painted white and set up in the Forum. Hence the edicts are sometimes called the *album*. As time went on, the edict became more and more stereotyped. Rules which had worked well, and had approved themselves to the public, were not altered and were handed down from one prætor to another. This part of the edict which the new prætor no longer ventured to change got the name of the *edictum tralaticium*, or the traditionary edict. The new prætor confined himself to making a few additions—*nova edicta, novae clausulae*. By the time of Cicero the greater part of the edict had already become tralaticious, so that he describes the prætorian law as a sort of customary law: *Consuetudine . . . jus esse putatur id, quod voluntate omnium sine lege vetustas comprobarit. . . . Quo in genere et alia sunt multa et eorum multo maxima pars quae praetores edicere consuerunt.*[1]

In this way a regular system of law grew up in the Prætorian Court which formed a very important addition to the statutory and customary law already in force. One might say the edict was a kind of Code of Civil Procedure, including a good deal of substantive law which the prætors slowly built up bit by bit. But in spite of the differences of form, the edict corresponds more closely to our judge-made law than to our statutory law. The prætor's attention was called to some defect or anomaly in the law applicable to a case which came before him. He laid down a rule which seemed to him to do justice in the particular case, and then declared that if similar facts again presented themselves he would give the same decision. The rule was then in all probability inserted in the next year's edict. The edict did not state general principles, but declared what the prætor would do in certain circumstances: "I will hold an agreement in such and such terms valid"; "In such a case I will grant an action"; "If a minor has been taken advantage of I will give him *restitutio in integrum*"; "In such a case the party must make exhibition."[2] As, originally, the edict was merely intended for one year, and expressed the promise only of the incoming prætor, the party desiring to avail himself of the remedy must raise his action during the year in which that particular prætor was in office. From this originated the rule that a prætorian action—that is an action

[1] *De Inv.*, ii. 22, 67. See Pernice, in *Zeit. Sav. Stift.*, xx. 156 and xxii. 59.

[2] This is one of the similarities between the influence exerted on the English law by the judges, and especially by the Chancellor, and the work of the Roman prætor. The changes made by both are mainly not by laying down new abstract rules, but by granting new remedies. As Mr. Bryce expresses it, "both were concerned with remedies; both acted through their control of procedure" (*Studies in History and Jurisprudence*, ii. 281).

not based on the old *jus civile*, but on the prætor's edict, must always be brought within a year after the cause of action had arisen. About 242 B.C. the increase of commerce made it necessary to appoint a second prætor. To him were assigned all cases arising between two peregrins—*i.e.* foreigners living at Rome, or between a Roman and a peregrin. He was called from this the *praetor peregrinus*. It was impossible for him to apply the strict *jus civile*, for a peregrin could not be a party to the forms of the *mancipatio* and *in jure cessio* which the *jus civile* required. The prætor was, therefore, obliged to seek out principles of equity applicable to traders of different countries in dealing with each other. The equitable rules which he introduced were what the Romans called the *jus gentium*, which I shall describe more fully a little later. One merit, and a great one, of the prætor's edict is peculiar to it, namely, the opportunity which it gave of trying legal experiments. It is legislation in fact if not in theory, but tentative legislation. If the prætor introduces a new remedy to meet a particular set of cases, there is nothing final about this. It can be tried for a year, and the profession and the public will see how it works. If on the whole it is approved of, the new prætor will retain it in his edict. On the other hand, if it has excited unfavourable comment it can be dropped. In modern systems of law defective statutes frequently remain for years unamended owing to the difficulty of getting parliaments to give time to them, or of finding citizens sufficiently anxious to press for the needed reform. And in like manner a case wrongly decided by a Court may stand as a stone of offence for a generation because the same point does not happen to come before a Court which can overrule the wrong decision. The elasticity in this respect of the prætor's edict is really admirable, and one can easily see how, in capable hands, it was made an exceptionally useful engine for the work of legal reform.[1]

[1] See Bryce, *Studies*, ii. 284.

Urban Prætor Borrows from Foreign Prætor.—Gradually the *praetor urbanus*, perceiving the simplicity and justice of these new rules which were thus introduced for the benefit of foreigners, began to think he might apply them to citizens. He took to borrowing a good deal from the edict of his colleague. In this way the *jus civile* became saturated with new and simpler forms and doctrines. The prætor could grant or refuse an action as seemed to him good. When his hands were freed from the chains of the old procedure by the passing of the *Lex Aebutia*, the edict rapidly became the chief engine of legal development. It became what Cicero calls it—the *viva vox juris civilis*.

And from Provincial Governors.—In addition to the edicts of the two prætors at Rome, the provincial governors each issued an edict for his province. They borrowed largely from the prætorian edicts, but made such alterations and additions as might make their edict suitable to the particular province. In this way where a province had customs and laws of its own, these might be retained if desirable by being put into the *edictum provinciale*. The provincial edicts also made regulations for the protection of quasi-property in land and quasi-real rights. For all land in the provinces belonged in theory to the State. The occupants had only a precarious enjoyment as long as they were left in possession by the State. But though this was their legal position, they had, practically, the right of ownership, for they were not disturbed, and they alienated their lands or left them by will just as if they had been absolute owners. These provincial edicts were, in their turn, studied by the *praetor peregrinus* at Rome, and helped him to see what rules were observed in different countries. They served him as collections of statistics.[1]

[1] On this introduction of foreign rules the work of Mitteis, *Reichsrecht und Volksrecht*, is very instructive.

Edicts of Ædiles.—The ædiles also issued edicts relating to the matters falling within their competence, such as police regulations and the rules of open markets for the sale of slaves or cattle. One or two of their regulations affected the general law —*e.g.* it was the ædiles who first laid down the rules which the French law among others still retains: (1) that the seller is bound for latent defects, even when they were not known to him, unless he stipulates that he sells without warranty; and (2) that the buyer in case he discovers the thing sold has such a latent defect or vice is to have an option. He may return the thing and get back the money by the *actio redhibitoria*, or, if he prefer it, he may keep the thing and sue for a return of a fair proportion of the price. This is the *actio quanti minoris.* But as to defects which the buyer might see for himself, there is no warranty. *Caveat emptor.* "His eye is his merchant." But except for a few provisions of which these are the most important, the ædiles introduced no changes into the general law.

Prætor's Edict Main Mode of Changing the Law.—The prætor's edict had already become in the time of Cicero the great organ of legal development. He complains that the Twelve Tables are no longer studied, and that philosophical speculation is neglected from the prevailing view that the best fountain of jurisprudence is the prætor's edict. *Non ergo, a praetoris edicto, ut plerique nunc, neque a XII. Tabulis ut superiores, sed penitus ex intima philosophia hauriendam juris disciplinam putas* (*De Leg.* i. 5, 17). The law made by the prætors was called *jus praetorium* or *jus honorarium.* We might translate the latter term by "magistrates' law"—law made by those who hold the *honores.* It would include the rules brought in by the ædiles. Most of the *jus praetorium* consisted of commercial law, and this formed the bulk of the *jus gentium.* But the prætors changed the law even in matters which concerned citizens only—*e.g.* to the *jus praetorium* belong the changes in the law of succession by the grants made by them of *bonorum possessio* to emancipated children or others who were not heirs by the *jus civile.* So also the *actio exercitoria* or the *actio institoria*, by which the shipowner or the shopkeeper, as the case may be, is sued for debts contracted by the captain of the ship or the manager of the shop, was part of the *jus praetorium*, though at first these actions seem to have been competent only against citizens as they presuppose *potestas.*[1] Papinian in a famous passage says, *jus praetorium est quod praetores introduxerunt, adjuvandi, vel supplendi, vel corrigendi juris civilis gratia propter utilitatem publicam.*[2] Before the *Lex Aebutia* the prætor's work was mainly *adjuvare vel supplere.* But afterwards he began boldly *corrigere.* At first his method was to apply the rule of law to cases not within the contemplation of its framer. He said, in effect, "This case is analogous to the case dealt with by the law. In extending the rule to it I shall be within the spirit if not within the letter." But just as the English Courts of equity came by a very similar process to create a body of rules overriding upon many points the rules of common law, so it was with the Roman prætor. After the *Lex Aebutia* the *judex* who heard the case was far more dependent than formerly upon the magistrate's instructions. He might in certain circumstances be directed to find for the defendant, though by the *jus civile* the defendant would have been liable, or he might be told to find for the plaintiff in circumstances where the civil law gave no remedy. As in England there might be a case in equity but none at common law, so in Rome there might be a case because the prætor thought it fair.

Moreover, when the prætor felt obliged to grant an action with which he did not sympathise, he might, if he chose, grant it only upon the plaintiff's finding security for costs. This might stop the suit, or deter others from raising similar ones.

[1] See D., 5, 1, 19, 3; Karlowa, i. 469.

[2] D., i. 1, 7, 1.

Character of Jus Gentium.—Nothing can be more misleading than to conceive of the *jus gentium* as in the least degree analogous to what is now called private international law. The fundamental principle upon which this system rests—viz. that in certain cases the Court will decide a question before it by the application of the law of a foreign independent power was never admitted at Rome. Indeed the birth of that science, as Huber has shown, was directly traceable to the break-up of the Roman Empire, and the conflict of laws which ensued on the rise of a number of different European States with their various laws and customs.

There was never any question at Rome as to whether either the *lex loci actus* or the *lex domicilii* should prevail over the *lex fori*. It was, indeed, very usual when a foreign country had been subdued and reduced to the rank of a province to leave it a limited "home rule," and allow it to retain its own laws; and the provincial constitution, the *lex* or *formula provinciae*, frequently contained a clause conceding to the people the right *suis legibus uti*. But the judge who administered this law was no more applying private international law than is the Judicial Committee of the Privy Council when it decides a case from Jersey by the law of that island.[1]

It is unfortunate that no uniform rendering of *jus gentium* has been adopted by English writers.[2]

The definition of the term with which the work of Gaius opens, adopted by the compilers of Justinian's *Institutes*, is "the law which natural reason settles for all mankind, which is equally observed among all peoples, and is called the law of the nations, being as it were the law which all the nations use."[3] This definition is obviously coloured by the philosophic specu-

[1] It is surprising to find *jus gentium* given as "international private law" by the translator of Mommsen (*History*, i. 166).

[2] Some of the Germans—*e.g.* Jörs—employ the word *Weltrecht* for *jus gentium*, and *Landrecht* for *jus civile*.

[3] Gaius, i. 1. "Law of Nations" is inseparably associated in English with international law.

lations of a later age than that at which the *jus gentium* took its rise. The closest modern parallel is the law-merchant, and Bell's definition of this in the preface to his *Commentaries on the Law of Scotland* would have been accepted by a Roman lawyer almost word for word, as an excellent account of the *jus gentium*. "The law-merchant is universal. It is a part of the law of nations, grounded upon the principles of natural equity, as regulating the transactions of men who reside in different countries and carry on the intercourse of nations independently of the local customs and municipal laws of particular states. For the illustration of this law, the decisions of Courts, and the writings of lawyers in different countries, are as the recorded evidence of the application of the general principle, not making the law, but handing it down, not to be quoted as precedents or as authorities to be implicitly followed, but to be taken as guides towards the establishment of the pure principles of general jurisprudence."

No doubt, ultimately, the *jus gentium* or the equitable principles underlying it invaded other branches of Roman law. But it was in its origin and in its important aspect for us, a body of principles of general mercantile law administered by a Court with wide equitable powers. In its root-conceptions, and in its animating spirit, the *jus gentium* was the antithesis of the *jus civile*. Before the one the foreigner had no rights, except such as flowed from the free grace of the Roman State. Before the other Roman and Greek, Carthaginian and Syrian, in a word, every free man, stood on the same footing.

To the one the letter—the *rigor juris*—is everything; the latter looks to the spirit, the *aequitas*. The question in the *jus civile* is, "Were the forms complied with?" in the *jus gentium*, "What was the intention of parties?" The spirit of the *jus gentium* was to have constant regard to the *bona fides* of the parties, and to prevent the technicalities of law leading to the denial of substantial justice. The *jus civile* asked only, "Is it so nominated in the bond?" The whole mercantile law of

Rome, including the law of sale, hiring, deposit, mandate, partnership, and agency, belongs to the *jus gentium*. And as Professor Sohm justly observes, it is the law of obligations, and especially the law of these consensual contracts, the *negotia bonae fidei*, which forms the really permanent contribution made by the Roman law to practical jurisprudence. What he says of Germany is true of other countries whose law is based on that of Rome.

"The Roman law of obligations will endure. It cannot be abolished. The intention of the purchaser, and hirer, &c., is the same in all ages, and it is this intention alone that the Roman law has made clear. The legislation of Germany may indeed repeal the Roman law on this subject; in point of fact, however, it cannot fail to be a substantial re-enactment of it."[1]

How were the Romans, stubbornly attached as they were to the old *jus civile*, and by no means free from narrowness and even philistinism on the intellectual side, induced to open their doors to a system so un-Roman? Jhering, in an eloquent passage in his *Geist des Römischen Rechts*, says: "It was a question of abjuring Rome in Rome herself, of detaching themselves from traditional ideas without abandoning them, and of applying upon an equal footing two opposite ideas to the whole system of the law, the national Roman idea and the cosmopolitan idea, of thinking as a Roman with regard to certain institutions and not others."[2] He compares the moral as well as intellectual qualities which the Romans needed to exert, in order to grapple successfully with the task, with those which a rigidly Catholic country would need to show in admitting Protestants to equal rights and liberties.

To attempt anything like an adequate examination of the causes which led to the admission of the *jus gentium* would be impossible in the space at my disposal. But the following points especially are to be kept in view:—

1. The growth of commerce and of intercourse with foreign

[1] *Institutes* (Ledlie's trans.), 1, 74.

[2] *Esprit*, 1, 331.

nations made great modification of the *jus civile* absolutely necessary, unless the progress of the city was to be arrested.

2. This intercourse itself had widened the mental horizon of the Romans by making them acquainted with foreign laws and customs. And among the influences which worked most strongly upon them was their contact with the Greeks, and their increased knowledge of Greek literature and philosophy. It was not that the Romans directly borrowed much of the substantive law, though the *Lex Rhodia de jactu* and the law of hypothec, in its origin, were importations from Greece. The Romans had undoubtedly as a nation a more decided legal bent than the Greeks, and it is quite characteristic of the difference that the Roman schoolboy learnt the Twelve Tables by heart at an age when the Greek boy was reciting stirring passages from the *Iliad* and the *Odyssey*.[1] But the spell which the brilliant and beautiful genius of Greece cast over the society of Rome was not without a powerful effect upon the law. In place of their narrow conceptions of citizen-law before which the alien had no rights, they were introduced to speculations about a natural law applying to citizen and alien alike, and about a commonwealth of all mankind governed by the impartial justice of the gods.[2] This idea of natural law drawn from the φυσικόν

[1] Cicero laments that this good old fashion has gone out—*a parvis enim, Quinte, didicimus "si in jus vocat ito" et ejusmodi leges alias nominare*—and *Discebamus enim pueri XII. Tabulas ut carmen necessarium quas jam nemo discit* (*De Leg.*, 2, 4, 9 ; *ibid.*, 2, 23, 59).

It is interesting to notice that towards the close of the Republic, the Romans of the upper class had much the same feeling about things Greek as the German noble class had about things French in the time of Louis XIV. The Roman nobles affected the Greek language, Greek dress, Greek mode of arranging the hair, and so forth, and looked down upon the simple Roman ways, just as in Germany French was the Court speech, and everything French was thought to have grace and distinction, while things German savoured of the *bourgeoisie*.

[2] Of course in the latest period, when the seat of Empire was at Constantinople, the influence of the Greek law upon the Roman became much more constant and powerful (see Mitteis, *Reichsrecht und Volksrecht*).

17

δίκαιον of the Stoa was like a new spirit breathing upon the dry bones of the *jus civile.* Cicero contemplates the training of the lawyer as directly based upon philosophy, instead of as formerly upon a literal knowledge of the Twelve Tables or the Edict.[1]

3. In addition to the growth of commerce and the leaven of Hellenism, the rise of the *jus gentium* was facilitated by a new class of learned and accomplished lawyers, themselves deeply imbued with foreign culture. These early jurists, who were almost all men of rank and wealth, were in the habit of giving advice without fee on matters of business as well as of strict law, and were consulted, Cicero roundly says, "about all things human and divine." The houses of those of them who attained a high reputation were thronged with citizens, who came to consult them about their litigations, the sale or purchase of land, the marriage of their daughters, and even the methods of farming. It is no wonder that we find Horace saying "the lawyer, when the client knocks at his door at cock-crow, envies the lot of the farmer."[2] It became usual for young Romans who were intended for a public career to be sent as pupils to the jurists, as Cicero himself was to Scaevola. They were allowed to be present at the consultations with clients, and the master discussed with them the legal questions which presented themselves. It is easy to see how in this way a more free and speculative treatment of law was rapidly engendered. The influence of the jurists rapidly increased, and with the rise of legal authorship, by which a systematic view of some branch of law was made possible, their influence became the dominant factor in developing a scientific body of legal principles. From the first penetrated with the Stoic philosophy, the jurisconsults gradually became more and more emanicipated from the narrow

[1] *Non ergo a praetoris edicto, ut plerique nunc, neque a XII. Tabulis, ut superiores, sed penitus ex intima philosophia hauriendam juris disciplinam putas* (*De Leg.*, i. 6, 17).

[2] *Sat.*, i. 1, 9.

rigidity of the traditional national jurisprudence, a tendency which must have been strengthened by the advent of foreign jurists to Rome. It is not without significance that many of the most famous jurists were themselves foreigners. Salvius Julianus, the compiler of the Edict, was born in Africa. Q. Cervidius Scaevola was a Greek, and of the five great "classical" jurists who belong to a somewhat later period, not one can be pronounced with certainty to have been a Roman. Such provincial lawyers, though they were Roman citizens, were not Romans of the type of Cato, belonged to no great Roman family, and had none of the passionate and exclusive conservatism of such Romans *de vieille roche.* In the eyes of these men the *jus civile* had no peculiar sanctity, and the *jus gentium* afforded an admirable field for the working out of general rules of law, and illustrating their application in particular cases. We have at Rome a body of learned lawyers imbued with the desire to rationalise the old law, and to reduce it to a philosophical system, and able to exert a strong influence upon the prætors whose edicts could be made so admirable an engine to effect this purpose. And it is these facts alone which can explain the remarkable evolution of the Roman law and the high degree of excellence to which it attained.[1]

Examples of Prætorian Law.

A few illustrations may be given of prætorian remedies

In Integrum Restitutio.—Suppose a minor has been cheated, or, at any rate, that advantage has been taken of his youth to lead him into an unprofitable transaction. The prætor said, "I will make the other party put things back in their former position. I will grant an *in integrum restitutio.*"

The Publician Action.—Or, suppose a *res mancipi,* which can be conveyed only by *mancipatio* or *in jure cessio,* has been bought

[1] The fullest work on the *jus gentium* is Voigt's *Das jus naturale aequum et bonum und jus gentium der Römer.*

and delivered to the buyer without employing either of these forms. By the *jus civile* the seller is still the owner. He can bring a *vindicatio* to get the thing back, even though he has the price of it in his pocket. But the prætor gave the buyer the *exceptio rei venditae et traditae.* Or, suppose the buyer in such a case has lost the possession of the thing which he had acquired *bona fide* but without the proper form of conveyance. The thing has got into the hands of another. The buyer cannot bring a *rei vindicatio* for his title as owner is defective. He has not the *dominium ex jure Quiritium.* But some prætor called Publicius invented an action called after him the *actio Publiciana*, by which the buyer, though, strictly speaking, he was not the owner, was given the right to sue by a legal fiction that he had become owner by *usucapion.* The case sent to the *judex* is, "If you, the judge, find that the plaintiff would have been owner of the thing *if he had held it for the period of usucapion*, then give judgment in his favour."

The buyer who has this right of action is called the bonitarian owner, as opposed to the quiritarian owner who has the strict legal title. He has an equitable title which the prætor protects, just as in England the Chancellors protected equitable rights which were not protected by the common law. And even if the quiritarian owner has recovered possession of the thing, the prætor will let the bonitarian owner bring the Publician action. The defendant may plead the *exceptio justi dominii*—that is, that he has the legal title. But to this the plaintiff may rejoin by the *replicatio doli* or *rei venditae et traditae.* Or, let us suppose, a thing has been acquired on a good title and in good faith from a man whom the buyer believed to be the owner, though in fact he was not—*a non domino.* If the possessor loses the possession he may recover the thing from a third party by the *actio Publiciana*, on the fiction that he has completed *usucapion.* As a *bonae fidei possessor* the prætor treats him as owner in a question with anybody but the true *dominus.* The first case, in which the thing was acquired from the quiritarian owner but by an informal conveyance, is called *in bonis possessio.* The second case where it was acquired *a non domino,* though perhaps by a valid form of conveyance, was *bonae fidei possessio.*

There are, therefore, two cases in which the *actio Publiciana* is available:—(1) When a *res mancipi* has been acquired without *mancipatio* or *in jure cessio;* and (2) when anything has been acquired *a non domino.* It is easy to see what a deadly blow was in the first case dealt by the prætor at the formal conveyances of the old law. In the second application of the Publician action we see a great step taken towards the doctrine that a purchaser in good faith deserves every protection, and that to make his position insecure is to shackle the advance of commerce.[1]

Negotiorum Gestio.—Again, take the doctrine called *negotiorum gestio.* If it appear that A. during B.'s absence has interfered to do something for B.'s advantage, then A. can claim compensation for his outlay from B., and, on the other hand, if A. has done harm, B. has an action against him. *E.g.* A. is absent in the wars. His house shows signs of falling down. B., his neighbour, has it repaired. B. can recover his expenses, provided they were spent to A.'s advantage *at the time.* If A. had abandoned the house, and it was of no value to him, B. could not recover, though he had spent money upon it in good faith. But if it was a valuable house, and his repairs saved it, he can recover, though later on, before A. came back, the house should chance to be burnt down.[2] *Negotiorum gestio* was quite a new doctrine. The early lawyers saw great difficulty in admitting that there could be a legal claim for repayment where there had been no contract between the parties, and no delict on the part of the defendant. The prætor brought in the idea of a quasi-contract or liability arising

[1] See Gaius, 4, 36; *Inst.*, 4, 6; Appleton, C., *Histoire de la Propriété Prétorienne,* Paris, 1889; Girard, *Manuel,* 5th ed. 351.

[2] D., iii. 5, 10, 1.

from a relationship which was like a contractual relationship.[1]

Slaves Irregularly Set Free.—Take again, as an illustration of the prætorian law, the case of a slave irregularly manumitted. By the civil law there are three ways only in which the master can free his slave: *censu, vindicta, testamento.* But a master might have neglected to comply with any one of these three forms, and might, nevertheless, have signified in an unmistakable manner that he desired to give liberty to his slave. In such a case the prætor will not allow the master or his heir to compel the ex-slave to return. *De jure* he is still a slave, but *de facto* he is protected in the enjoyment of his freedom. He is not a freeman, and what he earns is still his master's. His children also are slaves. But still he is protected to some extent. Later on the position of such slaves was dealt with by statute. The *Lex Junia Norbana* (*circ.* 25 B.C.) said they might earn money for themselves, but when they died their property reverted to the master. They lived as freemen, but died as slaves.

Bonorum Possessio.—Or, take one of the most important of all the prætorian doctrines—viz. *bonorum possessio*, by which, in course of time, the whole law of succession was altered. The prætor could not make an heir. He was not a law-maker. But he could give a man the possession of the succession of a deceased person, and protect him in it as if he had been an heir. Suppose—*e.g.* a father had emancipated his son. By law the son was now a stranger to his father. The father dies intestate. The emancipated son has no claim on his succession. But the prætor gives him *bonorum possessio* to an equal share with his unemancipated brothers and sisters. This is only one of many

[1] The doctrine of *negotiorum gestio* is admitted in the modern civil law, and under the English law in claims for salvage. But the common law does not admit it as a general principle (see Anson on *Contracts*, 14th ed. 434, and references; Pollock, *Contracts*, 7th ed. 13; and Keener, W. A., on *Quasi-Contracts*, New York, 1893).

cases in which the prætor enlarged or altered the class of persons entitled to share in a succession.

The edict was, as these illustrations have indicated, the main instrument by means of which the free principles of equity—*jus aequum*—gained their victory over the older *jus civile.* The prætorian edict reached its climax in the last century of the Republic. It was then fully recognised that the *jus honorarium*, most of which was now permanently settled or tralaticious, was entitled to rank side by side with the *jus civile.*

The history of "equity" in the English law, and the power of the Chancellor to grant relief when the common law was too rigorous, present many interesting parallels.

There is a striking resemblance between some of the prætorian remedies and some of those which were evolved by the Chancellors.

As at Rome, so in England, there is at a later stage a fusion of the two systems. The equitable system is taken into the "legal" system and gives it a new spirit. How far the English Chancellors were consciously borrowing from the Roman law is matter of dispute. In most cases, probably, the similarities are not due to borrowing but arose quite independently.

The Chancellor just like the prætor was much influenced by ideas of "natural law," and he was in a position to give practical effect to his views (Maitland, F. W., *Equity*, p. 8, Cambridge, 1913. See for some comparisons, Buckland, W. W., *Equity in Roman Law*, London, 1911).

CHAPTER XXIII

The Jurists

The Pontiffs.—In early Rome, as in the early history of most peoples, the first lawyers were the priests. Law and religion were inextricably intertwined. The members of the Roman College, or Corporation of Pontiffs, were long regarded as the sole guardians of the mysteries of the law. Every step taken without the advice of a pontiff was fraught with danger, and might draw down the wrath of the gods. They distinguished, it is true, between *Fas*, with which they were concerned primarily as priests, and *Jus*, with which they had to do as lawyers. But they were the only authorised interpreters of both the *Fas* and the *Jus*. It was their business to inform the inquirer as to *Fas* how he should perform rightly the services of religion, and the inquirer as to *Jus* what were the necessary solemnities which he must observe. Every legal step at this stage of development required the use of stereotyped forms—*certa et solemnia verba*. Moreover, the pontiffs alone knew what days must be kept sacred and not profaned by any legal business. This knowledge of juridical and non-juridical days — *dies fasti et nefasti* — was most jealously guarded, and was one of the chief sources of the influence of the pontiffs. If a magistrate unwittingly exercised his jurisdiction upon a holy day—a *dies nefastus—per quos dies nefas fari praetorem do, dico, addico*—he had to perform a sacrifice in expiation. If he acted wittingly, Q. Scaevola doubted if any expiation would wipe out so terrible a sin.[1] The pontiffs

[1] Varro, *De L. L.*, 6, 30 ; Festus, *s.v.* "Fastis" ; Ovid, *Fasti*, 1, 45 ; see Schulin, *Lehrbuch der Geschichte*, 510.

knew also the forms of action and the rules of interpretation which had become settled.

The oldest mode of settling a dispute was for the parties to apply to the pontiffs to tell them in what form the question could lawfully be raised for decision. They then went before the king, who heard the case. If he was in any doubt about the law he got an opinion from the pontiffs.

Publication of Pontifical Law.—The secrecy with which the pontiffs guarded their knowledge of the forms of actions and of the lawful and unlawful days was very unpopular. A decisive blow was dealt at this system of mystery by a publication issued in 304 B.C. by Cn. Flavius, the son of a freedman, and secretary to Appius Claudius, the censor. It was done, very likely, at the instigation of Claudius himself. Claudius was a patrician by birth, but a bitter opponent of his own order. How he procured his information about the secrets of the pontifical college is unknown. Probably by taking notes of the decisions pronounced and by making careful inquiry among those who had consulted the pontiffs, Claudius may have gradually collected enough information.[1] Flavius' book was called the *Jus Flavianum*. It was supplemented by a further collection of forms issued about 190 B.C. by Sextus Aelius, surnamed "Catus" or "cunning." [2] This is called the *Jus Aelianum*.[3] This secularisation of the law, by which it was taken away from the priests, marks undoubtedly an important point in the history of the law. And another important step was taken only half a century after the *Jus Flavianum*. This was the commencement of public instruction in law. Tiberius Coruncanius, the first plebeian *Pontifex Maximus*, was the first *publice profiteri*[4]—*i.e.* probably the first to admit students to his house who were

[1] Cuq, 2nd ed. i. 161.

[2] D., i. 2, 2, 7.

[3] The theory that Flavius or Aelius may have been the author or, at least, the publisher of the Twelve Tables has been discussed in the chapter on the Twelve Tables, *supra*, 104.

[4] D., i. 2, 2, 38. See Jörs, *Römische Rechtswissenschaft*, 76.

allowed to be present at his consultations with people who came to him for advice. After him there began a line of jurists, and a system like the English "reading in chambers" became common. The influence of the jurists in sharing the prætor's edict has already been touched upon. A young Roman of the upper class who intended to become a lawyer, or to adopt a political career, used to attach himself to some jurist of reputation. Thus Cicero says that as soon as he had assumed the *toga virilis* he was taken by his father to Q. Mucius Scaevola (the Augur—not the author of the Commentary), and as long as he could he never left the old man's side. The students were called *auditores*. It was considered so honourable for a jurist to have these pupils that even the most eminent men never refused to take them. The pupils were present at the jurist's consultations with his clients, and discussed with him, in private, the questions which arose. The master also gave them theoretical instruction, explaining the Twelve Tables and the other authorities, and supervising their reading of legal MSS. Even when the *auditores* had acquired a knowledge of law they frequently continued to read with the master and to help him, in much the same way as young barristers in London "devil" with a practising counsel. At this stage they were called *studiosi*.

The Work of the Lawyers.—The extraordinary growth of Rome and the constant influx of foreigners led to a great demand for legal advice, and the houses of the famous lawyers, such as Scaevola, were thronged from morning to night with clients. It is said that the Senate presented Scipio Nasica with a house on the Via Sacra that he might be able to see his clients with greater convenience.[1] The profession of a jurist differed in one somewhat important particular from that of a modern lawyer. It was purely gratuitous. Neither from their clients nor from their pupils did they accept any payment. The jurists of the Republic

[1] Pomponius in D., i. 2, 3, 37.

belonged almost exclusively to great and wealthy families. The chief personal advantage they derived from their services as jurists was that it brought them into notice and helped them if they became candidates for office. A great number of the Republican consuls were taken from this class. Cicero describes the professional work of these early lawyers—the *veteres* as they were called in later times—as consisting of *Respondere, Cavere*, or *Agere.*[1]

Respondere means the giving of an opinion as to the law of a case, either when consulted by a judge or by a private client.

Cavere was the drawing up of documents in the appropriate form.

Agere was the conducting of the case in Court.

Some of the *veteres* also wrote books. The first scientific Roman law book was by Q. Mucius Scaevola, the younger, called the *Pontifex Maximus*, to distinguish him from his namesake, the Augur. He wrote, about 100 B.C., a treatise on the *Jus Civile* in eighteen books. Scaevola was the first to explain clearly the nature of many of the most important legal institutions—*e.g.*, wills, legacies, partnerships, &c.[2]

The Responsa of the Lawyers.—The consulting of a jurist by the judge in a case is a very peculiar feature of the Roman system. It would seem strange with us if a judge before deciding a point of law should take the opinion of counsel upon it. But it is natural enough when we remember that the Roman *judex* was not a lawyer, but a layman. All through the Republic and down to the time of Diocletian, who began to reign in 284 A.D., cases were remitted for trial to a *judex*. Upon any point of law he required to be directed, and one of the chief duties of the

[1] *De Orat.*, i. 48. Sometimes (*e.g. Pro Mur.*, 9, 19) *Scribere* is used also. It does not seem to have any precise technical sense, and might be used either of the drawing of a document or of a written *responsum*. See Jhering, *Esprit*, 3, 102; Jörs, *Röm. Rechtsw.*, 91.

[2] See Roby, *Introd.*, cv.; Costa, *Storia delle Fonti*, 48; Krüger, *Geschichte der Quellen*, 59.

jurists was to give opinions—*responsa*—for the guidance of the *judex*, his *responsum* taking much the same place as a judge's direction to a jury in our system.

The *judex* was, in fact, more like a single juryman than a judge—*e.g.* if the *judex* wanted to know if the facts proved amounted to fraud (*dolus malus*), or if the *bona fides* of one of the parties ought to relieve him from penalty, or what amounted to accident (*casus*) and so forth, it was to the opinions of the jurists that he looked for instruction. In early times the jurist went to the Court and gave his opinion like an expert witness. Later on, he sent his *responsum* in writing to the judge. Still later, towards the close of the Republic, it was usual for the jurist to give his opinion to the party consulting him. He gave it in a sealed document which was opened and read in the Court.[1] Under the Empire, as we shall see afterwards, it became necessary to formulate precise rules with regard to the weight which was to be attached to the opinions of certain jurists.

[1] A particularly interesting and full description of the activity of the jurists is to be found in the unfinished work of Paul Jörs, *Römische Rechtswissenschaft zur Zeit der Republik*, Berlin, 1888.

CHAPTER XXIV

THIRD PERIOD—THE PRINCIPATE OR DYARCHY

The Princeps.—The period from 27 B.C., when Augustus voluntarily resigned his extraordinary powers and affected to restore the Republic, down to 284 A.D., when Diocletian ascended the throne, is often called either the principate or the Dyarchy. In theory the powers of the State during this period are divided between the emperor and the Senate. The emperor is the *princeps*, the first citizen of the Republic, and the outward forms of republicanism are preserved. It is true that the disguise becomes thinner and thinner as time goes on. The power of the emperor is always increasing at the expense of that of the Senate. But until Diocletian, the emperor is not an avowed despot. In addition to the emperor there exist, as authorities to some extent independent, the Senate, the magistrates, and the *Comitia*. The last, it is true, has become a mere *simulacrum*, and the others are dwindling away.

The Comitia.—Their judicial power as the supreme Court of Appeal in capital offences was taken from them under Augustus, and given to the *quaestiones* or large juries, each competent to deal with certain crimes only, which have been referred to in the chapter on Crimes.[1] The power of the *Comitia* to elect magistrates was taken away in the year 14 A.D. and given to the Senate. Their legislative power continued to be exercised during the reign of Augustus and the first half of the reign of Tiberius—*i.e.* to about 25 A.D. After that it disappears. The only *lex* in the sense of comitial enactment which occurs after that is the formal *lex regia de imperio*—the act conferring the *imperium* upon a new emperor.

[1] *Supra*, 215. See Dio Cass., 56, 40; Karlowa, i. 515.

The Senate.—The Senate had succeeded to the right of electing the consuls, prætors, &c. Certain of the provinces were placed specially under the administration of the Senate, and were called the senatorial provinces, in opposition to others which were called imperial, as being directly under the control of the emperor. The revenues of these two groups of provinces were kept distinct. The Senate had the management of the *aerarium* or public treasury, into which flowed the revenue of the senatorial provinces, while the emperor administered the *fiscus principis* which was sustained by the imperial provinces.

Moreover, early in the empire the Senate began to exercise genuine legislative powers. But the influence of the Senate was, throughout this period, and especially in the latter part of it, more apparent than real. The prince became more and more powerful, and the Senate more and more servile.

The Magistrates.—The emperor himself was the chief magistrate. In theory his powers were conferred upon him by the people. He had the consular *imperium*, and by that authority he was the commander-in-chief of the army. He had the *tribunicia potestas*, and in virtue of it his person was inviolable, and he could block the acts of any magistrate. The old republican magistrates, consuls, prætors, tribunes, &c., continue to be elected annually. And the consuls and prætors, when their year of office is expired, are sent as governors to the senatorial provinces. But the emperor takes care to leave no army in these provinces, and gradually assumes a greater degree of control over all the magistrates. He creates a new set of officials, appointed solely by himself and accountable only to him—such as the *praefectus urbi*, the chief of police, and the *praefectus praetorio*, the Captain or Captains of the Prætorian Guard. In time the authority of these great officers of the imperial household completely overshadows that of the elected magistrates.

The Sources of the Law during the Principate.—There are six sources of the law during this period, each of which will need to be mentioned. They are custom, *leges*, *edicta*, *senatus-consulta*, *constitutiones principum*, and *responsa prudentium*. The seventh source of the old law—viz. *plebiscita*—has now disappeared, and the *leges*, *edicta*, and *senatus-consulta* are really only various forms in which it suited the emperors for a time to express their own will.

1. Custom (*usus*, *mos*, *consuetudo*). This continues to be a source of law and also to abrogate laws.

2. *Leges*. We do not hear of any comitial legislation, except the formal *lex regia*, of later date than about 25 A.D.—*i.e.* the middle of the reign of Tiberius.

Augustus was fond of getting his wishes carried out by laws of the *Comitia*, and himself proposed some important measures which he brought before the *Comitia* in his character as tribune.

Among the *leges* of the early Empire there are some very famous enactments which it may be well to mention. Several of them are attempts to grapple with the great social problems of the time. It was a period of unusual corruption of manners. Marriage was avoided, and the population would have decreased but for the foreign immigration. The greatest possible laxity existed as to the marriage tie, and divorces upon the most frivolous grounds were extremely common. The corrupt state of society was attributed partly to the great number of freedmen. Many of these enfranchised slaves were Asiatics or Greeks. They were frequently persons of dissolute character, who, not content with the indigenous vices of the capital, introduced the depraved Romans of the wealthy class to every form of Oriental immorality.

Social Legislation.—Augustus tried by legislation to stem this tide of licence. The *Lex Julia et Papia Poppaea* and the *Lex Julia de maritandis ordinibus* were laws passed to encourage marriage, and at the same time to check alliances between persons of very unequal condition, such as between senators and freedwomen or actresses.[1] The *Lex Papia Poppaea* (9 A.D.) is often

[1] Gaius, 1, 145; Ulp., 16, 32.

called the *Lex Caducaria*, because it tried to encourage marriage by a system of *caduca* or forfeitures.[1] Men between twenty-five and sixty, and women between twenty and fifty, if *caelibes*—*i.e.* not married—were not allowed to take benefits under the will of any stranger unless they had some excuse satisfactory to the law as well as to themselves for not marrying. A married man who had not at least one child, or a married woman who had not at least three children, if she is a free woman, or four if she is a freedwoman, fell into the class called *orbi* and could only take one-half of what was left to them. The shares so forfeited were called *caduca*. They went to the other heirs or legatees not disqualified, and, failing any such, to the *fiscus*. Caracalla made *caduca* lapse directly to the *fiscus*.[2]

E.g. a testator appoints A., B., and C. as his heirs:—

A. is married and has children.

B. is married and has no children.

C. is unmarried and over twenty-five years old.

C. takes nothing under the will unless he betroths himself within 100 days after the opening of the succession, and marries within two years.

B. only takes half his share.

A. takes all C.'s and half B.'s share in addition to his own, until Caracalla sweeps the *caduca* into the net of the fisc.

But these rules did not apply when the testator was related to the heir or legatee within the sixth degree. The same law contained provisions which it is not necessary here to give in detail, limiting the capacity of a husband to succeed to his wife or *vice versa*, unless there have been children. This part of the *Lex Julia et Papia* was called the *Lex Decimaria*.[3] Other advantages in the way of public honours, eligibility for office and so on, are offered to fathers of several children, and patrimonial penalties are imposed on divorce.

[1] Ulp., 17, 1. [2] Ulp., 17, 2.

[3] Ulp., 15, 1; 16, 1; Girard, 5th ed. 875; Costa, *Storia del Diritto*, 531.

The *Lex Julia et Papia* was a well-meant measure, but it did as much harm as good. Innumerable devices were resorted to by ingenious schemers of the wealthy class to foist off the children of others as their own, and to prevent the marriage of persons whose shares if caducous might fall to the schemers.

The sons of Constantine abolished the penalties[1] of celibacy and childlessness, and the *Lex Decimaria* was repealed by Honorius and Theodosius.[2] Other provisions fell into desuetude, and in the time of Justinian all this legislation was a dead letter.

The Freedmen.—There were also important comitial laws passed in the early empire which attempted to deal with the dangers caused by the growing number of freedmen. These were the *Lex Aelia Sentia*, the *Lex Junia Norbana*, and the *Lex Fufia Caninia*.

The *Lex Aelia Sentia* (4 A.D.) placed restrictions on manumissions:—

(1) A master under twenty was not to be allowed to manumit a slave unless he did so *vindicta*, or for a reason approved of by a special *consilium* appointed under this law to inquire into manumissions. Examples of such a *justa causa manumittendi* might be some special service rendered by the slave to the master, some tie of blood between them, or a sexual relation between them which it was desired to convert into lawful marriage.

(2) A slave under thirty could not be manumitted except subject to the same restrictions.

(3) Manumissions in fraud of creditors were to be invalid.

(4) Slaves who had been guilty of serious crimes or had been kept as gladiators were in no case to become citizens when manumitted. They were to have the status of enemies surrendered at discretion—*dediticii*—and were prohibited from living within 100 miles from Rome.[3]

The *Lex Junia Norbana* cleared up doubts as to the exact

---

[1] C., viii. 58, 1.

[2] C., viii. 58, 2.

[3] Gaius, 1, 13; Ulp., 1, 12.

status of slaves who had been irregularly manumitted—*i.e.* not *vindicta, aut censu, aut testamento.*[1] Their position was to be something like that of the *Latini Coloniarii,* and hence they were called Junian Latins. Like the Latin allies they had *commercium* but not *conubium.* But unlike them they could not make a will. At death all their property reverted to their old master or to his heirs. The Junian Latin, it is said, lived as a freedman, but died as a slave.

The *Lex Fufia Caninia* (*circ.* 1 B.C.) forbade any owner to manumit by will more than 100 slaves, and in any case only allowed him to manumit a certain proportion of his slaves.[2] These laws were, to a great extent, obsolete before the time of Justinian, and so far as still in force they were entirely repealed by him.

But after this social legislation of the early Empire the legislative activity of the *Comitia* entirely ceases. And even in passing these *leges* the *Comitia* did not exercise any independent judgment, and would not have dared to reject a measure desired by the *Princeps.*

The Edicts of Magistrates.—With the establishment of the Empire it was natural that a change should come over the prætor's power of issuing edicts which should alter the law. This power was, as I have said, part of the sovereign authority which at the expulsion of the kings had devolved upon the Republican magistrates. It seemed to the emperors to be inconsistent with their own power to allow a magistrate to retain this right of making laws without the imperial sanction. And the *tribunicia potestas* of the emperor enabled him if necessary to veto any proposal of the prætor. The prætor's power of making law was not at first taken away. But he hardly dared to exercise it except at the suggestion of the Senate

[1] Gaius, 1, 22 ; *Inst.*, 1, 5, 3. The date of this law (perhaps 19 A.D.) and its relation to the *Lex Aelia Sentia* are controversial. See *Zeit. Sav. Stift.*, vi. 186, and vii. 31 ; Costa, *Storia delle Fonti*, 38 ; *Storia del Diritto*, 146.

[2] Gaius, 1, 42 ; Ulp., i. 24 ; *Inst.*, i. 7 ; *Cod.*, 7, 3.

or the emperor. *E.g.* when the Senate passed the *Senatusconsultum Velleianum,* providing that obligations of suretyship entered into by women, married or single, should be void, they directed the prætors to make rules to carry out this new principle.[1] Hadrian thought the time had come to close the chapter of prætorian legislation, or at least to reduce the prætor's power within very narrow limits. He conceived the plan of casting the edict in a permanent shape, and of depriving the prætors of the power to make further changes in the law there laid down. By this time the *praetor urbanus* had borrowed so much from the *praetor peregrinus* that the two city edicts were alike in all essentials, and the edicts of the provincial governors had been assimilated to these. Hadrian, about 128 A.D., directed the famous lawyer Salvius Julianus to revise the edicts of the two prætors, and to add to them the market regulations and so forth contained in the edict of the ædiles. When the revision was complete it was ratified by the Senate, and declared to be henceforth unalterable by the prætor. If changes are made they must be made by the emperor. This consolidated edict is called the *Edictum Hadrianeum* or *Julianum,* or sometimes the *Edictum Perpetuum,* using that word in a new sense.

It is probable that the edicts of the provincial governors were also consolidated and published as the *Edictum Provinciale.* In theory the distinction between *jus honorarium* and *jus civile* was not destroyed. The prætors and the governors continued to issue the edict on taking office. In principle the law contained in it was derived from the magisterial power. And the prætor on taking office can still publish a new edict, provided it is not in conflict with the *Edictum Julianum.*[2] But the prætor's law-making, on a serious scale, was at an end. The edict was no longer the *viva vox juris civilis.* Henceforth the work of developing the law passed from the prætor to the classical jurists and the emperors.

The edict has been lost, and it is impossible to tell with

[1] See Krüger, *Geschichte der Quellen,* 85.
[2] See C. Tanta, s. 18.

certainty exactly what it contained. But Paul and Ulpian, among others, wrote lengthy commentaries upon it, and many passages from these are preserved in Justinian's *Digest.* From these and from other fragments the edict has been to a great extent reconstructed. The best attempt is that by Lenel, published under the title of *Palingenesia juris civilis,* of which a second edition appeared in 1907.[1] The general order is pretty well established, and was to a great extent followed in the *Digest* of Justinian.

Senatus-consulta.—During a part of this period the Senate was a legislative body, and *senatus-consulta* are treated as having the binding force of laws. The Senate's ordinances as to the government of the provinces and other matters of public law had been recognised during the Republic as entitled to general obedience. And, in the sphere of private law, at the end of the Republic, the Senate had begun, if not to make laws, yet to dispense individuals from obedience to particular laws. The Senate also not uncommonly recommended the prætor to make by edict a change in the law, and the prætor generally complied with such a recommendation. Under the Principate the emperor used the Senate as his mouthpiece or *prête-nom.* The genuine legislative activity of the Senate lasted only for about 180 years—*i.e.* from about 26 A.D. to about 206 A.D. The Senate did not really exercise any initiative. The usual course was for the emperor to propose a measure, either coming himself to the Senate and making a speech to introduce it, or getting a quæstor to read a speech prepared by him. This *oratio principis in senatu habita* was adopted by the Senate as a matter of course, and generally passed in the identical words. Thus it happens that the historians often speak of the *oratio Severi* or *oratio Antonini* of a certain year, when they mean the *senatus-consultum,* passed to give effect to the *oratio.*[2] The *Institutes* explain the legislative authority of the Senate by saying merely that when the

[1] See *Zeit. Sav. Stift.*, xxx. 490. [2] See Costa, *Storia delle Fonti*, 67.

population had become so great that it was difficult to assemble them all together, it seemed right to consult the Senate as representing the people.[1]

Among the best known *senatus-consulta* I may mention—

1. *Sct. Velleianum*, 46 A.D., referred to later.[2]

2. *Sct. Claudianum*, 52 A.D., providing that a freewoman who continues to cohabit with a slave after receiving three formal warnings—*denuntiationes*—from the slave's master shall herself become a slave of the master of her paramour, and that her whole estate shall accrue to him.[3]

3. *Sct. Macedonianum, circa* A.D. 70, declaring that, apart from certain exceptional cases, no action should lie either against father or son to recover loans of money made to a *filiusfamilias*.[4]

4. The *Sct. Tertullianum, circa* A.D. 158, gave to mothers of three children, if the mother is freeborn, or of four children if the mother is a freedwoman, the *jus liberorum*. This entitled the mother to succeed to the estate of her children in preference to all relations, except a child of the deceased, or a *frater consanguineus*, or a *parens manumissor*.[5]

5. The *Sct. Orfitianum*, 178 A.D., gave to the children of a woman who died intestate a right to succeed to her estate in preference to all agnates.[6] Under the old law a woman's children were not *sui*, and not agnates, unless indeed their mother had been *in manu*, and then she would have had nothing to leave, as her whole estate would have passed to her husband at the marriage or subsequently.[7]

6. The *Sct. Trebellianum*, 56 A.D., regulating the position of a trustee under a universal trust; and (7) the *Sct. Pegasianum* of the time of Vespasian, which gave the trustee the right to keep one-fourth of the estate for himself.[8]

---

[1] *Inst.*, 1, 2, 5. [2] See *infra*, p. 352.

[3] Gaius, 1, 86, 91, 160; Ulp., 11, 11; Tac., *Ann.*, 12, 53.

[4] D., 14, 6, 1, pr. [5] Ulp., 26, 8; *Inst.*, 3, 3, 2.

[6] *Inst.*, 3, 4, pr. [7] *Inst.*, 1, 3, 4, pr.

[8] Gaius, 2, 254; Ulp., 25, 14, 15; Paul, 4, 2; *Inst.*, 2, 23, 5.

Constitutiones Principum.—The authority of the emperor to make laws is said in the *Institutes* to be based on the *lex regia de imperio*, by which it is said the people confer upon him all their own power, so that he makes law as their mouthpiece. This is an attempt at a philosophical explanation. As a matter of fact the declared will of the emperor was before very long—at any rate before Gaius—regarded as having *legis vicem.*[1] The most general term for declarations of the imperial will was *constitutiones*—a word sometimes applied to decrees of the prætor and even to opinions of jurists. There seemed nothing novel or unconstitutional to the Roman mind in the emperor having this power, for, as we have seen, every magistrate who had the *imperium* might issue an edict and compel obedience to it. But whereas in the case of the magistrate—*e.g.* the prætor—the force of his edict depended on his own power to oblige people to conform to it, the emperor had the advantage that his orders were binding upon every other magistrate. The ways in which the emperor declared his will were various:—

(1) *Edicta;* (2) *Rescripta;* (3) *Decreta;* and (4) *Mandata.*

1. *Edicta.*

Every magistrate, and *a fortiori* the emperor, had the *jus edicendi.* The emperor's issuing an edict and expecting it to be obeyed shocked no one, and the reason why he adopted the method in the early Empire so little is that it seemed as easy to put his law in the form of a comitial law, or of a *senatus-consultum*—forms which were more imposing from their historical associations. In the earlier Empire the emperor's edict was not law after the death of the emperor who promulgated it. It might be renewed or tacitly kept in force by his successor, and in time came to be treated as continuing in force like any other law.[2] During the later Empire the emperors legislated extensively by *edicta.*

[1] Gaius, i. 5.

[2] Karlowa, i. 647; Costa, *Storia delle Fonti*, 68.

2. *Rescripta.*

These are answers to legal questions submitted to the emperor for his opinion. Magistrates and governors of provinces who had difficult questions of law to decide were encouraged to refer them to the emperor for solution. In this case, the emperor replied in a formal document giving his opinion and the reasons for it pretty fully. A rescript of this kind was called an *epistola.*

But even private individuals might petition the emperor for his opinion, and in replying to them he generally gave his answer very briefly, and wrote it at the foot of the petition itself. This was called *subscriptio* or *subnotatio. Rescriptum* as a general term covered both. After the second century, A.D., it became a very common practice for a party to an action to obtain beforehand the emperor's opinion upon the point of law involved. This was given, as counsel's opinions are given now, upon the assumption that the facts have been stated fully and fairly by the petitioner. The facts had then to be proved in the ordinary way before the judge, and he thereupon applied the law as directed in the emperor's rescript. The emperor's law must be taken as sound, if the facts turned out to be as they had been stated to him. But it was often a matter of difficulty to know whether the emperor had not meant to lay down a general rule, which a judge ought to follow if the same point presented itself again. This was a question of intention. The judge had to decide:—

First, Did the emperor who had given a rescript in a previous case intend to lay down a general principle of law?

Second, Was the second case really analogous?

These questions had generally to be determined by studying the language in which the rescript had been expressed. In many of them the emperor clearly gave an opinion limited to the special circumstances before him. If so, it was called a *constitutio personalis.* In others, again, his reasons seemed general in their nature, and applicable to similar cases in the future. These were *rescripta generalia*, or *constitutiones generales*. The rescripts of deceased emperors required, therefore, to be construed, and this was one of the duties of the jurisconsults under the Empire.

In all this, it is not to be supposed that the emperors had the legal knowledge, or could spare the time, to give these numerous opinions on points of law. Just as the prætor in preparing his edict had been wont to call in the aid of lawyers of repute, so the emperor had a *consilium* or board of which distinguished lawyers were members. This *consilium* sat in a room at the palace—the *auditorium principis*—and considered all petitions, and drew up rescripts for the emperor to sanction. As a rule it was in points of detail that the law was modified by rescripts.

3. *Decreta.*

These are judgments rendered by the emperor in cases in which he sat as judge. The emperor might sit as a judge of first instance like the prætor, and some of the early emperors did this a good deal. Suetonius says in praise of Augustus, *Jus assidue dixit.* But by the time of Domitian this had become unusual.[1] The emperors generally contented themselves with their appellate jurisdiction. This was based on their *tribunicia potestas.* The emperor might, if so requested, veto the judgment of any Court, or in other cases the magistrate before whom a case was pending might refer it to the emperor. He then examined the case and issued a *decretum.* Here as with rescripts the judgment might apply to the particular case only, or it might lay down a general rule. If it did so it was binding law in future cases.[2]

4. *Mandata.*

These were official instructions given to dignitaries, especially to governors of provinces. They contain directions as to their conduct, and seldom touch private law. More often they contain provisions as to criminal or administrative law.

[1] Suet., *Dom.*, 8. [2] Karlowa, i. 649.

Hence, in the *Institutes*, *mandata* are not included among the *constitutiones*. But occasionally a rule of law was made in such governors' instructions. *E.g.* the rule that a governor was not during his term of office to marry a lady of the province.[1] Such a rule if intended to be general would be a binding law.[2]

Responsa Prudentium.—Augustus saw the importance of attaching to himself the leading lawyers whose influence was considerable.[3] He saw also the danger of allowing great weight to be given to the private opinions of men, some of whom, like the great Labeo, were known to be ardent Republicans. He accordingly chose out some of the most distinguished lawyers, and gave them a quasi-official position. He conferred upon his favourites the *jus respondendi ex auctoritate principis*.[4] The creation of this privileged class of patented counsel did not prevent their less favoured *confrères* from giving *responsa*. But the *responsa* of the jurists who had the *jus respondendi* carried with them a higher degree of authority. Indeed, it seems that if a party got a *responsum* from one of these official counsel it was binding upon the *judex*, provided the facts were proved to be as assumed by the counsel.[5] The *responsum* must be in writing and sealed, and given to the party. But it might happen that conflicting *responsa* were produced. Hadrian dealt with this difficulty by a rescript. He said if there were more *responsa* than one, and they all agreed upon the law, the judge was bound by this view. If they differed, he must use his own judgment.[6] Some writers, notably Puchta, think that Hadrian's rescript applied to the books of jurists living and dead, as well as their opinions given for the particular

[1] Karlowa, i. 653.

[2] D., 24, 1, 3, 1.

[3] D., 1, 2, 2, 48.

[4] D., 1, 2, 2, 48.

[5] Karlowa, i. 660; Girard, *Manuel*, 5th ed. 70; *contra* Machelard, *Dissertations de droit Romain*, 654; Accarias, *Précis de droit Romain*, 59; Bruns-Pernice, s. 47.

[6] Gaius, i. 7.

case in hand. But this is a controversial matter.[1] Our information is scanty as to the manner in which Hadrian's rescript was administered. Probably if one party brought a *responsum* in his favour this was accepted as sound law, unless his opponent produced another *responsum* in the opposite sense.[2] Muirhead suggests that the number of patented counsel was very small, and that the judge was only bound by a *responsum* in which they all concurred.[3] It is, however, difficult to believe that their number can have been so restricted.[4]

The Proculians and the Sabinians.—The Augustan age saw a curious split among the jurists into two rival schools or sects. These came to be known by the names of the Proculians and the Sabinians.[5] Curiously enough, neither school is named after its real founder. M. Antistius Labeo was considered the head of the Proculians, and C. Ateius Capito the head of the Sabinians. These two men were the most famous lawyers of the time of Augustus. They differed widely in political views. Labeo was a stalwart Republican, who viewed the rise of the imperial power with dislike and suspicion. When a motion was made in the Senate that the senators should take turns in standing guard over the Cæsar when he slept, Labeo said, "I snore, and therefore am not suited to be a guard in an ante-chamber."[6] Capito, on the other hand, was a pliable courtier, anxious to win favour with the new monarch. As a lawyer Labeo was by far the more distinguished. He was a voluminous writer, a man of wide general culture, and well versed in the Greek philosophy. His opinions are frequently referred to with great respect in Justinian's *Digest*. Capito

[1] *Inst.* i. s. 117; Puchta, *Cursus*, 1, s. 117; Karlowa, i. 660; Eisele, in *Zeit. Sav. Stift.*, xi. 199; Costa, *Storia delle Fonti*, 77; Machelard, *Dissertations*, 662; Accarias, 60; Appendice I. by M. E. Bonnier to vol. ii. of Labbé's edition of Ortolan, *Les Instituts de Justinien.*

[2] Bonnier's Appendice I. to vol. ii. of Labbé's Ortolan.

[3] Second edition, 293.

[4] See Krüger, *Rechtsquellen*, 113; Bruns, note by Pernice to s. 47.

[5] Pomponius, in *Dig.*, i. 2, 2, 47, 48.

[6] Roby, *Introd.*, cxxv.

is rarely mentioned in the texts of Justinian, and but little is known of him.[1] Labeo's follower, Proculus, gave his name to one school, and Sabinus, a disciple of Capito, to the other. A good deal of rather fruitless labour has been expended on the attempt to discover some broad lines of distinction between these two schools. We frequently read that the Proculian view upon some question was so and so, and that the Sabinian view differed from it in such and such respects. But many of the disputes were on very small points, and it is difficult, if not impossible, to detect any underlying differences of principle. According to the traditional view the Proculians clung more closely to the legal doctrines of the Republic, while the Sabinians were more inclined to the equitable tendencies of more modern times, and this is borne out by some of the illustrations cited by the authors.[2] The two schools continued to exist for a considerable time, for Gaius, whose *Institutes* were written probably after the middle of the second century, reckons himself as a Sabinian, and speaks of the writers of the other school—*diversae scholae auctores*—as still living. It is not at all improbable that each of the two schools became associated with a college, and that a succession of teachers and students at one of these *stationes jus docentium* kept up a traditional attachment to Sabinian views, while at the other *statio* they honoured the names of Proculus and Labeo. No doubt the two schools were inclined to take different views, and the opposition between them may have been something like the vague rivalry between two neighbouring Universities such as Oxford and Cambridge, or Harvard and Yale.[3] It is probable that other similar schools existed, the names of which have been lost.

[1] The fullest account of Labeo is in the valuable work of Pernice, *Marcus Antistius Labeo*, Halle, 1873, 1900.

[2] *Cf.* Gaius, 1, 196; Ulp., 11, 28; Ulp. in D., 12, 1, 9, 9; Gaius, 2, 123.

[3] See on this obscure subject Roby, *Introduction to the Digest*, 124 *seq.*; Karlowa, i. 664, where a good many examples of the controversies between the two schools are collected; Costa, *Storia delle Fonti*, 80; Clark, *Hist. of Roman Private Law—Sources*, 107.

CHAPTER XXV

The Classical Jurists

Julian, Pomponius, and Papinian.—We come now to the group of writers who are known as the classical jurists. It is from their works that Justinian's *Digest* and his *Institutes* are mainly compiled. The first, and one of the greatest of those whom we need mention, was Salvius Julianus. He occupied the highest offices of the State during the reigns of Hadrian and Antoninus Pius, being twice consul and finally *præfectus urbi.* Hadrian charged him with the important task of consolidating the edict. Julian published a still more important work called his *Digesta,* in ninety books. Like many of the great lawyers of this period, he was not of Roman birth. He was born at Hadrumetum, in the province of Africa. After him comes Pomponius, who contributed considerably to the *Digest.* A long extract from a work ot his, called the *Enchiridion* or Handbook, is our principal authority for a good deal of the early history of the law. Except for an introductory passage from Gaius, it forms the whole of the Title *De Origine Juris.*[1] Pomponius seems to have been more esteemed as an antiquarian than as a practical lawyer, though some of his doctrinal writings are also referred to. Passing over some of the less known names we come to Aemilius Papinianus. Papinian is generally regarded as the greatest of all the Roman jurists. Justinian lavishes upon him such epithets as *acutissimi ingenii vir et merito ante alios excellens*[2] *disertissimus, splendidissimus, pulcherrimus, summi ingenii vir,*[3] and so on. And in more

[1] D., i. 2.
[2] C., vi. 42, 30; *Const. Omnem,* ss. 1, 4.
[3] C., vii. 45, 14.

modern times the great French lawyer Cujas has spoken of Papinian as "the greatest lawyer that has been or will be, as pre-eminent among lawyers as Homer is among poets."[1] The distinction of his career, the noble integrity of his life, and the courage with which he faced death rather than disgrace, all contributed to place Papinian on a plane by himself. And in comparing his writings with Paul and Ulpian—his only possible rivals among the Roman jurists—we have to remember that they were his pupils, and had absorbed his teaching.

Papinian flourished under Marcus Aurelius and Septimius Severus. He filled many high offices, including that of *magister libellorum*, or Master of Petitions—the officer who drew up the imperial rescripts for approval.[2] He was an intimate friend of Severus, and in 204 A.D. held the great office of Prætorian Prefect. This dignitary was a kind of grand vizier who was at the head of every department of State. He was at once prime minister, supreme judge, and adjutant-general. Sometimes the office was put in commission, or held by two or three Prætorian Prefects.

Papinian accompanied the Emperor Severus to Britain to suppress a rebellion, and a law of Severus dated at York in 210 A.D. was probably drawn by Papinian. For three years the two highest tribunals sat at York. Papinian, with Paul and Ulpian as his successors, sat on the bench there. As a writer on Papinian says, it was rather as if the House of Lords and the Judicial Committee were to sit at Uganda.[3] And Papinian, Paul, and Ulpian must have constituted as strong a Court as could be imagined. Severus at his death specially commended his sons Caracalla and Geta to the care of Papinian. The story goes that after Caracalla had murdered Geta, he called on Papinian to address the Senate in defence of the

[1] *Unus Papinianus erit, ut Homerus unus poetarum princeps, sic unus princeps jurisconsultorum Papinianus. Praef. ad Comment. in Quaest. Papin.* (ed. Mut. 1777).

[2] D., xx. 5, 12, pr.

[3] N. J. D. Kennedy in the *Juridical Review*, Edinburgh, v. 312.

murder. Papinian replied, "Parricide is not so easy to defend as to commit."[1] On account of his refusal, Caracalla caused Papinian and his son, who was a quæstor, to be killed. The excerpts from Papinian, 595 in number, are by no means so long as the extracts from Paul and Ulpian. But they quite bear out his reputation, and are admirable specimens of legal reasoning. In Justinian's time Papinian's *responsa* formed a main part of the work of law-students in their third year. The students at that stage were called *Papinianistae.*[2] The course of study lasted then for five years.

Ulpian.—Domitius Ulpianus was a Tyrian.[3] He was guardian of the young Emperor Alexander Severus, and at the same time was Prætorian Prefect. In fact, for some years Ulpian virtually governed the Empire. He incurred the hostility of the guard by taking away some of their privileges, and was attacked one night by some of the soldiers. He fled for refuge to the palace, but was followed and slain there. His works were most of them written in the reign of Caracalla, between 212 and 217, though some of them belong, probably, to a rather later period.[4] He was a most voluminous writer. He wrote a commentary on the edict in eighty-one books, and one on Sabinus in fifty-one books, as well as many smaller treatises. Of these the best known is his Book of Rules—*Liber Singularis Regularum*—which was first printed in Paris in 1549. Ulpian is not, perhaps, a writer of marked originality. He borrows with great freedom from earlier writers. But his works are remarkable for lucidity of style and arrangement. Mommsen says of the Rules—*Ulpiani Regulae ea brevitate, perspicuitate, proprietate, conscriptae sunt quam adhuc secuti sumus omnes, assecutus est nemo.* The extracts from Ulpian form the heart of the *Digest.* He is much more drawn upon than any other writer, and the passages from him occupy one-third of its pages.

[1] *Hist. August.*, 88. See Gibbon, 1, 159.

[2] *Const. Omnem*, s. 4; see Roby's *Introduction*, 28.

[3] D., 50, 15, 1, pr.

[4] See Krüger, *Röm. Rechtsquellen*, 292; Clark, *Sources*, 137.

Julius Paulus.—After Ulpian comes his contemporary, Paul, who was a Prætorian Prefect under Alexander Severus. Paul was a voluminous writer. Among his works I may mention *Institutionum Libri Duo; Sententiarum ad Filium Libri Quinque,* commonly called Paul's *Sentences;* a commentary on Sabinus in sixteen books; and a commentary on the edict in seventy-eight books. Paul was, possibly, as good a lawyer as Ulpian, but he had not Ulpian's grace of expression. His style is crabbed and difficult. There are 2081 extracts from Paul in the *Digest,* but their average length is less than that of Ulpian's 2464 extracts. Paul's proportion of the *Digest* is about one-sixth, so that Ulpian and Paul together wrote half the *Digest.* Paul's *Sentences* is a very valuable little work for the law of the classical period.

It is not possible to assign precise dates of Paul's various writings. They extend in all likelihood over the period 193-222 A.D., from Severus to Alexander. The *Sentences* must have been published after 206 A.D.[1]

Modestinus.—After Ulpian and Paul there is only one writer who is reckoned among the classics, and he occupies a rank much lower than theirs. This is Herennius Modestinus, a pupil of Ulpian. He seems to have been a Greek, or at least from a Greek-speaking province, and some of the extracts from him in the *Digest* are in that language. He was teacher of the younger Emperor Maximinus, who was killed in 238 A.D. There are in the *Digest* 345 passages from Modestine. They exhibit him as a rather tiresome and quibbling kind of lawyer.

After Modestine there is a rapid decline, and no other name needs to be mentioned. This may be partly due to the fact that after the end of the third century the emperors discontinued making grants of the *jus respondendi.* Henceforth the imperial rescripts were the only *responsa* which were of authority.

Gaius.—One jurist I have purposely omitted, though his date

[1] See Roby, *Introd.,* cciii.; Karlowa, i. 749; Clark, *Sources,* 133; Costa, *Storia delle Fonti,* 108.

is earlier than Papinian. This is Gaius. He occupies a somewhat peculiar position. Of the man himself we know nothing —not even his cognomen. Gaius, less correctly written Caius, is either a prænomen, by which the lawyer was popularly designated, or, as is perhaps more likely, is the single name used by Greeks or Greek-speaking provincials.[1] From internal evidence it seems that he lived in the reign of Antoninus Pius and Marcus Aurelius, and he must have survived 178 A.D., for he wrote a book about the Orfitian Senatusconsult which was passed in that year. The first book of his *Institutes* and a part of the second were written about 161 A.D., though the precise date is disputed.[2] The peculiarity about Gaius is that his fame came to him so long after his death. There is a doubtful allusion to him by Pomponius, who speaks in one place of *Gaius noster*. But many writers think he means Gaius Cassius Longinus.[3] Except for this, Gaius is never mentioned by his contemporaries or by the great jurists who succeeded him. Yet suddenly, in the middle of the fifth century, nearly three hundred years after his works appeared, we find Gaius distinctly recognised as being in the same class with such luminaries as Papinian and Ulpian. And we find in Justinian's time, a century later, that Gaius' little work—his *Institutes*—is the text-book in the hands of all law students. Justinian's own compilers of the *Institutes* base their work on that of Gaius, and pay it the compliment of borrowing from it so freely that half of Justinian's *Institutes* is taken bodily from the older book.

Why was Gaius so obscure in life, and so famous three or four centuries after his death?

[1] Costa, *Storia delle Fonti*, 102, where see references.

[2] In *Inst.*, 2, 195, he refers to *divus* Pius Antoninus. Antonine died in 161 A.D., and the form of the reference to him seems to make it clear that this part of the work was after that date. See Karlowa, i. 727; Clark, *Sources*, 125.

[3] D., 45, 3, 39. See Karlowa, i. 720. The bold conjecture that Gaius and Gaius Cassius were one and the same person will not bear examination. See Herzen in *Zeit. Sav. Stift.*, 1899, xx. 211; Muirhead, 2nd ed. 301, and Appendix, 432; Costa, *Storia delle Fonti*, 102.

The probable explanation is that Gaius was not a statesman occupying a great position like Papinian, Ulpian, or Paul. Indeed he was so far from that rank that it is almost certain he never possessed the *jus respondendi*. He seems to have been a professor of law at one of the law-schools or *stationes jus publice docentium*. Gaius was, apparently, familiar with Greek; he wrote a commentary on the provincial edict, and he is particularly full in his treatment of the law affecting peregrins or foreigners living at Rome. Mommsen has inferred from these facts that Gaius was a provincial professor of law, who was most likely an Asiatic, and he thinks there is some ground for supposing that he lectured at Troas in Asia. Karlowa disputes this inference and thinks it more likely that Gaius taught at Rome, but perhaps at a law-school attended specially by provincials.[1] But it is generally agreed that Gaius was a professor and not a statesman, and that his works slowly won their way by their intrinsic merit and did not possess at first such authority as belonged naturally to the writings of the leading men of the day like Papinian.

Besides his *Institutes* and his treatise on the *Edictum Provinciale*, Gaius wrote other works, and particularly one called *Libri rerum cotidianarum*, which afterwards went by the name of the *Aurea* of Gaius.

The *Institutes* have been thought from their style to be Gaius' notes for his own lectures.[2] In the *Institutes* of Gaius we find for the first time a systematic division of the whole field of law into the law of persons (*jus quod ad personas pertinet*), the law of property and obligations (*jus quod ad res pertinet*), and the law of actions (*jus quod ad actiones pertinet*). This division of the subject was followed in the *Institutes* of Justinian, and has been adopted with various modifications in modern codes and treatises. Whether Gaius invented it or took it from some older authority is doubtful, but, as Gaius is by no means conspicuous for originality, the latter is more probable.

[1] i. 722. [2] Costa, *Storia delle Fonti*, 101.

He is very cautious, and on controversial points seldom gives an opinion, but contents himself with stating the views held by the opposing authorities. The re-discovery of the long-lost MS. of the *Institutes* of Gaius is one of the romances of literary history. Considerable extracts from it existed in other compilations, especially in Alaric's Breviary, but the complete work had utterly disappeared. In 1816, Niebuhr, in passing through Verona, took the opportunity of glancing through the collection of MSS. in the Library of the Cathedral. He found among them a MS. of the Epistles of St. Jerome which he at once perceived to be a palimpsest—that is, written over an older MS. The monks, as their manner was, had attempted to erase the old writing with pumice stone in order to use the parchment for copying St. Jerome. The first writing was very difficult to decipher, but Niebuhr just made out that it dealt with law. Being so well known as a scholar he got leave to borrow the MS. and sent it to Savigny for examination. It turned out to be the long-lost *Institutes* of Gaius. The Berlin Academy sent antiquarians to attempt to decipher it, but unfortunately one of them used such strong chemicals as to make it more unintelligible than before. A subsequent attempt to reproduce it by photography has been more successful, and it is now possible, with the aid of many conjectures, to make out the greater part of the work. The discovery really marks an epoch in the history of Roman law, for as Gaius states the law as it was some four centuries before Justinian, we can compare his account with Justinian's, and in that way understand many things which before had been full of obscurity.[1]

[1] There is a voluminous literature about Gaius. I may refer particularly to Krüger, *Römische Rechtsquellen*, s. 24; Costa, *Storia delle Fonti*, 100; and Greenidge's Introd. to the 4th ed. of Poste's Gaius.

CHAPTER XXVI

FOURTH PERIOD—THE ABSOLUTE MONARCHY, 284 A.D.-565 A.D. (DEATH OF JUSTINIAN)

Absolutism.—From the accession of Diocletian in 284 A.D. to the end of our period the emperor is to all intents and purposes an autocratic sovereign. The republican checks altogether disappear.

The *Comitia* have faded away.

The Senate gets weaker and weaker, loses its imperial character more and more, and tends to become a kind of municipal assembly for the city of Rome. When Constantine founds the new Rome, or Byzantium, he furnishes it also with a Senate.

The old magistrates, consuls and prætors have only the shadow of their former power. The *praetor urbanus* and the *praetor peregrinus* are still judges in the city of Rome. But they are now only judges of first instance. An appeal lies from them to the *praefectus urbi.*

High above every power in the State stands the emperor. No longer content to be the first citizen of the Republic—the *Princeps*—he has now come to be called *dominus*, even *deus*, and receives divine honours. Below him is an elaborate hierarchy of new officials by whom the work of governing the vast Empire is carried on.

Italy a Province.—The whole position of Rome and of Italy has undergone a profound change. The provinces and subject states no longer look up to the Romans as to a sovereign people. The different degrees of citizenship—so to speak—the status of Latins, Junian Latins, peregrins, and so on have become of much less importance. For, about 212 A.D.,[1] Caracalla had given the full Roman citizenship to all the free inhabitants of the Empire except the class called *dediticii*.[1] It is probable, however, that Caracalla's law extended only to the Junian Latins and peregrins living at its date. It did not apply to the future, and, therefore, a new brood of Junian Latins and peregrins must have grown up before Justinian's time. He abolished altogether the status of Junian Latinity and that of the *dediticii*.[2] But after Caracalla's law, broadly speaking, the romanised Teuton in Gaul and the romanised Jew in Palestine are Roman citizens just as much as the natives of the capital. And Italy is merely one among many provinces.

The Division of the Empire.—This new conception of the Roman Empire as an enormous and heterogeneous group of provinces all equally free, and all equally subject to the commands of the emperor and of the new bureaucracy, made it seem desirable to reorganise the whole system. Moreover, the Empire was exposed to constant attacks from the Teutons on the north and west, and from the Parthians and the Persians on the east. It was impossible for an emperor, living at Rome, to defend the Empire at all its vulnerable points. Diocletian devised an elaborate scheme of administration for the whole Empire. He divided it into four grand divisions called præfectures, and set a *praefectus praetorio* over each. The præfectures were subdivided into dioceses, each governed either by the *praefectus* in person or by a *vicarius*. The præfectures were—(1) the East; (2) Illyricum; (3) Italy; and (4) Gaul.[3]

[1] D., 48, 19, 17, 1; D., 48, 22, 6, pr. See *Zeit. Sav. Stift.*, ix. 42. It is doubtful if the law can have applied to some parts of the Empire not divided into *civitates*, *e.g.* Corsica and Sardinia. See Mommsen, *Staatsrecht*, 3, 1, 699; Ferrini, C., *Pandette*, s. 56; Savigny, *Vermischte Schriften*, i. 27.

[2] *Inst.*, i. 16, 2; Cod., 7, 5; 7, 6. See Muirhead, *Introd.*, 2nd ed. 319, 391; Cuq, 2, 148, 790; Karlowa, i. 929.

[3] See (dioecesis) Karlowa, i. 830, 850; Marquardt, *Röm. Staatsverwaltung*, i. 81; Bethmann-Hollweg, *Röm. Civil Prozess*, iii. 11; Pauly-Wissowa, *s.v.* "Dioecesis."

The præfecture of the East included, speaking roughly, the modern countries of Palestine, Egypt, Asia Minor, and part of Turkey and Roumania. Illyricum included Greece and the Balkan States, so far as not in the East. Italy included, besides the peninsula, the province of Africa. The præfecture of Gaul covered Spain, France, Britain, and Germany, so far as they had been subdued.[1]

The two eastern præfectures—*i.e.* the East and Illyricum, and the two western—*i.e.* Italy and Gaul, were, respectively, to be governed by an Augustus assisted by a Cæsar. The two Augusti were to be joint-emperors, each administering a separate part of one Empire. Legislation was to be agreed to by both, and to apply to the whole Empire. This grand scheme was not uniformly carried out. Sometimes the two halves are reunited again under a single ruler. The last emperor to rule the whole Empire alone was Theodosius the Great. At his death in 395 A.D., he divided the Empire again between his two sons, giving the West to Honorius and the East to Arcadius. After that time there are two great divisions of the Empire—the East, with its capital at Constantinople, and the West, with its capital at Rome, or more often at Ravenna.[2]

Such, in brief outline, is the history of the division of the Empire.

During the absolute monarchy the only source of law is the emperor. He declares his will in rescripts or in edicts. Speaking broadly, all important changes in the law are made by edicts, *leges edictales*, addressed to the Senate, to the whole people, or, very often, issued to the prætorian præfects, with instructions to publish them in their respective jurisdictions.

The Authority of the Jurists in the Later Empire.—After

[1] See the Table of the Divisions of the Roman Empire at the Beginning of the Fifth Century in Bury, *History of the Later Roman Empire*, i. xv.

[2] It is common, but not very accurate, to speak of the Eastern and the Western Empire. In theory there was one Empire, though there might be two emperors. See Freeman, *Historical Essays*, 3rd series, 251 ; ch. xxii. s. 191 ; Bury, *History of the Later Roman Empire*, i. vii.

about 250 A.D., the date of Modestinus, there were no great jurists. The practice of conferring the *jus respondendi* died out. This may have been due in part to the want of great lawyers, and in part to the disinclination of the emperors, who were getting more and more autocratic, to give to another an authority which they could exercise themselves. It seemed to them unfitting that a private citizen should be a *conditor et interpres legum*.[1] Instead of obtaining a *responsum* in their favour from a living jurist, the lawyers got into the habit of relying on passages from the works of the great jurists of the past. They supported their arguments by citations from Papinian or Ulpian, or from one of the famous commentators. The works of these old writers were now spoken of as *jus*, and were relied upon as absolutely correct. The old *leges* or *edicta* or *senatus-consulta* were never looked at. They were taken as they stood in the writings of these commentators. But the classical jurists were numerous. They did not always agree in their views, and the unlearned *judex* was often greatly perplexed to know which guide he ought to follow in forming his decision. As to Papinian, the highest authority of all, there was a peculiar difficulty. His pupils, Ulpian and Paul, had annotated his writings, and had not seldom dissented in the notes from the opinion of the master given in the text. Was the judge, in such a case, to prefer Papinian's view or Ulpian's? Constantine, in 321 A.D., came to the help of the distracted judge by enacting that the notes of Ulpian and Paul should be of no authority, and must be disregarded altogether.[2] He also enacted, in 327, that Paul's *Sentences* should be a work of authority.[3] But a more decided and detailed attempt to define the authority of the jurists was made a century later. This was the law passed in 426 A.D. by Theodosius II. and Valentinian III., and generally referred to as the Valentinian Law of Citations.[4] It provided that for the future five jurists should

[1] Karlowa, i, 932.
[2] Cod. Th. i. 4.
[3] *Ibid.*
[4] See the text in Cod. Th., i. 4. 3.

be of paramount authority. All their writings are declared to be authoritative. The select five are Papinian, Paul, Gaius, Ulpian, and Modestine. It is expressly declared that Gaius is to have the same weight as the others. This implies that he had hitherto been in an inferior position. But not only were the great five to be of authority—they were to give authority to all jurists whom they cited—*eorum quoque scientiam, quorum tractatus atque sententias praedicti omnes viri suis operibus miscuerunt, ratam esse censemus.* If Paul cited a passage from Marcellus, this was sufficient to make all the works of Marcellus authoritative. But this was subject to the condition that the accuracy of the passages cited from the old authors should be proved by producing the manuscripts of their works—*si tamen eorum libri propter antiquitatis incertum codicum collatione firmentur.*[1] The precise sense of the words "*codicum collatione*" has been much disputed. It appears to mean that before a passage from Marcellus is to be accepted as binding, two manuscripts, at least, of Marcellus must be produced in order to see if the passage is genuine.[2] But the object of the law seems to have been to make the works of the great five practically the sole authorities. The emperors did not like to take away the authority of such famous lawyers as Scaveola, Sabinus or Julian. But manuscripts of their works were rare, and they were, in practice, unknown, except by the passages which Ulpian or one of the classical jurists had cited from them. To

[1] Cod. Th., i. 4, 3.

[2] Roby, *Introduction*, lxxxv.; Krüger, *Rechtsquellen*, 263; Karlowa, i. 934. This seems to be the most natural meaning. Girard thinks *codicum collatione* means "by the production of an original manuscript of the jurist cited" (*Manuel*, 5th ed. 73). Others interpret the law as giving authority only to the passages cited by one of the five, and then only subject to the condition that its accuracy shall be proved by producing a manuscript of its author showing that it has been correctly quoted (Costa, *Storia delle Fonti*, 123). But this seems inconsistent with the word *scientia*. It is not the individual passage but the legal learning of its author which is officially approved.

say to a lawyer "you may refer to Marcellus, but you must show me a manuscript or even two manuscripts of his work," was practically to exclude Marcellus, for the condition could hardly ever be fulfilled. Indeed, it was only in the large cities or at the law schools that manuscripts of the great jurists could be found. In the country the lawyers and the judges had to get on with hardly any books. The ordinary working library of the country lawyer consisted of Gaius' *Institutes* and Paul's *Sentences.*[1] After fixing what books might be referred to, the Valentinian Law dealt with conflicts of opinion among the authorities, by providing that the judge was to accept the view of the majority. If the jurists expressing an opinion upon the point were equally divided, and Papinian had given his view about it, the side which included Papinian was to prevail. It was only in cases of equality on some point as to which Papinian was silent that the judge could use his own discretion.

This cast-iron rule, which reduced the function of the judge to the mechanical art of counting the votes of legal writers two hundred years old, points unmistakably to a period of great decay. There was no modern authority to be compared in weight with these *veteres*, and there were no judges who could be relied upon to come to a sound conclusion if they were left to exercise their own discretion.

Justinian's *Digest* was compiled from the authors chosen in the Valentinian Law—either the great five, or some writer whom they cite. But he did not bind down his compilers by the same iron rules as had been imposed on the judges by the Law of Citations. The collation of manuscripts was not insisted on; the compilers might, as a modern judge may, accept the view of a single writer, even against the great Papinian himself; and lastly, the notes of Paul and Ulpian on Papinian were not to be thrown out of account.[2]

State of the Empire at the Time of Justinian.—The great

[1] Bruns-Pernice, s. 67.

[2] See the *De Conceptione Digestorum*, 6 (first constitution at beginning of *Digest*).

compilations of the Roman law were made at Constantinople. Before the death of Theodosius in 395 A.D., he divided the Empire into two parts, assigning one to each of his two sons, giving the West to Honorius, and the East to Arcadius. Henceforth there is a western part of the Empire, with Rome, or sometimes Ravenna, for its capital; and an eastern part of the Empire, of which the capital was Constantinople. Both had reached, long before the time of Justinian, a condition of great feebleness. Italy was occupied over and over again by hordes of barbarians, who at first contented themselves with sacking the country and then retiring with their booty, but as time went on became more exacting, and established themselves on the land. In 410 A.D., Alaric the Goth appeared with his army before the gates of Rome, and sacked the city. The Goths under his successor occupied Gaul, and established there three kingdoms. The Franks seized the north, the provinces near the Loire and the Seine; the Burgundians the east of Gaul; and the Visigoths the south. In 455 Rome was again sacked by the Vandals under Genseric. After that time the Western Empire languished on for twenty years. The barbarians made and unmade the emperors. The last of these phantom holders of the imperial dignity was Romulus Augustulus, son of an ambassador of Attila, King of the Huns. He was soon dethroned by Odovacar, and Italy was divided among the barbarians. The western part of the Empire was lost in this way in 476 A.D., half a century before Justinian's compilations. It was not finally destroyed until 1453 A.D., when the Turks took Constantinople.

Justinian, b. 483; *imp.* 527; *d.* 565.—Justinian, it has been said, rose from an Illyrian hut to the imperial throne. He has been claimed as a Slav, and his real name said to have been Upranda.[1] He was born on the borders of Thrace

[1] Apart from the fact that it is extremely doubtful whether at that time the Slavs had penetrated so far, the authority for Justinian's Slavonic origin is late and suspicious. See Bryce, J., in *Eng. Hist. Rev.*, 1887, 2, 657; Kuhlenbeck, *Entwicklungsgeschichte des röm. Rechts*, 351.

and Illyricum, at Tauresium, perhaps in the country now called Bulgaria, or perhaps in Macedonia.[1] His marvellous rise was due in great part to the equally marvellous rise of his uncle Justin. Justin was a military adventurer who had become prætorian prefect, and by the favour of the soldiery had made himself emperor. Having no children of his own, he had long before this brought his young nephew to Constantinople, had given him the best education, and had placed him in the position of a son. Justin himself could not write his name. The nephew bore his uncle's name with the suffix "ian"—the mark of adoption. In 527 he was raised by his uncle to the position of joint-emperor, and a few months later, on the death of Justin, Justinian was allowed to succeed him. He was then forty-five years of age. He was married to Theodora, an actress and ballet-dancer of great beauty, but of doubtful reputation. Justinian had persuaded Justin to repeal the law forbidding senators to marry actresses. Theodora was created his colleague on the throne, and the oath of allegiance had to be taken before both. The Empire in Justinian's day was in a state of corruption and decline. Of the ancient Roman Empire nothing but its vices had been preserved at Constantinople. Society, rotten to the core, was divided into different religious sects, and into factions called the blues and the greens, which strove with one another with indescribable violence.

Justinian himself was a rank persecutor and strong partisan. He ordered a cruel massacre of all the Samaritan Jews who had been concerned in a rebellion in Palestine. When he began his reign, Africa had been seized by the Vandals, Spain by the Visigoths, Gaul by the Franks, Burgundians and Visigoths, Italy by the Ostrogoths, and other parts of the

[1] Tauresium has not been identified with certainty. It is generally thought to be the same place as the modern Küstendil, but it may be Usküb in Turkey (the ancient Skupi), Bryce, J., under "Justinian," in *Ency. Brit.* Justinian may very well have belonged to the old Thracian race.

West by various tribes of barbarians. But for a time, by the help of his great general Belisarius, the armies of Justinian achieved much success. The Empire of the Vandals was destroyed, Africa again made a province, Sicily recovered, and the Goths were driven from Rome. Belisarius in his old age fell into disgrace, was accused of treachery, and stripped of his honours. He was succeeded as commander by the eunuch Narses. Narses completed the reconquest of Italy, and was created viceroy or exarch of that country. He established his capital at Ravenna. In the East Justinian was less fortunate. He had several times to save himself from destruction by buying off Chosroes, the Persian king, and he ended by paying an annual tribute to the Persians, the Huns, and the Saracens.[1]

But Justinian aimed at success in other ways, as well as by arms. He was a man of restless ambition, of great physical strength, full of new plans, and childishly vain. His buildings perpetuate his name more than his wars; his laws more than his buildings. He built an enormous number of churches and public buildings all over the empire. The most famous of all was the great church of St. Sophia, which the Turks have turned into a mosque. It is said that, when St. Sophia was finished, Justinian exclaimed, "Solomon, I have surpassed thee!" and that he caused to be set up a statue of Solomon looking with sad eyes at Justinian's work, which threw his own temple into the shade. This boast is not without much justification. A high authority on architecture says, "There was nothing erected during the ten centuries from Constantine to the building of the great mediæval cathedrals which can be compared with it. Indeed, it remains now an open question whether a Christian church exists anywhere, of any age, whose interior

[1] The fullest and best account of Justinian's wars is in Hodgkin's *Italy and Her Invaders*.

is so beautiful as that of this marvellous creation of old Byzantine art." [1]

Tribonian used to flatter the vanity of Justinian by telling him that he would never die, but would be translated to heaven, and by calling his laws "divine oracles."

Like Henry VIII. and James I. of England, Justinian was a great theologian, and imagined that he could settle disputed points of doctrine by his *ipse dixit.*

But it is on his legislative works that Justinian's fame rests. He found the law a chaos. To discover what the law was upon any point, it was necessary to ransack the *leges* and *plebiscita* of old Rome, the prætors' edicts, thousands of law books of greater or less authority, and a vast number of imperial laws of earlier emperors. He left it a system so well ordered and so sensible that his compilations have shaped the law of the civilised world. How much credit is due to the emperor himself it is impossible to say. Tribonian was his great lieutenant in this work of rearranging the Roman law and putting it into a form adapted for the needs of that time. But Justinian's name will always remain associated with the Roman law, just as the name of Napoleon is associated with the French code.[2]

Decline and Fall of the Eastern Empire.—The Eastern Empire was not finally destroyed until 1453 A.D., when the Ottoman Turks, whose power had been growing for a long time, took Constantinople and made it the Capital of the Turkish Empire and the political centre of the Mohammedan world.

---

[1] Fergusson, *History of Architecture*, ii. 444; Gibbon, *Decline and Fall*, ch. xl. 85 (1823 ed.).

[2] With Gibbon's account of Justinian compare those of Bury, J. B., *History of the Later Roman Empire*, i. 333; Hodgkin, T., *Italy and Her Invaders*, 3, 537 *seq.*; and Finlay, G., *History of Greece*, i. 192. Justinian's reputation, and still more that of Theodora, have suffered greatly from the stories related in the "Secret History" attributed to Procopius. It is now generally believed, however, that the statements found there are largely malevolent scandals. See Bury, *op. cit.*, i. 359; Hodgkin, T., *Italy and Her Invaders*, 3, 536.

The Eastern Empire had its vicissitudes but was frequently in a state of great weakness. There was a certain revival of learning in the ninth, tenth, and eleventh centuries which affected law as well as letters, and is mentioned later in speaking of the fate of the *corpus juris* in the East.[1]

[1] *Infra*, p. 337. For the last two centuries and a half before its overthrow by the Turks, the Empire exhibited a most curious picture of slow decay.

CHAPTER XXVII

The Contents of the Corpus Juris

Corpus Juris.—The *Corpus Juris Civilis Justiniani,* in the form in which we now have it, consists of four parts :—

(1) The Institutes—*Institutiones ;*

(2) The Digest, or Pandects—*Digesta seu Pandectae*—*i.e.* collections ;

(3) The Code—*Codex ;*

(4) The Novels—*Novellae Constitutiones.*

The name *Corpus Juris Civilis* is not a title originally given to the whole work. It was used by Denys Godefroi in his famous edition of 1583, and its convenience for the purpose of distinguishing the work from the compilation of the Canon law called the *Corpus Juris Canonici* led to its general adoption.[1]

The Institutes.—The Institutes is a brief manual of the whole law. It was published 21st November 533 A.D. Justinian tells us in the *Prooemium* that he meant the Institutes to be a text-book for students. It was compiled by a commission of three—Tribonian, Theophilus, and Dorotheus. Probably Theophilus and Dorotheus, both of whom were professors of law, did all the work of compilation, and Tribonian acted as chairman and decided doubtful points. The Institutes is founded largely upon the earlier book of the same elementary character, the Institutes of Gaius, but contains many passages from another work of Gaius, the *Res Cotidianae,* and possibly also from other elementary works

[1] Justinian himself uses the expression *corpus juris* to denote the whole Roman Law (Code, 5, 13, 1), and the phrase *corpus juris civilis* is occasionally employed by the glossarists.—Savigny, *Geschichte des röm. Rechts im Mittelalter.*

such as the Institutes of Marcian and of Florentinus. The passages from the longer commentaries of the jurists and from the imperial constitutions were taken, not from the originals, but from the Digest and the Code. These compilations, it is true, had not been published, but the material had been collected and revised, and it was no doubt available to the editors of the Institutes.[1] There is in this small book little citation of authority, and questions of difficulty are, so far as possible, avoided. The Institutes has remained the usual text-book for students. This is in some respects to be regretted, as, on the one hand, it contains a good deal of matter which is now only of antiquarian interest, and, on the other hand, it is not very full upon subjects like obligations which the modern law has taken chiefly from the Digest. A text-book of the same size written for students of the twentieth century instead of the sixth might, naturally, contain more of the living Roman law. But, upon the whole, the work possesses no little merit as a text-book. It is written in a clear style, and is arranged in a natural and logical order.

It must not be forgotten that the Institutes, though intended for use as a text-book, was binding law, and had the same statutory force as the Digest or the other parts of the Corpus.

The mode of citation by the old writers is *Instit. lib.* 3, *tit.* 1, § 2, *de haereditatibus quae.* The English way is shortest and best—viz., *Inst.* 3, 1, 2. In Germany they often cite thus: § 2, I. *de haereditatibus quae* (3, 1).

The Institutes is divided into four books; each book into titles; and each title into numbered paragraphs. The first paragraph is called the *principium*—cited as pr.—and the second paragraph is number 1.

The Digest.—The Digest is a work of great bulk compared

[1] See Krüger, *Röm. Rechtsquellen*, 341; Karlowa, i. 1015; Mispoulet, in *Nouv. Rev. Hist.*, 1890, xiv. 7; Costa, *Storia delle Fonti*, 136; Kübler, in *Zeit. Sav. Stift.*, 1902, xxiii. 509.

with the Institutes. It consists of selected passages from the works of legal writers of admitted authority. If, in compiling a work like the *Pandectes Françaises*, the editors had simply arranged under each heading—*e.g.* Gifts *inter vivos*—a string of passages from Pothier, Toullier, Demolombe, or if the *Encyclopædia of English Law* consisted of a catena of extracts from Littleton, Blackstone, Story, and other sages of the law, we should have a work on the plan of Justinian's Digest, except that in it the subjects are not arranged in alphabetical order. The arrangement under each title of the passages themselves is rather perplexing. I shall refer to it later.

The Digest was published, less than a month after the Institutes, on 16th December 533 A.D. It is divided into fifty books; each book into titles; each title into *leges* or fragments; and the *leges* into a *principium* and numbered paragraphs. Each *lex* is the whole of a clipping or extract from some writer, and begins with his name and the reference to the book. *E.g.* *Ulpianus libro vicesimo nono ad edictum*, and then the extract.

In citing the Digest, the old writers followed the awkward plan of giving the subject of the title and the number of the fragment and of the paragraph, without giving the reference to the book or the title. *E.g.* ff. L. 2 *Qui petant tutores;* ff. L. 1, 85 *De reg. jur.*[1] This was well enough when the Digest was continually in the lawyer's hands, and he knew where the titles came. Now it is inconvenient. In England the Digest is cited thus: D. 17. 1. 2. pr. The Germans cite L. 2 pr. D. *mandati* (17, 1), or Fr. 2 pr. D. 17, 1 (*de mandatis*). When it is desired to name the author of the fragment cited the citation will be in the form Ulp., D. 1. 1. 1. The curious symbol ff. is very old as a reference to the Digest.[2] It is a sort of conventional way of writing a "d" with a line through it.[3]

[1] See Civil Code of Lower Canada, arts. 251, 1062, references by the Commissioners.

[2] It is used in Godefroi's edition.

[3] *Cf.* the symbol, &c., for etc., Roby, ccxlv.

Some have said it was for π (*pandectae*), but that is a mistake, for we find *ff*[orum], not [arum], and the process of development from đ to *ff* can be traced in the MSS.[1]

The Code.—The Code was published about a year after the Digest, 16th November 534 A.D. It is really a second edition, —*codex repetitae praelectionis.* The first edition was published in 529, and was the earliest of all the compilations. But it was superseded by the second edition, compiled after the Digest, and this second edition is the only one which has come down to us.

The Code is a collection of decrees and laws enacted by the emperors, and of rescripts issued by them. The most general word for such laws is *constitutiones.* The emperors, being despotic rulers, made a law simply by issuing a proclamation. The Code, in a general way, resembles the collections of *Edits et Ordonnances* of the French kings, which were to all intents and purposes as efficacious as the decrees of an absolute monarch, though in France there were a few formalities such as registration by the several *Parlements.* But the form of the Code differs from a collection of *Edits* in this, that in the Code most of the laws are in the form of answers to particular individuals, and addressed to them, whereas the French kings did not issue rescripts of this kind.

Many of these *constitutiones* are given in the Code in an abridged form. The work is divided into twelve books, each book into titles, which are much shorter than those of the Digest, and each title into *leges* or *constitutiones.* If the *lex* is long it is also divided into paragraphs. By the old writers it is cited thus: Cod. L. 2 *de testibus.* The English way is Cod. 4, 34, 11. The Germans cite L. 11, § 1 C. *depositi* (4, 34) or c. (for *constitutio*) 11 *depositi* (4, 34). The citation now frequently begins with the name of the emperor who issued the *constitutio.*

[1] See for other modes of citation employed by some writers, Roby, *Introd.*, ccxlv.

Each *constitutio* begins with the name of the emperor who issued it, and that of the official or other person to whom it is addressed. They are arranged chronologically, and, what would be very odd now, the compilers had the power to alter and correct the constitutions which were inconsistent with later ones. They are often quite short. *E.g.* this is the whole of a title. *De Confessis. Imp. Antoninus A. Juliano.* "Those who have confessed judgment are in the same position as those against whom judgment has been pronounced. Accordingly you have no right to claim to withdraw your confession now that you are being forced to pay."[1]

The Code is for us a book of far less value than the Digest. A good deal of it consists of public law, criminal and ecclesiastical, which is not applicable to modern times. And a great many constitutions are answers as to particular small points. But sometimes we have to refer to the Code for important discussion of general principles.

The Novels.—The Novels did not form part of the original compilations of Justinian, for the sufficient reason that they were not written until after its publication. They are, in fact, a supplement to the Code, consisting of the laws made by Justinian after the issuing of the Code. The full name for these later laws is *Novellae constitutiones post codicem.* The bulk of them fall between the years 535-556. A good many are undated. One or two are put by some as late as 565—the year of Justinian's death. The Novels are addressed to some one or other of the high officials of the Empire, and contain the emperor's instructions upon some public matter. A great many of them deal with ecclesiastical laws. As Greek was the language of most of Justinian's Empire, it is natural to find that most of the Novels are in Greek. In many cases they were not intended to lay down a law for the whole Empire, but to contain instructions as to what was to be done in some particular province. A few were published both in Greek and

[1] C., 7, 59.

Latin, and those intended for the Latin-speaking provinces—viz. Illyricum, Africa, and Italy, which Justinian had for a time won back from the Goths, were in Latin only. Most of them are addressed in the first instance to the *praefectus praetorio Orientis*—the highest dignitary in the official hierarchy. His duty was to transmit them to the *rectores provinciarum*, by whom they were posted up as official proclamations.[1] The most important of the Novels dealing with church matters were addressed first to the Patriarch of Constantinople. Justinian had intended to make an official collection of all his Novels. But this he did not carry out. But collections of them were made by the lawyers for their own convenience. Three of these private collections of Novels have come down to us. They are:—

1. The *Epitome Juliani*.
2. The *Authenticum*.
3. The collection of 168 Novels.

The *Epitome* is an abridged Latin translation of 124 Novels. It includes a few Novels which were Latin originally. It was made by Julian, a professor of law in Constantinople, and dates from Justinian's own time. It was probably intended for use in the Province of Italy.

The *Authenticum* or *Versio Vulgata* is a fuller Latin version of 134 Novels. This was the collection used in Europe during the Middle Ages. It is given in the new stereotype edition of Schoell, as well as the third collection. It is probably a translation of a collection of the Novels which was made in Justinian's time, and perhaps by his instructions, with a view to official publication in Italy, or it may be a private translation made in Italy of an official collection.[2]

The third and fullest collection of 168 Novels gives the Greek Novels in the original. Of these, 152 are genuine Novels of

---

[1] See Karlowa, i. 1019.

[2] See Costa, *Storia delle Fonti*, 139.

Justinian, four (140, 144, 148, and 149) are by Justin II., who succeeded him, and three by Tiberius II. (161, 163, and 164) belong to a collection of edicts generally printed as a supplement; two occur twice over (75=104 and 143=150), one is given separately in Greek and in Latin as if it were two Novels (32=34), and three are edicts of the prætorian præfect (166-168).[1]

Many of the Novels deal with ecclesiastical law, or with administration. But some of them make important changes in the private law. In particular, the Novels completely recast the law of succession. Novel 118 becomes the leading text upon that great branch of the law. The law of succession in most of the countries of Europe is largely founded upon Novel 118, though feudalism introduced many changes.

The Novels are not divided into books. They are cited thus: Nov. 118, cap. 3, sec. 1.

[1] Krüger, *Röm. Rechtsquellen*, 357; Kroll's Preface to Schoell's edition; Biener, F. A., *Geschichte der Novellen Justinian's*, Berlin, 1824.

CHAPTER XXVIII

Justinian's Codification and the Works from which it was Compiled

Jus Vetus and Jus Novum.—Leaving out of sight the Novels, which are merely supplementary to the Code, and the Institutes, which is a short text-book intended to be an introduction to the study of the Digest, we see that Justinian's two great books are first, the Digest, and the second, the Code. Each of these is intended to be a codification of one of the two main divisions of the law which presented themselves in the time of Justinian. These were—(1) *Jus* or *Jus Vetus*, and (2) *Leges* or *Jus Novum.*

The lawyers of the sixth century had to find their law either in the books of certain famous lawyers of a former day, called the classical jurists, or else in some enactment made by an emperor. The law which was laid down by the old writers they called the *jus*. *Jus* in this connection is equivalent to jurisprudential law. The laws made by the emperors were called *leges* or statutes, to distinguish them from the common law, if we may so call the *jus vetus*.

The Digest is a codification of the *jus*, and the Code is a codification of the *leges*.

Common Law and Statutes.—The Digest corresponds in a general way with the codes of countries such as France or Italy which have codified their law. It is a condensation of an immense mass of law, itself deprived from various sources, but taken at the date of codification from certain authors of established reputation. The civil codes of Europe are much more abstract and much shorter than the Digest, because instead of giving the string of passages from authorities in support of a particular proposition, the codifiers merely state the proposition in its naked form. The fact that the Digest gives the *ipsissima verba* of the writers instead of condensing what they say and stating the result, makes the Digest much more lively and varied than a modern code can be. The law which was codified in the Digest had been made in a variety of ways. Part of it was really statute law, laws passed by the old legislative bodies of the Republic, or by the Roman Senate during both the Republic and the early Empire. But practically its source was disregarded. It was accepted because it was laid down by Papinian or Ulpian. The line of these great writers was long closed. The latest author cited in the Digest is Arcadius, whose date is about 339 A.D.—*i.e.*, roughly, 200 years before the Digest was compiled. The bulk of the Digest is taken from writers a hundred years earlier than Arcadius, and they often stated law which had been accepted for centuries before them. It is not curious, therefore, that in Justinian's time they called the law of the jurists *jus vetus*.

Of the *leges* the bulk consisted of constitutions made by the later emperors coming down to Justinian. Compared with the *jus*, it was most of it modern, and was not unnaturally called *jus novum*.

Speaking roughly, we may say that the Digest was a work on the same plan as the Civil Code of France or of the Province of Quebec, which, like it, contain a great deal of law the origin of which is lost in antiquity. The Code, on the other hand, was not very unlike an official edition of revised statutes. It consisted of particular enactments abridged and rearranged. Each enactment had a known date and origin, and its origin was not extremely remote. A still closer analogy may be found in the division between common law and statute in the English law. The Digest was a systematised dictionary of the old common law, and the Code was an edition of statutes revised and abridged by authority.[1]

[1] See Brunner, *Deutsche Rechtsgeschichte*, i. s. 50.

The Code.—The work of codifying the *leges* or imperial enactments was facilitated by the fact that already several collections of these had been made. The earlier compilations were :—

1. The *Codex Gregorianus.* This is a collection of imperial laws made by a certain Gregorianus of whom nothing more is known. It was published about 295 A.D., and, probably, gave the constitutions up to that time. But the extracts which have come down to us contain only constitutions issued between the years 196-295.

2. The *Codex Hermogenianus* was a supplement bringing the code of Gregorian down to date. When it was published is not certain, but there are grounds for assigning it to between 314 and 323 A.D.[1]

We do not possess either of these codes in their original form, though a good many fragments of them remain in various collections, especially in the work called Alaric's Breviary. They must have been very voluminous, for Justinian's Code gives some 1200 rescripts by Diocletian and Maximian alone, and it is not likely that he had any other source for them than the Hermogenian Code. So far as we know, Gregorian and Hermogenian were both private lawyers who made these collections for the use of the profession.[2] They were not issued under the imperial authority. But they were so carefully made, and proved so useful, that they came to be regarded as of the highest authority, and were in constant use in the Courts, both in the East and the West. They were superseded in the time of Justinian by being taken into his Code.

These two old collections of imperial laws were made use of by Justinian in his Code. But, rather curiously, they were before his day included in the *jus* and not in the *leges.*[3] The reason for this is not very clear. It may be that they were

[1] Karlowa, i. 754 ; Costa, *Storia delle Fonti*, 114.

[2] Karlowa, i. 941 and 959.

[3] See Puchta, *Inst.*, i. 134 ; Karlowa, i. 931.

so treated because the collections of Gregorian and Hermogenian were not official. This is confirmed also by their position in the work called Alaric's Breviary, which I shall speak of more fully later. That work consists of two parts—(1) the *leges*, (2) the *jus*; and the extracts from the Gregorian and the Hermogenian Codes are given in the second part, just as if Gregorian and Hermogenian had written and not merely arranged the laws which they give in their collections.[1] And an additional reason may have been that they were collections chiefly of rescripts and not of *leges edictales*. After the time of Constantine the emperors legislated extensively by lengthy proclamations, called sometimes *leges generales*, sometimes *edicta*. Before his time there had not been much direct imperial legislation of a general character. The emperors either clothed their laws in the forms of *senatus-consulta*, or else issued rescripts which, in most cases, dealt with some particular point raised by a petitioner. The *leges* or *jus novum* consisted of these imperial laws issued by Constantine the Great and his successors.[2]

Codex Theodosianus.—A third compilation of imperial laws of greater importance than these is the Codex Theodosianus. This was a code prepared under the direction of Theodosius II., Emperor of the East, and published in 438 A.D. Valentinian III., the Emperor of the West at the time, agreed that the Code should have authority in the West also. It was arranged also that laws subsequently promulgated by either emperor should be communicated to the other, who might, if he chose, proclaim them as law in his own dominions. This arrangement was acted upon, somewhat fitfully, until the loss of the western part of the Empire in 476 A.D.

The *Codex Theodosianus* was a work of great size in sixteen books, and gave constitutions from the time of Constantine down to its date. We do not possess it in its complete form,

[1] See Glasson, *Hist. du Droit*, i. 214, note; and Brunner, *Deutsche Rechtsgeschichte*, i. s. 50.

[2] Karlowa, i. 939, 945.

but a large part of it has been discovered in recent times, and it is a valuable work, throwing great light on the state of the Empire in the fifth century.[1] The separate constitutions promulgated after its date down to the fall of the Western Empire were called the *Post-Theodosian Novels.*

It is interesting for us to notice that the old French law is based upon these earlier codes, especially the Theodosian, and not upon the compilations of Justinian. This is because Gaul had ceased to be a province of the Empire, and had been overrun by the barbarians after Theodosius, but before Justinian, so that Justinian's Code superseded the Code of Theodosius in the East, but not in Gaul.

Theodosian Code in Gaul.—The *Corpus Juris* exercised a great influence on the French law from the twelfth century onward, and the learned lawyers introduced from it into the French law the main doctrines of obligations, besides much else. But in the fifth century the great authority was the Code of Theodosius. Gaul had by that time assimilated in a remarkable degree the civilisation of Rome. The immense mass of the population remained Celtic. The Roman element was composed of a small class of officials, a few merchants, and here and there a group of soldiers to whom grants of land had been made.[2] But the Celts seem to have had a pliability of nature which enabled them to become romanised more quickly and more profoundly than other races which Rome had conquered. The Latin language became widely used, and was made compulsory in the courts. After the famous law of Caracalla, by which all free inhabitants of the Empire were granted the rights of Roman citizens, the Celtic laws rapidly disappeared.[3] Some local peculiarities in the law of landownership remained, but in general the whole country became

---

[1] Much use is made of it in the interesting book of Mr. S. Dill—*Roman Society in the Last Century of the Western Empire*, London, 1898.

[2] See Glasson, *Histoire du Droit, &c.*, i. 191.

[3] *Circa* 212 A.D. See *supra*, 292.

subject to the Roman law. The works best known and most used in Gaul were the Codes of Gregorian and Hermogenian, the *Institutes* of Gaius, and the *Sentences* of Paul. When the Theodosian Code came out, part of Gaul was already occupied by the Visigoths, the Burgundians, and the Franks. But the Theodosian Code at once took effect in the centre of Gaul and on the left bank of the Rhone. And so strong a hold had the Roman law obtained upon the country that, as we shall see, the barbarians themselves allowed their new subjects to retain it. Of this law, which survived the conquest, the Theodosian Code formed the most important part.[1]

The Code of Justinian, therefore, was compiled of imperial laws taken from these three earlier codes, and of separate enactments, issued in the East from 476 to the date of Justinian's own compilation. The Code was prepared by a commission of ten members, including Theophilus, a professor of law in Constantinople, the rest being high officials, two eminent advocates, and Tribonian. They were empowered to leave out all enactments which had become obsolete, to abridge freely those which they included, and to remove inconsistencies between earlier and later laws. The *leges* having been collected to so great an extent in the earlier codes, it is not so surprising to find that Justinian's Code took only a little over a year to complete. It was declared that it should now supersede all the laws which it consolidated. Henceforth all reference in the Courts to the earlier enactments was prohibited. It was not permitted to refer to the laws in their original shape as a means of interpreting the law as abridged and amended by the codifiers. The Code and the Code alone was now to be the statute-book of the Empire. As I have already said, this first edition of the Code was soon superseded by a second which was sanctioned on 17th November 534 A.D., after the Digest. It is this *Codex repetitae praelectionis* which we possess.

[1] See Glasson, *op. cit.*, i. 215.

Compilation of the Digest.—The preparation of the Digest was a work of much greater difficulty. A vast number of legal treatises and text-books existed. They were, naturally, of very unequal value, and contained, like modern law-books by different authors, innumerable passages which sometimes were flatly contradictory, and, more often, were inconsistent with each other in a slighter degree.

Many of the MSS. were extremely rare; still more were very costly. No library contained anything like all of them, and most lawyers had to work with the aid of very few books. It continually happened, in the more remote parts of the Empire, that cases had to be decided without either the judge or the counsel being able to refer to works which might have thrown great light upon the point at issue. Tribonian, whose own library was one of the finest in existence, estimated that there must be about two thousand books which ought to be gone through if the legal literature was to be fully examined.

Quinquaginta Decisiones.—Before attacking this mass of material, it was thought well to clear the ground. There were a large number of well-known moot-points of law about which the lawyers had wrangled for generations. The Commissioners would be certain to differ about some of these, and it seemed desirable to relieve them of the responsibility of deciding them. Justinian therefore published a number of rulings by which he settled for ever these old controversies, and he afterwards directed the Commissioners to adopt his view as to all these points. This little book was called the *Quinquaginta Decisiones.*[1] We do not possess it, but we know from references in the Institutes and the other books what some of these old moot-points were.[2]

Method of Compilation.—These preliminary difficulties being

[1] *C. Cordi de emend.*, *Cod.* Just., i.; Karlowa, i. 1007; Costa, *Fonti*, 131.

[2] See some examples in Ortolan, *Histoire dela Législation Romaine*, (ed. Labbé), i. 431.

cleared away, the work of compiling the Digest was at once taken up. Its object was to reduce the chaotic mass of law-books into an ordered system. Suppose, *e.g.*, a lawyer had a question about a right of way. As things were, he might consult the works of, say, Papinian, Paul, Gaius, and Ulpian. They might not entirely agree upon the point. Moreover, Gaius might be a little fuller with regard to some one aspect of the matter, and Paul more complete upon another side of it.

The scheme of the Digest was for the Commissioners to ransack all the writers of authority who treated of this subject of right of way; to decide in cases of conflict which opinion was the sounder; to put down the best and fullest statement of the law, which might be, *e.g.*, by Papinian, and to supplement it by passages from Paul or others which contained something omitted by Papinian. The Commissioners were to avoid repetitions, to reconcile inconsistencies, and to omit statements which were obsolete. But, so far as possible, they were to give the passage in the words of the original writer, and the reference to the work from which it was quoted. It was declared beforehand that the Digest was to consist of fifty books, and that when it appeared it was to supersede all the old law-books. As a matter of fact, the compilers made use of the works of thirty-eight authors, and included passages from 1544 books (*i.e.* rolls or volumes).[1] Henceforth it was not to be permissible to cite any of these works in court. The Digest was to be the sole and final authority for the text of the jurists.

Authors Selected.—The Commission to prepare the Digest consisted of sixteen members besides Tribonian, who acted as chairman or superintendent. They were directed to make excerpts only from the works of writers whose authority had been officially recognised—*quibus auctoritatem conscribendarum interpretendarumque legum sacratissimi principes praebuerunt.*[2] These all belonged to the limited class of

[1] Roby, *Introd.*, xxiv.

[2] Const., *Deo Auctore*, s. 4.

lawyers whose works had been stamped by the Valentinian Law of Citations as possessing authority. The name *juris auctores* was limited to this class, except that we must add the *veteres*, who lived before the days of imperial patents.

The compilers departed from their instructions to a trifling extent by admitting a few extracts from the works of Arcadius Charisius, and a larger number from those of Hermogenianus,[1] neither of whom were "patented counsel." They also give a few passages from three of the old lawyers of the Republic who lived before this system of official recognition was introduced. But, with these slight reservations, we may say that the Digest consists of select passages bearing on the same subject taken from a group of lawyers who enjoyed a peculiar degree of authority.

The Arrangement of the Digest.—The general order of the Digest is not very clearly indicated, and there are so many digressions and interpolations that it is not always easy to see in what order the subject-matter is intended to be treated. It is very different from the simple division of the Institutes—which treat first of Persons, secondly of Things or Property, and thirdly of Actions. But, of course, a short and elementary book is more easily arranged than a large work like the Digest. And after all, the simplicity of the arrangement of the Institutes is gained by the rather unfair means of dragging in the law of succession and the law of obligations under the head of Property. The scheme, however, of the Digest is quite different, and was probably based on the order of the edict. Roughly speaking, the arrangement is:—

1. Jurisdiction, parties, and bars to action.

2. Kinds of actions, and to whom they are competent; actions *in rem;* vindications; actions for damages; actions for partition, &c.

[1] Possibly, but not certainly, the author of the *Codex.* See Roby, *Introd.*, ccviii.; Karlowa, i. 754; Clark, *Sources*, 143.

3. Actions on contracts; explanation of commercial contracts.

4. Family law; marriage; tutory.

5. Successions.

6. Judgment and execution.

7. Injunctions or interdicts; special pleas, such as *res judicata;* prescription; fraud, &c.; and bonds and sureties.

This concludes the matters of actions purely civil.

Then come—

8. Punishment of wrongs, civilly and criminally; actions for penalties; and criminal law.

9. Public law, including municipal law, and general rules as to interpretation.[1]

Bluhme's Theory.—How are the different extracts arranged in the separate titles? The order of the extracts is extremely difficult to follow. There is, however, a clue which was discovered by a young German—Friedrich Bluhme—and published in his thesis for his degree when he was only twenty-three years old.[2] The plan seems to have been something like this: the whole of the juristic literature was divided into three great masses:—

1. Books of an elementary character, such as the *Institutes* of Gaius and special treatises on the old civil law—the *jus civile.* In this group the most important work was a voluminous treatise by Sabinus, upon which Ulpian had written a commentary. After this book, the group or mass was called by Bluhme the Sabinian Mass.

2. Works on the prætor's edict; the *jus gentium*—Edictal Mass.

3. Miscellaneous works, especially works of "casuistry," in which difficult questions of law were raised and discussed. In

[1] See the useful analysis by Mr. Roby, *Introduction to the Digest*, xxxiii. *seq.*

[2] His paper was published in the *Zeitschrift für geschichtliche Rechtswissenschaft*, 1820, iv. 257 *seq.*

this group the great name was Papinian; hence the mass is called by Bluhme the Papinian Mass.

Tribonian seems to have assigned each of these masses or groups of works to a separate committee. In addition, there was a much smaller mass containing, as it would seem, extracts from books procured after the original assignment into three "masses." The committee which had the Papinian "mass" took charge also of this minor "mass," and it forms a sort of appendix to their part of the Digest.[1]

When the Commissioners met as a body, each committee had prepared a string of extracts upon the subject in hand. These were then compared. Those extracts which contained only the same law as was given in some other fuller extract were struck out; and each committee was left with a shorter string of useful passages. These were then adopted by the Commissioners. If the edictal committee happened upon a particular subject to have the longest string of extracts, they were put first in the title; then came the next longest string; and then the third. It is not denied that there are many places in the Digest where this plan has not been rigidly followed. But on the whole, Bluhme's theory has won its way to such complete acceptance that in Mommsen's great edition of the Digest you will find the extracts marked S., E., or P., according as they belong to the Sabinian, the Edictal, or the Papinian group.[2]

No Commentaries.—The preparation of the Digest occupied about three years, a remarkably short time considering the magnitude of the undertaking. Tribonian estimates that it reduced the bulk of the juristic literature to one-twentieth of what it had been. Although so many books were consulted, and

[1] See Roby, *Introd.*, liv.; Krüger, *Röm. Rechtsquellen*, 338.

[2] Bluhme's theory has been called in question, but without success. In the opinion of the best judges it still holds the field. See Mommsen in *Zeit. Sav. Stift.*, 1901, xxii. 1, and P. Krüger, *ibid.*, 12; Karlowa, i. 1011; Costa, *Fonti*, 133.

so many writers cited, it turned out that five well-known authors contained most of the law which the compilers thought it worth while to preserve. These were Papinian, Paul, Ulpian, Gaius, and Modestine. About two-thirds of the whole Digest comes from the works of the great five. When the Digest appeared, Justinian issued a proclamation called *Tanta*, which now stands as a preface to the work. By it he declared it should be henceforth unlawful to cite the original writers. All commentaries were forbidden. Only literal translations (*κατὰ πόδα*), *indices*, *i.e.* summaries, and *paratitla* were to be allowed. *Paratitla* were references to parallel passages in other parts of the Corpus.[1] And, by another constitution, Justinian organised the course of study in the law-schools, enacting that it should extend over five years, of which the first should be devoted to the Institutes and to the preliminary books of the Digest, the second, third, and fourth to the remaining books of the Digest, and the fifth to the Code.[2]

Napoleon had the same idea that his code ought to stop the tide of the legal literature, and he exclaimed "*mon code est perdu*" when he heard of the first commentary on the Code Napoléon. If Justinian could have foreseen the libraries of huge tomes which were to be composed to explain the Digest, he would probably have regarded his compilations as a failure.

[1] C. *Deo Auctore*, 12; C. *Tanta*, 21.
[2] C. *Omnem*, 2-5.

CHAPTER XXIX

Leges Romanae Barbarorum

The Gothic Kingdoms.—Before the time of Justinian, as we have seen, the Western Empire had been overthrown. Belisarius and Narses won back Italy for a few short years. But it was overrun by the Lombards only three years after Justinian's death. Gaul had fallen for ever under the power of the Teutons. The Empire had fought a stubborn rear-guard fight for centuries. As early as the third century the seat of the provincial government had been moved from Trêves to Arles, to be farther from the hordes pressing in from the North-East. Great numbers of the barbarians served in the Roman armies. Their leaders obtained lands held by military tenure, and some of them rose to the highest positions in the Roman official hierarchy.[1] Before the fifth century the tribes, which had been brought in closest contact with the Empire, had embraced Christianity. It was in the course of that century that the barbarians established permanent kingdoms within the territory of the Western Empire. The countries which now occupy Europe began at that time to have a separate existence. Those which specially concern us here are three:—

1. The Visigoths, or West Goths.

They established, about 412 A.D., a kingdom which included nearly all Spain and Southern France, as far north as the Loire and as far east as the Rhone. The capital was Toulouse. The North of France and Central Germany were occupied by the Franks.

2. The Burgundians.

---

[1] See—*e.g.* Freeman, *Historical Geography*, 87.

Between the Alps and the Rhone, in south-east Gaul, at about the same time, the Burgundians established a kingdom, of which the capital was Geneva.

3. The Ostrogoths, or East Goths.

In 493 A.D. Theodoric, King of the East or Ostrogoths, founded a kingdom which included Italy, part of Austria, and the sea-coast along the Riviera (coast of Provence). Theodoric acknowledged nominally the suzerainty of the emperor at Constantinople, but he was in reality an independent king. His capital was Ravenna.

System of Personal Laws.—These tribes had been for centuries harassing the Western Empire, and during that time they had become to some extent romanised. When they came in this way to set up permanent seats of government, the question presented itself, what law was to prevail in these new kingdoms?

It was answered in a rather singular way. The German tribes themselves had been migrating from place to place, being governed all the time each by its own tribal customs. It seemed to them natural that a Goth should be under Gothic law, or a Burgund under Burgundian law, wherever he might happen to find himself. And they were willing to apply the same principle to the Roman provincials whom they had conquered. Let the Roman keep his law, and the Goth keep his law, although they might live side by side in the same city. This was the system called that of personal laws, as opposed to territorial. A man's law did not depend on whether he lived in Gaul, but on whether he was by race a Goth or a Roman. A contemporary writer says, *Nam plerumque contingit ut simul eant aut sedeant quinque homines, et nullus eorum communem legem cum altero habeat.* "It often happens that of five men who chance to be sitting together, every one is under a different system of law."[1] In order to distinguish clearly the different

[1] Bp. Agobard of Lyon, cited in Brunner, *Deutsche Rechtsgeschichte*, i. s. 34. In countries like Egypt, where foreigners retain their personal law in matters of status, this might easily happen to-day.

systems which governed their different subjects, the Gothic kings found it necessary to codify them. They had codes of Roman law drawn up to show what law governed their Roman subjects, and Gothic codes to show what were the laws of the Goths.

The Gothic Codes.—Each of the three kingdoms had its code of Roman law. Two of them were in force only for a few years and had little influence on the development of the law. These two were:—

1. The *Edictum Theodorici*, published, probably, about 500 A.D.[1] This code is drawn chiefly from Paul's *Sentences* and from the codes of Gregory, Hermogenian, and Theodosius. Unlike the others it applied to both the Gothic and the Roman subjects in the kingdom of the Ostrogoths. But the reason seems to be that it contained hardly any private law. The Goths in Italy were willing to adopt the public and criminal law of the Romans, but as regards the law of the family and of succession it is probable that the system of personal laws prevailed, and that the Goth was under his old Gothic customs, and the Roman under Roman law. When Justinian's generals overthrew the Ostrogothic kingdom the Edict of Theodoric fell with it and Justinian's *Corpus* became the law of Italy (554 A.D.).[2]

2. *Lex Romana Burgundionum, or Papian.*—This was published either by Sigismund, son and successor of Gundobald, or, as some writers think, by Gundobald himself,[3] about 517 A.D.[4] For themselves the Burgundians had a code, now generally

[1] There has been some controversy as to the date, and it has been assigned by one writer to as late a period as 524. See, for references, Costa, *Fonti*, 125; Calisse, *Storia del Diritto Italiano*, i. 3, and in vol. i. of the *Continental Legal Series* (General Survey, p. 10); Karlowa, i. 947.

[2] For some interesting information as to Theodoric's edict, and, especially, as to the history of the manuscripts, see Hodgkin, *Italy and Her Invaders*, 3, 276 and 309.

[3] See Krüger, *Quellen*, s. 40.

[4] The date is not certain. It may be before 506 A.D. Costa, *op. cit.*, 127.

called, after King Gundobald, the *loi Gombette.* It was founded partly on native customs, but borrowed much from Roman law. The Burgundian kingdom was overthrown by the Franks in 534, so that *Papian* was law only for about seventeen years.[1]

3. *Lex Romana Visigothorum or Alaric's Breviary.*—By far the best and the most important of these Roman codes published by the Gothic kings is that of the Visigoths. It is known as *Lex Romana Visigothorum,* or, popularly, as Alaric's Breviary (abridgment). This compilation was published by the authority of Alaric II., King of the West Goths, at Aire in Gascony, in 506 A.D. In Spain, more of the spirit and intellectual power of Rome survived the ruin of the Western Empire than in any other part of Europe except Italy. In preparing this code for his Roman subjects, who were very numerous, Alaric had the assistance of learned Roman lawyers. Like Justinian's *Corpus* the Breviary is taken from the two sources, the *Jus* and the *Leges.* The extracts from the *Jus* consist of an epitome of the *Institutes* of Gaius cut down here to two books, Paul's *Sentences,* a few excerpts from the Gregorian and Hermogenian Codes, and a single passage from the *Responsa* of Papinian. The selections from the *Leges* include extracts from the Theodosian Code and a number of the post-Theodosian Novels. Until the modern discovery of the MSS. of Gaius our knowledge of his work was almost wholly based on the Breviary, as was also our knowledge of the Theodosian Code so far as private law is concerned. Alaric's Breviary was much used in Western Europe from the sixth century to the twelfth. It was, in fact, for 500 years the *Corpus Juris* of the West, as Justinian's was of the East, and from it was derived, broadly speaking,

[1] The name "Papian," by which this code used to be called, is due to a curious blunder of a copyist. His MSS. included the *Lex Romana Visigothorum,* the last title of which was headed "Papian," an abbreviation for Papinian. The copyist mistook this for the name of the *Lex Romana Burgundionum,* which followed. The blunder has been unjustly ascribed to *Cujas.* See Glasson, *Hist. du Droit,* ii. 148.

such knowledge of the Roman law as existed in Europe before the time of the glossators. It was used for purposes of instruction and as a compendium of Roman law in the West Gothic kingdom even after it had ceased to be of binding authority.[1] In the south of France the Breviary continued to hold the highest authority until, in the twelfth century, it began to be superseded by the *Corpus* of Justinian. In the monkish schools it was used as the text-book for legal education. When the Digest of Justinian began to be known in the West, as I shall describe later, it was natural that the Breviary should give way to it. The compilers of the Breviary had discarded, because they found them too difficult, the real masterpieces of Roman jurisprudence—viz. the writings of Papinian, Ulpian, and Paul. The permanent value of the Roman law lies in the excerpts from the great jurists which we possess in the Digest. The Imperial enactments, and such books of elements as the *Institutes* of Gaius or the *Sentences* of Paul, might well enough strike the unlettered Goths as wonderfully refined when compared with their own rude legal records. But as Europe became civilised Alaric's Breviary would have been found hopelessly inadequate to meet the wants of growing trade and of changed social conditions. On the other hand, the rules of contract, and much else which the Roman jurists of the classical period had worked out with so much elaboration and subtlety, were well fitted to serve as the framework upon which the modern law could be constructed.[2]

Forum Judicum.—For themselves the West Goths retained their national customs. About a century and a half later, Recessuinthe, a king of the Visigoths, promulgated a new code

---

1 Krüger, *Rechtsquellen*, s. 40.

2 There are numerous editions of the barbarian Codes. Abridgments of them, with useful notes, may be found in Gengler, H. G., *Germanische Rechtsdenkmäler*, Erlanger, 1875. See on these Codes generally, Glasson, *Hist. du Droit*, ii. 134 ; Brunner, *Deutsche Rechtsgeschichte*, ii. ss. 49 *seq.*

called the *Forum Judicum*, which is the basis of the law of Spain. It borrowed largely from the Roman law, but modified it a good deal, under the influence of the Church. The *Forum Judicum* applied to all the subjects of the West Gothic kingdom, and the Romans were expressly forbidden to invoke their old law.[1]

[1] See Glasson, *Histoire du Droit et des Institutions de la France*, ii. 164.

CHAPTER XXX

The System of Personal Laws

The Professio Juris.—During a great part of the Middle Ages the curious system of personal laws continued to exist in several countries of Europe. The first thing the judge had to do was to ask the defendant *qua lege vivis?*[1] The defendant's answer is called by modern writers his *professio juris.* It was noted in the record. *E.g. Interrogaverunt ipso comiti supradicto qua lege vivebat? Ille autem praesens stetit, et taliter dixit quod lege sàlica vivebat.* It is thought by some writers that the defendant might choose for himself whether he would live under the Roman or the Gothic law.

Out of the conflicts which arose when the parties had different personal laws were evolved many of the rules which form the beginning of the branch of law now called Private International Law. *E.g.* the rule that the penalty was fixed by the *lex loci delicti commissi*—the rule that legitimate children follow the personal law of their father; illegitimate, that of their mother; and many others.

Capitularia.—In addition to the personal law which differed for Goth and for Roman, there were laws made by the Gothic kings—the *capitularia,* which applied to all subjects—Goths and Romans alike. The position was just what it would have been in Canada, if the English at the conquest had said: "We will be under our own law; let the French keep theirs. New statutes will apply to both." There were, in fact, some who advocated this plan.

The personality of laws in Europe lasted, roughly, till about the tenth century, when territorial law began to be established.

[1] Brunner, *Deutsche Rechtsgeschichte,* i. s. 34.

CHAPTER XXXI

The Fate of the Roman Law in the West

Disappearance of the Digest.—During the dark and confused period between the second conquest of Italy and the Lombards, just after Justinian's death, and the beginning of the twelfth century, the *Corpus Juris* is almost lost to sight. The old civilisation of the Empire was becoming more and more a faint tradition. The rude and turbulent tribes, out of which the modern nations of Europe were to grow, had little time or taste for learning of any kind. So far as the Roman law was studied at all, it was mainly in the mutilated fragments preserved in Alaric's Breviary.

There was an old story, at one time universally believed, that Justinian's *Corpus Juris* was for centuries utterly lost. It was said that a MS. of it was discovered at the sack of Amalfi in 1137, and was presented by Lothaire II. to the Pisans, who had helped him to take the town. Lothaire at the same time declared that the Roman law should be binding in his dominions. From Pisa it afterwards came by conquest to Florence. The famous Florentine MS. of the Pandects, which is by far the best in existence, does appear to have come from Pisa. It is referred to by the Glossarists as *litera Pisana*. But though it came to Florence from Pisa, the probability is that its first home in Italy was at Ravenna.[1] The rest of the story is a fable, now altogether discredited. It embodies, however, an element of truth, viz. that the *Digest* was long

[1] See Mommsen's Preface to his edition of the Digest (*Justiniani Digesta*, Berlin, 1870), xii., and *Zeit. Sav. Stift.*, vi. 500 ; xi. 302 ; Costa, *Fonti*, 140. The MS., which belongs to the sixth or the beginning of the seventh century, is being reproduced by photography. It is in the Laurentian Library at Florence.

neglected. There were schools of law at Ravenna—the old capital of the exarchate—and at Padua, where the Lombards had established their capital, and the Code, the Novels, and the Institutes were to some extent studied.[1] But the Digest was almost, if not entirely, ignored.

Irnerius at Bologna.—At the beginning of the twelfth century there began a remarkable awakening, which has been called the Twelfth Century Renaissance. It was due largely to the rise of the Italian cities. After centuries of invasions and confused fighting there had come a period of tranquillity, and commerce began to make rapid advance. With the spread of trade came the necessity for rules of law fitted to meet the complicated relations which now emerged. The first famous teacher of the Roman law at this time was Irnerius (*circa* 1100). He gave lectures at Bologna, to which students flocked from all parts of Europe. The school founded by him gained such celebrity that it is said to have had at one time 10,000 students—clerk and lay, boys and greybeards. Irnerius, called by his admirers *lucerna juris*, was the first of the school of Romanists known as the Glossators.[2] They were so styled because they wrote *glossae*, or notes, upon the Roman texts. These were, primarily, explanations of hard passages, but the glossators also helped the student by inventing *casus*—*i.e.* hypothetical cases raising the point stated theoretically in the text; and *summae*—*i.e.* short abstracts of the subject under consideration. Irnerius' immediate following were the "four doctors" of Bologna, whom he himself described in the lines,

Bulgarus os aureum Martinus copia legum.
Mens legum est Hugo, Jacobus id quod ego.

After the "four doctors" came Odofredus. "Chi non ha Azo, non vada a Palazzo," was a popular saying. It meant

[1] Muirhead, 2nd ed. 405.

[2] See Rashdall's *History of Universities of Europe in the Middle Ages* (Oxford, 1895); Fitting, *Anfänge der Rechtsschule zu Bologna* (Berlin, 1888); Flach, *Études Critiques sur l'histoire du droit romain* (Paris, 1890).

that in some places a lawyer could not become a judge unless he possessed a copy of the *Summa* of Azo.

Accursius and the Glossators.—The notes of these writers accumulated in volume. They were scattered about in many places, and, as might be expected, were not by any means always in agreement with each other. Franciscus Accursius (*circa* 1260) brought all these *glossae* together, analysed them, and published the whole *Corpus Juris* of Justinian with the most important notes of his predecessors, and with many notes of his own opposite the text. This great work is called the great Gloss—*Glossa ordinaria.* The books of Justinian in this edition are not arranged as they are now. The glossators adopted a curious division, probably due to the fact that they did not become possessed of all the MSS. at the same time. They divided the whole into five volumes:—

(1) *Digestum Vetus* (books i. to xxiv. ; tit. 2).

(2) *Infortiatum* (books xxiv., from tit. 3 to end of book xxxviii.).

(3) *Digestum Novum* (books xxxix. to l.).

(4) Code (first nine books only).

(5) *Volumen parvum;* the *Institutes;* the *Authenticum* or Latin translation of 134 of the Novels; and the last three books of the Code. In this volume was also put a compilation of feudal law called the *Libri Feudorum.*[1]

In the Code they also inserted as notes abstracts of the Novels which had modified the law of the Code. These were called *Authenticae.*

This arrangement of the works of Justinian lasted after the invention of printing, and was not discontinued until the sixteenth century.

The *Infortiatum* is perhaps so called (Digest Strengthened), because it was discovered after the other parts.

The Great Gloss.—The gloss of Accursius was for centuries

[1] See, especially, Savigny, *Hist. de Droit Romain au Moyen-Age* (trad. Guenoux), iii. ss. 157-192.

the great fountain of legal learning. It was held as of the highest possible authority—even greater than that of the text itself. Raphael, a professor at Padua, taught his students that it was better to have the gloss on one's side than to have the text. If a lawyer cited the text the judge would retort, "Do you think the great Accursius had not studied the text and that he did not understand it better than you?"

When the Roman law was accepted bodily, as in Germany, it was the glossated texts alone to which the Courts paid attention. Certain parts of the *Corpus* which the glossators had not annotated, generally because they dealt with institutions no longer existing, were likewise treated by the judges as inapplicable to modern life. *Quicquid non agnoscit glossa nec agnoscit forum.* This maxim does not mean that the non-glossation was the reason why the passage was not "received." It merely states the historical fact that it was the Roman law of the glossators which was held binding.[1]

Characteristics of the Gloss.—It can hardly be said that the notes of the glossators, at one time regarded with such veneration, are much looked at nowadays. If we glance over them we are apt to be more struck with some absurdity of medieval thought than with any merit of the commentator. The glossators regarded the *Corpus* in much the same way as the old commentators regarded the Bible. They made no attempt to take into account the date, and the authorship of the separate parts, or the circumstances in which each was composed. The glossarists looked upon all this collection of writings by many different hands as if it had been a new code just published at Bologna. It was all the word of the great Justinian. The text was for them sacred. On the other hand, they had little scruple in twisting the literal words of a passage into a sense which they were never intended to bear. Obviously a good deal of this had

[1] See Dernburg, *Pandekten*, 6th ed. i. s. 4 (Berlin, 1900). The Institutes were all glossed; the *Digest* all except parts of two titles. Only 96 Novels were glossed. For the unglossed constitutions of the Code and the Novels see Vangerow, *Pandekten*, 7th ed. i. s. 6, amm. 1 (Marburg, 1876).

to be done if the laws of the second century were to be made to fit the society of the twelfth. Of what we now call historical criticism they had not the faintest trace. We are startled sometimes by the depth of their ignorance. In one place Justinian is spoken of as a contemporary of Jesus Christ.[1] The habit of mind with which they regarded the texts is characteristic of their age. Just as Aristotle was treated by the school-men as infallible, and his statements accepted as applicable to all circumstances, so the glossarists took no account of what to a modern would be the first thing to bear in mind—viz. that Justinian's *Corpus* had been compiled more than 500 years before their time, and was made up of extracts from works of a still earlier date. It did not strike them that this fact alone made it impossible that the Roman law should be applicable to many circumstances which arose in a society which had undergone a complete re-casting. The modern view, which looks upon the Roman law as upon the other remains of antiquity with the detachment of the critic, would have been unintelligible to the glossarists. We drop out whole chapters of the Roman law as clearly belonging to a past age, and inapplicable to our circumstances. The glossators thought they were bound to take the law, the whole law, and nothing but the law.[2]

Versio Vulgata.—But in spite of much that strikes us now as absurd, the glossators did a great and valuable service to the science of law. Their crowning merit was that they went back to the original texts. Before them the law was to be found partly in the crude and meagre codes of the Gothic kings, partly in custom, partly in rules laid down by the Church. Every-

[1] Gl. ad Nov. 47, c. 1.

[2] The fullest information about the glossarists is still to be found in Savigny, *Geschichte des römischen Rechts im Mittelalter* (7 Bände, 2nd ed. 1834-1851). There is a French translation (abridged) by Guenoux, published at Paris, 1839. I may also refer to Rivier, *La Science du droit dans la première partie du moyen-âge* (in *Nouvelle Revue Historique du Droit Français*, 1877, i.), and to Fitting, *Zur Geschichte der Rechtswissenschaft in Mittelalter* (in *Zeit. Sav. Stift.*, vi. and vii.).

where it was dark and obscure. The law of the Digest was incomparably better than the law of Europe in the Dark Ages. The glossarists went back to the great monuments of the Roman law, gathered together all the texts, explained them, and showed their connection with each other. By comparison of several MSS. they constructed the text of the whole *Corpus*, which was for centuries the authorised and received text, and is called the *versio vulgata*. Secondly, the glossarists by the most patient study showed the relation of the parts of the *Corpus* to each other. Their references to parallel passages, and their notes showing where a provision of the Digest or the Code has been modified or repealed by a Novel, are still of great utility and have been retained in modern editions of the *Corpus*. We undoubtedly owe to them the preservation of the text and the marginal references. All else of value in the Gloss has long since passed into other works where it is easier to find than in the cumbrous folios of the glossarists.

Bartolus and the Post-Glossators.—To the schools of the glossators there succeeded the post-glossators or Bartolists, as they were called, after the most celebrated of them, Bartolus de Sassoferrato (1314-1357). As Accursius is the typical lawyer of the thirteenth, so is Bartolus of the fourteenth century.

The post-glossators applied to the law the methods of the school-men who annotated Aristotle. Casuistical and fond of hair-splitting, they gradually drifted further and further away from the original texts. Their work was *glossare glossarum glossas.* They cited great numbers of opinions, and generally accepted the *opinio communis* which had the mass of commentaries in its favour, though sometimes it had neither the Roman text nor common sense on its side. As commentaries on the Roman texts, their works are of no value. Cujas said of them, in language which applies to annotators of all ages, *Verbosi in re facili; in difficili muti; in angusta diffusi.*[1] But

[1] Lib. 5, Respon. Pap. ad L. 17, *de injusto rupto;* see Flach, *Cujas et les Glossateurs*, 16.

they did a good deal in the way of adapting the Roman law to the modern world, and had considerable influence in shaping the modern civil law which the French call the *Droit Civil,* and the Germans the *Heutiges Römisches Recht.* In his day Bartolus enjoyed a fame and a position greater perhaps than any lawyer has gained before or since. He was called the Pilot of Jurisprudence, the Prince of Legislators, the Light of the Law, the Miracle of Nature.[1] In Spain and Portugal his writings were declared to have the force of statute, at Padua a chair was established for *lectura textus glossae et Bartoli,* which, as Mr. Flach says, is much like saying, "the law and the prophets."[2] Even more curious, the Emperor Charles IV., among other high distinctions, gave to Bartolus and those of his descendants who should be professors of law, the right to legitimate any of their students who might be illegitimate, and to emancipate any from the disabilities of minority. The school of the Bartolists produced a vast mass of enormous tomes now hardly ever consulted. The revival of letters in the fifteenth century brought about in the sixteenth a revival in the study of the Roman law in the original texts.[3]

Cujas and Doneau.—As Bartolus and his school dominate the fourteenth and fifteenth century, so Cujas is the great name of the sixteenth. Cujas was the most eminent example of what was called the *mos gallicus* or French School of Jurisprudence, as opposed to the *mos italicus* or Italian School of the glossators and post-glossators. The Italian School, which the Germans mostly followed down to the end of the eighteenth century, was the method of gathering together the authorities *pro* and *con.* The French School aimed at going back to the pure Roman law. Cujas (1522-1590) was a learned scholar possessed of immense antiquarian knowledge. He studied with the greatest acumen

[1] Berriat Saint Prix, 309.

[2] *Cujas et les Glossateurs,* 17.

[3] See on Bartolus and his school, Savigny, *Geschichte des römischen Rechts im Mittelalter,* vi. 137-184; Flach in *Nouv. Rev. Hist.,* 1883, 218; Brissaud, *Manuel d'Histoire,* i. 213.

the original texts of the Roman law and did much to elucidate them. He was a most voluminous writer, and his works were for centuries the great quarry out of which lawyers extracted the material for their arguments. Cujas is still occasionally cited in the Courts, but most of what is valuable in his works has found its way into more modern books.

His great rival was Doneau (Hugo Donellus, 1527-1591), who singularly enough was a fellow professor of Cujas at the little University of Bourges.

Doneau was the first writer who attempted to give a synthetic view of the whole Roman law arranged as a logical system.

Domat and Pothier.—This is not the place to make any attempt to review the history of the law in modern times. In the seventeenth century the great work of Domat (1625-1696), *Les Lois Civiles dans leur Ordre Naturel*, did much for the shaping of the Roman law to fit a different age. In the eighteenth century this operation was carried on by other legal writers, and more particularly by Pothier (1699-1772). Partly owing to Pothier's remarkable merits, and partly to the fact that his works were published just before the close of the *ancien régime*, Pothier's influence on the modern law has been immense. Through his writings, which were greatly relied upon by the compilers of the Code Napoléon, a great deal of Roman law may be said to have been definitely received into the law of France. It is worth noting that the French law takes its Roman doctrines not directly from the Roman texts, but through the French commentaries, and especially through Pothier. Pothier was a great student of the Roman law, but he was not infallible. When he trips, as he sometimes does, in his interpretation of the texts he generally leads the Code Napoléon into the same error.[1] From this necessarily brief sketch we see that in the French law the Roman law has always been, so to speak, the centre and nucleus of the whole. Other elements

[1] Girard, *Manuel*, 5th ed. 5; *Pandectes Françaises*, *s.v.* "Obligations," note 27.

contributed to its formation, but without the Roman law it never would have assumed its present shape at all.

Portalis, after the Code Napoléon was introduced, could still say, "Une législation civile vient d'être donnée à la France, mais n'allez pas croire que vous puissiez abandonner comme inutile tout ce qu'elle ne renferme pas. Jamais vous ne saurez le nouveau code civil si vous n'étudiez que ce code. Les philosophes et les jurisconsultes de Rome sont encore les instituteurs du genre humain. C'est, en partie, avec les riches matériaux qu'ils nous ont transmis, que nous avons élevé l'édifice de notre législation nationale. Rome avait soumis l'Europe par ses armes, elles l'a civilisée par ses lois."[1]

And what Portalis said of the French law might be said with no less truth of the Italian, or of the German, or of the Roman-Dutch law, to mention only some of the systems which are based upon the Roman. In the Roman-Dutch law John Voet (1647-1714) holds a position analogous to that of Pothier in France. The elaborate treatises of both bridge the gulf between the classical Roman law and the modern world, and exhibit in a clear and systematic manner the Roman law as it has been modified by legislation and custom.

[1] Berriat Saint Prix, 277.

CHAPTER XXXII

THE FATE OF THE CORPUS JURIS IN THE EAST

Theophilus.—The history of the Justinianian compilations in the East is widely different from that in the West. Their very merits made them from the first unsuitable as the working law-books for the Eastern Empire. It was not only that they were of great volume, and that the arrangement of them was very difficult to understand. But they were essentially Roman, were written in the Latin language which in the East was known only to a few scholars, and were saturated with doctrines only intelligible as the outcome of Roman civilisation.

Although the emperors of the East kept up the theory that they were the Roman emperors, Constantinople became more and more Greek. The Roman law became more and more a foreign law written in a foreign tongue. Before the lawyer could be sure that he was in possession of the law upon any point, he had to wade through a number of opinions not always very consistent, as they had been roughly thrown together in the Digest, and then to make sure that the law had not been changed by any of the myriad constitutions contained in the Code and the Novels. In spite of Justinian's prohibition of abstracts and commentaries, such works were quickly found to be indispensable. The professors of law in the schools of Constantinople and Berytus (Beirout, in Phœnicia) were compelled for the benefit of their students to attempt to extract the essential and practical parts of the Justinianian books, and to explain and paraphrase the passages which were ambiguous. These abstracts found their way from the class-rooms to the Courts, and led to the preparation of other summaries of parts of the law not treated of in the academic prelections. The Digest and the Code in their original form seem to have dropped almost completely out of use at an early period. Of the Institutes, a Greek paraphrase, which contains a good many explanations not found in the Latin, was largely used. It has commonly been ascribed to Theophilus, one of the three compilers of Justinian's Institutes, and is said to have been intended primarily for his students at Constantinople, where Theophilus gave a course of lectures on the Institutes, and where the position of its author gave it great authority. It was widely circulated in the East.[1]

The Basilika.—In the ninth century there was a considerable revival of legal activity in the East. There had been by that time so many changes made by imperial laws that it was very difficult to find out what the law was upon any point. To remedy this, the emperors Basil the Macedonian (867-886), and his son Leo the philosopher (886-911), caused to be prepared an elaborate compilation in Greek, which is called the *Basilika* or royal laws. In it the law of Justinian is rearranged. The whole law of each subject is gathered together from Institutes, Digest, Code, Novels, and the laws since Justinian's time. The *Basilika* consisted of 60 books which we do not possess in a complete form. The *Basilika* was the law of the Eastern Empire until Constantinople was taken by the Turks in 1453. It is noteworthy, as showing how completely the *Corpus* of Justinian had been forgotten in the East, that among the many thousand MSS. which found their way to

[1] There is a new edition of "Theophilus," by E. C. Ferrini, under the title, *Institutionum Graeca Paraphrasis Theophilo Antecessori Vulgo Tributa* (Berlin, 1884-1897). Ferrini believes the ascription of the paraphrase to Theophilus to be erroneous, but does not doubt that it belongs to the age of Justinian. The traditional view is much strengthened by the discovery that the paraphrase was ascribed to Theophilus before the end of the sixth century. See Zachariä von Lingenthal, in *Zeit Sav. Stift.*, 1889, x. 257.

Europe from the libraries of Constantinople after the siege, there was none of any part of the *Corpus* of Justinian except the Novels. Learning was at a very low ebb in the tottering Eastern Empire for some centuries, though between the ninth and the eleventh century there was a certain revival of letters. The lawyers in practice disregarded the *Basilika* almost as completely as Justinian's *Corpus*. They used meagre epitomes or abstracts. One of these—the *Hexabiblos*—said to be a poor epitome of previous epitomes, which goes back to 1345, was, strange as it sounds, made the law of the restored kingdom of Greece in 1835, though since then Greece has got new codes largely based on French, Italian, and German models.

CHAPTER XXXIII

The Distinction between Law and Morals and the Definition of Law

Ulpian's Definitions.—The Institutes, like most modern compendia of law, begin with a preliminary attempt to explain the nature of law and of jurisprudence. The compilers did not find anything of this kind in Gaius, so they borrowed three passages from Ulpian's Rules which struck them as suitable,—

1. *Justitia est constans et perpetua voluntas jus suum cuique tribuens.*

This was a traditional definition. We find it in Plato's Republic (I.) cited from Simonides, *τά οφειλόμενα ἑκάστῳ αποδιδόναι δίκαιόν ἐστι.* Cicero has a similar definition: *animi affectio suum cuique tribuens.*[1]

2. *Jurisprudentia et divinarum atque humanarum rerum notitia, justi atque injusti scientia.*

3. *Juris praecepta sunt haec: honeste vivere, alterum non laedere, suum cuique tribuere.*

Jus and Fas.—These general precepts and definitions are obviously unsatisfactory. They do not distinguish sharply between the sphere of law and the sphere of morals, and they were probably retained by the compilers of the Institutes merely for the sake of old association. All primitive peoples mix up law and religion, and in early times the priest is at the same time the lawyer, as the pontiffs were at Rome. But the Romans perceived earlier than most peoples that the field of law was not co-extensive with that of morals. They distinguish very early between *Fas* and *Jus.*

[1] *De Fin.*, v. 23.

Fas = the sum of the duties owed by man to the gods.

Jus = the sum of the duties owed by man to man.

It is true that for a long time the pontiffs were the interpreters of both *jus* and *fas.*

These old and familiar *praecepta juris* did not lead the lawyers astray. We find the jurist Paul, *e.g.*, expressly declaring, *Non omne quod licet honestum est.*[1]

Justice.—Consider for a moment the three definitions. "Justice is a steady and fixed intention," &c. It is not enough to make a man just that he should occasionally do just acts. He must have a just character; a fixed habit of justice. This is according to the Aristotelian philosophy, by which every virtue must be a fixed or ingrained habit (ἕξις προαιρετική), that is, a habit or trained faculty of choice (Nic. Eth., 2, 6, 15), which manifests itself in virtuous acts as a good tree brings forth good fruit. But, clearly, the law cannot enforce justice in this sense. It may insist on the *jus suum cuique tribuens*, if by *jus suum* we understand a man's legal rights. The law will see that a man gets his legal rights, but it will not pretend to see that his debtor pays him with a *constans et perpetua voluntas.* On the contrary, even a grudging and enforced performance will satisfy the law's demands.

Jurisprudence.—So with the second definition. One would think that everything conceivable must belong either to the sphere of the divine or the sphere of the human. If so, jurisprudence would be, according to the definition, the science of the universe.

But Ulpian, certainly, does not mean to say this, though it is true that the Romans looked upon law as the most necessary of all sciences; calling it, sometimes, *scientia civilis*, or *sapientia civilis.* In this passage Ulpian seems to be referring in a somewhat flowery and rhetorical manner to

[1] D., 50, 17, 144.

the distinction between *fas* and *jus*, and declaring that jurisprudence includes both.[1]

It is worth nothing that jurisprudence is a term which is used by English and French writers in different senses. In the English sense jurisprudence means the science of law, as *jurisprudentia* meant in Latin; though as we have seen *jus* was sometimes understood by Roman writers very broadly. If we restrict "law" to its modern meaning, then by jurisprudence, or the science of law, we mean the investigation of one or more legal systems in order to discover the fundamental principles. Just as the geologist or the astronomer takes a great number of facts and tries to co-ordinate them, and to show their relation with each other, so the scientific lawyer collects and observes a number of laws — either statutes or customs—and tries to find out what common principles underlie them. Professor Holland describes jurisprudence as "a scheme of the purposes, methods, and ideas, common to every system of law."[2] This is rather a definition of comparative jurisprudence than of jurisprudence pure and simple. In discovering what principles are primary or fundamental, it is often a great help to compare several legal systems. If the same rule runs through them all, it will incline one to think that this is an "idea common to every system of law." But Mr. Holland would probably admit that even if there were only one legal system in the world, we might still speak of jurisprudence in the sense of a scientific attempt to explain and correlate the elementary principles upon which that system was based.

In French legal language *jurisprudence* is not generally used in its original sense of the science of law. In its ordinary sense it may be defined as being that solution of a legal problem which the courts have agreed to regard as correct and as finally settled. It is, in fact, equivalent to what English lawyers mean when they say that a point is settled

[1] Accarias, *Précis*, 5. [2] *Jurisprudence*, c. 1.

by judicial decisions. But it has to be remembered that under the French system a lower court is not bound by the decisions of the courts above it to the same extent as in England. We say in this sense the jurisprudence of the Court of Appeals at Quebec differs upon a certain point from that of the Court at Montreal. In a still looser way, *jurisprudence* is used to mean merely the cases which have arisen under a certain provision. It is used in opposition to *la doctrine*, that is, the teaching of the commentators.

E.g. the list of cases which have been determined as to the sense of a particular article of the Code is called the *jurisprudence* upon that article, and is contrasted with the *doctrine—i.e.* the views of the writers of commentaries of accepted reputation.

This meaning of jurisprudence as merely the decided cases is quite incorrect, but is pretty well established.

Law versus Morals.—Ulpian's definitions did not really deceive the Roman lawyers. They saw that law and morals were two things. Morality generally includes law, because most laws enjoin the performance of duties which are at the same time moral duties and legal duties. The law, which compels a man to pay a debt for which he has given a promissory-note, compels him to do what it is also his moral duty to do. Still it is easy to suppose a law which should enjoin the doing of a wrong thing—*e.g.* by ordering the massacre of some innocent persons who happened to belong to some sect or class not in favour with the Government. It would still be a law, but an unrighteous law. In such a case there would be a conflict between law and morals. It might be the moral duty of the good citizen to disobey the law. Rebellion might be more righteous than helping in cold-blooded murder. So, likewise, decisions of judges may settle the law, but settle it in an unjust sense. As the jurist Paul says: *Praetor quoque jus reddere dicitur, etiam cum inique decernit.*[1]

[1] D., 1, 2, 11. *Cf.* Gaius, 4, 115, and 1, 84.

Most laws, happily, command right things, not wrong things, to be done. But they do not command all right things, but only certain ones. *E.g.* morals would require that a man paid his debt, though the creditor might not be able to prove his claim. But law says, "unless such and such evidence is produced, the debt will not be held to exist." *E.g.* I borrow £100 from A. on the simple security of my word of honour. A. dies, leaving his only son as his heir. The son (*a*) knows nothing about the transaction, or (*b*) has no evidence to prove it. I have no legal duty to pay him the £100, but I have a clear moral duty to do so. A man is compelled under severe penalties to fulfil his legal duties, but he cannot be compelled to fulfil all his moral duties. And morals require that I shall perform my duties willingly, and not under compulsion. There must be a conformity between the will and the act. I must not only do the right thing, but I must do it from the right motive. A moral act can only proceed from a moral motive. But an act may be legal though done from a bad motive, and may be illegal though done from the best motives in the world.

Motives in the Law.—It is true that there are some branches of the law in which the character of an act is determined greatly by the motive with which it was done. This is so as to crimes. *Actus non facit reum nisi mens sit rea.*[1] If I strike a man with a stick, intending to kill him, and cause his death, I am guilty of murder. If I strike him a comparatively slight blow, never imagining that I am likely to cause him serious injury, and he is killed, I am guilty of manslaughter. If I am striking at a rat and, without any carelessness of mine, I hit the man instead, and kill him, this is excusable homicide by misadventure. The *mens rea* makes all the difference.

But in civil matters the general rule is that the legality or illegality of an act does not turn at all upon the motive with

[1] There is a valuable discussion as to the extent and application of this maxim in *Reg.* v. *Tolson*, 23 Q.B.D. 168.

which it was done. *Nullus videtur dolo facere qui suo jure utitur.*[1] If I invade the civil rights of another person, I commit a legal wrong, and incur liability to make reparation for any loss which may be the natural consequence of my act. The excellence of my motive will not excuse me, though it may be a good moral justification.

The converse case is more difficult. Suppose I do an act in itself legal, but I do it from a bad motive, and with the intention of injuring my neighbour. Will the badness of my motive make illegal the act which would otherwise be legal? According to the later Roman law it might do so. Where it was possible to show that a man's act was done solely from a desire to injure another, this was sufficient to make unlawful what otherwise would have been lawful. *E.g.* if I can show that my neighbour is sinking a shaft in his land not for his own advantage, but merely to cut off the water which would otherwise flow down to me, or is building a screen for no purpose except to block my view, I can get him restrained. Ulpian says, *Denique Marcellus scribit, cum eo, qui in suo fundo fodiens vicini fontem averterit, nihil posse agi. Nec de dolo actio est; et sane non debet habere, si non animo vicino nocendi, sed suum agrum meliorem faciendi id fecit.*[2]

An act is unlawful if it is done *animo vicino nocendi. Malitiis non indulgendum est.* It is not explained how the proof of malice is to be made, and in many cases a landowner would be able to find some plausible excuse for the act which was injurious to his neighbour.

It is indeed a striking fact, in spite of Ulpian's vague and misleading definitions, that one of the distinctive features of

[1] D., 50, 17, 55. Cf. *ibid.*, fr. 129 and fr. 151.

[2] D., 39, 3, 1, 12. Probably the few texts in which this doctrine is laid down are interpolations and do not represent the law of the classical period. See Pernice, *Labeo*, 2, 1, 64; Ferrini, *Pandette*, 461. For a review of the development of this theory in the modern law, see an article by the present writer on "Motive as an Element in Torts," in the *Harvard Law Review*, 1909, xxii. 501.

the Roman law is the sharp line drawn between law and morality.[1]

The Greeks, with all their genius for art and philosophy, never arrived at any satisfactory demarcation between these two spheres. With them almost every question was left to be decided by the verdict of a large jury, which arrived at its decision upon what seemed to them to be grounds of general equity. These juries, as might be expected, were continually led away by appeals to passion and prejudice.

At Rome, especially in the early days, the field of law was remarkably narrow, but it was well defined. The procedure was highly technical, and the judge was bound to decide according to the strict letter of the law. The law was a precise and special science. On the other hand its field was limited. A great deal was left outside the law. Much was trusted to good faith. Public opinion and a high sense of honour led the primitive Romans to deal honestly by each other. Polybius says, "If you have to trust a single talent to the care of others in Greece you will need ten written documents, ten seals, twenty witnesses, and after all you will be cheated; at Rome you will have no security but the word of the depositary, and it will be religiously kept."[2]

Morals Wider than Law.—Within the family the Roman *paterfamilias* was absolute. The law does not interfere with him. The lives and property of his wife and children were at his mercy. And yet the reciprocal duties of husband and wife, parent and child, were never more scrupulously performed than when they were left to the mere discretion of the *paterfamilias*, and removed outside the range of the law. And it would be very erroneous to imagine that a society is likely to be more healthy in which the law attempts to make men act up to all their moral duties. When we find many laws which aim at

[1] This is well treated by Gide in his work, *Sur la Condition Privée de la Femme*, 91.

[2] Polybius, vi. 56 (abridged).

making men moral, it is generally a sign that the social system has become corrupt. In the later Roman law the husband and the wife, the son and the father, are bound by heavy penalties to perform their duty to each other. It is because morals are in a state of decay that law tries to take their place. As M. Gide pointedly puts it, *Le législateur n'a commencé a y faire de la morale que lorsqu'il n'y avait plus de mœurs.*[1]

Law May Permit Wrong.—It must be remembered that though the sphere of law is narrower than the sphere of morals, there being many moral duties which the law does not enforce, yet on the other hand the law may permit a man to do something which is forbidden by morality. Shylock says—

> "The pound of flesh, which I demand of him,
> Is dearly bought, 'tis mine, and I will have it.
> If you deny me, fye upon your law!
> There is no force in the decrees of Venice."

A man is not always morally justified in standing on his legal rights. *E.g.* my widowed sister, who is a tenant of mine, cannot pay her rent. The law allows me to seize her furniture and turn her into the street. But such an act, though legal, would, assuredly, not be moral. *Non omne quod licet honestum est.*

Jus and Justus.—It is worth noticing that the terms *jus* and *justus* are used in various senses, which need to be carefully distinguished. When Ulpian says jurisprudence is *justi atque injusti scientia,* he merely means the knowledge of right and wrong. The same definition is twice applied by Cicero to *sapientia.* But by the classical jurists *justus* is generally used in a more technical sense. It denotes that which satisfies the requirements of the strict civil law. *E.g. justae nuptiae,* as has been shown in the chapter on "Marriage," means more than legal marriage. It means a marriage between a Roman citizen and a woman with whom he has *conubium*—a marriage which has certain consequences which do not flow from every legal

[1] *Condition Privée de la Femme,* 127.

marriage. By the old law *justae nuptiae* brought the wife into *manus*, and the children into *potestas*. In Justinian's time *manus* was obsolete, but *potestas* survived as a consequence of this kind of marriage. The marriage of a Roman with a peregrin with whom he had no *conubium* was quite legal. But these consequences did not flow from it. It was a good marriage, but not a Roman marriage.[1]

So *injustum dominium* = property acquired in some way which does not satisfy all the conditions necessary for quiritary ownership. *Injusta manumissio* = any way of freeing a slave except one of the three *legitimae manumissiones*. It does not mean a manumission which the law does not recognise at all, for the slave manumitted in one of these less regular ways was nevertheless protected in his freedom.

Jus, again, is a most ambiguous word. It includes two ideas—viz. (1), *jus*—the *norma agendi* = law, in the sense of the law which directs and regulates. *Jus* is here used objectively. (2) *Jus*, the *facultas agendi* = right, the right which is sanctioned and protected by the law. *Jus* is here used subjectively. An example of—(1) is *jus gentium;* or (2) *jus in re aliena.*[2]

Law and Right.—There is the same ambiguity in the French *droit*, the Italian *diritto*, the German *Recht*, as we see in such expressions as *le droit civil, mes droits, droit réel. Droit, diritto, Recht,* all mean both law and right. English has the advantage of two words. It is the *law* which gives and protects a man's *rights*. *Droit* and *Recht* are metaphors from geometry, to be compared with "right" line; with "tort," which is a crooked line; and with *règle*, by which such a line is drawn. Besides this broad division between *jus* in the sense of law and *jus* in the sense of right, the term *jus* is

[1] *Supra*, 165.

[2] *Jus* is from a root *ju*, to bind—*jugum*, ζεύγνυμι. *Lex* is from a root *leg* connected with *legere*, to collect, bring together. In both there is the same metaphor of *binding*. It is possible that the primary meaning of *lex* is the joining of the hands in sign of agreement to a contract. See R. Meringer, in *Indogerman. Forschungen*, xvii. 100.

also used with various other meanings. It may mean, for example—

1. *The* law; as *jus civile; studiosus juris.*
2. A law; as *jura condere* = to pass laws.
3. *Potestas;* as *sui juris.*
4. Legal position in general—*i.e.* status, as when it is said that an adopted son who is emancipated by his adoptive father returns *in pristinum jus*—*i.e.* recovers his original status.
5. The place where the prætor sat to administer justice—*e.g. jus dicitur locus in quo jus redditur.* This is a very common and technical sense of *jus. E.g. in jus vocare,* to summon before the prætor. When the proceedings are before the *judex* the case is said to be *in judicio.*[1]

Definition of Law.—Although English has the good fortune to possess the word "right," which serves to express *jus* in its subjective meanings, the word "law" is, notwithstanding, difficult and ambiguous. Among the many definitions which have been attempted, I think one of the best is this, which I owe to the late Professor Muirhead, of Edinburgh: "The law of any country is the aggregate body of rules which the Courts of that country will enforce for limiting, in the interest of the whole number, the freedom of action of the individual; for guaranteeing freedom of action within these limits; and for restraining it beyond them."

A man's legal Rights = the measure of the free-will which the law allows him, together with his title to have that free-will recognised and protected.

A man's legal Duties = the measure of the respect which one man is obliged to show to the rights of others.

[1] See D., 1, 1, 11 and 12 where one or two other meanings are also given.

CHAPTER XXXIV

Jus Publicum and Jus Privatum

Public and Private Law.—After laying down the general maxims which I have just discussed, Justinian says that there are two branches of the law—viz. public law and private law.

Huius studii duae sunt positiones, publicum, et privatum.

Publicum jus est, quod ad statum rei Romanae spectat, privatum quod ad singulorum utilitatem pertinet.[1]

Positiones literally means points of view. We may look at the law from the point of view of the State, or from that of the individual. This is one of those convenient distinctions which the Roman lawyers made, and every modern system has retained. It does not mean that there is an absolute division between the two branches, so that in private law the State has no interest, or that public law has no concern with the advantage of the citizen. It merely means that for purposes of convenience we may keep apart those branches of law in which our attention is mainly directed to the State, from those branches in which our attention is mainly fixed on the individual.[2] The public interest often exists in matters which at the first blush strike one as purely of private concern. *E.g.* if a man steals my watch or breaks my head, it might seem that this was my private affair, as I am the sufferer. But, of course, it concerns the State to see that thieves are repressed, and that harmless citizens escape violence. Similarly, though as a general rule the State allows its subjects to make any bargains among themselves which they think desirable, there are limits to this freedom of contract. Certain persons such as minors and married women are to some extent protected against themselves.

[1] I., 1, 1, 4.

[2] See Markby, *Elements of Law*, s. 292.

And even persons of unlimited capacity are not allowed to make a contract which is against public order and good morals. It concerns the State to discourage such dealings, even though primarily they would seem to affect only the parties themselves. Papinian puts it shortly and well, *jus publicum privatorum arbitrio mutari non potest.*[1] There is no description in the Institutes of what subjects fall under public law. In the Digest it is said *publicum jus in sacris, in sacerdotibus, in magistratibus consistit,* but this is a rather meagre statement of the matter.[2]

Public law, generally speaking, is the law which regulates the relations between the State and the subject.

Private law regulates the relations between subject and subject.

Public Law.—Public law will, therefore, include :—

1. Constitutional Law.

All the laws which determine by what organs the sovereign authority in the State is to be exercised. Such are the laws relating to the election of members of legislative bodies, the laws defining the powers of these bodies, the laws fixing the authority of government officials, and so on.

Modern classifiers would add administrative law as a separate branch of constitutional law. Under this would fall all laws dealing with the privileges and duties of public officials, laws as to collection of revenue, poor-law, education, recruiting for army and navy, &c., &c. The Roman law included all such law under the general head of constitutional law. In a general way laws of this kind referred to *magistratus.*

2. The *Jus Sacrum.*

The rules which the State lays down as to the ceremonies of an established Church, its right to tithes, &c., the privileges of its priests, &c. At Rome in the early days the pontiffs were

[1] *Cf.* D., 2, 14, 38 ; D., 50, 17, 45, 1 ; D., 2, 14, 31.
[2] D., 1, 1, 1, 2.

the lawyers, and in the latest times the organisation of the Church was regarded as a very important part of the work of the State, as we see from the large number of constitutions in the Code and Novels which deal with ecclesiastical law.

3. Criminal Law.

Crimes, which the State feels it ought to punish, are to be distinguished from delicts or torts which concern the injured individual, and not the State. Mere negligence is not criminal unless it is of so gross a character as to amount to wilful intention to cause injury. The State will not punish a man for carelessly running over me and breaking my leg. It leaves me to bring an action of damages. And in early laws, as has been shown in the chapter on "Crimes," the field of delict is much wider, and the field of crime much narrower than in later times.

Laws of Public Order.—In addition to these subdivisions of public law, comes the application of that term to a large number of laws which belong to the field of private law.

There are many laws which belong in one sense to public law, and in another to private law. These are "the laws of public order and good morals." They are laws which affect only the relations of subjects *inter se*, and would therefore appear to fall under private law. But the private rights which they affect are so important that the State feels bound to protect them. To allow shameless dishonesty or gross immorality to go unreproved would harm the State. It is in this sense that Papinian uses *jus publicum*, when he says, *jus publicum privatorum arbitrio mutari non potest.*

Contrary to the general rule that parties may make any agreements they please, and the State will enforce them—*pacta dant legem contractui*—there are some agreements which the State will refuse to enforce, because they conflict with the principles of good morals and public order. *E.g.* to take a few examples from the Roman law.

The law would not allow a man by any agreement to

deprive himself of the right of making a will in any terms which he chose. He could not tie his hands beforehand. A promise that he would leave all his property or any part of it to a particular person would not bind him. The law would not enforce it, because it was a matter of public policy that people should be free to make their testamentary provisions as they chose when they came to die. If they wanted to make donations during their lifetime, they must make them out and out. There was one reasonable exception to this. A promise made in a contract of marriage is not like an ordinary donation. On the faith that it will be fulfilled, the man and the woman take a step which is irrevocable. It is right, therefore, that the law should enforce donations made in contracts of marriage, even though they are not to take effect until after the donor's death. Public policy demands that testaments shall be revocable *ad nutum.* There is no rule more firmly fixed in the law. A testament is essentially revocable, or ambulatory, as English lawyers call it. And a donation of something to be paid after the donor's death is, so far as it goes, a testament, and, like a testament, it may be revoked. But a donation made in a marriage-contract is different, for there the donee has given a *quid pro quo* by entering into the marriage.[1]

Again, it was a long time a rule of public policy at Rome that an heir instituted by a will should be an heir in reality as well as in name. He must get a substantial share of the estate. The testator could not appoint A. B. his heir and then leave his whole estate to legatees. A. B. was entitled by the *Lex Falcidia* to one-fourth of the estate, by the mere fact of his being instituted as heir. Justinian came to the conclusion that public policy did not require to go so far. He provided that if the testator did not expressly declare otherwise, the heir was to get his quarter. But if the testator

[1] See Esmein, *Mélanges*, 59. *Cf.* D., 39, 6, 13; 1, 35, 4, Labbé *sur* Ortolan, liv. ii., app. iv. i. 733.

declared in so many words that he wished to give the whole estate to the legatees, and that his intention was that the heir should not take a fourth of it, this declaration was not, in Justinian's view, so contrary to public policy that effect ought to be denied to it.[1]

So also it was made a rule of public policy that a woman should not be a party to obligations of suretyship. If a creditor accepted a woman as a surety, he did so at his own risk. She could not be compelled to fulfil her obligation. She could shelter herself behind the defence or *exceptio*, called the *exceptio senatus-consulti Velleiani*. Not married women only but women in general were thus protected from entering into obligations of this kind for the benefit of their male friends, or of each other.[2]

Again, a vendor who was not very sure about his title to the property he was selling, might declare that he was not to be liable in damages if the buyer should be evicted by the real owner. The buyer might say, "I will not hold you responsible for the title. I will take my chance." Public policy did not forbid such a bargain. But the law would not allow a vendor, or, indeed, anyone else, to stipulate that he was not to be held responsible for his own fraud.

Again, a person appointed to act as a tutor could not, arbitrarily, refuse to act. Tutorship was a *munus publicum*, and it was a rule of public order that the tutor appointed must act unless he had some legal excuse.

Public Policy.—Each country has its own views as to what contracts are against public policy, and these views are liable to change. So public policy as understood by us does not protect a woman, as such, from her own folly or over-kindness in becoming a surety, any more than it protects her against other acts of administration which involve her in loss. If

[1] Nov. 1, 2, 2.

[2] There are a few exceptional cases in which the woman is bound. See Cod., 4, 29, 23, 2.

she is a widow, or unmarried, she can play ducks and drakes with her fortune as freely as a man can. If she is married it is true that she is to a great extent protected. But the incapacity of married women has a different history, and depends upon different principles.

For a long time the Velleian *senatus-consultum* was followed in France, both in the north and in the south. Public policy seemed as clearly in its favour there as at Rome. But after much division of opinion lawyers came round to the view that if a woman in contracting an obligation as a surety renounced the benefit of the Velleian, the renunciation should receive effect. This clause of renunciation naturally became a clause of style in dealing with women-sureties, and finally the Code Napoléon abolished the last vestiges of the Velleian.[1] The view of public policy had completely changed.[2]

Again, in all systems of law, the institutions of the family are protected from modifications made by private parties which would be contrary to the views held by the community as to the respective duties of the consorts to each other and to their children. A man and a woman could not, for example, agree that they would be married, but that the marriage should be terminable at the expiration of ten years. They could not agree that the husband should follow the wife's domicile, or that the children should not have any rights of succession.

These are a few illustrations out of many of public law in the sense of public policy.

Public law, in the widest sense of the term, includes, therefore, all those provisions of law which relate to the citizen in his citizen-capacity. As a citizen he has certain political rights. As a citizen he may have certain duties to an established church, in countries where one particular form of

---

1 See an article, " Des Renonciations au Moyen-Age," by M. Ed. Meynial, in *Nouv. Rev. Hist.*, 1900, 108. See Viollet, *Histoire du Droit Civil Français*, 2nd ed. 798 *seq.*

2 Gide, *Condition Privée de la Femme*, 405, 414. C. N. 1123.

religion is specially recognised by the State. As a citizen he must respect the laws which the State has laid down for repressing crime. And, as a citizen also, he must in his dealings with his fellow-citizens refrain from contracts which by the law of his State are regarded as immoral or injurious. At any rate the courts will not lend the public authority to enforce contracts of such a character.

Public law, in a word, has to do with the rights and duties of citizens. In private law it is not the citizen as a citizen, but the individual as an individual who is the subject of the right. In the very last title of the Institutes there is a brief outline of the laws relating to the trial and punishment of criminals.[1] But, otherwise, the Institutes do not deal with public law except incidentally. Their field is the field of private law.

[1] I., 4, 18.

CHAPTER XXXV

The Tripartite Origin of Private Law

Three Sources of Private Law.—Every rule of private law is derived, according to Justinian, from one or other of three sources; *ex naturalibus praeceptis, aut gentium, aut civilibus*—*i.e.* either from natural law, or from the law of nations, or from the *jus civile,* the special law of Rome.

The Jus Naturale.—The rules of law which are derived from the precepts of nature form, when looked at in the mass, the law of nature—the *jus naturale.* This law, Justinian says, following Ulpian, extends to the lower animals. *Jus naturale est quod natura omnia animalia docuit.* Even the fishes of the sea and the birds of the air follow these precepts which nature has planted in the breast of every living thing. As examples he gives the union of the sexes in marriage, and the rearing and training of the young. No doubt some of the higher animals, and many birds, live in pairs, and are examples of conjugal fidelity and of parental care. But other animals set but a low standard of decorum, and by no means all of them show any care for their young, but leave them to take care of themselves at an age when they are sadly unable to protect themselves against their many enemies. Among fishes, for instance, it would not be easy to find much of that training of the young, *liberorum educatio,* which Ulpian says is a universal law of nature.[1] What Ulpian means is pretty much what we mean when we say that a man who is cruel to his wife or child

[1] For an interesting account of the degree of parental care exercised by *omnia animalia,* see Westermarck, *History of Human Marriage,* 2nd ed. 9 *seq.*

is worse than a beast. Even the brutes, though hardly *omnia animalia,* defend their consorts and watch over their young.

As a matter of fact, the expression *jus naturale*, like its modern equivalent, the law of nature, is a very vague one. It is hardly ever used by two writers in the same sense. Ulpian uses it here as meaning the elementary instincts which lead men, and even some animals, to form families and to restrain their natural ferocity in dealing with other members of the family. In another passage of the Institutes *jus naturale* is expressly identified with the *jus gentium ;—jure naturali, quod, sicut diximus appellatur jus gentium.*[1] Here Gaius is speaking, and Justinian cites his words without pointing out that they are inconsistent with Ulpian's, or attempting any reconciliation of the two texts. And, to add to the confusion, in other passages the *jus naturale* and the *jus gentium* which Gaius says are identical are found contrasted with each other. Thus, in this second title it is said that, whereas by the law of nature all men were born free, by the law of nations slavery has come in.[2] And whereas nature meant peace to reign over the earth, the law of nations has brought in wars and leadings into captivity. It is in these and similar passages that the term "natural law" is used in its ordinary sense. Neither Ulpian who says the *jus naturale* extends to *omnia animalia,* nor Gaius who says it is the same thing as the *jus gentium,* is upon this point quite in accord with most of the jurists. The author of the Greek paraphrase, who is generally supposed to be Theophilus, one of the compilers of the Institutes, says that it is a mistake to confound the *jus naturale* with the *jus gentium.*[3] What the jurists generally mean by *jus naturale* is not any law which actually exists as a positive enactment or custom. It is a philosophical conception, borrowed from the Stoics, of an ideal justice with which positive law ought, so far as possible, to be brought into harmony. When the writer or the judge declared that the law of nature was in favour of a particular determina-

[1] I, 2, 1, 11. [2] I., 1, 2, 2, *cf.* I., 1, 5, pr. [3] I., 1, 2, 2. See *supra*, 338.

tion, what he meant was that this determination struck him as equitable and right. So Paul says, *Id quod semper aequum ac bonum est, jus dicitur, ut est jus naturale.*[1] It is, in fact, the same thing as what English lawyers call equity, when they use that term in its general sense, and not as meaning a definite set of rules.

Cicero, following the Stoics, speaks of *jus naturale* as an eternal and immutable law which it is sinful for the legislator to attempt to change. *Est quidem vera lex recta ratio, naturae congruens, diffusa in omnes, constans, sempiterna—huic legi nec obrogari fas est neque derogari ex hac aliquid licet neque tota abrogari potest, nec vero aut per senatum aut per populum solvi hac lege possumus, neque est querendus explanator aut interpres eius alius, nec erit alia lex Romae alia Athenis, alia nunc alia posthac, sed et omnes gentes et omni tempore una lex et sempiterna et immutabilis continebit unusque erit communis quasi magister et imperator omnium deus.*[2] But Ulpian does not dispute that a positive law may conflict with the law of nature.[3] *E.g.* natural law may be said to forbid a creditor from exacting payment of his debt twice over, because his debtor is unable to prove that he has already paid it. It forbids Shylock from claiming his pound of flesh, even though a court would be bound to give judgment in his favour. A man is not to take unfair advantage even of his legal rights. He must act fairly and honestly with all men, and follow the maxim, *Quod tibi fieri non vis alteri ne feceris.* The most elaborate study of the *jus naturale* as it was understood by the Romans, is that of M. Voigt.[4] From his analysis its characteristic features may be thus summarised :—

1. It is capable of being applied to all men. It knows no distinction between slave and freeman.

---

[1] D., 1, 1, 11.

[2] *De Repub.*, **3**, **22**, **33**, and see other citations to a like effect in Krüger, *Römische Rechtsquellen*, s. 6.

[3] D., 50, 17, 32 ; D., 1, 5, 24.

[4] *Das Jus Naturale, &c., der Römer.*

2. It extends to all peoples. Before it the citizen and the alien are equal.

3. It is the same in every age. What is just to-day cannot be unjust to-morrow in identical circumstances.

4. It corresponds with the innate sense of right.

From this conception of natural law Voigt says the jurists eventually came to recognise :—

1. The claims of natural relationship — of cognation — whereas the early lawyers considered only agnation. Thus the prætors, following the dictates of natural law, admitted emancipated children to share equally with their unemancipated brothers and sisters in the father's succession. Similarly, they ranked collateral kindred through females with those related through males, whereas by the old law an emancipated child or a relative on the mother's side was looked upon as an absolute stranger.

2. Through natural law the later lawyers came to feel the duty of faithfulness to engagements, even to engagements not entered into with due regard to legal form. This led them to give effect to what they called natural obligations—viz. such as from some defect of form or from the position in which the parties stood to each other were unenforceable by the *jus civile.* They did not go the length of saying that a man might base an action on a natural obligation, but they said he might at least be allowed to found on a mutual obligation as a defence against an unjust claim.

3. Natural law dictated that gains and losses should be apportioned according to equity. No man must be allowed to enrich himself unjustly.

4. In the interpretation of any declaration, oral or written, the guiding rule is to discover, if possible, the intention of the party. The judge is not to be bound to slavish adherence to the letter. He must get at the true mind of the party.[1]

[1] See Voigt, *Das Jus Naturale, &c., der Römer,* esp. i. 52-64, 89-96 ; and Muirhead, *Roman Law,* 2nd ed. 279.

Two remarks may be made upon this theory of natural law. Firstly, such generalisations are not without value, but when all is said they carry us only a very little way. Natural law is not a code of precise rules, but is merely an expression for that abstract justice which ought to be embodied in every rule of positive law. As Burke says, "All human laws are, properly speaking, only declaratory. They may alter the mode and application, but have no power over the substance of original justice." [1]

But, after all, where there exists a rule of positive law which is applicable to the point in question, it is the duty of a judge to give effect to it, even though it may seem to him contrary to "natural law." [2] *Dura lex sed lex.* To say, "Let us burn our law-books and direct that every judge shall decide all cases by natural law" would be to introduce the rule not of ideal justice but of caprice.

And, secondly, it is a profound error to believe, with some philosophers ancient and modern, that, in his primitive state, man followed the dictates of a pure conscience, and that natural law in the sense of ideal justice was the governing rule of society. On the contrary, nothing is more certain than that primitive man was immensely further away from natural law than we are to-day. If we want to find laws which are the embodiment of sound reason and equal justice, we must not look for them among savages. Even in matters of form, simplicity is not the mark of ancient but of modern law. Primitive man delights in cumbrous ceremonies and in blind devotion to traditional forms. With him the letter is everything, the spirit nothing.[3] No better evidence for this could be adduced than the history of the Roman law itself. In

[1] *Tracts on the Popery Laws*, cap. iii. pt. i.; and see Lorimer, *Institutes of Law, passim.*

[2] *Cf.* Gaius, 4, 115, 1, 84. See Ferrini, *Pandette*, 7.

[3] Interesting illustrations of primitive laws and customs are given in the works of A. H. Post. See especially *Grundriss der Ethnologischen Jurisprudenz.*

it we can trace without difficulty a continual advance towards equity and simplicity. The harshness and unreasonableness of the early law and its pedantic love of legal technicality gradually give place to a system so reasonable, so clear, so orderly, that all nations of the world reject their own laws and adopt the Roman.

It may freely be admitted that the tendency of the later law towards equity was largely due to the philosophical theory of an abstract and ideal justice, to which it was the duty of lawyers to bring the law into conformity. But the *jus naturale* as a separate source of law is very little insisted upon in our texts. The reason why this threefold division, into *jus naturale, civile, et gentium,* plays so small a part is that the distinction between the *jus naturale* and the *jus gentium* is of so little importance. The doctrines of the *jus naturale,* or, more correctly, its one essential doctrine that justice or equity is the ideal to be aimed at came to be incorporated, so far as practicable, in concrete cases by the prætor. And the body of equitable rules which grew up in this way was the *jus gentium.* So far as the natural precepts of equity could be reduced to positive laws, this was done in the *jus gentium.* The jurists therefore found it sufficient to make a twofold instead of a threefold division, and to say that every rule of law belonged either to the *jus gentium* or to the *jus civile.*

The history of the growth of the theory of natural law in modern Europe is interesting, but lies outside the scope of this book.[1]

[1] An acute and valuable criticism is given in the work entitled *Natural Rights,* by D. G. Ritchie (London and New York, 1895).

CHAPTER XXXVI

The Jus Gentium

Definition.—The definition given of the *jus gentium* in the Institutes is not much more satisfactory than that of the *jus naturale.* The text-writers are often weakest in their philosophical or would-be philosophical statements. It is said to be that law *quod naturalis ratio intes omnes homines constituit, id apud omnes populos per aeque custoditur vocaturque jus gentium, quasi quo jure omnes gentes utuntur.*[1] This is borrowed from Gaius. He says that in every country the law consists of two branches, one the special local law peculiar to the country, and the other the universal law which is the same everywhere. It assumes:—

1. That certain institutions or rules of law are found to be identical everywhere.

2. That they are so identical because based on *naturalis ratio,* by which is meant that they accord with their true nature, or are in harmony with the order of the universe, that they are *κατὰ φύσιν* as the Stoics said.

Gaius here identifies the *jus gentium* with the *jus naturale,* which, as we have seen, is not consistent with the views of other jurists.[2] But a more serious fault of the definition is that firstly, as a matter of fact, such identity of principles among all nations could not be established, and certainly had not been established by the Romans, and secondly, as is pointed

---

[1] Gaius, *Inst.* i. 1. *Cf.* on *Jus Gentium,* Mommsen, *Staatsrecht,* iii. 603 *seq.*

[2] See Krüger, *Römische Rechtsquellen,* s. 17 ; Muirhead, 2nd ed. 283.

out immediately afterwards, some of those institutions which are the most universal—*e.g.*, slavery—are not according to nature.

A reader of the definition might suppose that what was meant by the *jus gentium* was a series of doctrines of law which observation had shown to be practised throughout the civilised world. This, however, would be completely misleading. Gaius writes as if the *jus gentium* had been arrived at by a conscious selection, and as if the philosophic Roman had surveyed the world from Persia to Britain, and had found certain laws everywhere the same, while each country had in addition certain customs peculiar to itself. Those which were everywhere the same he called the *jus gentium.* Theophilus gives these examples. Everywhere we find contracts of sale, lease, deposit, partnership, loan. We find donations and wills. By the *jus gentium* murderers are put to death and thieves are fined, because it is natural that the punishment should fit the crime—that people should be punished *eo genere quo deliquerunt.* By the *jus gentium* a debtor shows gratitude to one who comes to his help when he is in straits for money. By the *jus gentium* a slave ought to obey his master, unless the master orders him to do something unlawful. Nothing, however, is more certain than that the *jus gentium* was not introduced as a result of any study of comparative jurisprudence. It grew up slowly and unconsciously, bit by bit, and it existed long before lawyers had taken to philosophising about the law.

Foreigners' Law.—The classical jurists, who wrote in a philosophical age, perceived upon a survey of the Roman law that it was made up of two separate elements. Certain parts of it—*e.g.* the *patria potestas*—the rules as to the powers of the head of the family—or as to *mancipatio*—the characteristic form of conveyance of real property—were extremely ancient, belonged to the primitive law of Rome, and had always been confined strictly to Roman citizens. It was Roman law *par excellence*—the law of the Romans only. This they called the *jus civile.* A *mancipatio* was null if one of the parties, or even if one of the witnesses was an alien. An alien could not be a *paterfamilias* in the Roman sense. The rules applying to this branch of the law were rigid and formal. They perceived, on the other hand, that there was another element, including—*e.g.* the law of sale of moveables, and the law of partnership, in which there was no such formality. Here the rules were free and equitable, and the minimum of form was prescribed. And this branch of the law clearly did not belong to the primitive stock. It had been grafted upon it at a later date. It was applicable not to Romans only, but to foreigners at Rome. This part of the law the jurists called the *jus gentium.* Every man—*i.e.* according to ancient ideas, every free man, be he Roman or be he foreigner, can be the subject of the *jus gentium.* Everything which is capable of being held in private property, every *res in commercio,* can be its object. In the *jus civile* the form is everything. It matters not however clearly the parties may have shown their intention, if they have not clothed it in the strict forms prescribed by law, there is nothing which the courts can recognise.

In the *jus gentium* the intention is everything, the form unimportant. For the *jus civile* it is essential that the Latin language should be employed. For the *jus gentium* any language is equally good if it is understood by the parties.

Victory of Jus Gentium.—The history of the Roman law is to a large extent the history of the gradual invasion of the *jus civile* by the *jus gentium.* The rapid development of the *jus gentium,* if not its origin, was due to the growth of foreign trade at Rome. The prætorian edicts, and especially the edict of the *praetor peregrinus,* formed the vehicle by which it was introduced. Its evolution was aided by the spread of philosophical culture, and the consequent decline of the exclusive sentiment which at first prevented the Romans from admitting that a foreigner could claim to be heard before a Roman tribunal, or that the Romans could have any laws in common with foreign nations.

The dawn of the *jus gentium* is found in the treaties with their Italian allies, by which the latter were admitted to share to a limited extent in the Roman law. These favoured nations received by treaty grants of *commercium* and *recuperatio.* This meant that they could enter into contracts according to the forms of the *jus civile.* Commercial treaties were made with important trading communities such as Carthage and Massilia. The treaties frequently declared that questions arising as to contracts entered into in virtue of them were to be decided not by the ordinary Roman tribunals, but by *recuperatores.* A question between two Carthaginian merchants at Rome, or between a Roman and a Carthaginian, was probably decided by *recuperatores.*[1] They were a kind of special juries. It has been suggested that they consisted partly of Roman citizens and partly of citizens of the foreign country to which one or both of the parties belonged. But it is more probable that the *recuperatores* were all Romans.[2] But as Rome became more and more a great commercial centre, numbers of traders began to flock thither who did not belong to any nation which enjoyed such treaty-rights. It was against the interests of the citizens, as well as of the foreign merchants, to prevent them from dealing with each other.

Method of Prætor.—This influx of foreigners led, about 242 B.C., to the appointment of a special prætor to act as judge in questions between two foreigners or between a Roman and a foreigner.[3] He was called the *praetor peregrinus*, or foreign prætor, and in the chapter on the "Edict" I have described the machine by which his reforms were introduced. What law was he to administer? The peregrins could not be parties to the forms of the *jus civile,* so that was out of the question. It would hardly have occurred to a lawyer of that period to collect

Livy, 43, 3.

[2] Puchta, *Institutionem*, 1, s. 83.

[3] D., 1, 2, 2, 28, Pomponius.

statistics as to the laws of other countries, and to select from them those which seemed the most suitable. What the prætor did, when a case occurred, was to ask himself not if the forms of the *jus civile* had been complied with, but if their spirit had been satisfied. *E.g.* by the *jus civile* one could not sell real property, or beasts of draught or burden, without going through a curious and ancient ceremony called *mancipatio*, before five witnesses. If a peregrin sold his horse to a Roman, *mancipatio* was impossible. But the prætor held that there was a valid contract of sale, if there had been a declaration of intention on the part of the owner of the horse to deliver it to the other for a certain price which the latter bound himself to pay. There had not been *mancipatio*, but there had been something which in the circumstances ought to be treated as equivalent. In some such way as this the prætor came to examine the institutions and doctrines of the *jus civile* itself, and to see how they might be stripped of their formality and be made applicable to foreigners. It is not to be supposed that any considerable mass of new law was at one stroke thus introduced. It grew up bit by bit as the occasion presented itself. At the time when the peregrin prætor was appointed, Rome was becoming a great power. Italy had been conquered, and foreign conquests had begun. The Romans were beginning to notice the laws of other countries, and they were becoming conscious of the extreme technicality of the *jus civile*. In his work of simplification the prætor was encouraged by finding that other nations, and especially the Greeks, who traded in the Mediterranean, had devised forms of contracts simpler than the cumbrous ceremonies of *mancipatio* and *in jure cessio*, and that these simple forms had been found to answer every actual need. Here and there he introduced bodily a foreign bit of law, such as the *Lex Rhodia de Jactu*, concerning jettison of goods to save a struggling ship; or the law of hypothec, where the Greek name betrays the origin of the law. But such a case was quite exceptional. More often he did not take the Greek law but he modified the Roman law in the Greek spirit of equity as opposed to formality.[1] But, broadly speaking, the *jus gentium* was home-grown law worked out at Rome by Roman magistrates. It is, in fact, a vexed question if it had not made considerable progress before there was any noticeable influx of foreigners. The better opinion seems to be that the *jus gentium* in the beginning grew up out of the needs of Roman citizens themselves. The old forms were found too cumbrous, and the prætor simplified them. Later on, when foreign trade arose, these prætorian rules were found to be well adapted for doing justice between a Roman and foreigner, or two foreigners—a system of Roman equity which at a later stage of the history was extended to foreigners, and was greatly amplified as time went on and as the increase of foreign relations raised new questions which had to be solved.[2] According to the other view, still held by many writers, the *jus gentium* was introduced in the first place as a consequence of the foreign trade, and was, so to say, "peregrin-law," which at a later stage was applied between citizens themselves.[3]

Jurists Improve Jus Gentium.—Once in operation its advantages were obvious, and after the edict had become stereotyped by the Julian compilation, the jurists of the classical period improved and developed the *jus gentium*. In their time the Stoic philosophy had leavened the thought of the educated Roman world. The lawyers were all on the look-out for principles which seemed to flow from natural reason, and to square with the eternal fitness of things. The *jus civile*, of which the old lawyers of the Republic had been so proud, seemed to the new class of philosophical jurists to be narrow, formal, and bigoted. They wanted to find doctrines applicable not to the citizens of Rome, but to the citizens of the world, and in their hands it was that the *jus gentium*

[1] *Cf.* Gide, *Condition Privée de la Femme*, 124, with Bruns-Pernice, s. 19.

[2] Karlowa, 1, 454; Cuq, 2nd ed. i. 169.

[3] See, *e.g.*, Ferrini, *Storia delle Fonti*, 18.

was moulded into the shape which made it of permanent value.

The *jus gentium* consisted first almost entirely of commercial law. It was practically the law of contract and the law of personal property. Justinian says sale, lease, partnership, loan, deposit—*omnes paene contractus*—belong to it. Some modern writers of high authority confine the term *jus gentium* to this branch of law.[1]

Jus Gentium not Confined to Mercantile Law.—But as the *jus gentium*, in the sense of the law-merchant, was introduced by the prætor, it is not unnatural that the same term should be applied to other new rules of the law which came in by the same means. *E.g.* a marriage between a Roman and a peregrin was not *justae nuptiae*, because there was no *conubium* between the parties. The husband had no *patria potestas* over the children. Still, it was out of the question to treat as mere concubinage the permanent and honourable union of two foreigners at Rome, or of a foreigner and a Roman. The children were lawful, though not *in potestate.* The father was bound to aliment them and so forth. So a marriage *juris gentium* came to be recognised side by side with a strictly Roman marriage.[2] So the prætorian changes in the law of succession are included by some writers in the *jus gentium.*[3] The passage already cited from Theophilus shows that the term was applied in this general sense by ancient writers.

We must be careful to remember that *jus gentium* does not mean international law. It has nothing to do with the law, positive or ideal, which is to be applied in regulating the differences between independent States. In the seventeenth century, it is true, *jus gentium* was commonly used in this sense. Grotius and the other founders of international law who were seeking for a philosophical basis upon which to rest their theories found the *jus gentium* a convenient term. The

[1] Bruns-Pernice, s. 19.
[2] Muirhead, 2nd ed. 227.
[3] *E.g.* Ferrini, *Pandette*, 9.

rules of humanity and justice which they were anxious to introduce in the relations of States were supported partly by the practice of the more civilised nations and partly by an appeal to the natural sense of right. These rules fell well enough under Gaius' definition of *jus gentium* as *quod naturalis ratio inter omnes homines constituit.* But Gaius and Grotius were thinking of quite different things.

CHAPTER XXXVII

The Jus Civile

Citizens' Law.—The term *jus civile* is used in two senses—(1) to describe the whole of the law applicable to all those enjoying legal rights in Roman territory, whether they are citizens or aliens, that is in the same sense as a Frenchman uses the term *droit civil* to mean the private law applicable to all persons amenable to the jurisdiction of French courts; and (2) to denote the law peculiarly applicable to Roman citizens, except in so far as by grants of *jus commercii* or *jus conubii*, or both, foreigners might be admitted to its enjoyment. *Quod quisque populus ipse sibi jus constituit, id ipsius proprium est vocaturque jus civile.*[1] In the wider sense *jus civile* is used of the whole body of the Roman law, including the *jus gentium.* In this sense Cicero writes:—*Quod civile, non idem continuo gentium; quod autem gentium, idem civile esse debet.*[2] It is in its narrower sense that we are now concerned with it. So we find *jus civile* used in antithesis to the *jus gentium* or the *jus praetorium.* Papinian in a well-known passage says *jus civile* is all the Roman law made by the legislative assemblies, by the emperors, and by the jurists, as opposed to the *jus praetorium* which the prætors had made.[3]

Local Peculiarities.—Each State has its own *jus civile* peculiar to itself, based on its own history and applicable to its own special requirements. We do not expect to find here that universality which is characteristic of the *jus gentium* or the *jus naturale.* Mercantile laws have to be much the same among the countries which carry on trade with each other or

[1] Gaius, 1, 1; *Inst.*, 1, 2, 1. [2] *De Off.*, 3, 17, 69. [3] D., 1, 1, 7, 1.

commerce would be restricted. Human nature is much the same everywhere, and certain broad principles of equity are likely to be recognised by all civilised States. But outside these there is a field within which diversity and not similarity is to be looked for. Theophilus gives some illustrations.[1]

Athens, like England, could not support her own population, and depended largely on imported corn. It was therefore advisable for Athens to have free trade in corn, and this was part of the Athenian *jus civile.* But Egypt was a great corn-producing country, and it would, according to Theophilus, have been as ridiculous for Alexandria to have free trade in corn as it was politic for Athens.

Sparta, like China, hated foreigners, and believed that their presence in the country was likely to corrupt the State. Sparta had therefore a law—the ξενηλασία—under which foreigners were expelled from her territory when it seemed to the Government desirable to do so.[2]

Athens, on the other hand, like England, believed in the "open door" to immigrants.

Taking *jus civile* in this sense of the local law confined to citizens, it is clear that the peculiar and unparalleled success of the Roman law was due not to this *jus civile* but to its abandonment. The peculiar *jus civile* of Rome, based on the Twelve Tables, and on their extension by the interpretation put upon them by the Jurists, was, as time went on, transmuted bit by bit by the new doctrines of the *jus gentium.* Its restriction to *cives* became of less and less importance as the citizenship was extended. When the Emperor Caracalla (*circa* 212 A.D.) made all the free subjects of the Empire Roman citizens all the civilised world was under the Roman sway, so that the *jus civile,* instead of being the law of a small body of privileged inhabitants of a little town in Italy, had become the law of the world.[3] And, as we have seen, its

[1] I., 1, 2, 11. [2] See Thuc., 1, 144. [3] D., 1, 5, 17.

content had changed as much as its extent. The continual inroads of the *jus gentium* had left hardly anything intact of the primitive *jus civile.*

Jus Scriptum—Jus non Scriptum.—All the law, whether public or private, and whether belonging to the *jus civile* or the *jus gentium,* is either written law or unwritten law.[1]

By written law is meant law which is formulated in a precise shape and at a particular point of time by some body or person having authority to make law.

Unwritten law is the law which rests upon custom, which has grown up unconsciously, and the introduction of which cannot be referred to a definite moment. Customary law does not become written by being put in writing. It must be put in writing by a particular authority having the power to legislate. It must be enacted as a statute, though at Rome this did not necessarily mean by a legislative assembly. But it must be done by someone authorised to make it written law, by one or other of the recognised law-givers, or *νομοθέται,* as Theophilus calls them.[2] So Cicero can speak of the prætor's edict as the chief vehicle for introducing customary or unwritten law, though it became *jus scriptum* by being taken into the *corpus juris.*[3] Written law must be written by the State, not by an individual. In the time of Justinian there is only one source of written law, namely, the declarations of the emperor.

[1] D., 1, 1, 6, 1; *Inst.*, 1, 2, 3. *Cf.* Cic., *De Fin.*, 2, 22, 74, and D., 1, 2, 2, 13; Costa, *Storia delle Fonti*, 78.

[2] Theoph., 1, 1, 4.

[3] *De Inv.*, 2, 22, 67; *De Fin.*, 2, 22, 74. See Pernice in *Zeit. Sav. Stift.*, xx. 156, and xxii. 59; Costa, *Storia delle Fonti*, 43, 78.

CHAPTER XXXVIII

The Seven Sources of the Law

Enumeration.—There are, according to Justinian, seven sources of the Roman law—*i.e.* seven ways in which, at one time or another, laws had been made at Rome. The written law was the work of one or other of no less than six authorities who, at various periods in the long history of the State, had possessed the power to legislate by making a statute or by changing the law as the prætor did in his edict, or even as an official lawyer might do in a *responsum*.

The unwritten law springs from one source—viz. custom.

The written law, he says, consists of *leges*, *plebiscita*, *senatusconsulta*, *principum placita*, *magistratuum edicta*, and *responsa prudentium*. Long before Justinian's time, however, the sources of law have been reduced to two, viz. (1) the declarations of the emperor, and (2) custom; and custom, as a source of law, has become of much less importance than formerly.

External and Internal History.—The description of these sources of the law, or, in other words an account of the legislative machinery of Rome at various epochs, is called by the modern writers the external history of the law. It is, in fact, a part of the constitutional law. Opposed to it is the internal history; that is to say, an account of the growth of the particular legal institutions and doctrines. *E.g.* the explanation of the powers of the Senate or of the prætor belongs to the external history, while the explanation of the doctrine of *patria potestas*, and the modifications which it underwent, belongs to the internal history.

I have already spoken of the six sources of the written law. It remains to explain the source of the unwritten law.

Custom as a Source of Law.—Ex non scripto jus venit quod usus comprobavit. Nam diuturni mores consensu utentium comprobati legem imitantur.[1]

Among the Greeks, Justinian says that the Lacedæmonians had little written law, whereas most of the Athenian law was written. He makes the puerile remark on this that customary law seems to have its origin at Sparta, and written law at Athens. Justinian rests the authority of all law upon the consent of the people. It binds them because they have agreed to be bound by it. There are different modes in which this consent is declared. The people may meet in one of the regularly constituted assemblies, and there pass a law. The magistrates, and certain of the lawyers, may make laws subject to particular restrictions. And the emperor, the highest magistrate of all, may make laws. But the legislative power of these officials, including the emperor, is derived from the people. Their authority to legislate has been conferred upon them. It is analogous to the legislative power of our members of Parliament. As a matter of fact the emperor was a despot. But in theory he enjoyed his unlimited power because it had been conferred upon him by the people. In all these various ways there may be an express act of legislation. But besides these there may be, so to speak, a tacit act of legislation. The people may make laws, not only by enacting a statute themselves or by permitting some representative to enact a statute for them, but also by accepting a custom. By following a custom they as clearly show their consent that it should be law as if they had expressly enacted it.

Quid interest suffragio populus voluntatem suam declaret an rebus ipsis et factis?[2]

This is a good enough reason why custom should be binding. But it must be understood that much of the customary law goes

---

[1] I., 1, 2, 9.

[2] D., 3, 32, Julian; Gell. v. 13; D., 1, 3, 33, Ulpian; D., 1, 3, 35, Hermogenian.

back to a remote antiquity. At an earlier period the customs observed by a particular people were believed to derive their validity not from the consent of the people, but from the will of the gods. In primitive societies in which writing is unknown, the old men are the guardians of the customs, and doubtful questions are referred to them. The law is preserved in the memory of the old men. Often the chief rules of custom are enshrined in proverbs. *E.g.* an African tribe—the Bogos—say "Woman is a hyena"—meaning that she has no legal rights.[1]

Primitive Customs.—The Romans perceived clearly that a custom could not be considered as binding unless it had been sanctioned by long and continuous observance. It must belong to the *mores majorum.* It must be a *diuturna consuetudo, inveterata consuetudo, per annos plurimos observata.*[2] In fact the origin of most customary law is lost in antiquity. And customary law in the Roman sense plays a much slighter part in the development of the law in historical times. But some important rules were introduced by custom even during the Republic, as, *e.g.*, the prohibition of donations between husband and wife.[3]

There is no doubt that in early times custom is the main fountain of law. The fundamental institutions of the family, the main rules as to the rights personal and patrimonial of husband and wife, the law as to the rights of the children of the marriage are in most countries part of the traditions of the race. Certainly this was so among all the Aryan peoples. Very often the early legislation does not consist in the making of new law, but in drawing up in precise language and formally enacting what has been the law from time immemorial. The Twelve Tables—the early Roman Code—as has been explained

[1] Post, *Grundriss der Ethnologischen Jurisprudenz*, i. 11.

[2] D., 1, 3, 32 and 33. *Cf.* Serv. ad Verg, *Aen.*, 7, 601; *mos est communis consensus omnium simul habitantium, qui inveteratus consuetudinem facit.* See Ferrini, *Pandette*, 22.

[3] D., 24, 1, 1; see Karlowa, i. 450.

in an earlier chapter, was mainly of this declaratory character.[1] Nor is it necessary to declare all the law, because much of it is so familiar that no one disputes it. This is one reason why such early codes can be so short. They take a great deal for granted. In France, in the fifteenth and sixteenth centuries, two thousand years later than the Twelve Tables, we see the same process of giving statutory shape to traditional customary law in the *rédaction* of the *Coutumes*. The *Coutume*[2] *de Paris* does not, for example, make the rules as to the community of property between the consorts. It merely declares a Frankish custom of immemorial antiquity.

How Custom Becomes Law.—The exact way in which custom becomes law has been much disputed. The old view was that people acted for generations in a particular way, until gradually the practice became so settled that to depart from it shocked the sense of the community and was treated as unlawful. By a slow process, and unconsciously, the custom hardens into law. Savigny rightly points out that this is an inadequate explanation. A community does not adopt merely at random a particular practice. Its character, its composition, and its history impel it in a certain direction. The custom springs from the national consciousness, and is its outward sign. The reason a uniform practice is followed is that it corresponds with the national view of right (*Rechtsgefühl* or *Rechtsbewusztseyn*). The principle precedes the practice.[3]

Custom as Interpreter of Statute.—Besides this more important way in which custom becomes law, there are also certain other ways in which law grows out of custom. One of these is when a particular construction of a statute comes by custom to be regarded as the correct one. Statutes are frequently ambiguous, and two or more interpretations of a clause may

1 Karlowa, i. 113.

2 See Esmein, *Hist. du Droit Français*, 3rd ed. 743.

3 *System*, i. 34 *seq.*; see Holland, *Jurisprudence*, ch. v.; Maine, *Early History of Institutions*, chaps. xii. and xiii.; Karlowa, i. 450; Jenks, *Law and Politics in Middle Ages*, 56 *seq.*

be at first equally plausible. One of them may, however, by custom come to be firmly established as the right one. Paul says *optima enim est legum interpres consuetudo.*[1] Even a construction which is really unsound in the sense that the authors of the statute never intended it, may nevertheless come in this way to be regarded as unassailable.

E.g. the Twelve Tables gave an intestate succession in default of *sui* to the agnates of the deceased. No distinction was made between male and female agnates. But the jurists interpreted the term agnates in the case of women to mean sisters only, and they declined to allow a female cousin, for example, to take a succession as an agnate, though a male cousin might do so. Justinian says this was never intended by the Twelve Tables, but by custom it became a fixed rule that the provision should be construed in this sense.[2]

Judicial Precedents.—Somewhat analogous to the authority of custom as interpreting an ambiguous enactment is the authority of previous decisions by the courts upon a doubtful point. The Romans did not admit that previous decisions actually made law, though they cited such *exempla* as guides to the correct decision. So Justinian does not include *res judicatae* among the sources of law.[3] Cicero, in another enumeration of the sources of the law, includes *res judicatae;* but his enumeration is not scientific, but popular.[4] And although prior decisions may have gone far to influence the courts, it is not correct to treat them as having been under the Roman system, among the direct sources of law. Justinian himself says *non exemplis sed legibus judicandum est.*[5] In the rescript which contains this famous phrase Justinian says, "for if a question has been wrongly decided it is not right that this error should lead other judges astray as well."

[1] D., 1, 3, 37.

[2] I., 1, 2, 3. *Cf.* C., 8, 48 (49), 6; Ferrini, *Pandette,* 24.

[3] Karlowa, i. 451.

[4] Cic., *Top.,* v.; Bruns-Pernice, s. 29.

[5] C., 7, 45, 13.

But, in another place, Justinian points out very clearly that this rule does not apply when the emperor himself has decided a point, whether judicially or in answer to a petition. Here he says, "Let all judges subject to our rule know that the emperor's decision is law, not only for the particular case in which it was pronounced, but also for all similar cases."[1]

Even a code does not altogether prevent the growth of customary law. The discussion of writers and the decisions of the courts lead to certain rules being followed in preference to others. It is by a kind of custom that we have a settled *jurisprudence.* And there are still a considerable number of cases in which under most codes the judge is bound to take account of local usages or customs.

Custom as Abrogating Law.—As custom can make law, so it can unmake it. This is an easy doctrine when we consider merely the question whether an old custom can pass away, or be superseded by a newer custom. Here the affirmative is clear. The only sanction of the custom is that it shall be a custom which is in observance. A custom fallen into decay is a custom no longer.

But a much more difficult question is whether a statute can cease to be law because people cease to regard its provisions. We sometimes speak of an Act of Parliament as being a "dead-letter." But is it so much a dead-letter that the courts will decline to enforce it? Can a statute be abrogated by desuetude? Upon this point the Institutes contain a clear statement that the tacit consent of the community is sufficient to abrogate even a statute.[2] And in the Digest there is a still more explicit opinion in the same sense by Julian. "What difference," he asks, "does it make whether the sovereign people declare their will by votes or by acts? Wherefore it has, most properly, been admitted that laws should be abrogated by disuse, by the

[1] C. 1, 14, 12. See the interesting discussion by Mr. Strachan-Davidson in *Problems of Roman Criminal Law*, 1, 79.

[2] I., 1, 2, 11.

tacit consent of everybody, as well as by the express vote of the legislator."[1]

There is no doubt that during the greater part of the history this view was accepted as sound law. Many laws, statutory as well as customary, are said by the jurists to have fallen into desuetude. *E.g.* Gaius says that the two early forms of wills—the *testamentum calatis comitiis*, and the *testamentum in procinctu*—have passed away by disuse—*in desuetudinem abierunt.*[2] And Ulpian says, speaking of the Lex Aquilia—the great statute dealing with reparation for injuries—that the second chapter of that law has passed into desuetude.[3] Against this there is a constitution of the Emperor Constantine (319 A.D.) which seems to lay down as a general statement that custom cannot overrule statute. *Consuetudinis ususque longaevi non vilis auctoritas est: verum non usque adeo sui valitura momento, ut aut rationem vincat aut legem.*[4] Various attempts have been made to reconcile this passage with the passages cited from the Institutes and the Digest. According to one view, Constantine means that a general law can only be abrogated by a general custom to the contrary. The law of a country cannot be abrogated by a contrary custom of a particular town in that country.[5] Nor can the general law be overruled by the local custom of some part of the empire.[6]

According to another view, Constantine means that custom cannot abrogate a statute if the statute itself contains a provision to the contrary. But it is hard to see why such a declaration should have any greater efficacy than the rest of the

[1] *Nam quid interest suffragio populus voluntatem suam declaret an rebus ipsis et factis? Quare rectissime etiam illud receptum est ut leges non solum suffragio legislatoris, sed etiam tacito consensu omnium per desuetudinem abrogentur* (D., 1, 3, 32, 1).

[2] G., 2, 103.

[3] D., 9, 2, 27, 4. Cf. *Nov.*, 89, 15, where a law of Constantine is said to have fallen into desuetude.

[4] C., 8, 52, 2.

[5] Puchta, *Inst.*, i. s. 20.

[6] Mitteis, *Reichsrecht und Volksrecht*, 163; Costa, *Storia delle Fonti*, 44.

enactment. The utmost weight that it would be reasonable to give to such a declaration would be to hold that in this case mere custom would not be sufficient. There must be a custom resting on the conviction that the statute is no longer in force.[1] Many writers think it best to recognise frankly that there is an antinomy. The passages are not reconcilable without doing violence to the texts. In their opinion it is possible that the law of Constantine was intended to revoke the law laid down in the passages which afterwards found their way into the Digest, and the compilers of the Institutes may have overlooked the change.[2] The view which I am disposed to accept is that of Ferrini. Constantine intends to declare that an earlier custom cannot prevail against a later enactment, and that even though the enactment does not refer in express terms to the previous custom on the matter, yet, nevertheless, this custom must be considered as no longer in operation after the coming into force of the enactment. It has been argued with a good deal of plausibility that the case specially in view by Constantine was that of some classes of persons who claimed that, by old custom, they were exempt from certain public burdens, and maintained that this exemption had not been taken away by a general constitution imposing these burdens upon provincials in general.[3] Whether this be the true explanation of Constantine's constitution or not, we are, I think, bound to believe that it was not intended to overrule the general principle that a statute can fall into desuetude.

[1] See Windscheid, *Pandekten*, 8th ed. i. s. 18, note 3.

[2] See Dernburg, *Pandekten*, i. s. 28; Accarias, *Précis de Droit Romain*, 4th ed. i. 23. See references also in Ferrini, *Pandette*, 25.

[3] Ferrini, *Pandette*, 26. *Cf.* C., 11, 65 (64), 1; D., 47, 12, 3, 5.

INDEX

www.ingramcontent.com/pod-product-compliance
Lightning Source LLC
LaVergne TN
LVHW101455200926
848483LV00001B/133
* 9 7 8 1 5 8 4 7 7 9 6 6 7 *